3301446892

C000184779

STREET ATLAS

Shropshire

Bridgnorth, Ludlow, Oswestry, Shrewsbury, Telford, Wrexham

www.philips-maps.co.uk

First published in 2003 by

Philip's, a division of
Octopus Publishing Group Ltd
www.octopusbooks.co.uk
2-4 Heron Quays, London E14 4JP
An Hachette Livre UK Company
www.hachettelivre.co.uk

Second edition 2008
First impression 2008
SHRBA

ISBN 978-0-540-09052-5 (spiral)

© Philip's 2008

Ordnance Survey®

This product includes mapping data licensed
from Ordnance Survey®, with the permission of
the Controller of Her Majesty's Stationery Office.

© Crown copyright 2008. All rights reserved.
Licence number 100011710

Data for the speed cameras provided by
PocketGPSWorld.com Ltd.

Ordnance Survey and the OS symbol are
registered trademarks of Ordnance Survey, the
national mapping agency of Great Britain

Printed and bound in China by Toppan

Contents

Digital Data

The exceptionally high-quality mapping found in this atlas is available as digital data in TIFF format, which is easily convertible to other bitmapped (raster) image formats.

The index is also available in digital form as a standard database table. It contains all the details found in the printed index together with the National Grid reference for the map square in which each entry is named.

For further information and to discuss your requirements, please contact james.mann@philips-maps.co.uk

On-line route planner

For detailed driving directions and estimated driving times visit our free route plannner at www.philips-maps.co.uk

Mobile speed cameras

The vast majority of speed cameras used on Britain's roads are operated by safety camera partnerships. These comprise local authorities, the police, Her Majesty's Court Service (HMCS) and the Highways Agency.

This table lists the sites where each safety camera partnership may enforce speed limits through the use of mobile cameras or detectors. These are usually set up on the roadside or a bridge spanning the road and operated by a police or civilian enforcement officer. The speed limit at each site (if available) is shown in red type, followed by the approximate location in black type.

Mike Harrington / Alamy

A5
- NSL Aston
- NSL Gobowen, Moreton Bridge
- 60 Montford Bridge
- NSL West Felton

A41
- 40,NSL Albrighton Bypass
- NSL Chetwynd nr Newport
- 40 Tern Hill
- NSL Whitchurch Bypass

A49
- 30 Dorrington

A442
- 40 Crudgington

A456
- 30 Newnham Bridge

A458
- 40 Morville
- 30 Much Wenlock

A528
- 30 Shrewsbury, Ellesmere Rd

A5064
- 30 Shrewsbury, London Rd

B4368
- 40 Hungerford

B4373
- 40 Telford, Castlefields Way
- 40 Telford, Wrockwardine Wood Way

B5060
- 40 Telford, Castle Farm Way

B5062
- 60 Newport, Edgmond Rd
- 30 Shrewsbury, Sundorne Rd

UNCLASSIFIED
- 30 Newport, Wellington Rd
- 30 Shrewsbury, Monkmoor Rd
- 30 Shrewsbury, Longden Rd (Rural)
- 30 Telford, Britannia Way
- 40 Telford, Stafford Park 1

Key to map symbols

III

22a	**Motorway** with junction number
	Primary route – dual/single carriageway
	A road – dual/single carriageway
	B road – dual/single carriageway
	Minor road – dual/single carriageway
	Other minor road – dual/single carriageway
	Road under construction
	Tunnel, covered road
30 30	**Speed cameras - single, multiple**
	Rural track, private road or narrow road in urban area
	Gate or obstruction to traffic (restrictions may not apply at all times or to all vehicles)
	Path, bridleway, byway open to all traffic, road used as a public path
	Pedestrianised area
DY7	**Postcode boundaries**
	County and unitary authority boundaries
	Railway, tunnel, railway under construction
	Tramway, tramway under construction
	Miniature railway
Walsall	**Railway station**
	Private railway station
South Shields	**Metro station**
	Tram stop, tram stop under construction
	Bus, coach station

◆	**Ambulance station**
◆	**Coastguard station**
◆	**Fire station**
◆	**Police station**
✚	**Accident and Emergency entrance to hospital**
H	**Hospital**
✛	**Place of worship**
i	**Information Centre** (open all year)
🛒	**Shopping Centre**
P	**Parking**
P&R	**Park and Ride**
PO	**Post Office**
⋏	**Camping site**
🚐	**Caravan site**
▶	**Golf course**
✕	**Picnic site**
Prim Sch	**Important buildings, schools, colleges, universities and hospitals**
	Built up area
	Woods
River Ouse	**Tidal water, water name**
	Non-tidal water – lake, river, canal or stream
	Lock, weir, tunnel
Church	**Non-Roman antiquity**
ROMAN FORT	**Roman antiquity**
◀ 94	**Adjoining page indicators and overlap bands**
164	The colour of the arrow and the band indicates the scale of the adjoining or overlapping page (see scales below)

Acad	**Academy**	Inst	**Institute**	Recn Gd	**Recreation**
Allot Gdns	**Allotments**	Ct	**Law Court**		**Ground**
Cemy	**Cemetery**	L Ctr	**Leisure Centre**	Resr	**Reservoir**
C Ctr	**Civic Centre**	LC	**Level Crossing**	Ret Pk	**Retail Park**
CH	**Club House**	Liby	**Library**	Sch	**School**
Coll	**College**	Mkt	**Market**	Sh Ctr	**Shopping Centre**
Crem	**Crematorium**	Meml	**Memorial**	TH	**Town Hall/House**
Ent	**Enterprise**	Mon	**Monument**	Trad Est	**Trading Estate**
Ex H	**Exhibition Hall**	Mus	**Museum**	Univ	**University**
Ind Est	**Industrial Estate**	Obsy	**Observatory**	W Twr	**Water Tower**
IRB Sta	**Inshore Rescue**	Pal	**Royal Palace**	Wks	**Works**
	Boat Station	PH	**Public House**	YH	**Youth Hostel**

■ The small numbers around the edges of the maps identify the 1 kilometre National Grid lines ■ The dark grey border on the inside edge of some pages indicates that the mapping does not continue onto the adjacent page

The scale of the maps on the pages numbered in blue is 5.52 cm to 1 km • 3½ inches to 1 mile • 1: 18103	0 ¼ ½ ¾ 1 mile 0 250m 500m 750m 1 kilometre
The scale of the maps on pages numbered in green is 2.76 cm to 1 km • 1¾ inches to 1 mile • 1: 36206	0 ¼ ½ ¾ 1 mile 0 250m 500m 750m 1 kilometre

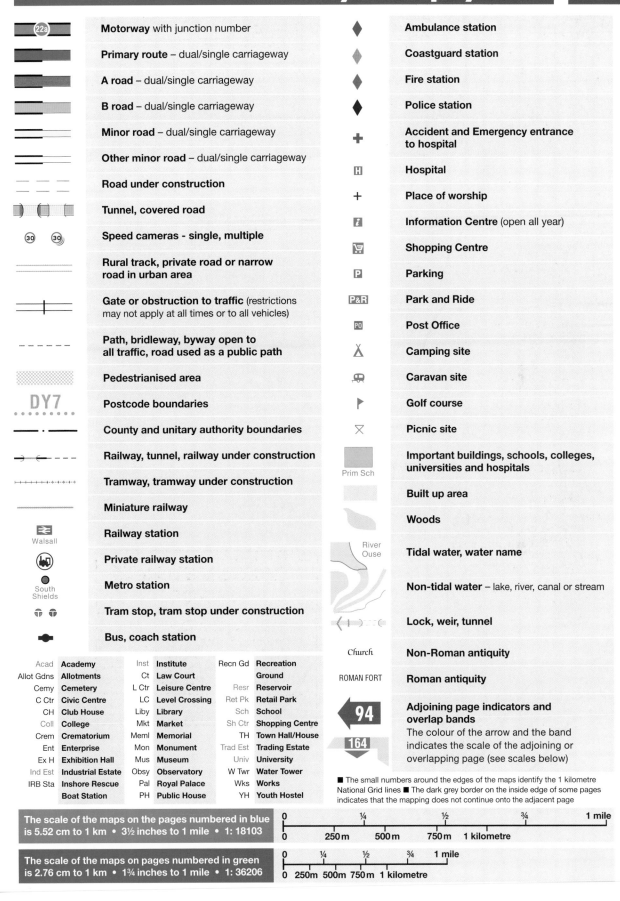

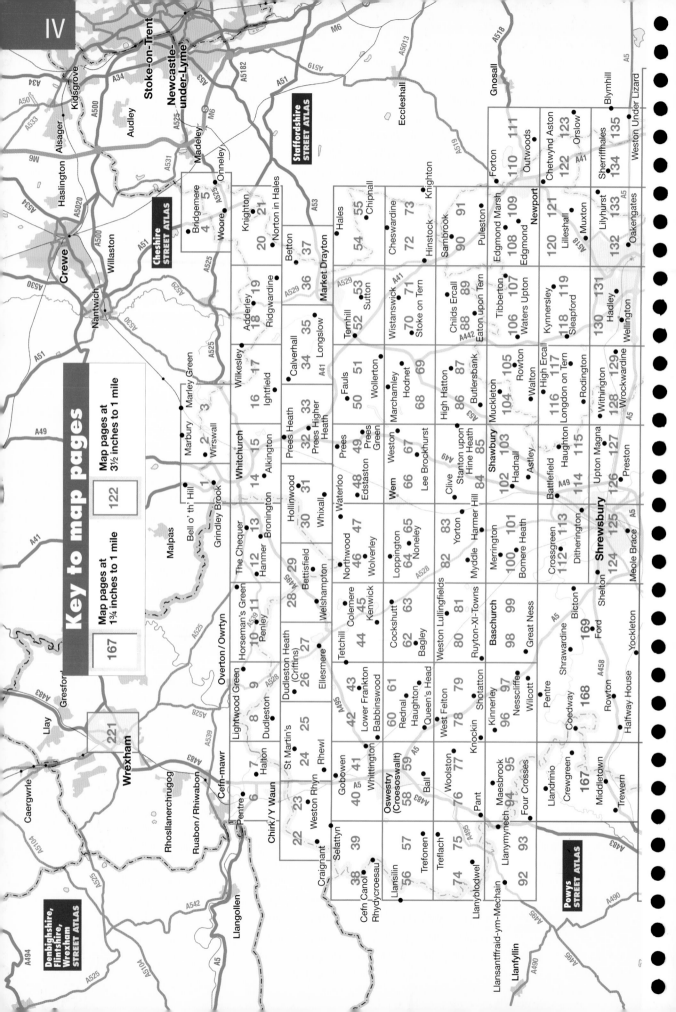

M54 · Codsall · A41 · A449 · A442 · A442 · Kidderminster · A451 · A443

Bishops Wood **148** · Nurton **157** · Pattingham **166** · Seisdon **190** · Wombourne · Swindon · Kinver · Stourport on Severn

Worcestershire STREET ATLAS

Albrighton **157** · Boningale **156** · Beckbury **165** · Ackleton · Worfield **189** · Claverley · Bobbington · Quatt **201** · Alveley · Romsley · Shatterford · Trimpley **211** · Bewdley

Tong **147** · Shifnal **145** · Kemberton **155** · Ryton **164** · Burnhill Green · Crowgreaves · Stanmore **219** · Eardington · Hampton **200** · Woodhill · Kinlet · Buttonoak **210** · Lem Hill

Shifnal **146** · Strichley **144** · Madeley **154** · Ironbridge **163** · Norton **162** · Astley Abbotts **188** · Bridgnorth **218** · Chelmarsh · A4117

Telford · Lawley **143** · Little Wenlock · Broseley **161** · Willey · Acton Round **187** · Morville · Chetton · Neenton **199** · Sidbury · Oreton **209** · Cleobury Mortimer · Newnham Bridge **215** · Lindridge

Lawley **142** · Wyke **160** · Acton Round **458** · Stanton Long · Burwarton **198** · Stottesdon · Cleeton St Mary **208** · Doddington · Boraston · **220** Tenbury Wells

Uppington **141** · Buildwas **151** · Sheinton · Harley · Much Wenlock **159** · Bourton · Brockton **186** · Ditton Priors · Cockshutford · Bromdon **208** · Cleehill · Nash **214**

Donnington **140** · Cressage **149** · Stanton Long **158** · Clee St Margaret · Caynham · Brimfield **213**

Atcham **138** · Cross Houses **139** · Pitchford · Acton Burnell **179** · Ruckley · Plaish **185** · Holdgate **197** · Munslow · Bitterley **207** · Caynham **213** · Ashford Bowdler

Bayston Hill **137** · Annscroft · Dorrington **178** · Longnor · Leebotwood · Cardington **184** · Wall under Heywood · Shipton · Alcaston **196** · Diddlebury · Stanton Lacy **207** · Ludlow **217** · Ludford · Batchcott **212** · Richards Castle · Orleton

Bayston Hill **136** · Stapleton · All Stretton · Church Stretton **184** · Little Stretton **216** · Seifton · Onibury **206** · Bromfield

Hanwood · Longden **173** · Pontesbury · Habberley · Picklescott · **177** Ratlinghope · Minton · Marshbrook **183** · Craven Arms **195** · Broome · Clungunford · Shelderton **205** · Leintwardine · Adforton · A4110

Herefordshire, Monmouthshire STREET ATLAS

Westbury · Aston Rogers **172** · Minsterley · Snailbeach · Stiperstones **176** · Hope · Wentnor · Lydham **182** · Totterton · Lydbury North · Kempton **194** · Clunbury · Clunton · Hoptonheath · Bucknell **204** · Brampton Bryan

Rowley **171** · Worthen · Marton · Rorrington · Chirbury **174** · The Marsh **175** · Priest Weston · Snead · Bishop's Castle **181** · Pentre · Whitcott Keysett · Clun **193** · Churchbank · Purlogue · Knucklas **203** · Stowe

Welshpool (Trallwng) **170** · Kingswood · Forden/Ffodun · Montgomery **174** · Pentrehylng · City **180** · Mardu · Acton · Newcastle **192** · Llanfair Waterdine · Llangunllo · Knighton/Tref-y-Clawdd **202** · A488 · A490

Anchor **191** · Felindre · Beguildy

Presteigne

Scale
0 · 5 · 10 · 15 km
0 · 5 · 10 miles

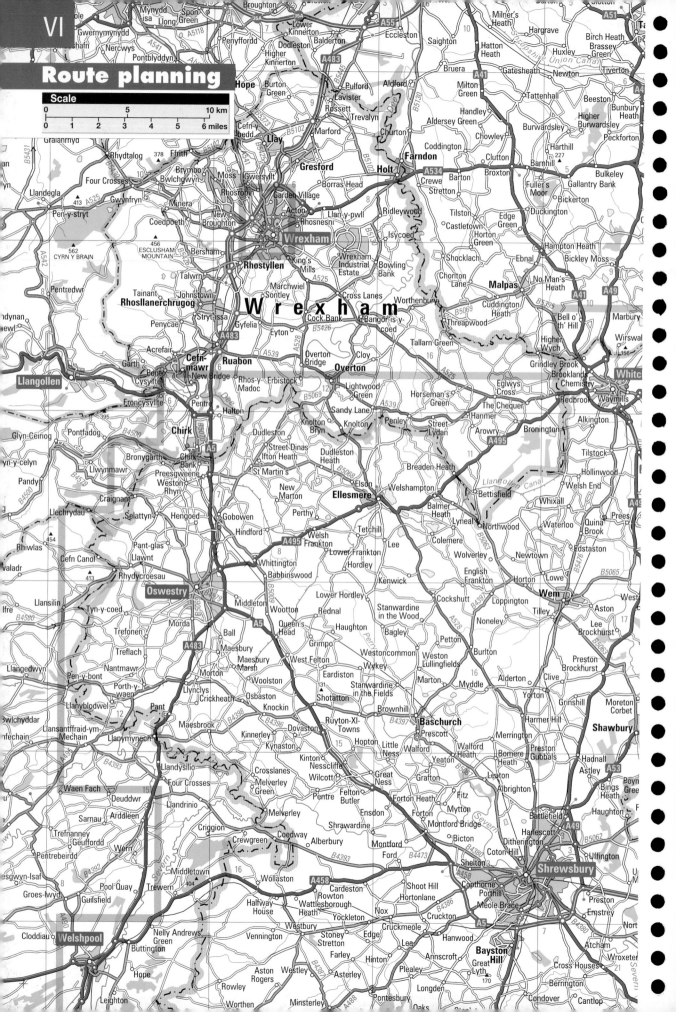

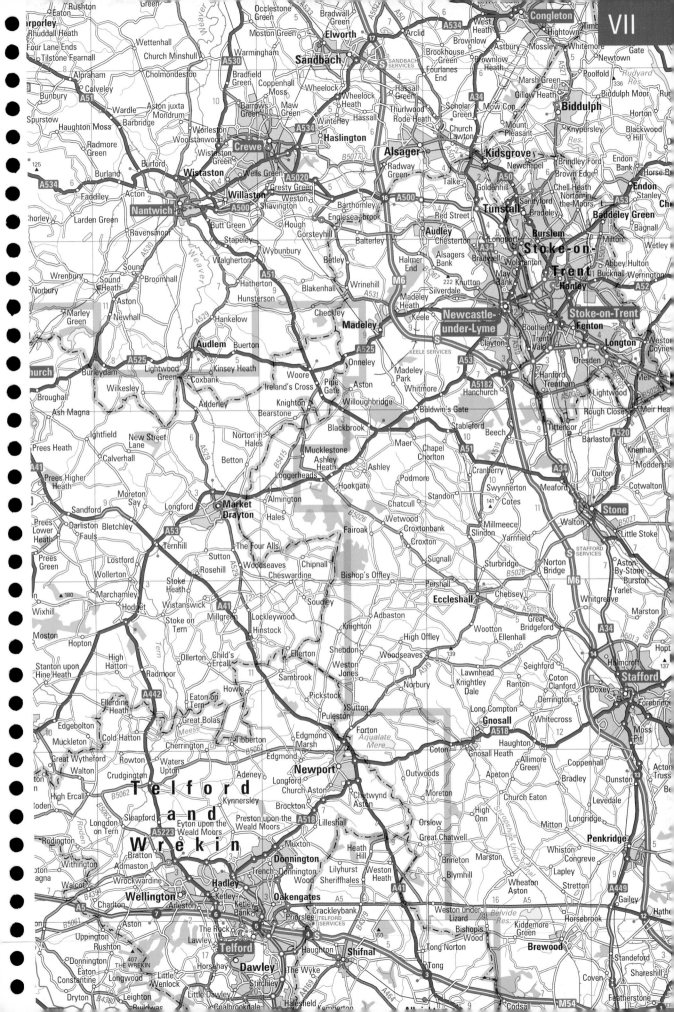

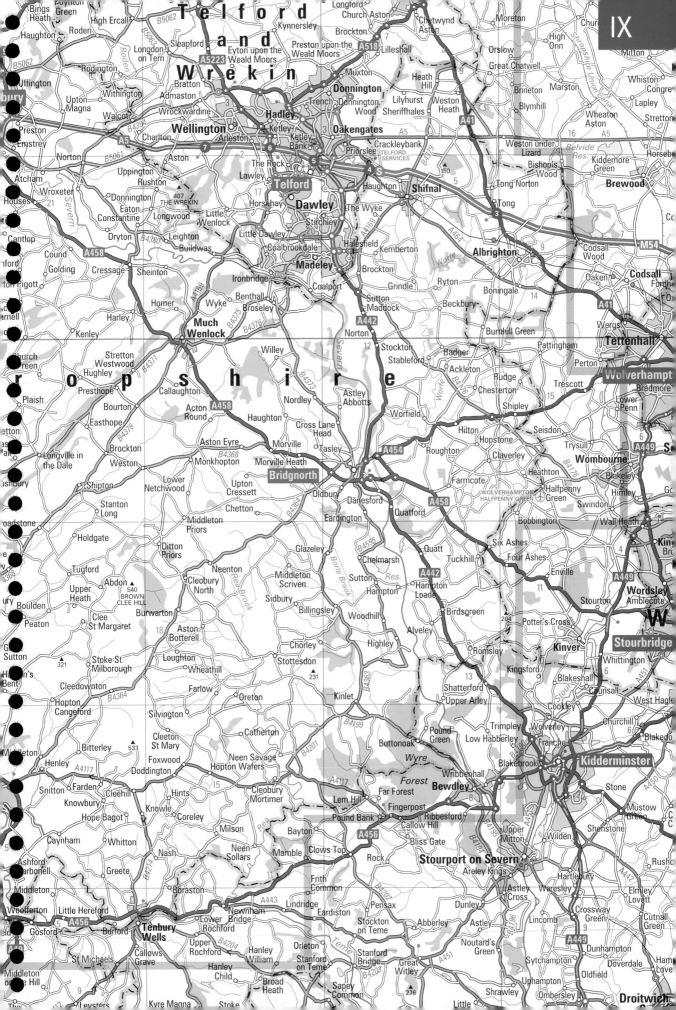

Administrative and Postcode boundaries

County and unitary authority boundaries

District boundaries

Postcode boundaries

Area covered by this atlas

Scale

0 5 10 15 20 25 km
0 5 10 15 miles

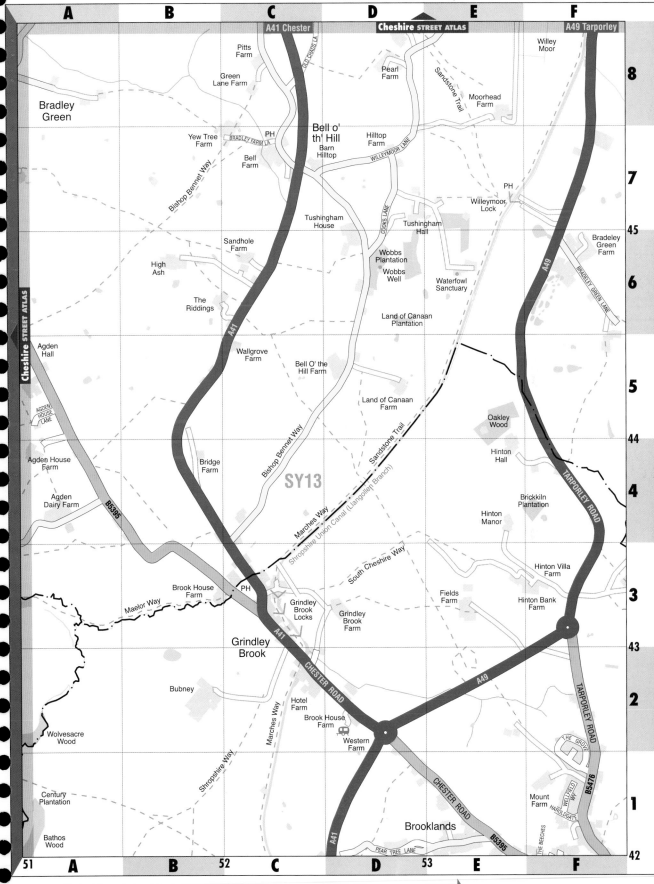

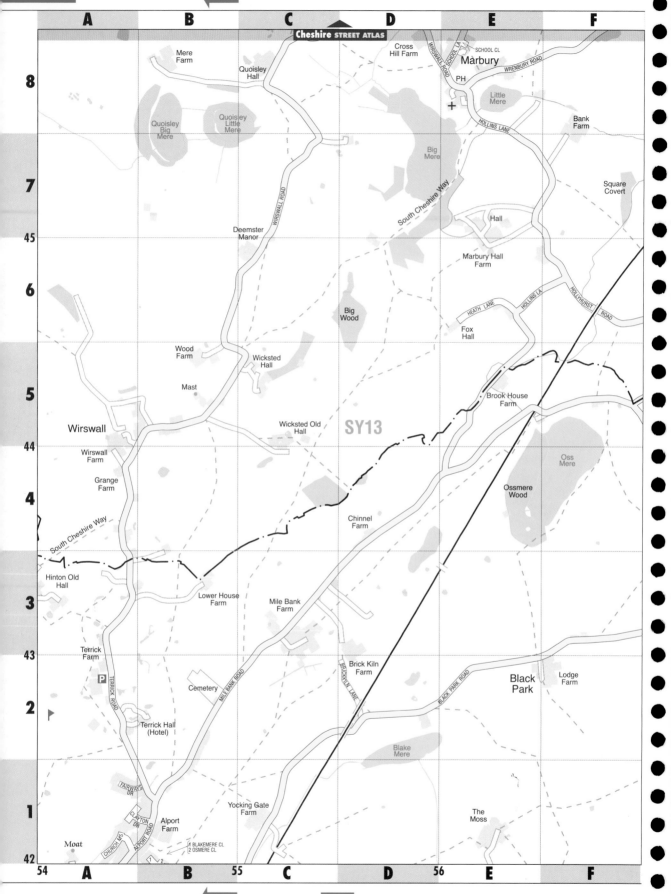

Cheshire STREET ATLAS

A B C D E F

8

45

7

6

5

44

4

3

43

2

1

42

54 A B 55 C D 56 E F

Mere
Farm

Quoisley
Hall

Cross
Hill Farm

SCHOOL CL

Marbury

WIRSWALL ROAD

SCHOOL LA

WRENBURY ROAD

PH

+

Little
Mere

Bank
Farm

Quoisley
Big
Mere

Quoisley
Little Mere

HOLLINS LANE

Square
Covert

Deemster
Manor

Big
Mere

South Cheshire Way

Hall

Marbury Hall
Farm

HEATH LANE

HOLLINS LA

HOLLYHURST ROAD

Big
Wood

Fox
Hall

Wood
Farm

Wicksted
Hall

Mast

Brook House
Farm

Wirswall

Wicksted Old
Hall

SY13

Oss
Mere

Wirswall
Farm

Grange
Farm

Ossmere
Wood

South Cheshire Way

Chinnel
Farm

Hinton Old
Hall

Lower House
Farm

Mile Bank
Farm

Brick Kiln
Farm

Terrick
Farm

P

Cemetery

MILE BANK ROAD

BRICKKILN LANE

BLACK PARK ROAD

Black
Park

Lodge
Farm

TERRICK ROAD

Terrick Hall
(Hotel)

Blake
Mere

FAIRWAYS DR

CLAYTON DR

Alport
Farm

Yocking Gate
Farm

The
Moss

Moat

CHURCH LAS

ALPORT ROAD

1 BLAKEMERE CL
2 OSMERE CL

1 2

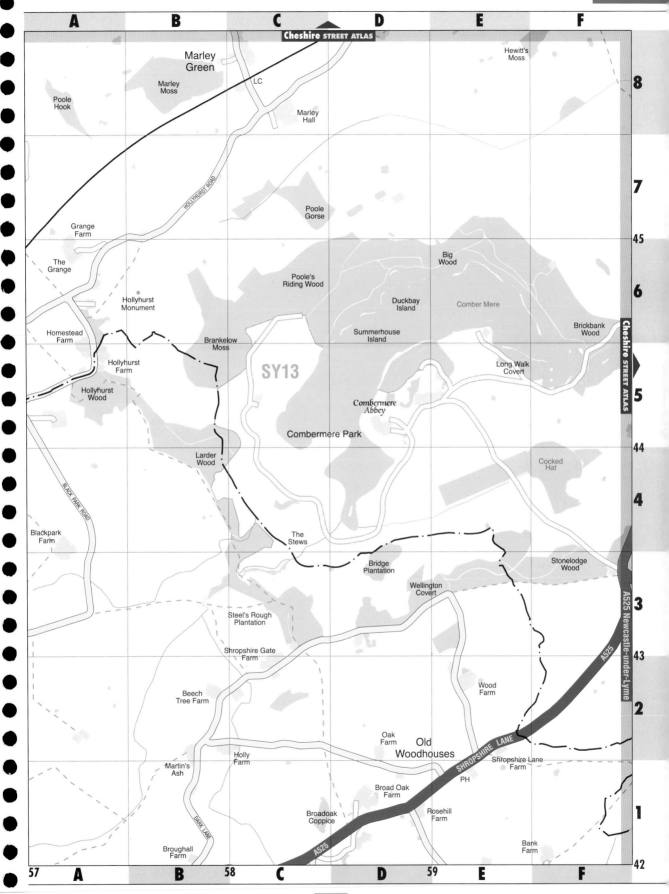

Cheshire STREET ATLAS

8

Marley
Green

Marley
Moss

LC

Poole
Hook

Marley
Hall

HOLLYHURST ROAD

7

Poole
Gorse

Grange
Farm

45

The
Grange

Poole's
Riding Wood

Big
Wood

Cheshire STREET ATLAS

6

Hollyhurst
Monument

Duckbay
Island

Comber Mere

Homestead
Farm

Brankelow
Moss

Summerhouse
Island

Brickbank
Wood

SY13

Long Walk
Covert

Hollyhurst
Farm

Hollyhurst
Wood

Combermere
Abbey

5

Combermere Park

44

Larder
Wood

Cocked
Hat

BLACK PARK ROAD

4

Blackpark
Farm

The
Stews

Bridge
Plantation

Stonelodge
Wood

Wellington
Covert

3

Steel's Rough
Plantation

A525 Newcastle-under-Lyme

Shropshire Gate
Farm

43

Wood
Farm

A525

Beech
Tree Farm

2

Oak
Farm

Old
Woodhouses

Martin's
Ash

Holly
Farm

Shropshire Lane
Farm

SHROPSHIRE LANE

PH

Shropshire Lane
Farm

DARK LANE

Broad Oak
Farm

1

Broadoak
Coppice

Rosehill
Farm

Bank
Farm

Broughall
Farm

A525

42

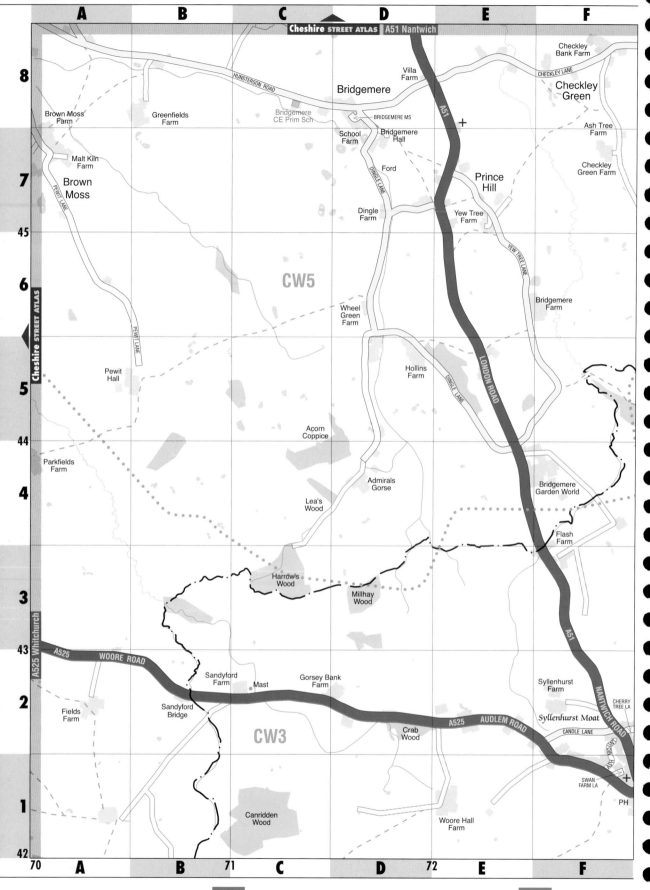

A B C D E F

8

HUNSTERSON ROAD

Bridgemere

Villa
Farm

Checkley
Bank Farm

CHECKLEY LANE

Checkley
Green

Brown Moss
Farm

Greenfields
Farm

Bridgemere
CE Prim Sch

BRIDGEMERE MS

School
Farm

Bridgemere
Hall

A51

Ash Tree
Farm

Malt Kiln
Farm

Ford

Checkley
Green Farm

7

Brown
Moss

PEWIT LANE

DINGLE LANE

Dingle
Farm

Prince
Hill

Yew Tree
Farm

45

YEW TREE LANE

6

CW5

Wheel
Green
Farm

Bridgemere
Farm

PEWIT LANE

5

Pewit
Hall

Hollins
Farm

DINGLE LANE

LONDON ROAD

44

Acorn
Coppice

Parkfields
Farm

Admirals
Gorse

Bridgemere
Garden World

4

Lea's
Wood

Flash
Farm

3

Harrow's
Wood

Millhay
Wood

A51

43

A525 Whitchurch

A525

WOORE ROAD

Sandyford
Farm

Mast

Gorsey Bank
Farm

Syllenhurst
Farm

NANTWICH ROAD

CHERRY
TREE LA

2

Fields
Farm

Sandyford
Bridge

CW3

Crab
Wood

A525 AUDLEM ROAD

Syllenhurst Moat

CANDLE LANE

A51

1

Canridden
Wood

Woore Hall
Farm

SWAN
FARM LA

PH

42

70 A B 71 C D 72 E F

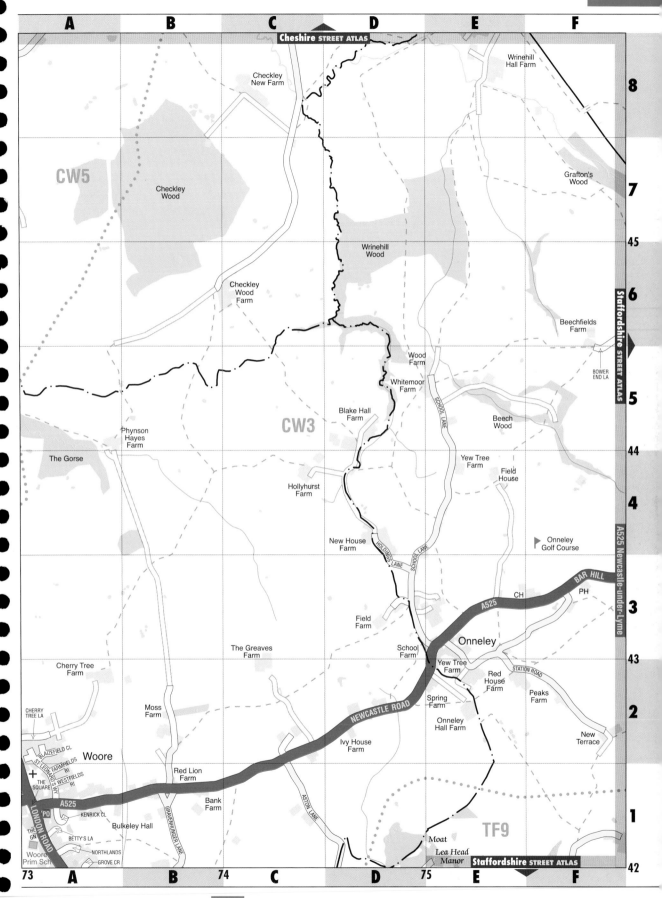

Cheshire STREET ATLAS

Staffordshire STREET ATLAS

A525 Newcastle-under-Lyme

CW5

Checkley
New Farm

Wrinehill
Hall Farm

Grafton's
Wood

Checkley
Wood

Wrinehill
Wood

Checkley
Wood
Farm

Beechfields
Farm

BOWER
END LA

Wood
Farm

Whitemoor
Farm

SCHOOL LANE

Beech
Wood

Blake Hall
Farm

CW3

Phynson
Hayes
Farm

The Gorse

Yew Tree
Farm

Field
House

Hollyhurst
Farm

New House
Farm

HOLDINGS LANE

SCHOOL LANE

Onneley
Golf Course

BAR HILL

A525

CH

PH

Field
Farm

School
Farm

Onneley

The Greaves
Farm

Yew Tree
Farm

STATION ROAD

Cherry Tree
Farm

Red House
Farm

Peaks
Farm

CHERRY
TREE LA

Moss
Farm

NEWCASTLE ROAD

Spring
Farm

Onneley
Hall Farm

New
Terrace

BLAIZEFIELD CL

ST LEONARD'S AV

Woore

FARMFIELDS
RI

WESTFIELDS
RI

Red Lion
Farm

Ivy House
Farm

THE
SQUARE

A525

PO

KENRICK CL

Bank
Farm

ASTON LANE

GRAVENHUNGER LANE

LONDON ROAD

BETTY'S LA

Bulkeley Hall

Moat

TF9

THE
GN

NORTHLANDS

GROVE CR

Lea Head
Manor

Woore
Prim Sch

Staffordshire STREET ATLAS

73   74   75

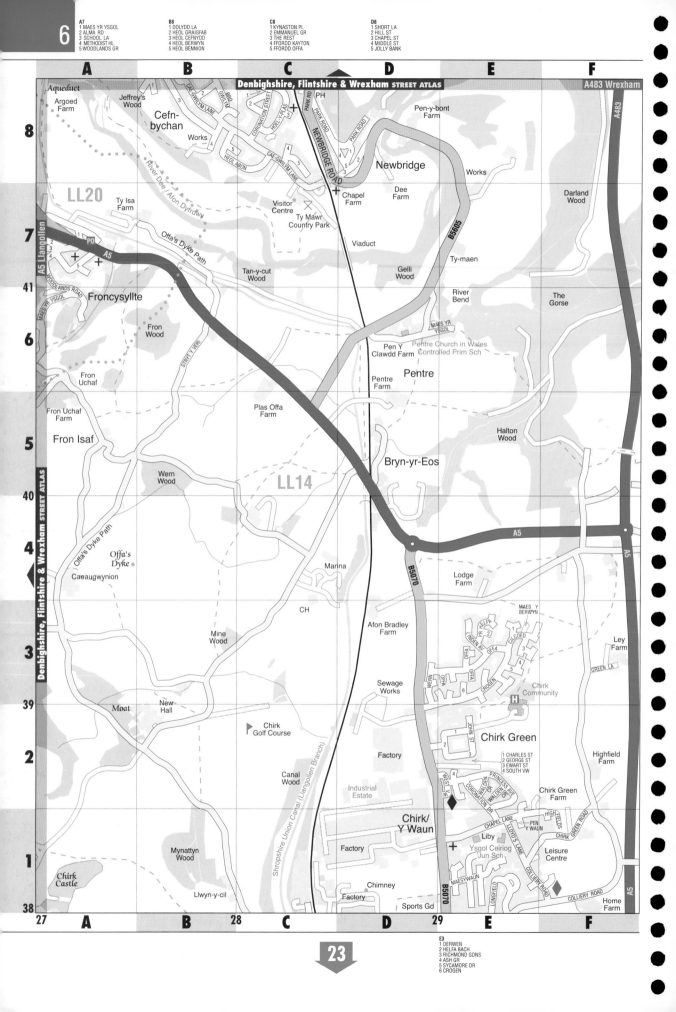

A7
1 MAES YR YSGOL
2 ALMA RD
3 SCHOOL LA
4 METHODIST HL
5 WOODLANDS GR

B8
1 DOLYDD LA
2 HEOL GRAIGFAB
3 HEOL CEFNYDD
4 HEOL BERWYN
5 HEOL BENNION

C8
1 KYNASTON PL
2 EMMANUEL GR
3 THE REST
4 FFORDD KAYTON
5 FFORDD OFFA

D8
1 SHORT LA
2 HILL ST
3 CHAPEL ST
4 MIDDLE ST
5 JOLLY BANK

Denbighshire, Flintshire & Wrexham STREET ATLAS

A483 Wrexham

Denbighshire, Flintshire & Wrexham STREET ATLAS

Aqueduct
Argoed Farm
Jeffrey's Wood
Cefn-bychan
Works
LL20
Ty Isa Farm
River Dee / Afon Dyfrdwy
A5 Llangollen
PO
A5
Offa's Dyke Path
Froncysyllte
WOODLANDS ROAD
MAES YR YSGOL
Fron Wood
STRYT Y VERN
Fron Uchaf
Fron Uchaf Farm
Fron Isaf
Wern Wood
LL14
Offa's Dyke Path
Offa's Dyke
Caeaugwynion
Mine Wood
Moat
New Hall
Mynattyn Wood
Chirk Castle
Llwyn-y-cil

Park Rd
PH
Pen-y-bont Farm
NEWBRIDGE ROAD
PARK ROAD
Newbridge
Works
Dee Farm
Chapel Farm
Darland Wood
Visitor Centre
Ty Mawr Country Park
Viaduct
Ty-maen
B5605
Gelli Wood
River Bend
The Gorse
MAES YR YSGOL
Pen Y Clawdd Farm
Pentre Church in Wales Controlled Prim Sch
Pentre Farm
Pentre
Plas Offa Farm
Halton Wood
Bryn-yr-Eos
A5
B5070
Lodge Farm
Marina
CH
Afon Bradley Farm
MAES Y BERWYN
Ley Farm
GREEN LA
LINDEN AV
PR HELFA
OFFA
GILCOED
CROGEN
WERN
OFFA
JOHN ST
Chirk Community
H
Sewage Works
Chirk Green
Chirk Golf Course
Factory
1 CHARLES ST
2 GEORGE ST
3 EWART ST
4 SOUTH VW
Highfield Farm
Canal Wood
Industrial Estate
Factory
WEST AV
CORONATION DR
PRINCESS AVE
WALDEN
Chirk Green Farm
HIGH FIELDS
CHIRK GREEN ROAD
Shropshire Union Canal (Llangollen Branch)
Chirk/ Y Waun
CHAPEL LANE
PEN Y WAUN
LLOYDS LANE
Liby
Ysgol Ceiriog Jun Sch
Leisure Centre
Chimney
Factory
MAESYWAUN
B5070
LONGFIELD
COLLIERY ROAD
Home Farm
A5
Sports Gd

E3
1 DERWEN
2 HELFA BACH
3 RICHMOND GDNS
4 ASH GR
5 SYCAMORE DR
6 CROGEN

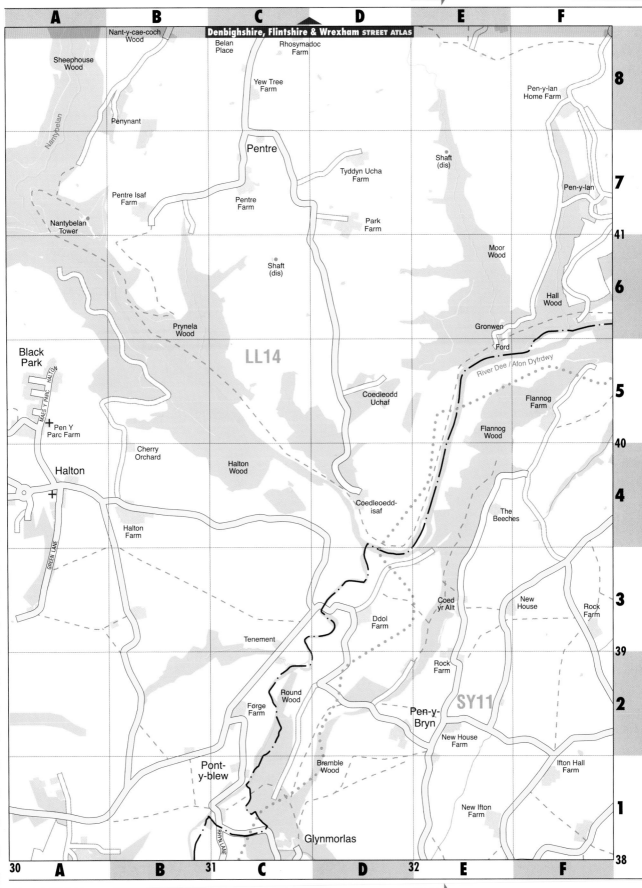

Denbighshire, Flintshire & Wrexham STREET ATLAS

Nant-y-cae-coch Wood

Sheephouse Wood

Belan Place

Rhosymadoc Farm

Yew Tree Farm

Pen-y-lan Home Farm

Penynant

Pentre

Shaft (dis)

Pen-y-lan

Tyddyn Ucha Farm

Pentre Isaf Farm

Pentre Farm

Park Farm

41

Moor Wood

Nantybelan Tower

Hall Wood

Prynela Wood

Shaft (dis)

Gronwen

Ford

6

LL14

River Dee / Afon Dyfrdwy

Black Park

Coedleodd Uchaf

Flannog Farm

5

Pen Y Parc Farm

Flannog Wood

40

Cherry Orchard

Coedleoedd-isaf

The Beeches

4

Halton

Halton Wood

Halton Farm

GREEN LANE

Coedleoedd-isaf

Coed yr Allt

New House

Rock Farm

3

Tenement

Ddol Farm

Rock Farm

39

Round Wood

Forge Farm

Pen-y-Bryn

SY11

2

Pont-y-blew

Bramble Wood

New House Farm

Ifton Hall Farm

RHYN LANE

New Ifton Farm

1

Glynmorlas

38

7

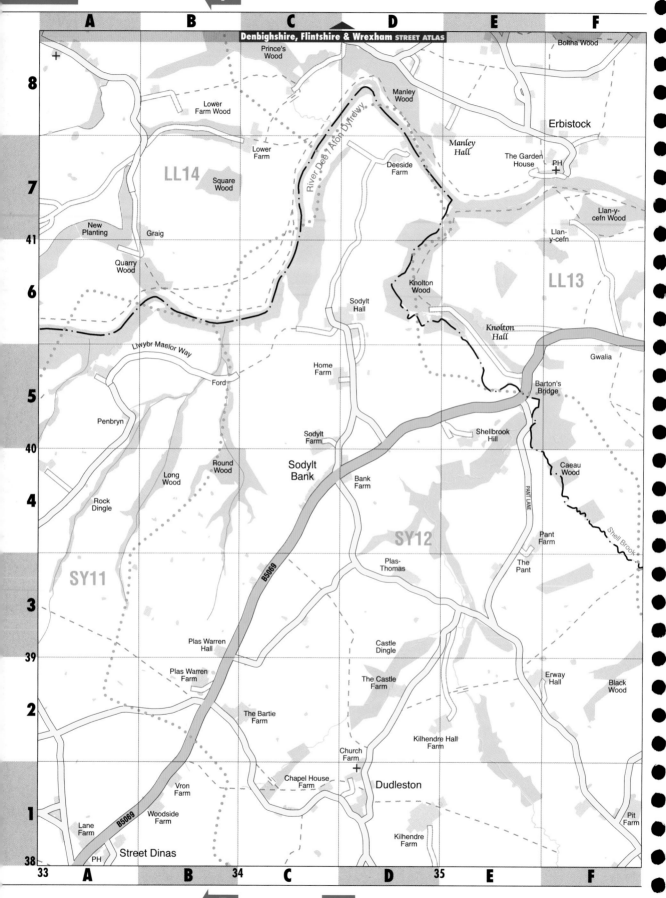

Denbighshire, Flintshire & Wrexham STREET ATLAS

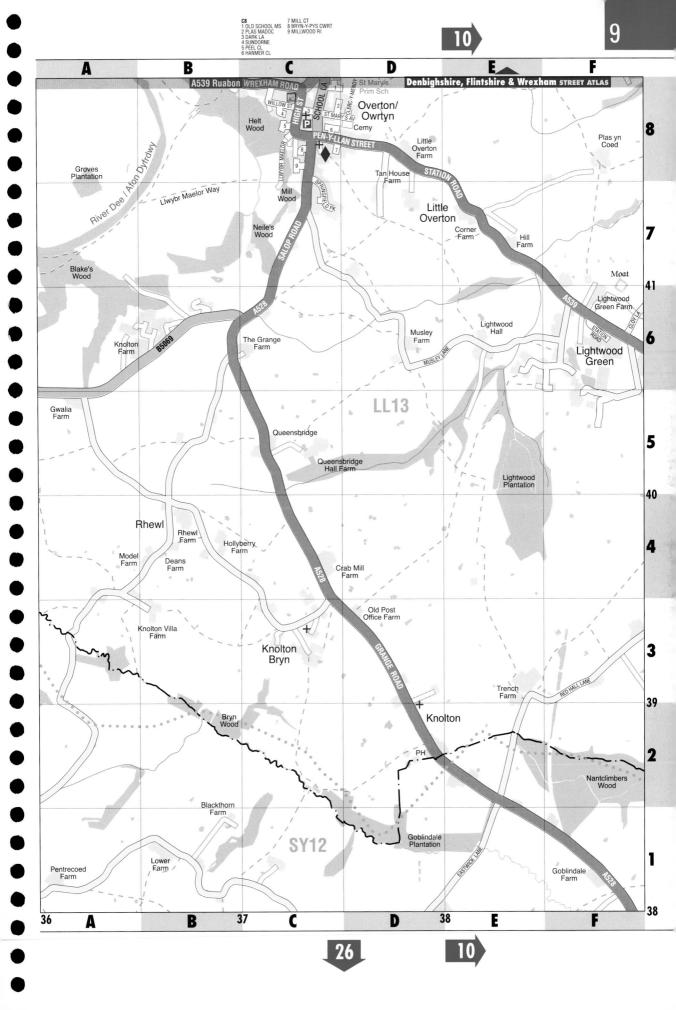

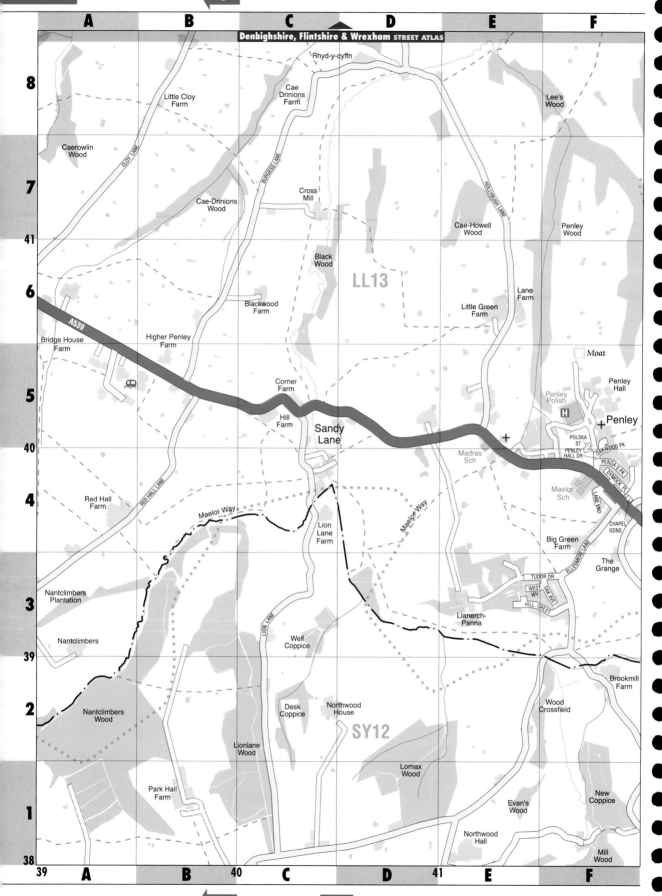

Denbighshire, Flintshire & Wrexham STREET ATLAS

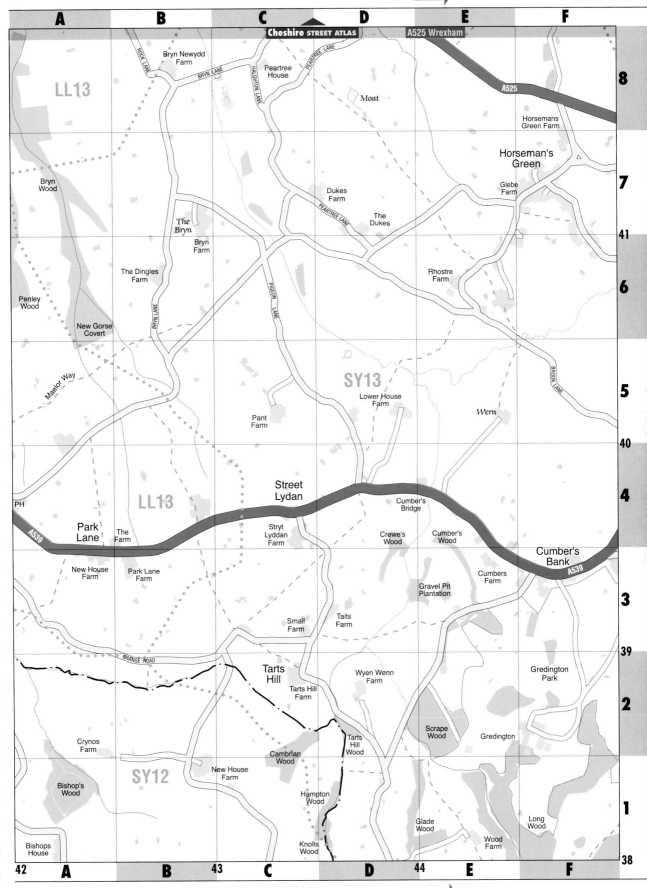

Cheshire STREET ATLAS

A525 Wrexham

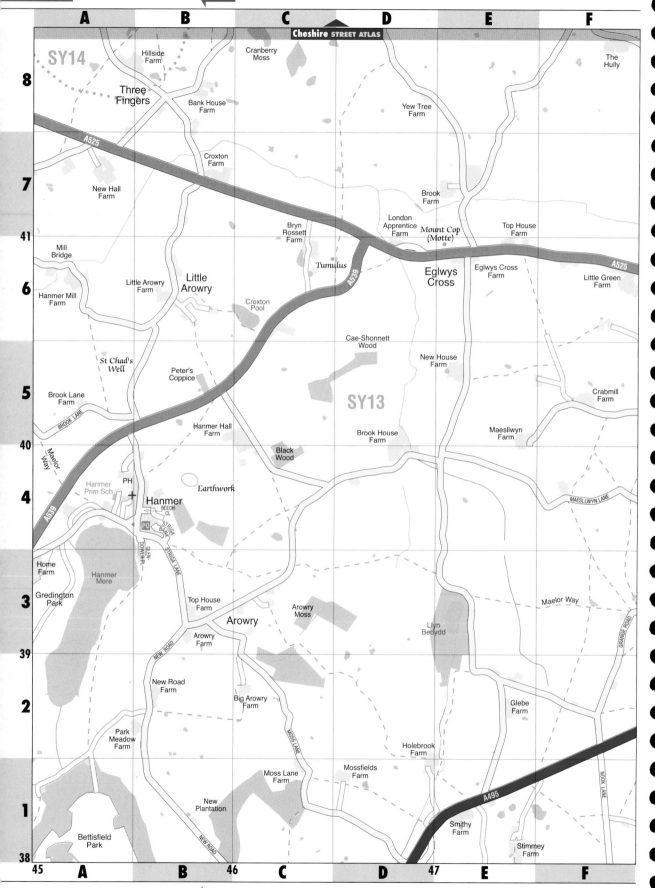

Cheshire STREET ATLAS

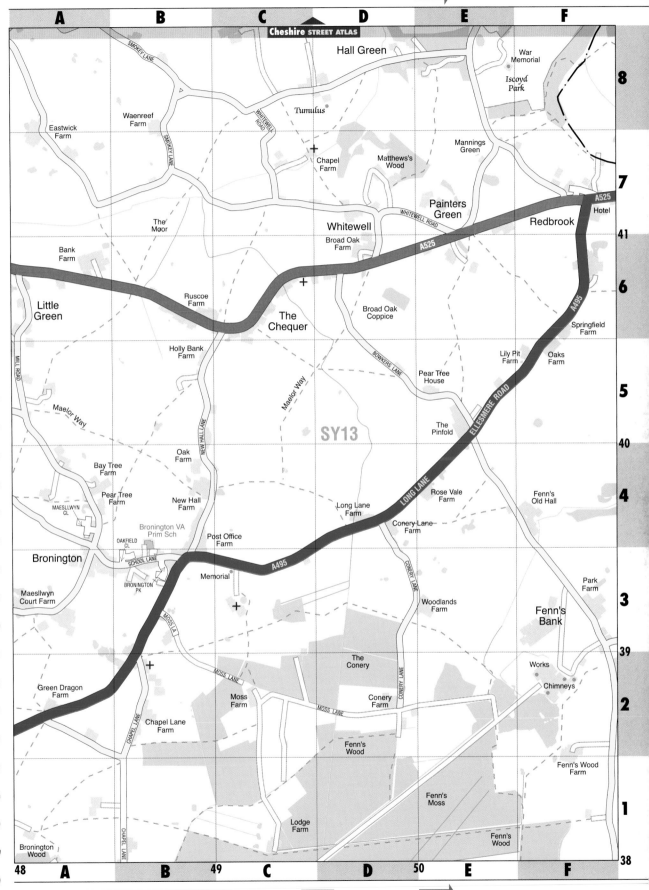

Cheshire STREET ATLAS

Hall Green
War Memorial
Iscoyd Park
8

Eastwick Farm
Waenreef Farm
SMOKEY LANE
Tumulus
Chapel Farm
Matthews's Wood
Mannings Green
7

The Moor
Painters Green
WHITEWELL ROAD
Whitewell
Redbrook
A525
Hotel
41

Bank Farm
Broad Oak Farm
A525
6

Little Green
Ruscoe Farm
The Chequer
Broad Oak Coppice
Springfield Farm
A495

MILL ROAD
Holly Bank Farm
Maelor Way
BOWKERS LANE
Pear Tree House
Lily Pit Farm
Oaks Farm
5

Maelor Way
Bay Tree Farm
Oak Farm
NEW HALL LANE
SY13
The Pinfold
ELLESMERE ROAD
40

Pear Tree Farm
New Hall Farm
Long Lane Farm
LONG LANE
Rose Vale Farm
Fenn's Old Hall
4

MAESLLWYN CL
Bronington VA Prim Sch
Post Office Farm
Conery Lane Farm
OAKFIELD CL
Bronington
SCHOOL LANE
Memorial
A495
CONERY LANE
Woodlands Farm
Fenn's Bank
3

BRONINGTON PK
Maesllwyn Court Farm
MOSS LA
Works
Chimneys
39

Green Dragon Farm
MOSS LANE
The Conery
CONERY LANE
2

CHAPEL LANE
Chapel Lane Farm
Moss Farm
MOSS LANE
Conery Farm
Fenn's Wood Farm

Fenn's Wood
Fenn's Moss
Fenn's Wood
1

Bronington Wood
Lodge Farm
38

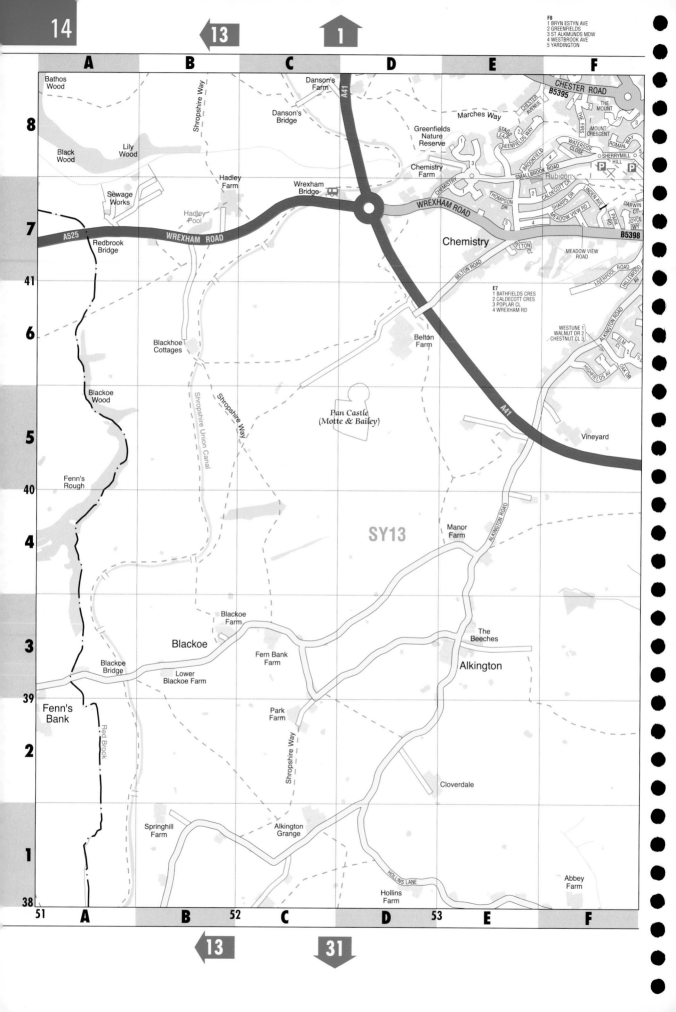

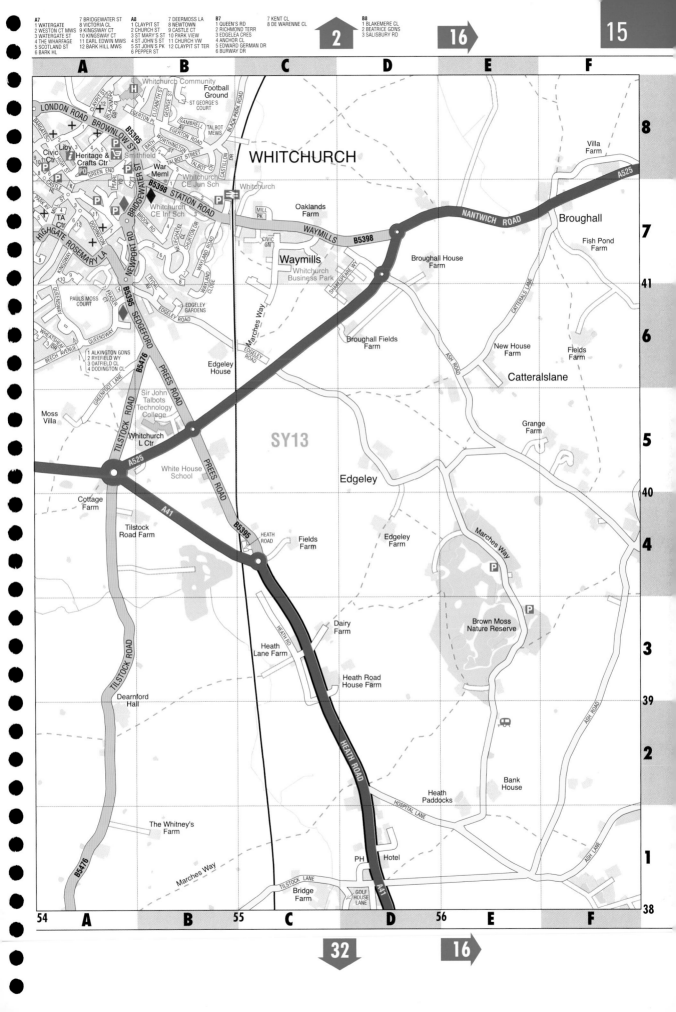

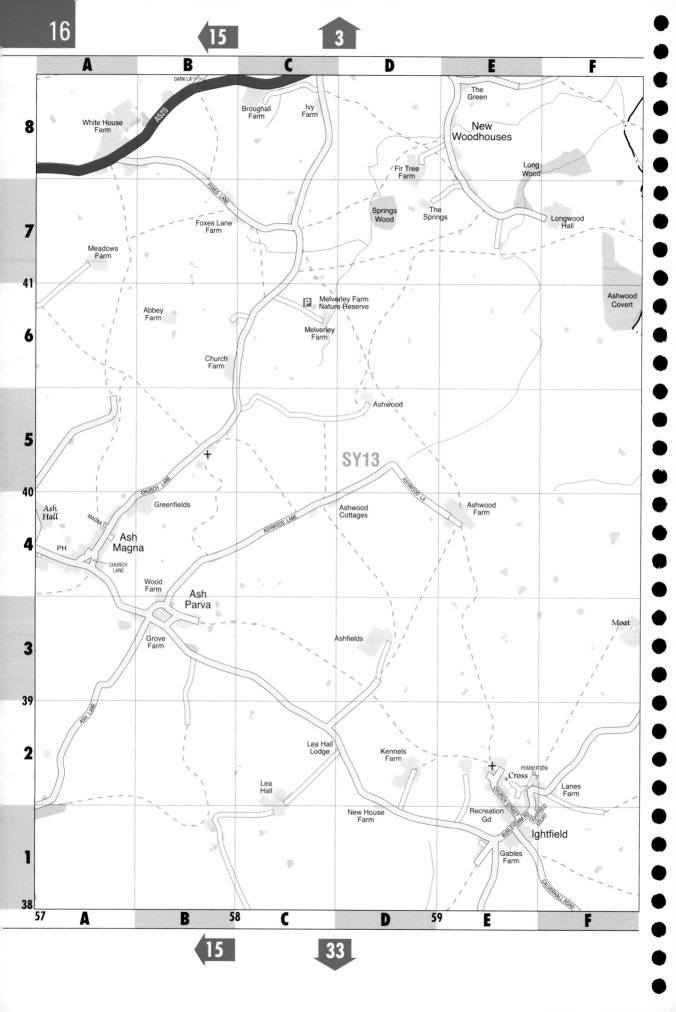

A B C D E F

8

White House Farm

DARK LA

A525

Broughall Farm

Ivy Farm

The Green

New Woodhouses

7

Foxes Lane Farm

FOXES LANE

Fir Tree Farm

Long Wood

Springs Wood

The Springs

Longwood Hall

Meadows Farm

41

Abbey Farm

P Melverley Farm Nature Reserve

Ashwood Covert

6

Melverley Farm

Church Farm

Ashwood

5

SY13

CHURCH LANE

40

Ash Hall

Greenfields

ASHWOOD LANE

Ashwood Cottages

ASHWOOD LA

Ashwood Farm

MAGNA CL

PH

Ash Magna

4

CHURCH LANE

Wood Farm

Ash Parva

Grove Farm

Ashfields

Moat

3

ASH LANE

39

Lea Hall Lodge

Kennels Farm

2

Cross

PEMBERTON CL

Lanes Farm

Lea Hall

CHURCH STREET

Recreation Gd

BURLEYDAM RD

HIGHFIELD COURT

New House Farm

Ightfield

1

Gables Farm

CALVERHALL ROAD

38

57 A 58 B C 59 D E F

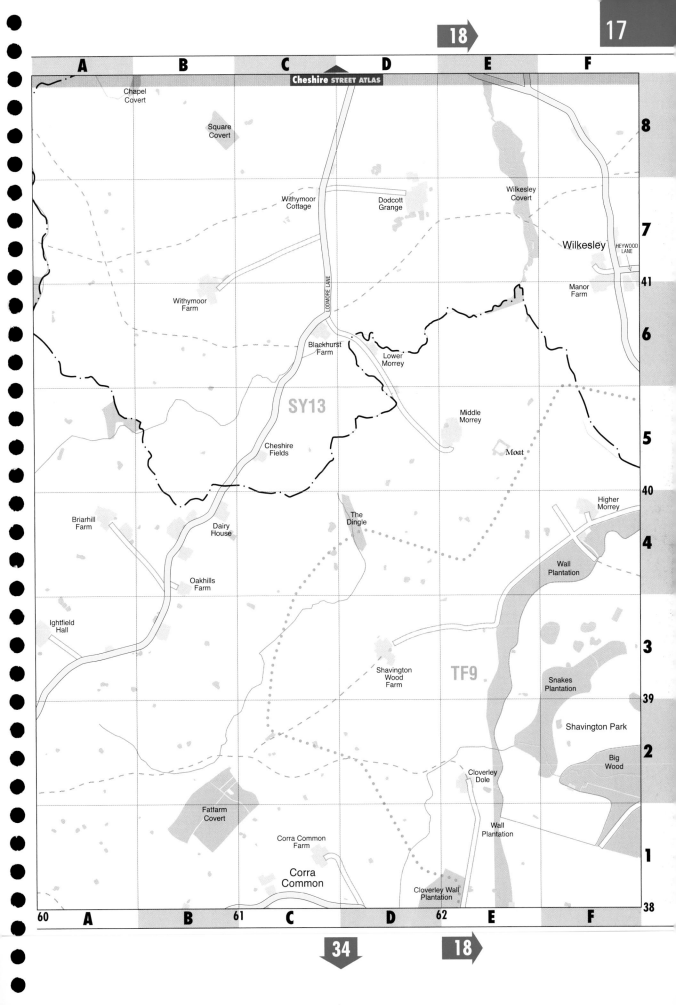

Cheshire STREET ATLAS

A　　B　　C　　D　　E　　F

8

Chapel
Covert

Square
Covert

Withymoor
Cottage

Dodcott
Grange

Wilkesley
Covert

7

Wilkesley

HEYWOOD
LANE

41

Withymoor
Farm

LODMORE LANE

Blackhurst
Farm

Lower
Morrey

Manor
Farm

6

SY13

Middle
Morrey

Moat

5

Cheshire
Fields

40

Briarhill
Farm

Dairy
House

The
Dingle

Higher
Morrey

Wall
Plantation

4

Oakhills
Farm

Ightfield
Hall

Shavington
Wood
Farm

TF9

Snakes
Plantation

3

Shavington Park

39

Fatfarm
Covert

Cloverley
Dole

Big
Wood

2

Corra Common
Farm

Wall
Plantation

1

**Corra
Common**

Cloverley Wall
Plantation

38

60　　A　　B　　61　　C　　D　　62　　E　　F

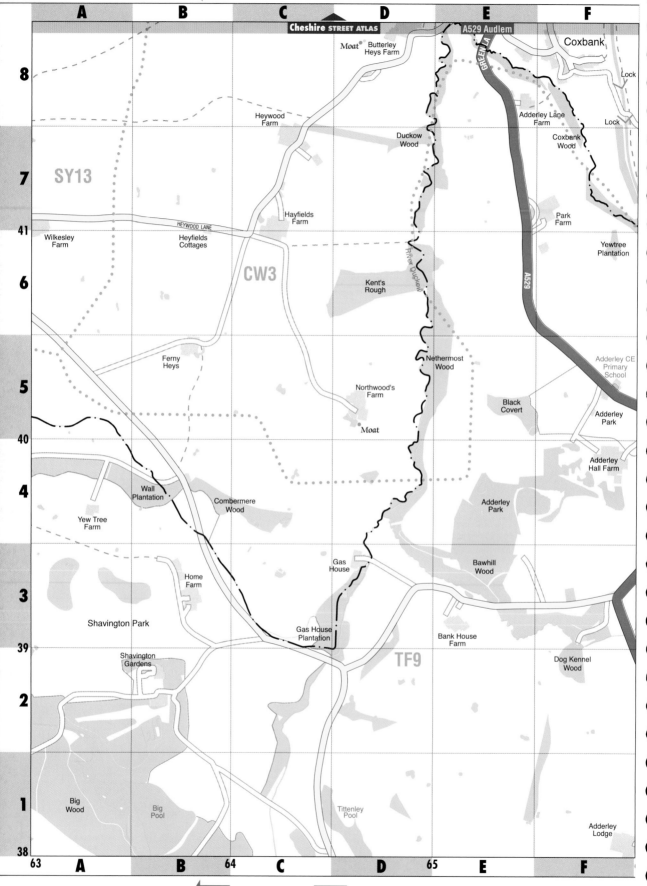

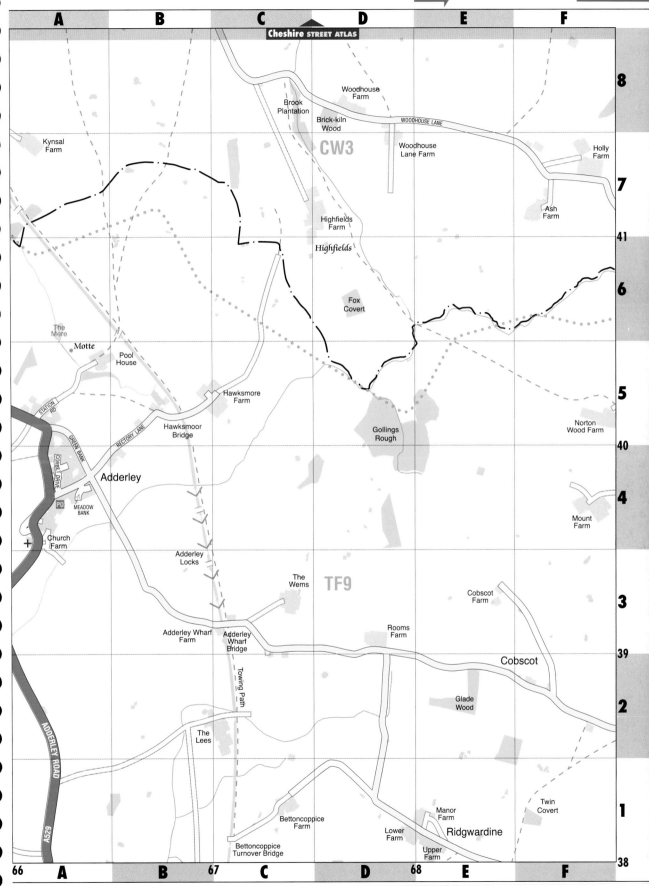

Cheshire STREET ATLAS

CW3

Kynsal Farm

Brook Plantation

Woodhouse Farm

Brick-kiln Wood

WOODHOUSE LANE

Woodhouse Lane Farm

Holly Farm

Ash Farm

Highfields Farm

Highfields

Fox Covert

Norton Wood Farm

The Mere

Motte

Pool House

Hawksmore Farm

Gollings Rough

STATION RD

GREEN BANK

RECTORY LANE

Hawksmoor Bridge

Mount Farm

CORBET DRIVE

Adderley

MEADOW BANK

PO

Church Farm

Adderley Locks

The Wems

TF9

Cobscot Farm

Adderley Wharf Farm

Adderley Wharf Bridge

Rooms Farm

Cobscot

ADDERLEY ROAD

A529

Towing Path

Glade Wood

The Lees

Twin Covert

Bettoncoppice Farm

Manor Farm

Lower Farm

Ridgwardine

Bettoncoppice Turnover Bridge

Upper Farm

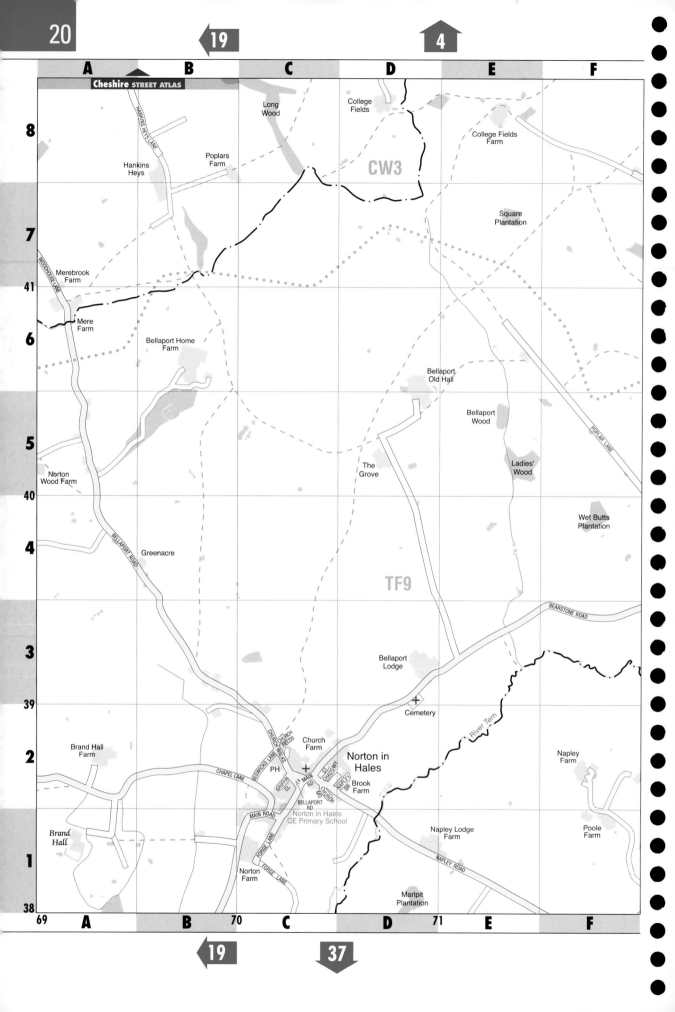

Cheshire STREET ATLAS

A B C D E F

8

Long
Wood

College
Fields

College Fields
Farm

CW3

Hankins
Heys

Poplars
Farm

Square
Plantation

7

Merebrook
Farm

41

Mere
Farm

6

Bellaport Home
Farm

Bellaport
Old Hall

Bellaport
Wood

5

The
Grove

Ladies'
Wood

Norton
Wood Farm

40

Wet Butts
Plantation

4

Greenacre

TF9

POPLAR LANE

BEARSTONE ROAD

3

Bellaport
Lodge

39

Cemetery

River Tern

Brand Hall
Farm

Church
Farm

Norton in
Hales

Napley
Farm

2

CHAPEL LANE

PH

Brook
Farm

BELLAPORT RD

Norton in Hales
CE Primary School

Poole
Farm

Napley Lodge
Farm

Brand
Hall

1

Norton
Farm

FORGE LANE

NAPLEY ROAD

Marlpit
Plantation

38

69 A B 70 C D 71 E F

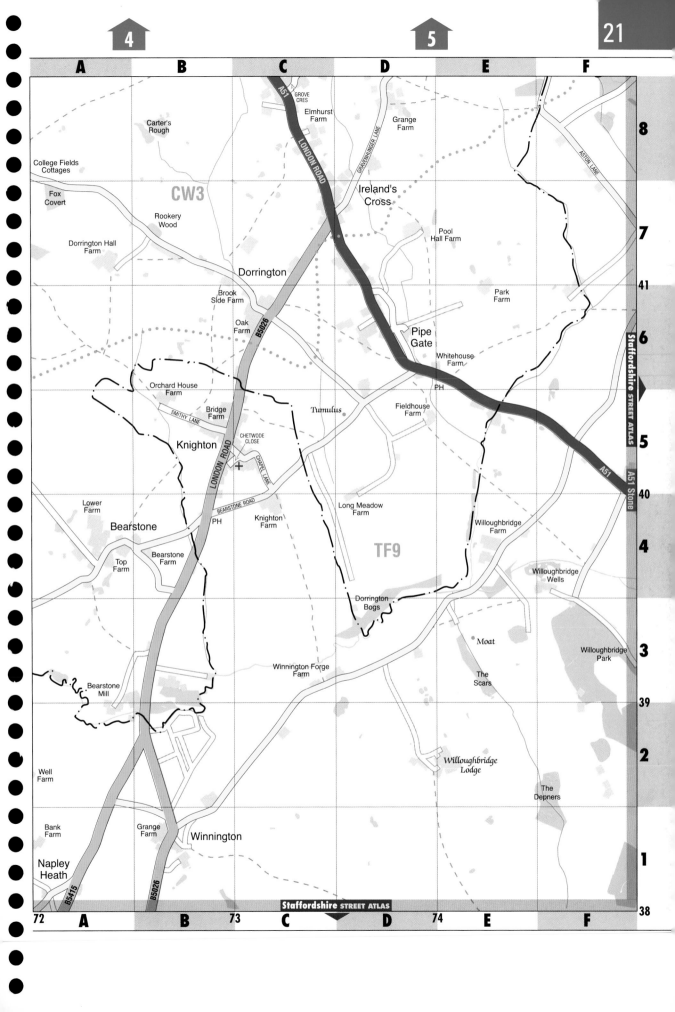

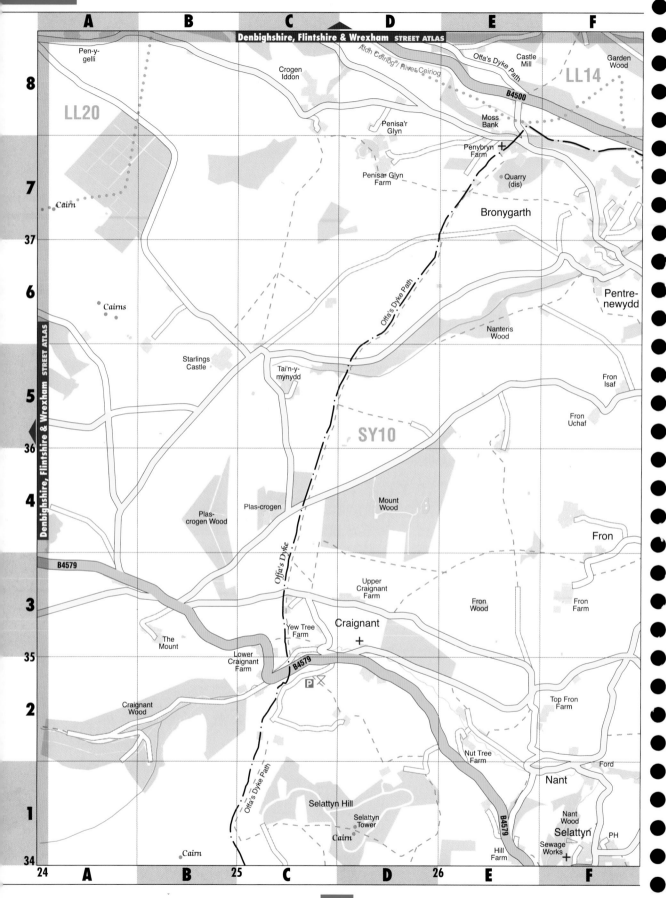

Denbighshire, Flintshire & Wrexham STREET ATLAS

Denbighshire, Flintshire & Wrexham STREET ATLAS

Pen-y-gelli

Crogen Iddon

Afon Ceiriog / River Ceiriog

Offa's Dyke Path

Castle Mill

Garden Wood

LL14

8

LL20

Penisa'r Glyn

Moss Bank

B4500

Penisar Glyn Farm

Penybryn Farm

Quarry (dis)

7

Cairn

Bronygarth

37

Pentre-newydd

6

Cairns

Nanteris Wood

Offa's Dyke Path

Fron Isaf

Starlings Castle

Tai'n-y-mynydd

Fron Uchaf

5

SY10

36

Plas-crogen Wood

Plas-crogen

Mount Wood

Fron

4

Offa's Dyke

B4579

Upper Craignant Farm

Fron Wood

Fron Farm

3

The Mount

Yew Tree Farm

Craignant

Lower Craignant Farm

B4579

P

Top Fron Farm

35

Craignant Wood

Nut Tree Farm

Ford

2

Offa's Dyke Path

Selattyn Hill

Selattyn Tower

Nant

Nant Wood

B4579

Selattyn

PH

1

Cairn

Cairn

Hill Farm

Sewage Works

34

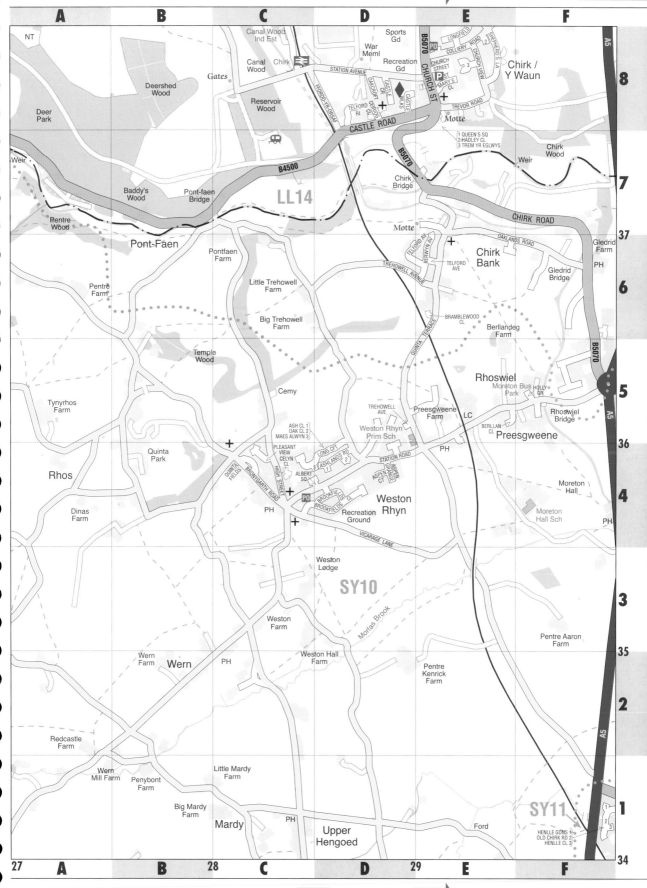

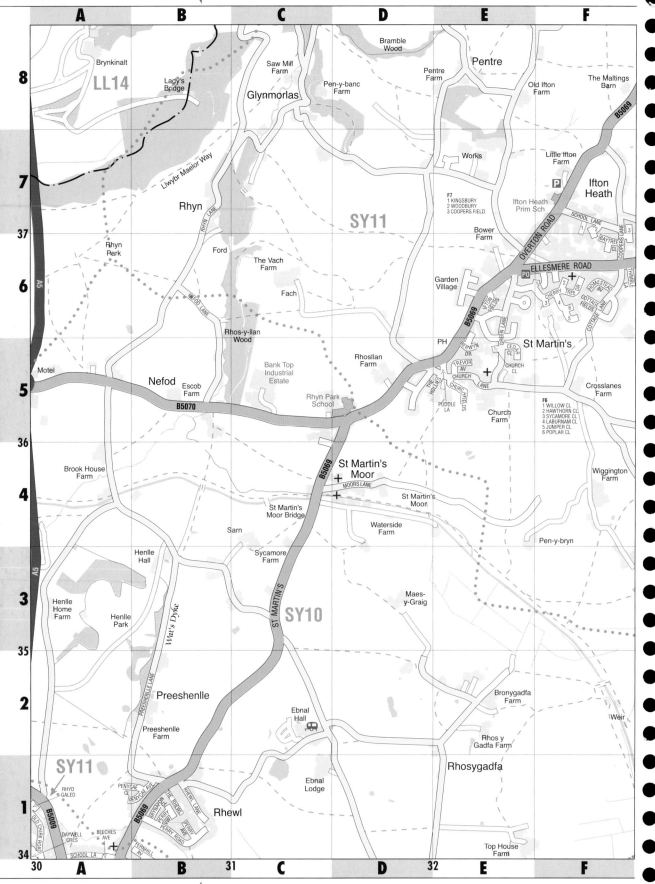

8 Brynkinalt
LL14
Lady's Bridge
Saw Mill Farm
Glynmorlas
Pen-y-banc Farm
Bramble Wood
Pentre
Pentre Farm
Old Ifton Farm
The Maltings Barn
B5069

7 Llwybr Maelor Way
Rhyn
Works
Little Ifton Farm
Ifton Heath
P
Ifton Heath Prim Sch

37 Rhyn Lane
SY11
F7
1 KINGSBURY
2 WOODBURY
3 COOPERS FIELD
SCHOOL LANE
BAYTREE
COOPERS LANE
THIMBLE LA

6 Rhyn Park
Ford
The Vach Farm
Fach
Bower Farm
Garden Village
ELLESMERE ROAD
OVERTON ROAD
PO
CHERRY TREE
HOMESTEAD AV
COTTAGE FIELDS
Rhos-y-llan Wood
Nefod Lane
B5069
IFTON FIELDS
GREEN LANE
St Martin's

5 Motel
Nefod
Escob Farm
Bank Top Industrial Estate
Rhyn Park School
Rhosllan Farm
PH
THE HOLLIES
BERWYN DR
TREVOR AV
CHURCH LANE
CHURCH MFIELDS
PUDDLE LA
CEDAR CL
CHURCH CL
Church Farm
Crosslanes Farm
B5070
F6
1 WILLOW CL
2 HAWTHORN CL
3 SYCAMORE CL
4 LABURNAM CL
5 JUNIPER CL
6 POPLAR CL

36 Brook House Farm
St Martin's Moor
MOORS LANE
B5069
St Martin's Moor
Wiggington Farm

4 St Martin's Moor Bridge
Sarn
Waterside Farm
Pen-y-bryn

3 Henlle Hall
Henlle Home Farm
Henlle Park
Sycamore Farm
Maes-y-Graig
Wat's Dyke
ST MARTIN'S
SY10

35 Preeshenlle Lane
Bronygadfa Farm
Weir

2 Preeshenlle
Preeshenlle Farm
Ebnal Hall
Ebnal Lodge
Rhosygadfa
Rhos y Gadfa Farm

1 SY11
RHYD GALED
B5009
PENYCAE CL
PENYCAE AVE
BRYNYAFON CL
THE RHEWL
RHEWL LANE
PERRY AVE
PERRY ROAD
PERRY RD
Rhewl
Ebnal
DAYWELL CRES
BEECHES AVE
FERNHILL AV
OLD CHIRK ROAD
SCHOOL LA
Top House Farm

34 A5

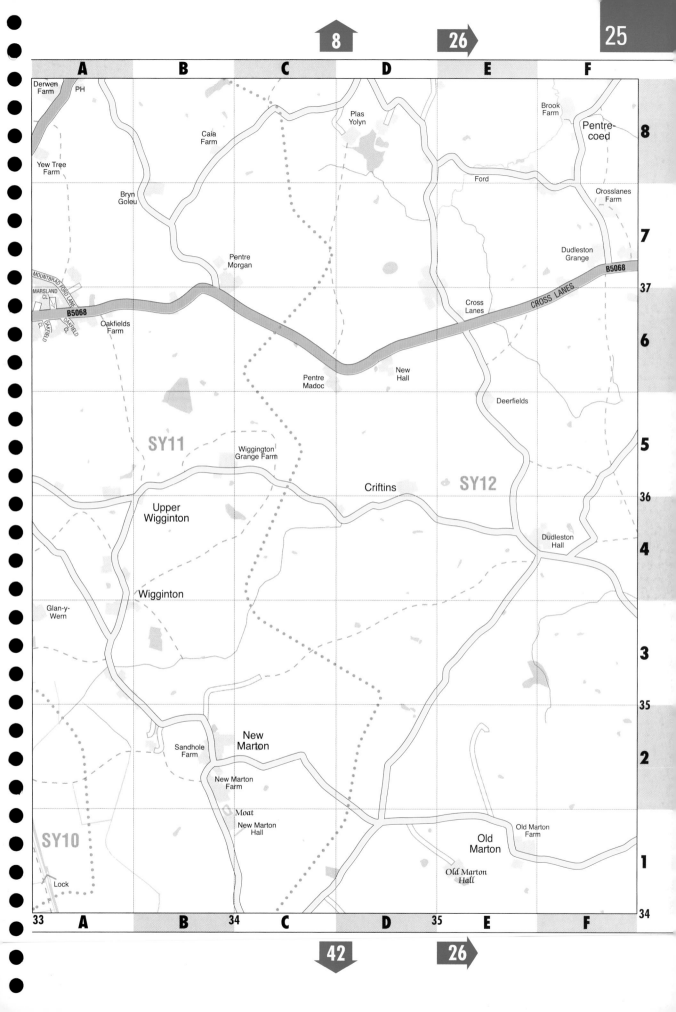

A B C D E F

Derwen Farm PH

Plas Yolyn

Brook Farm

Pentre-coed

Yew Tree Farm

Caia Farm

Ford

Crosslanes Farm

Bryn Goleu

Pentre Morgan

Dudleston Grange

B5068

MOUNTBRAD FORD LANE

MARSLAND CL.

Cross Lanes

CROSS LANES

B5068

OAKFIELD CL.

OAKFIELD CL.

Oakfields Farm

Pentre Madoc

New Hall

Deerfields

SY11

Wiggington Grange Farm

Criftins

SY12

Upper Wigginton

Dudleston Hall

Wigginton

Glan-y-Wern

New Marton

Sandhole Farm

New Marton Farm

Moat

New Marton Hall

Old Marton

Old Marton Farm

SY10

Old Marton Hall

Lock

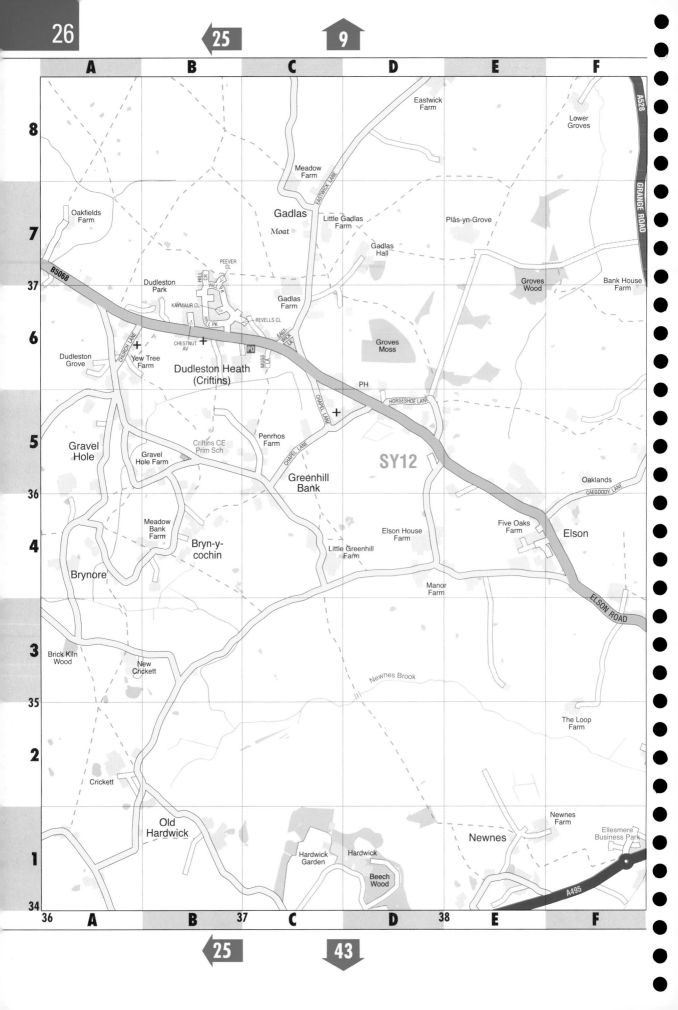

A   B   C   D   E   F

8

Oakfields
Farm

Eastwick
Farm

Lower
Groves

Meadow
Farm

7   Gadlas   Little Gadlas
Farm

Plâs-yn-Grove

Moat

Gadlas
Hall

B5068   PEEVER
CL
37   HILL CR   Groves
Wood   Bank House
Farm

Dudleston
Park   HILL ST   Gadlas
Farm

KAYMAUR CL   HILL PK

6   CHESTNUT   REVELLS CL
AV   EAST   Groves
Moss

CHURCH LANE   PO   WICK LA

Dudleston   Yew Tree   MOSS
Grove   Farm   LA   PH

Dudleston Heath   HORSESHOE LANE
(Criftins)   CHAPEL LANE

5   Criftins CE   Penrhos   SY12
Gravel   Prim Sch   Farm
Hole

Gravel   Greenhill
Hole Farm   Bank   Oaklands

36   CAEGOODY LANE

Meadow   Five Oaks
Bank   Elson House   Farm   Elson
Farm   Bryn-y-   Farm
4   cochin   Little Greenhill
Farm
Brynore   Manor   ELSON ROAD
Farm

Brick Kiln
Wood
3   New
Crickett

35   Newnes Brook

The Loop
Farm
2

Crickett   Newnes
Farm   Ellesmere
Business Park
Old   Newnes
Hardwick   Hardwick   Hardwick
1   Garden   Beech
Wood   A495
34
36   A   37   B   C   D   38   E   F

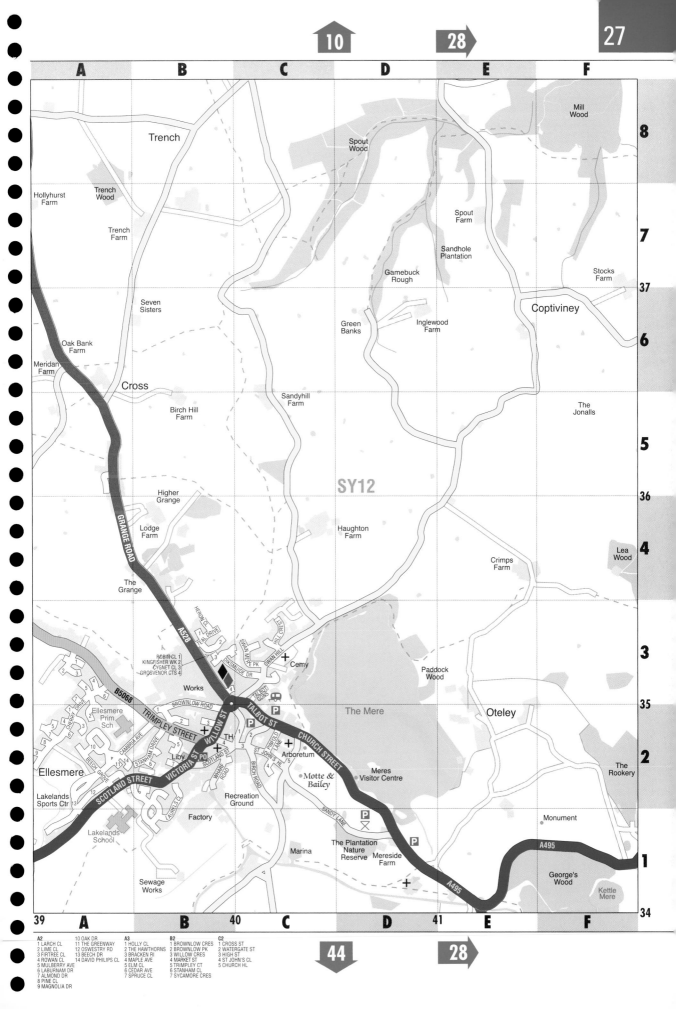

A   B   C   D   E   F

8
7
37
6
5
36
4
3
35
2
1
34

Mill Wood

Trench

Spout Wood

Hollyhurst Farm

Trench Wood

Spout Farm

Trench Farm

Sandhole Plantation

Stocks Farm

Seven Sisters

Gamebuck Rough

Coptiviney

Oak Bank Farm

Green Banks

Inglewood Farm

Meridan Farm

Cross

Birch Hill Farm

Sandyhill Farm

The Jonalls

SY12

Higher Grange

Lodge Farm

Haughton Farm

Lea Wood

The Grange

Crimps Farm

GRANGE ROAD

A528

HERON CL
TEAL DRIVE

SWAN MERE PK
HILL CREST
SWAN HILL

Cemy

Paddock Wood

ROBIN CL 1
KINGFISHER WK 2
CYGNET CL 3
GROSVENOR CTS 4

OAKSMUDE DR

Oteley

Works

BROWNLOW ROAD

TALBOT GDNS

TALBOT ST

The Mere

B5068

TRIMPLEY STREET

WILLOW ST

P
P

CHURCH STREET

Ellesmere Prim Sch

CAMBRIA AVE

TH

PINFOLD LANE

ST JOHN'S TR

Arboretum

The Rookery

CHERRY DRIVE

STANHAM DRIVE

Liby

VICTORIA ST PO

SCOTLAND ST

Meres Visitor Centre

Ellesmere

BEECH GROVE

SCOTLAND STREET

WINBE ROAD

BIRCH ROAD

Motte & Bailey

Lakelands Sports Ctr

LAURELS CL

Factory

Recreation Ground

SANDY LANE

P

Monument

Lakelands School

Sewage Works

Marina

The Plantation Nature Reserve

P

Mereside Farm

A495

A495

George's Wood

Kettle Mere

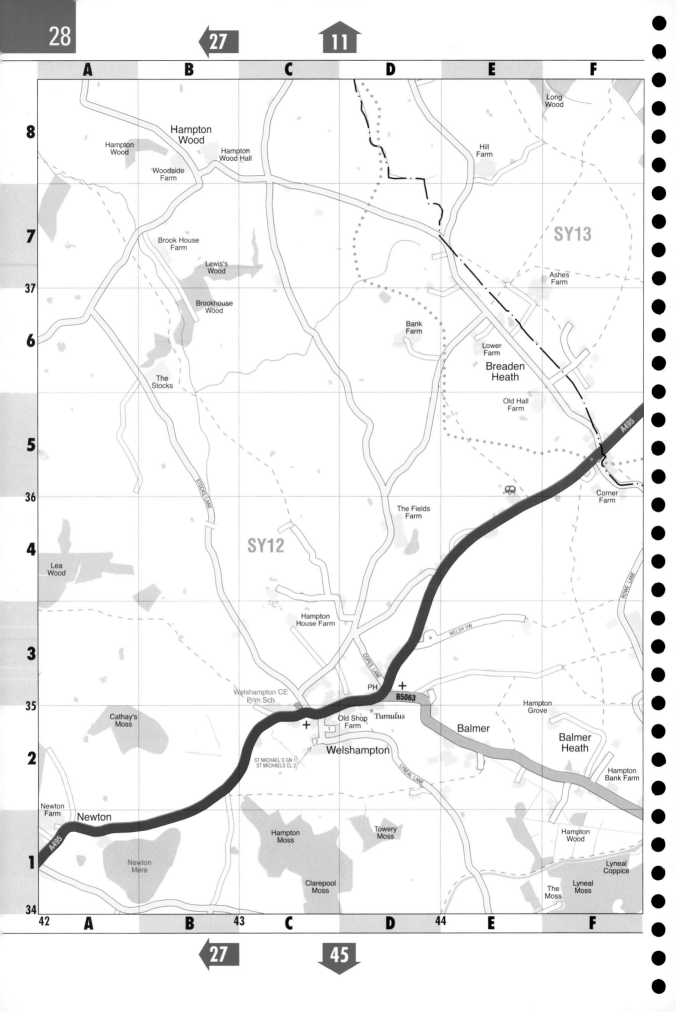

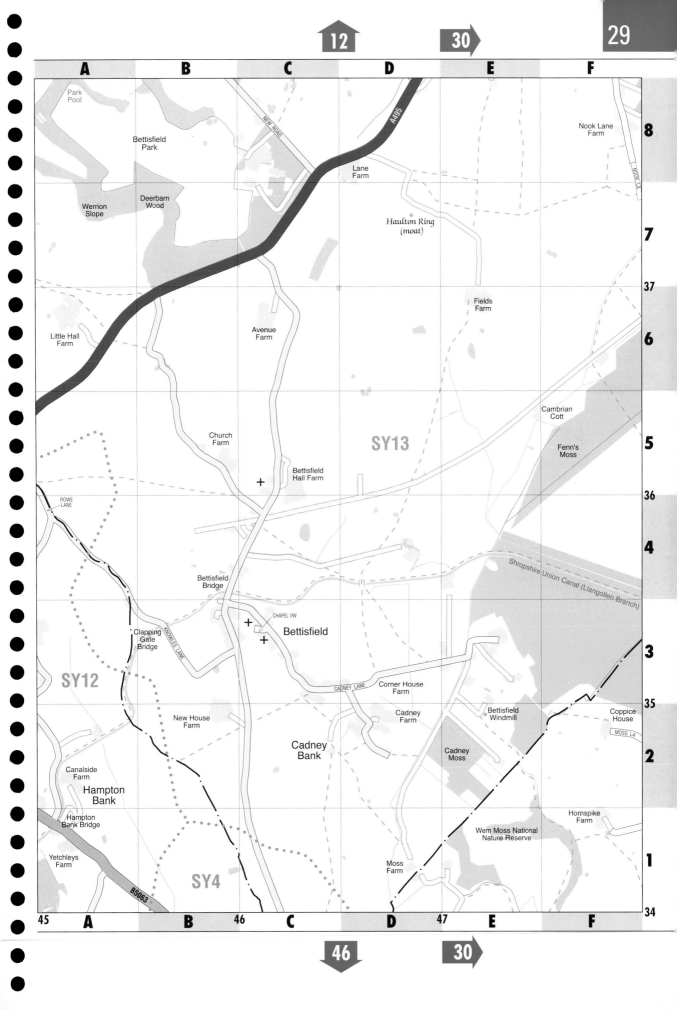

29 13

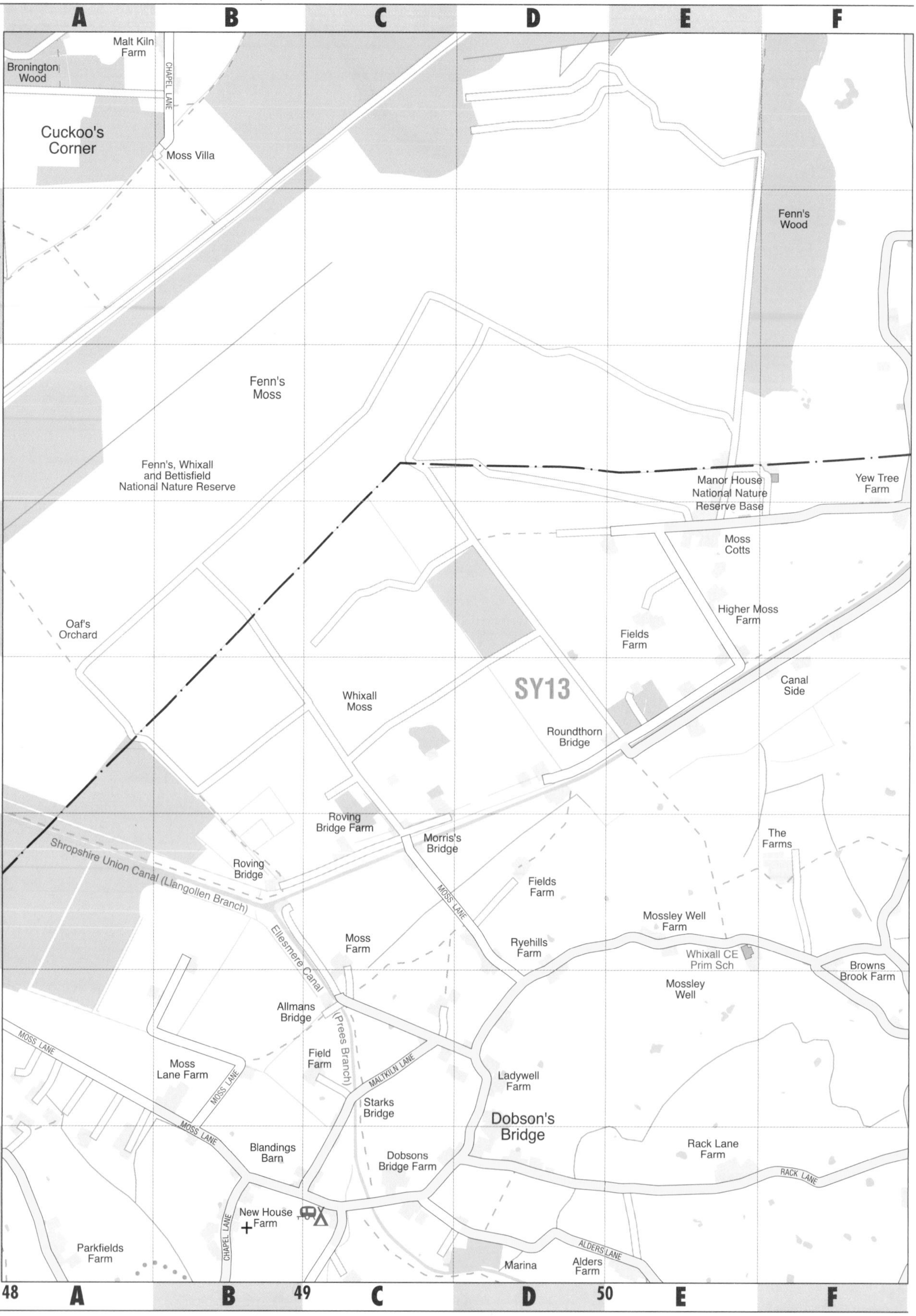

A B C D E F

8

Malt Kiln Farm
Bronington Wood
Cuckoo's Corner
Moss Villa
CHAPEL LANE

Fenn's Wood

7

37

Fenn's Moss

6

Fenn's, Whixall and Bettisfield National Nature Reserve

Manor House National Nature Reserve Base
Yew Tree Farm

Moss Cotts

5

Oaf's Orchard

Higher Moss Farm

Fields Farm

36

Canal Side

SY13

Whixall Moss

4

Roundthorn Bridge

Roving Bridge Farm

Morris's Bridge

The Farms

Shropshire Union Canal (Llangollen Branch)

Roving Bridge

Fields Farm

3

Ellesmere Canal

Moss Farm

Ryehills Farm

Mossley Well Farm

Whixall CE Prim Sch

Browns Brook Farm

35

Allmans Bridge

Mossley Well

(Prees Branch)

MOSS LANE

Field Farm

MALTKILN LANE

Moss Lane Farm

2

Starks Bridge

Ladywell Farm

Dobson's Bridge

Rack Lane Farm

RACK LANE

MOSS LANE

Blandings Barn

Dobsons Bridge Farm

1

CHAPEL LANE

New House Farm

ALDERS LANE

Parkfields Farm

Marina

Alders Farm

34

48 A B 49 C D 50 E F

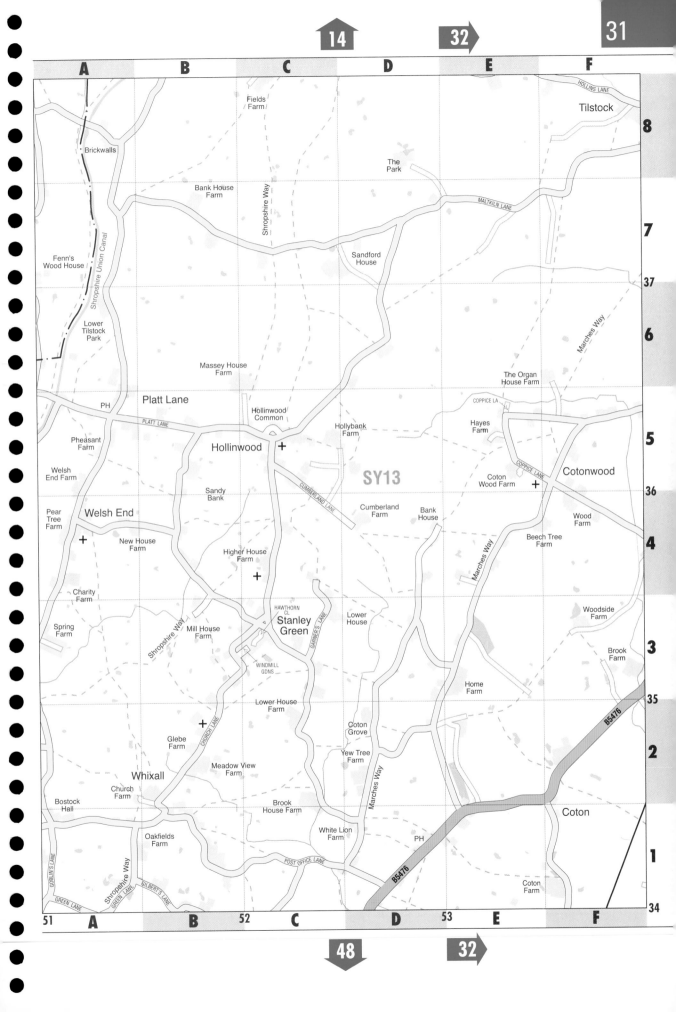

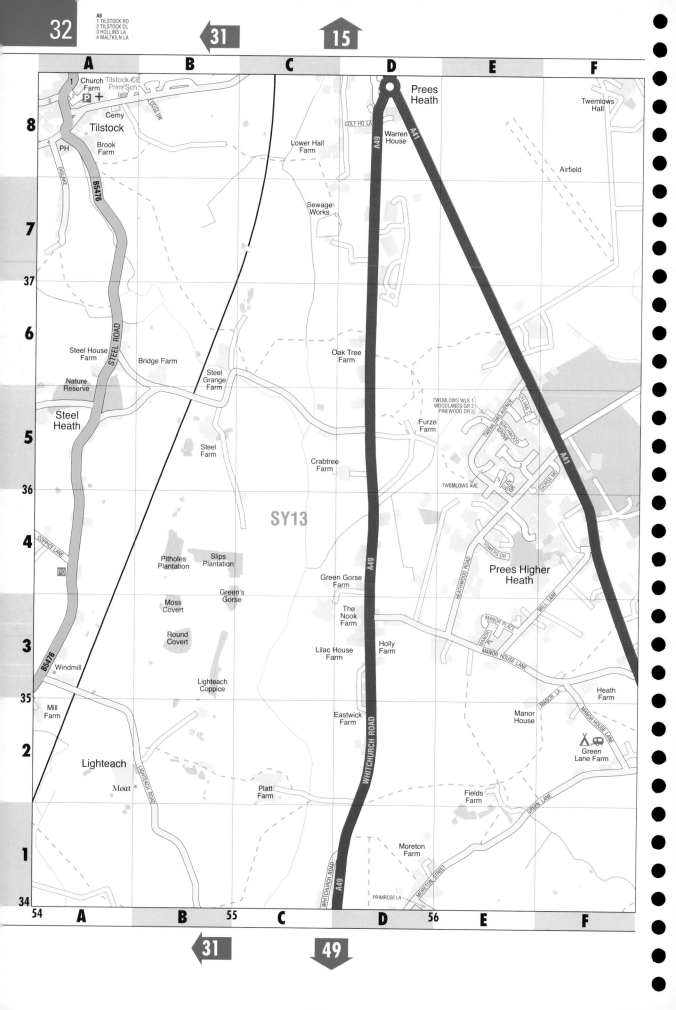

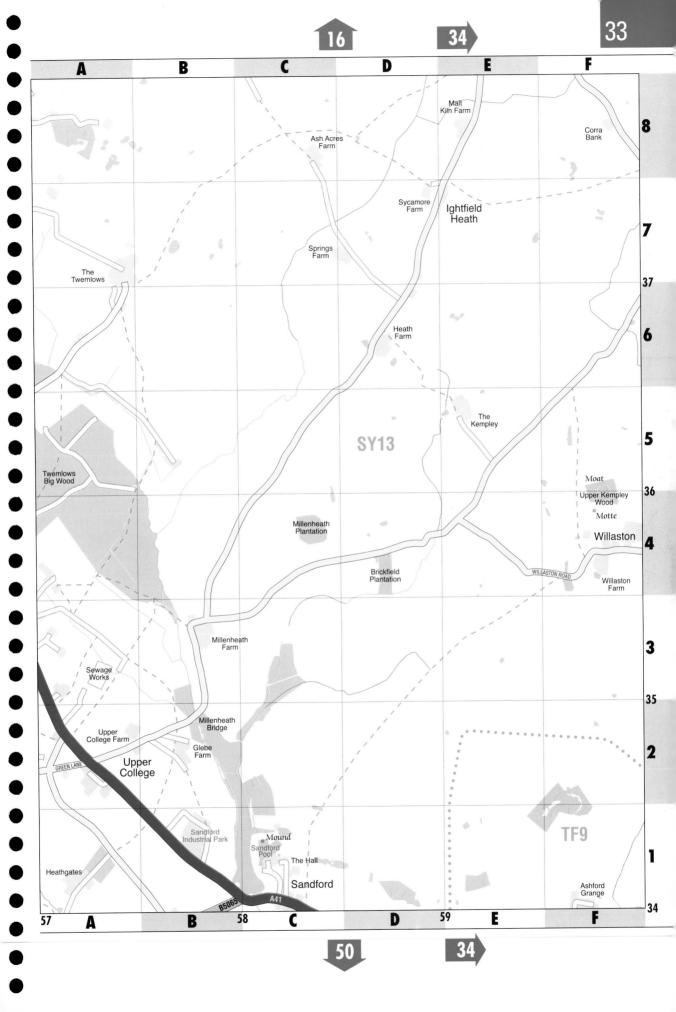

33
17

A B C D E F
8
7
37
6
5
36
4
3
35
2
1
34
60
61
62
Gorse Farm
Cloverley Wall Plantation
Big Wood
Moat
Church Farm
CORRA PL
CORRA MEADOWS
Calverhall
Manor Farm
PH
Springs Plantation
Newstreet Lane
Moat Farm
Moat
Moat Plantation
Churchwalk Plantation
Moat
Weston Farm
Cloverley Hall Farm
Cloverley Hall
PREES ROAD
BLETCHLEY ROAD
Cloverley Pool
Gravelhole Plantation
Little Cloverley Farm
Pedsmoor Plantation
Plantation Willow
SY13
WILLASTON ROAD
Pedsmoor Farm
Poole Farm
Oldfields Farm
Laurel Plantation
Wyrley
Moreton Wood Farm
Boundary Farm
WILLASTON ROAD
Hill Farm
Moreton Mill Farm
Lawns Cottage
White Gates Farm
BLETCHLEY ROAD
Moretonwood
TF9
Lawns Farm
Hightrees Cottages
Aychley Farm
A41
Church Farm
Hollies Farm

33
51

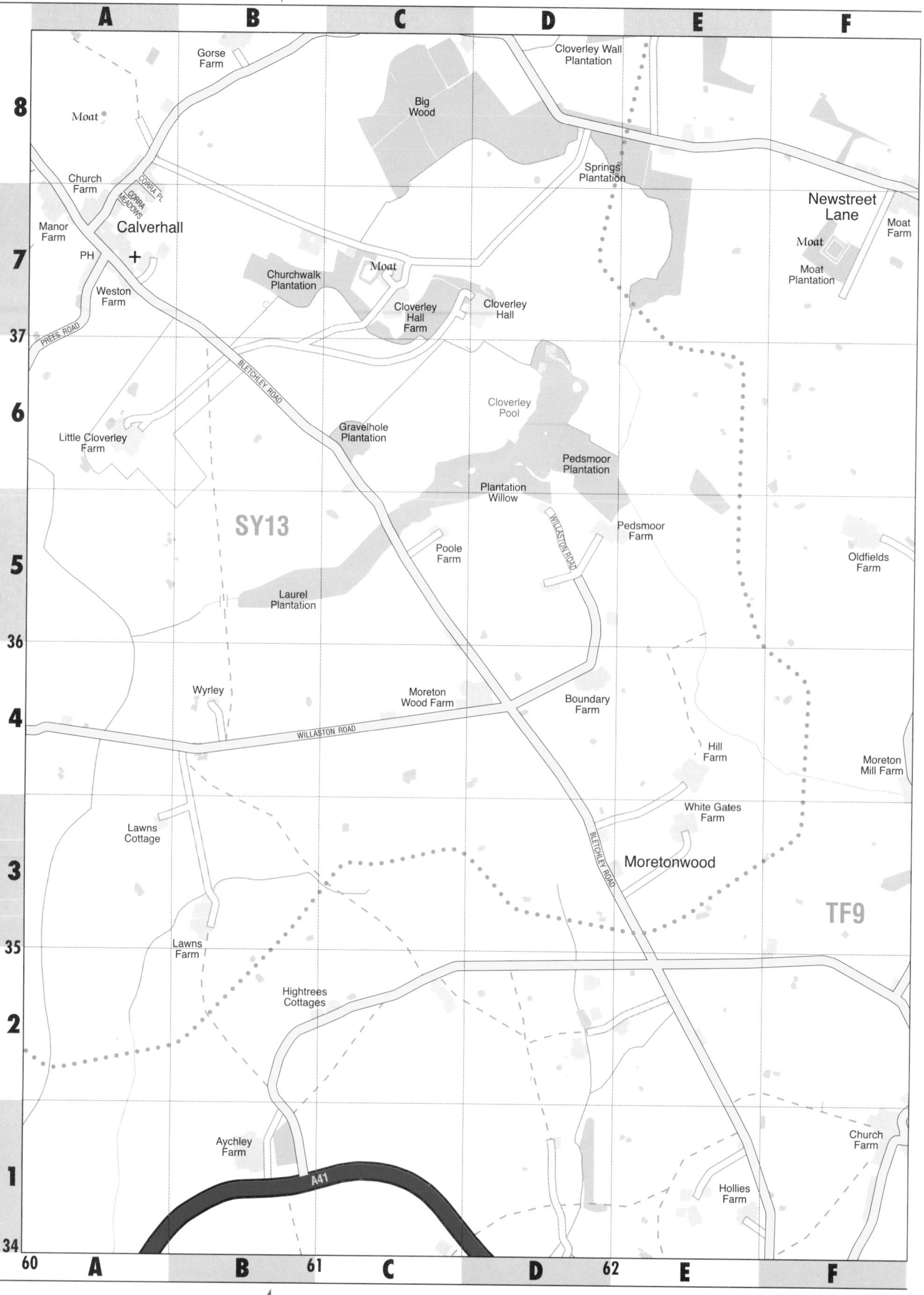

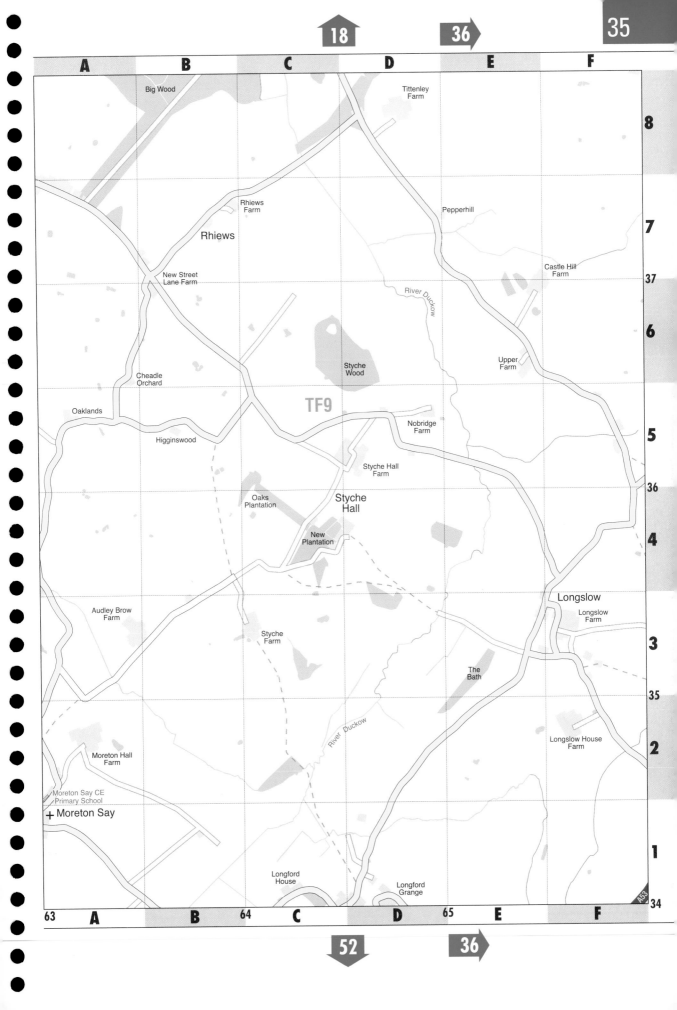

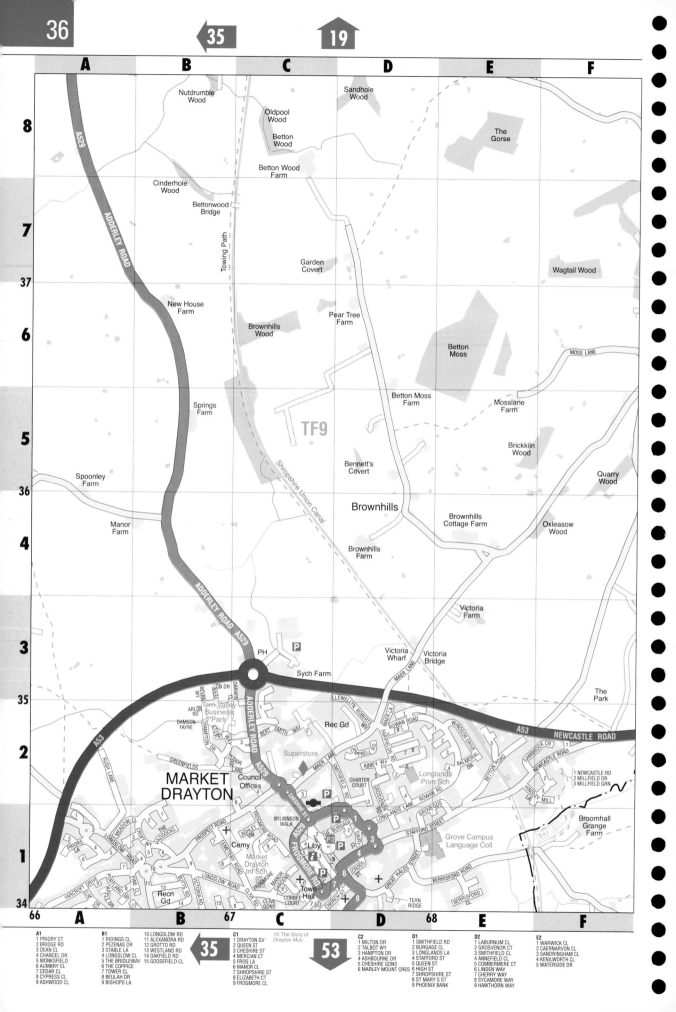

A · B · C · D · E · F

8

7

37

6

5

36

4

3

35

2

1

34

66 · 67 · 68

A529

ADDERLEY ROAD

Nutdrumble Wood

Oldpool Wood

Sandhole Wood

Betton Wood

The Gorse

Cinderhole Wood

Bettonwood Bridge

Betton Wood Farm

Towing Path

Garden Covert

Wagtail Wood

New House Farm

Brownhills Wood

Pear Tree Farm

Betton Moss

MOSS LANE

Springs Farm

Shropshire Union Canal

TF9

Betton Moss Farm

Mosslane Farm

Spoonley Farm

Brickkiln Wood

Bennett's Covert

Quarry Wood

Brownhills

36

Manor Farm

ADDERLEY ROAD A529

Brownhills Farm

Brownhills Cottage Farm

Oxleasow Wood

Victoria Farm

Victoria Wharf

Victoria Bridge

The Park

PH

P

Sych Farm

Maer Lane

A53

NEWCASTLE ROAD

Tern Valley Business Park

DARWIN WY
BEVAN WY
ARLON RD
DAMSON FAYRE
HAMPTON DR
STUART WY
TUDOR LANE

ADDERLEY ROAD A529

BERT SMITH WAY

Rec Gd

CAMPBELL RD
FAIRFIELDS RD
Maer La
ROWAN ROAD
WINDSOR DRIVE
BALMORAL DR
BETTON ROAD
SAMBROOK CR
NEWCASTLE ROAD
HINSLEY LA
MILL

1 NEWCASTLE RD
2 MILLFIELD DR
3 MILLFIELD GRN

GREENFIELDS

Superstore

Maer Lane

SMITHFIELD RD

ABBEY WY

CHARTER COURT

Longlands Prim Sch

MARKET DRAYTON

Council Offices

MEADOW CL
THE PADDOCKS
CROFT WY
TOWER CL
PROSPECT ROAD
ASHLEY VW
FROGMORE ROAD
A529
CHESHIRE ST
WILKINSON WALK
THE BURGAGE
DARBY RD
GROSVENOR RD
Longlands Lane
ROWAN RD
GROVE GDNS
Grove Campus Language Coll
STAFFORD STREET

Broomhall Grange Farm

PRIORS LA
LONGSLOW ROAD
CEMETERY ROAD
Cemy
FROGMORE RD
Liby
i
CROSS ST
GREAT HALES STREET
BERRISFORD ROAD
BERRISFORD CL

Market Drayton Inf Sch

MANOR GARDENS

Town Hall

CHURCH ST

TERN RIDGE

FARCROFT DRIVE
PORTLAND DR
ELM CL
PINE CL
MAPLE CL
Recn Gd
VICTORIA ROAD
BUTTS RD
CLIVE RD
CLIVE GDNS
CORBET COURT

LLEWELLYN ROBERTS WY

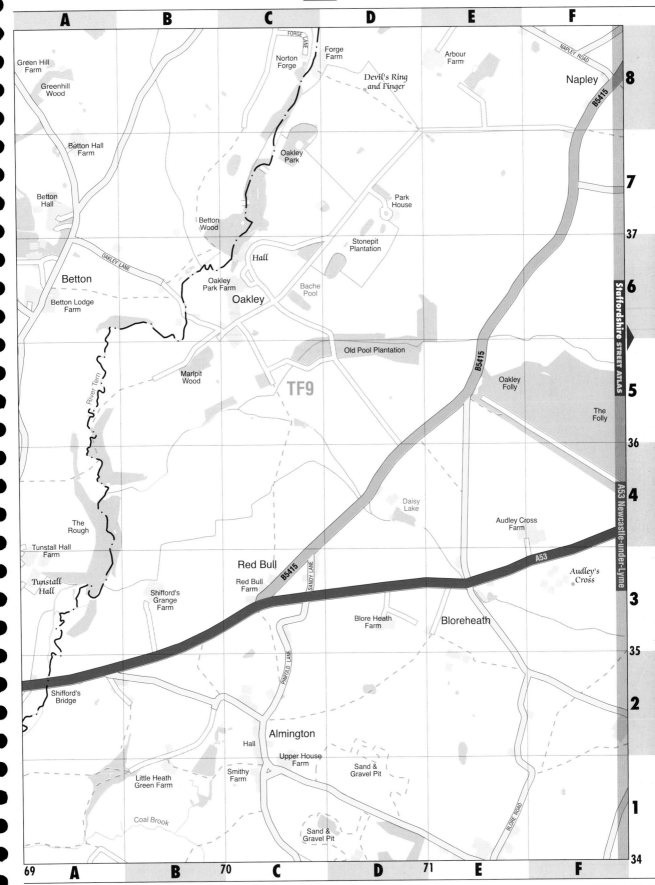

Staffordshire STREET ATLAS

A53 Newcastle-under-Lyme

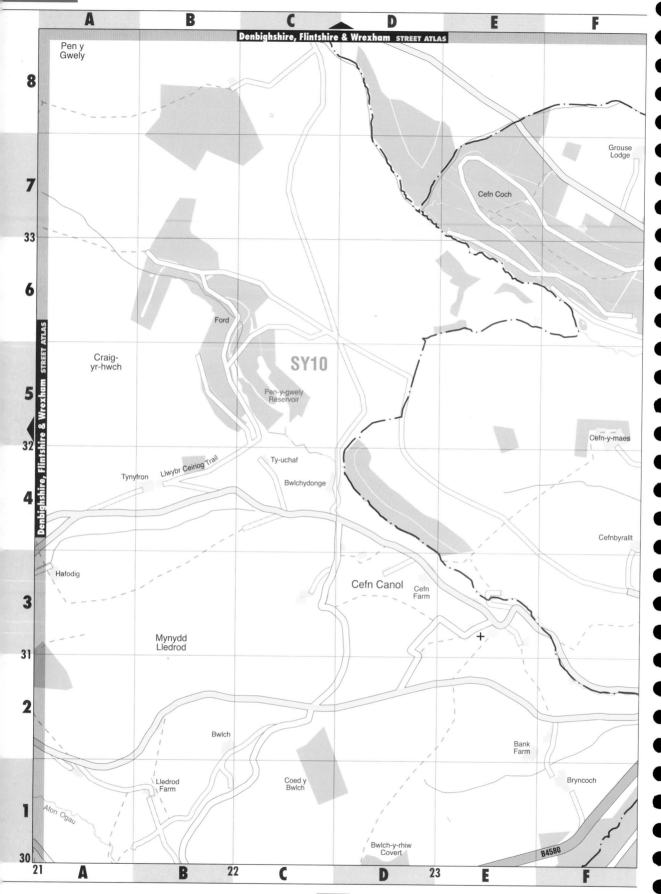

Pen y
Gwely

Grouse
Lodge

Cefn Coch

Denbighshire, Flintshire & Wrexham STREET ATLAS

Ford

Craig-
yr-hwch

SY10

Pen-y-gwely
Reservoir

Cefn-y-maes

Ty-uchaf

Tynyfron

Llwybr Ceiriog Trail

Bwlchydonge

Cefnbyrallt

Hafodig

Cefn Canol

Cefn
Farm

Mynydd
Lledrod

Bwlch

Bank
Farm

Lledrod
Farm

Coed y
Bwlch

Bryncoch

Afon Ogau

Bwlch-y-rhiw
Covert

B4580

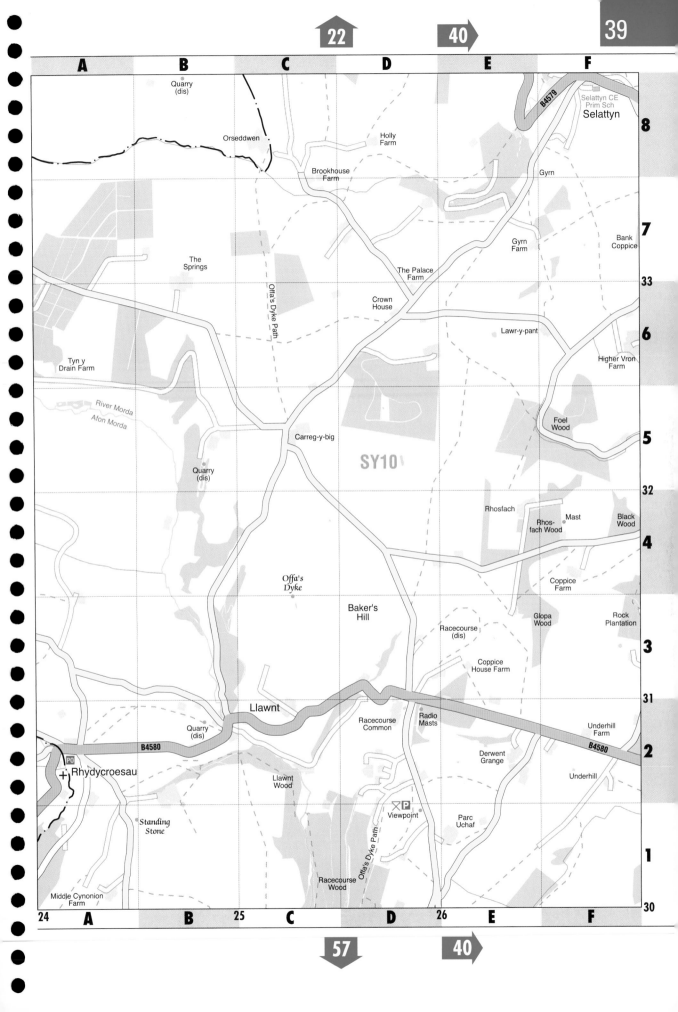

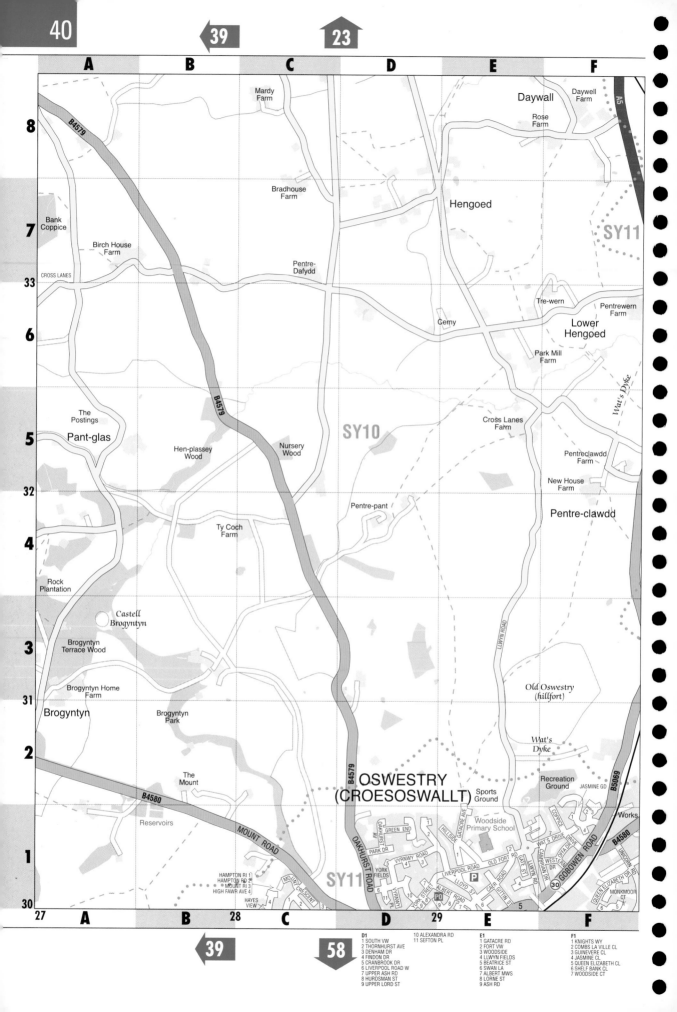

A B C D E F

8

7

33

6

5

32

4

3

31

2

1

30

27 A 28 B C 28 D 29 E F

B4579

Mardy Farm

Daywall

Daywell Farm

Rose Farm

A5

Bradhouse Farm

Hengoed

SY11

Bank Coppice

Birch House Farm

CROSS LANES

Pentre-Dafydd

Tre-wern

Pentrewern Farm

Cerny

Lower Hengoed

Park Mill Farm

The Postings

Pant-glas

B4579

Hen-plassey Wood

Nursery Wood

SY10

Cross Lanes Farm

Wat's Dyke

Pentreclawdd Farm

New House Farm

Pentre-clawdd

Pentre-pant

Rock Plantation

Ty Coch Farm

Castell Brogyntyn

Brogyntyn Terrace Wood

LLWYN ROAD

Old Oswestry (hillfort)

Brogyntyn Home Farm

Brogyntyn

Brogyntyn Park

Wat's Dyke

Recreation Ground

JASMINE GD

B5069

B4580

The Mount

B4580

B4579

OSWESTRY (CROESOSWALLT)

Sports Ground

Works

MOUNT ROAD

Reservoirs

Woodside Primary School

GOBOWEN ROAD

B4580

SY11

OAKHURST ROAD

30

UNICORN

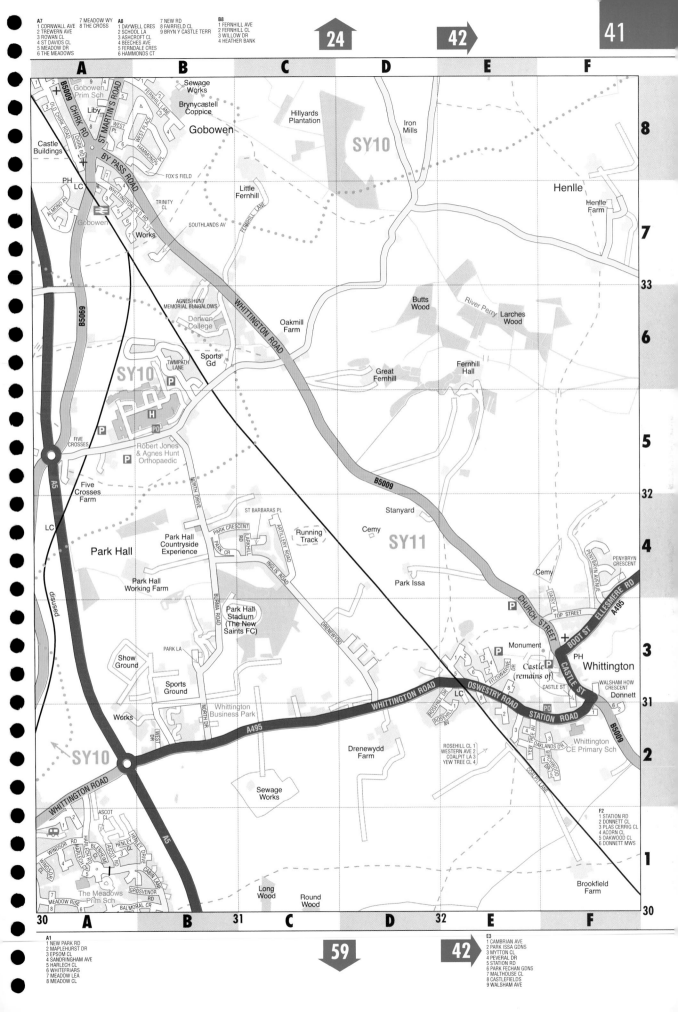

24
42

A B C D E F

8
7
33
6
5
32
4
3
31
2
1
30

30 A 31 B 31 C 32 D 32 E F

59
42

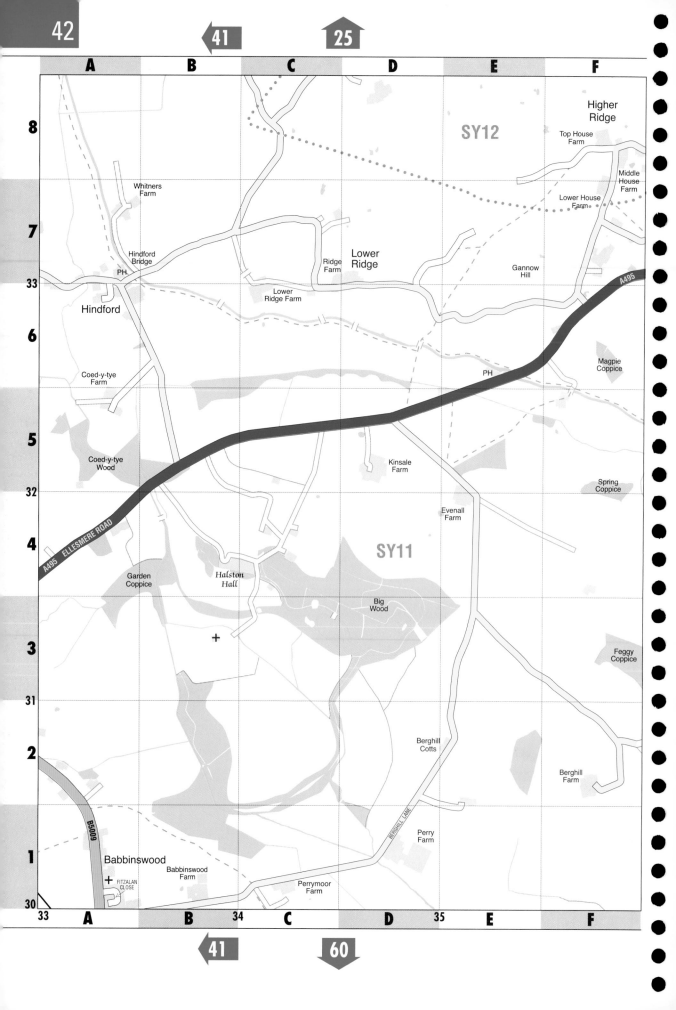

SY12

Higher Ridge

Top House Farm

Middle House Farm

Lower House Farm

Whitners Farm

Lower Ridge

Ridge Farm

Gannow Hill

A495

Hindford Bridge

PH

Lower Ridge Farm

Hindford

Magpie Coppice

Coed-y-tye Farm

PH

Kinsale Farm

Spring Coppice

Coed-y-tye Wood

Evenall Farm

A495 ELLESMERE ROAD

SY11

Garden Coppice

Halston Hall

Big Wood

Feggy Coppice

Berghill Cotts

Berghill Farm

BERGHILL LANE

Perry Farm

B5009

Babbinswood

FITZALAN CLOSE

Babbinswood Farm

Perrymoor Farm

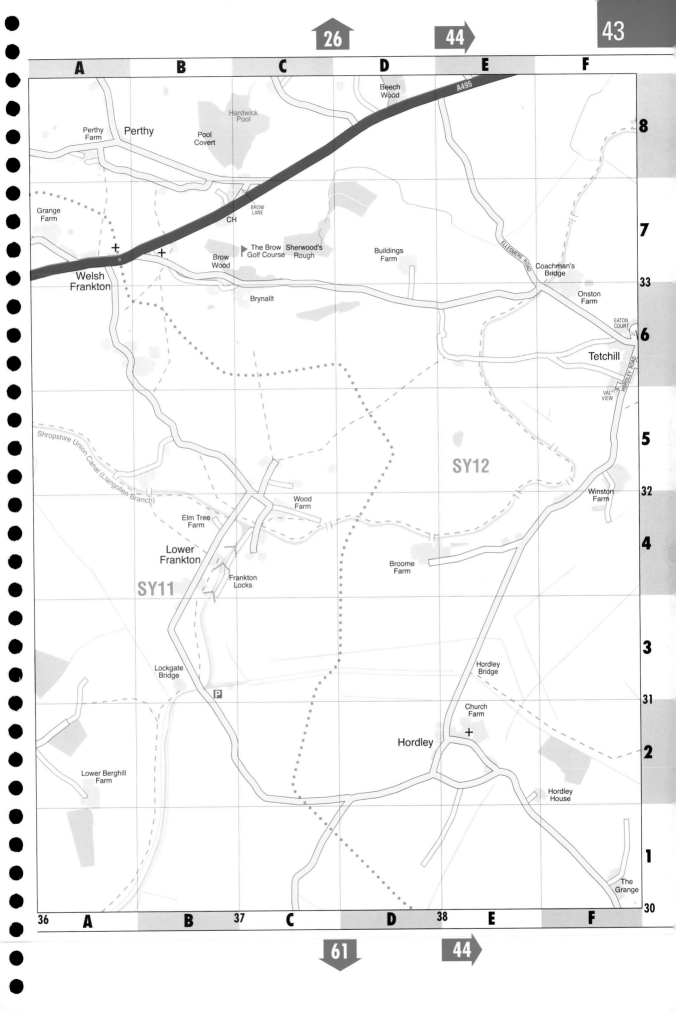

A B C D E F

8
7
33
6
5
32
4
3
31
2
1
30

Perthy Farm
Perthy
Hardwick Pool
Pool Covert
Beech Wood
A495

Grange Farm
BROW LANE
CH
Welsh Frankton
Brow Wood
The Brow Golf Course
Sherwood's Rough
Brynallt
Buildings Farm
ELLESMERE ROAD
Coachman's Bridge
Onston Farm
EATON COURT
Tetchill
HORDLEY ROAD
VAL VIEW

Shropshire Union Canal (Llangollen Branch)

SY12

SY11

Elm Tree Farm
Lower Frankton
Wood Farm
Frankton Locks
Broome Farm
Winston Farm

Lockgate Bridge
P

Hordley Bridge
Church Farm
Hordley

Lower Berghill Farm

Hordley House

The Grange

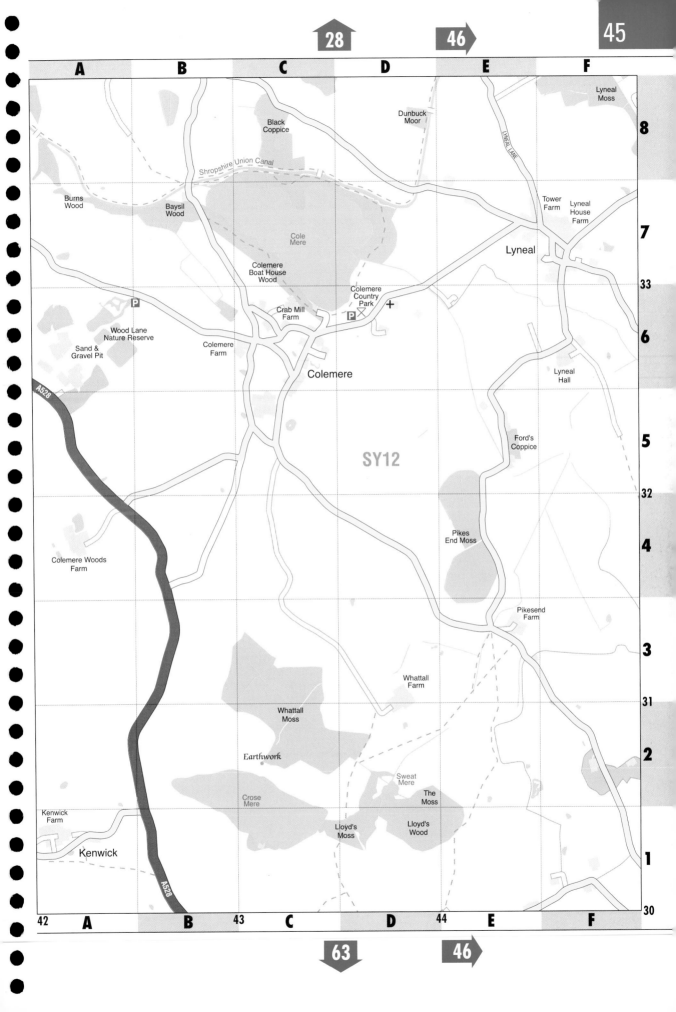

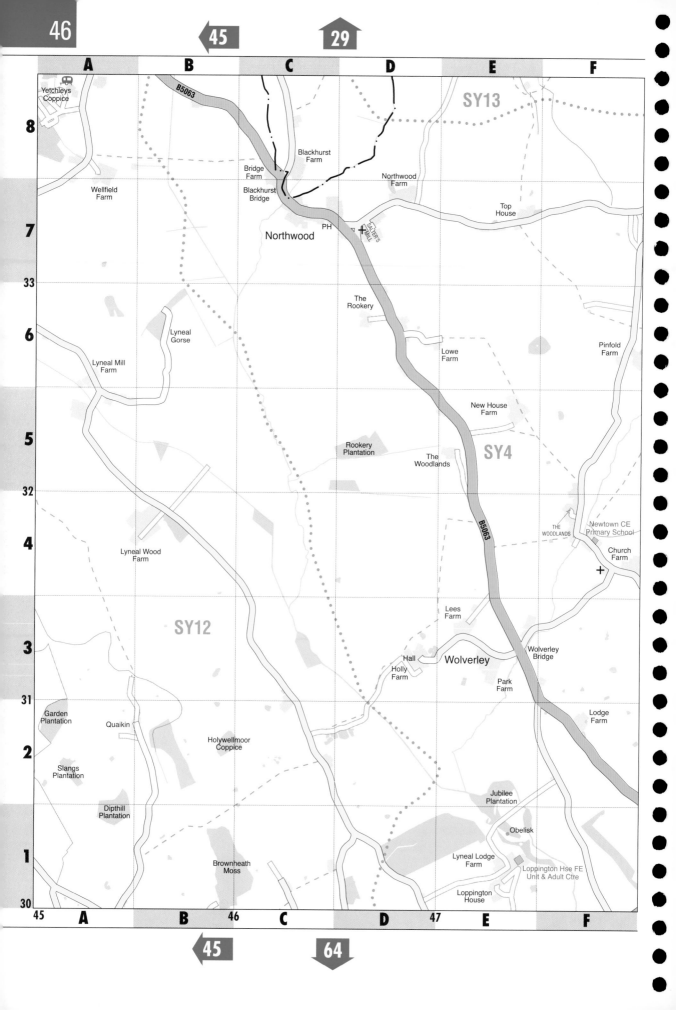

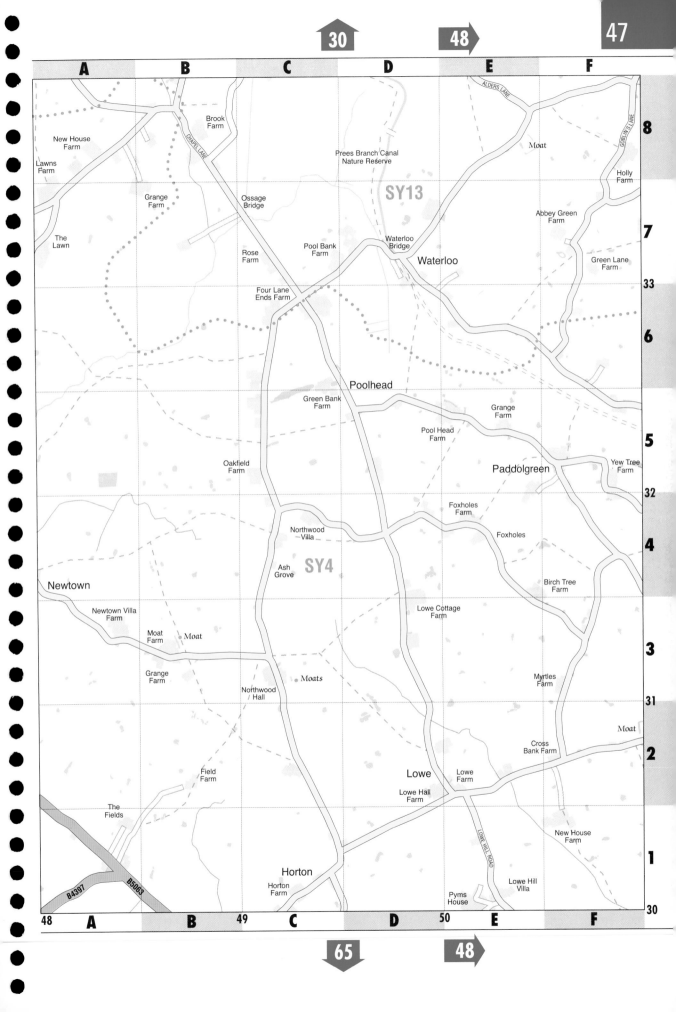

A **B** **C** **D** **E** **F**

8

New House Farm

Brook Farm

Lawns Farm

Prees Branch Canal Nature Reserve

Moat

ALDERS LANE

GOBLIN'S LANE

Holly Farm

Grange Farm

Ossage Bridge

SY13

Abbey Green Farm

7

The Lawn

Rose Farm

Pool Bank Farm

Waterloo Bridge

Waterloo

Green Lane Farm

33

Four Lane Ends Farm

CHAPEL LANE

6

Poolhead

Green Bank Farm

Grange Farm

5

Pool Head Farm

Oakfield Farm

Paddolgreen

Yew Tree Farm

32

Foxholes Farm

Northwood Villa

Foxholes

4

Ash Grove

SY4

Birch Tree Farm

Newtown

Lowe Cottage Farm

Newtown Villa Farm

Moat Farm

Moat

3

Grange Farm

Myrtles Farm

Northwood Hall

Moats

31

Moat

Cross Bank Farm

2

Field Farm

Lowe

Lowe Farm

The Fields

Lowe Hall Farm

New House Farm

1

B4397

B5063

Horton

Horton Farm

LOWE HILL ROAD

Pyms House

Lowe Hill Villa

30

A 49 **B** **C** 50 **D** **E** **F**

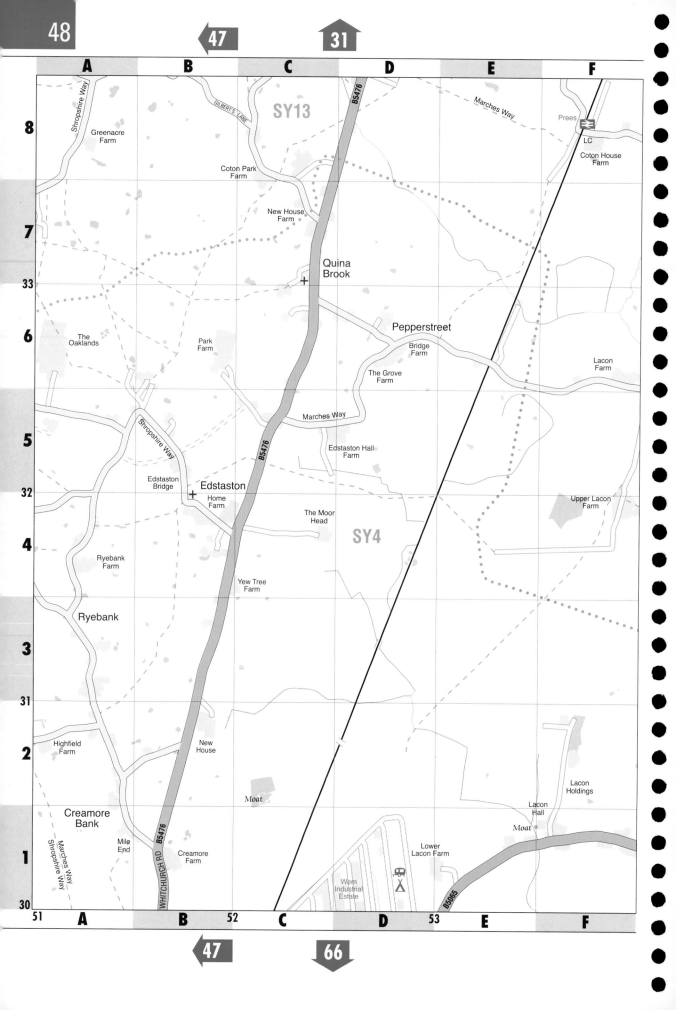

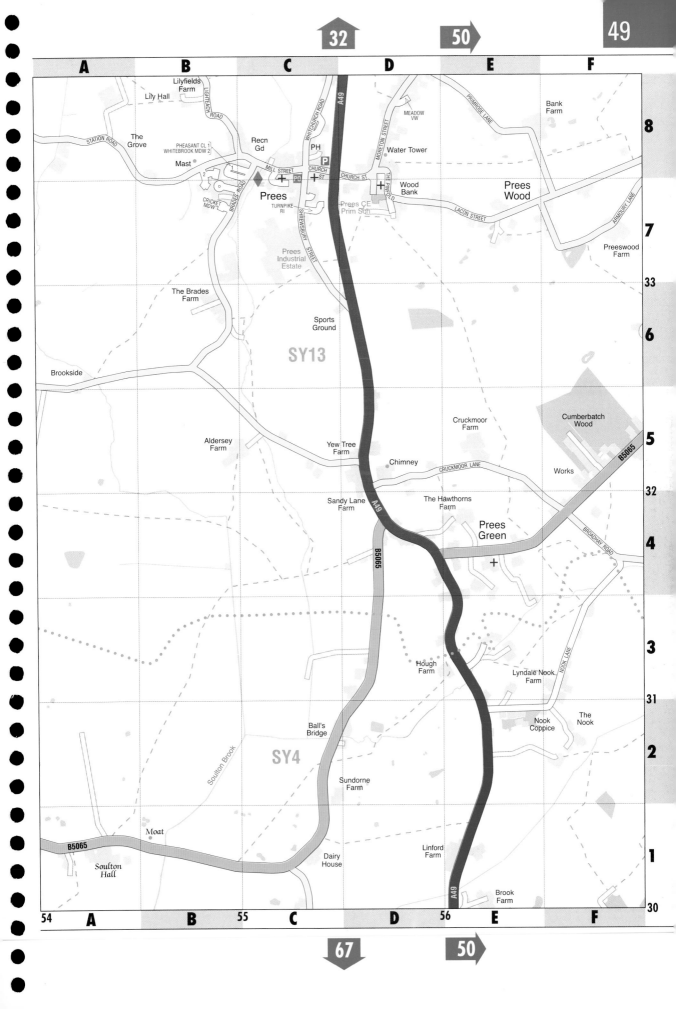

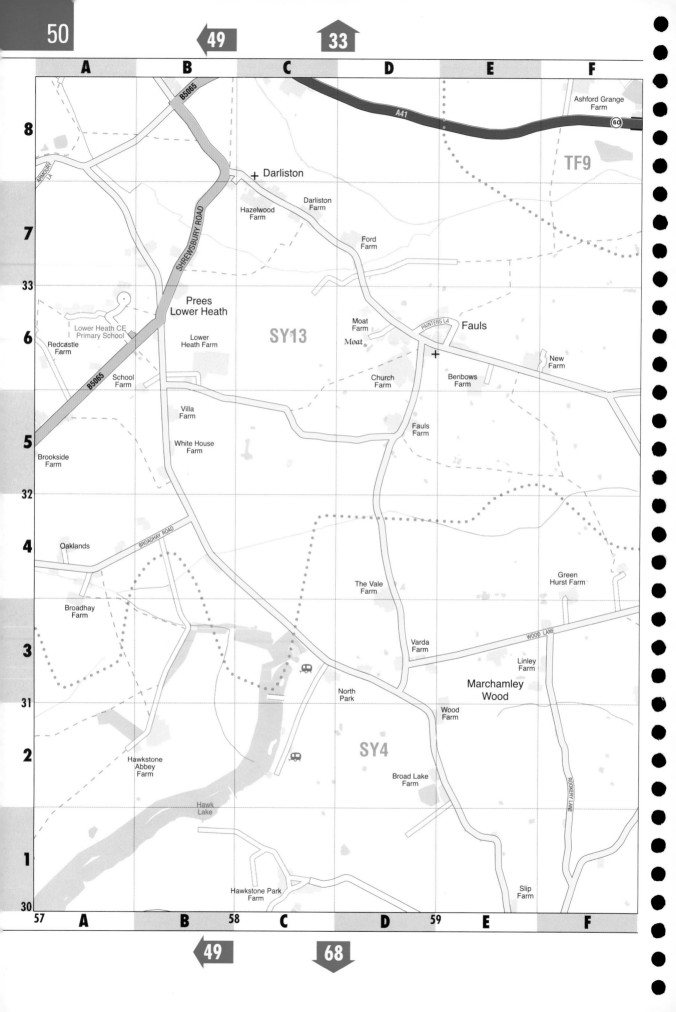

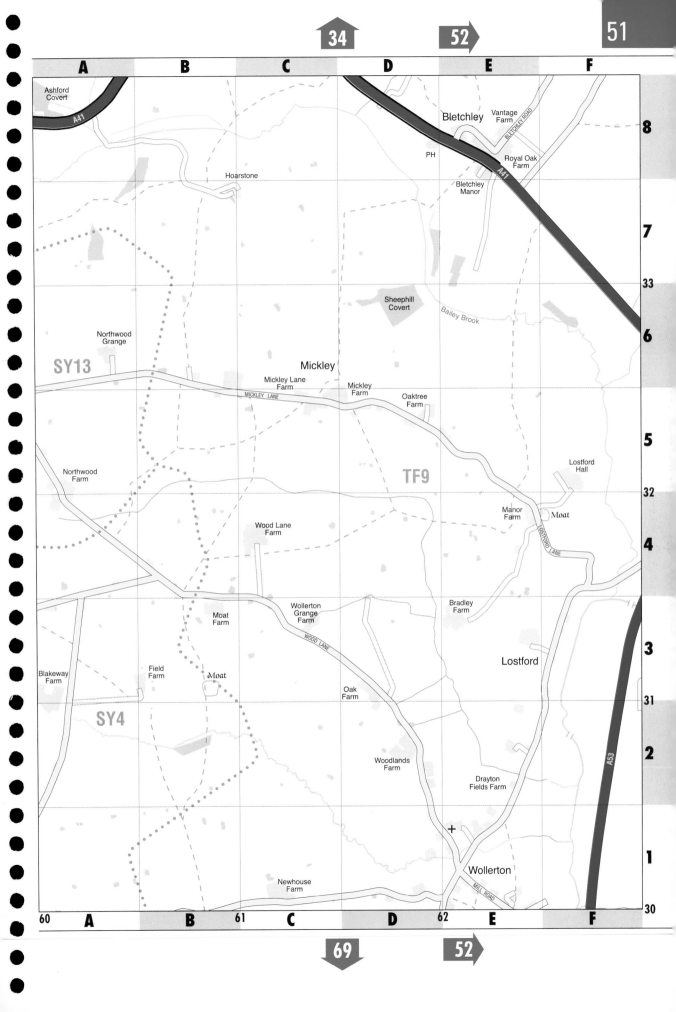

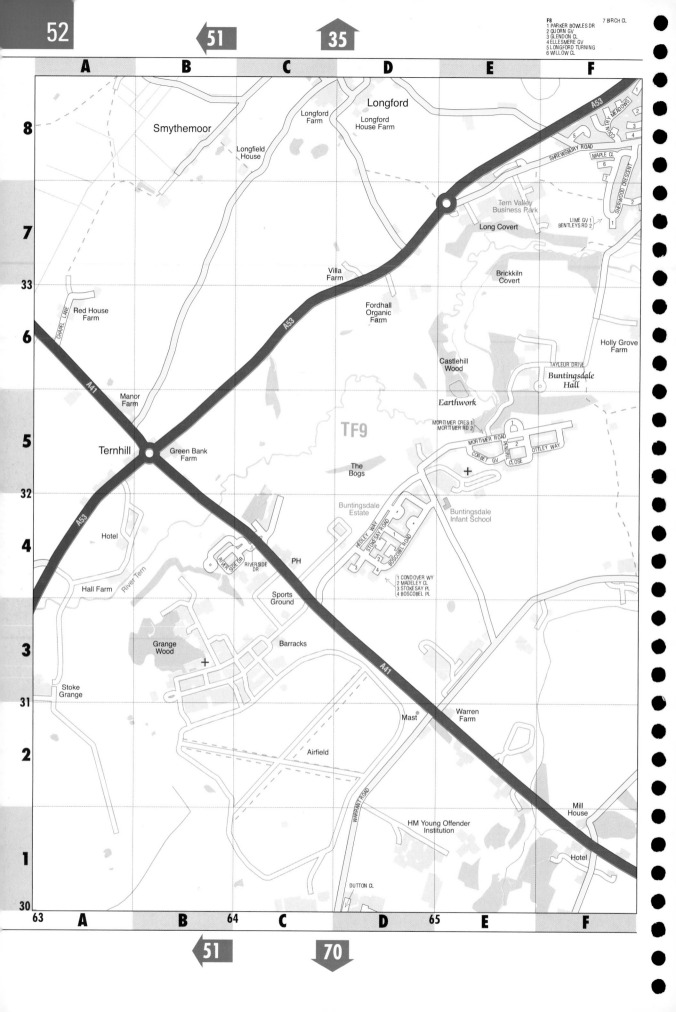

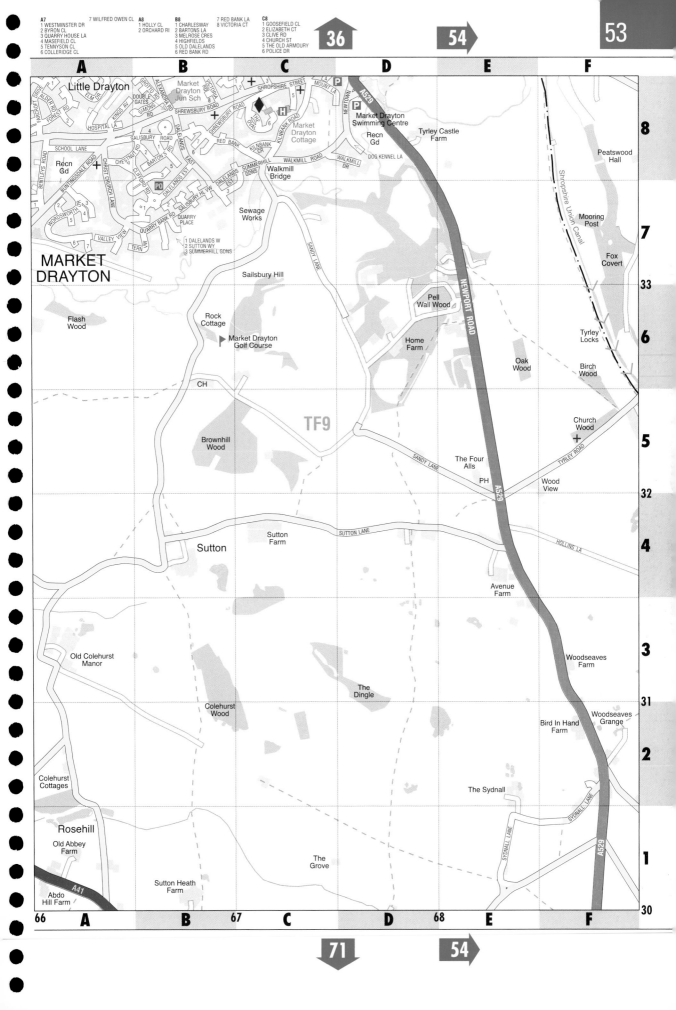

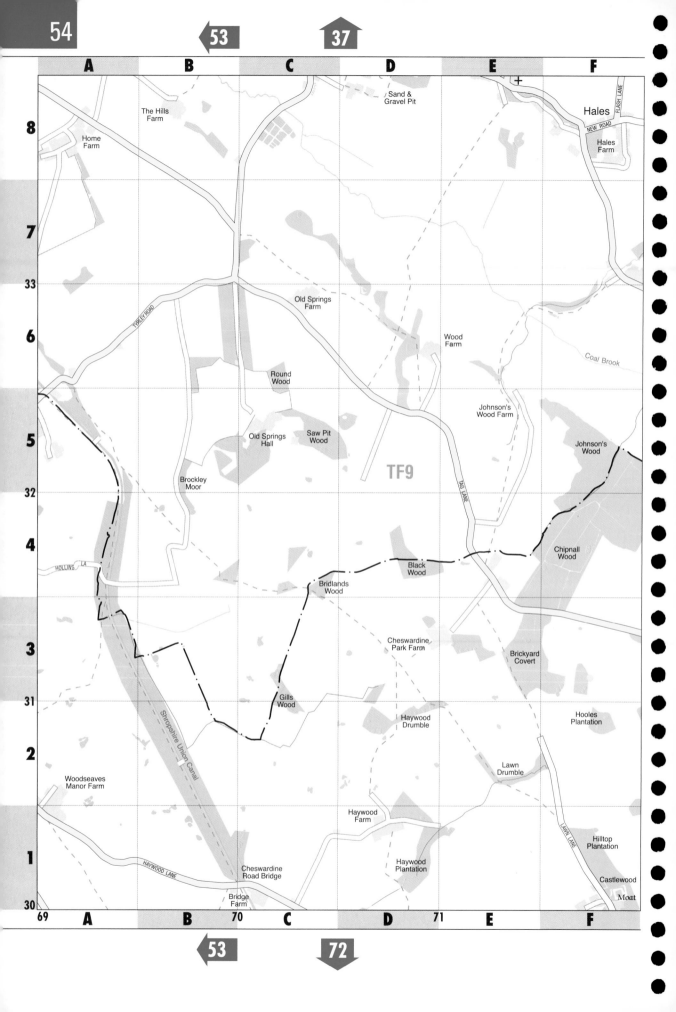

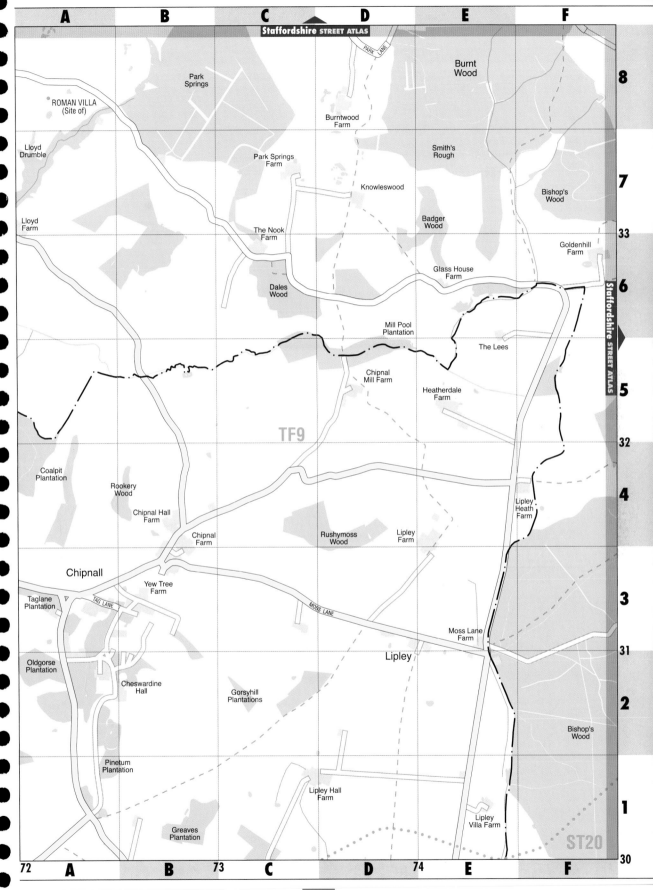

A B C D E F

8

Park
Springs

ROMAN VILLA
(Site of)

Burnt
Wood

Burntwood
Farm

Lloyd
Drumble

Smith's
Rough

Park Springs
Farm

7

Knowleswood

Bishop's
Wood

Lloyd
Farm

The Nook
Farm

Badger
Wood

33

Goldenhill
Farm

Glass House
Farm

6

Dales
Wood

Mill Pool
Plantation

The Lees

Chipnal
Mill Farm

5

Heatherdale
Farm

TF9

32

Coalpit
Plantation

Rookery
Wood

Lipley
Heath
Farm

4

Chipnal Hall
Farm

Chipnal
Farm

Rushymoss
Wood

Lipley
Farm

Chipnall

Yew Tree
Farm

3

Taglane
Plantation

TAG LANE

MOSS LANE

Moss Lane
Farm

31

Oldgorse
Plantation

Lipley

Cheswardine
Hall

Gorsyhill
Plantations

2

Bishop's
Wood

Pinetum
Plantation

Lipley Hall
Farm

1

Greaves
Plantation

Lipley
Villa Farm

ST20

72 A B 73 C D 74 E F 30

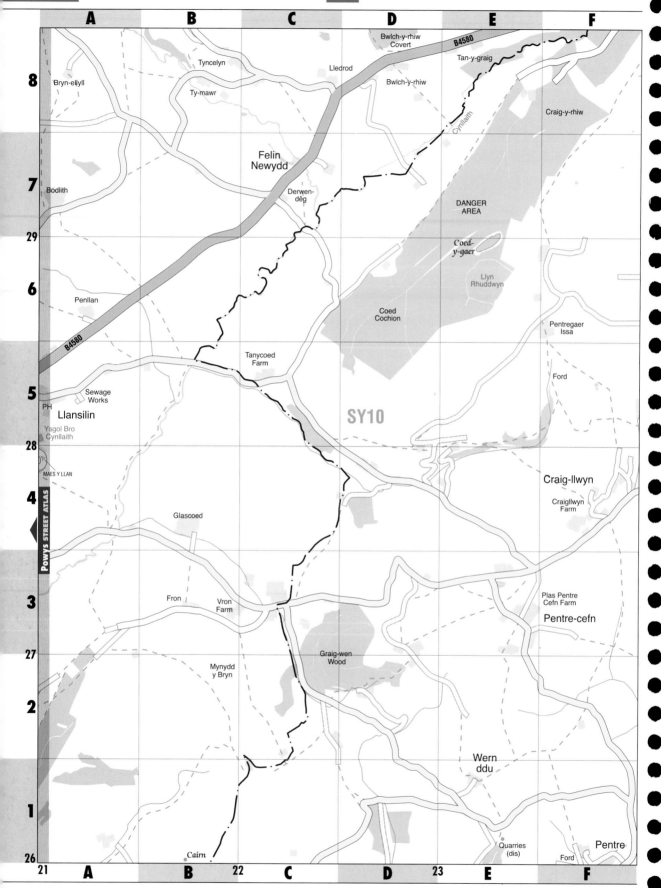

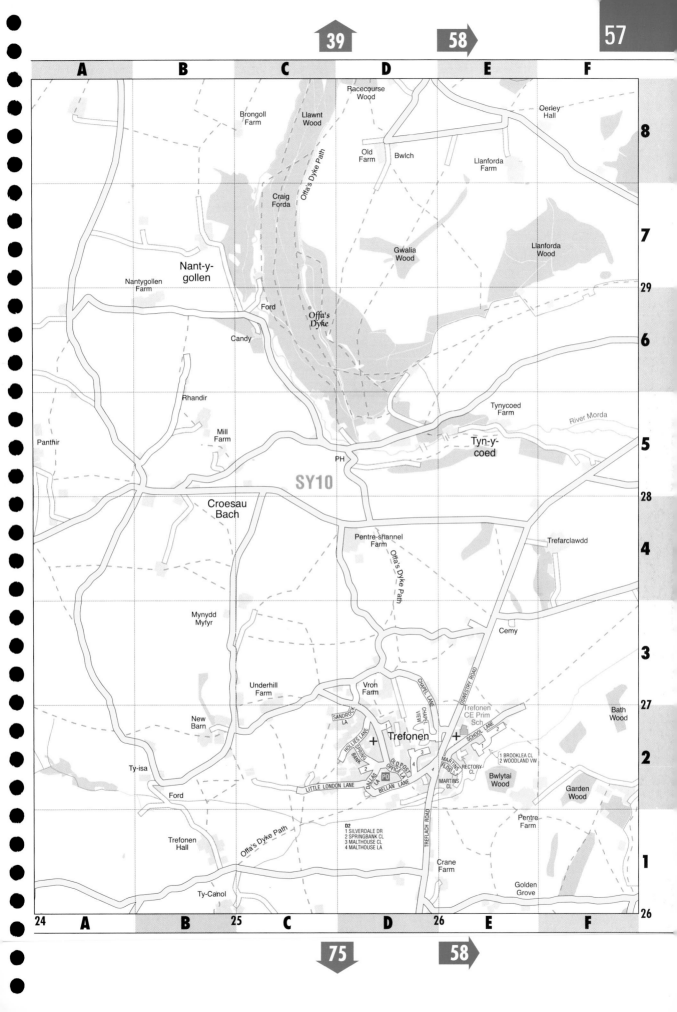

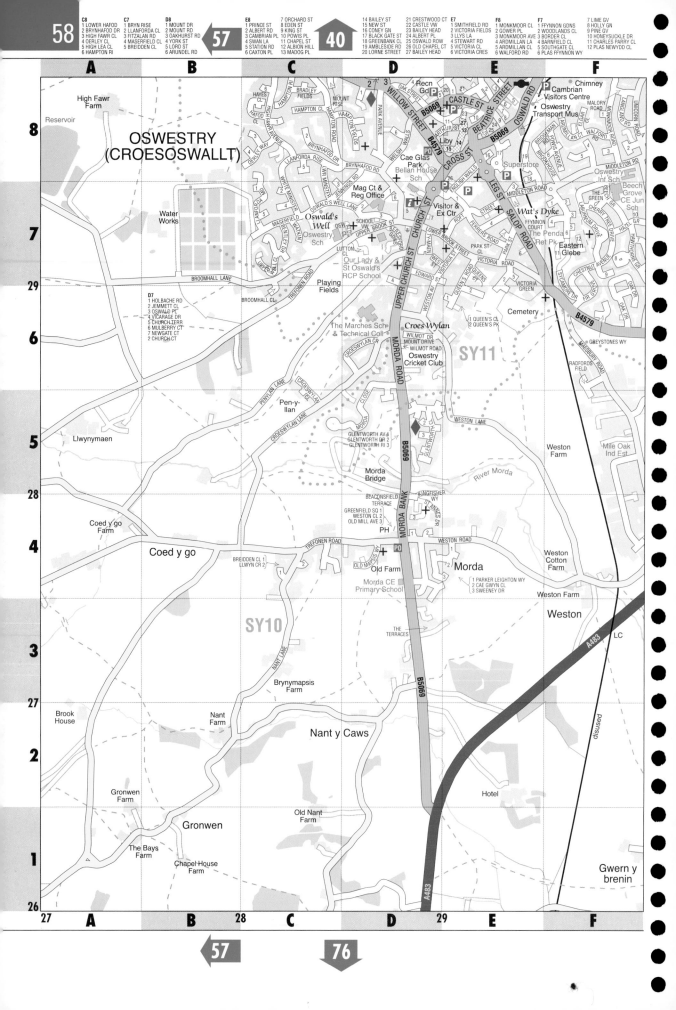

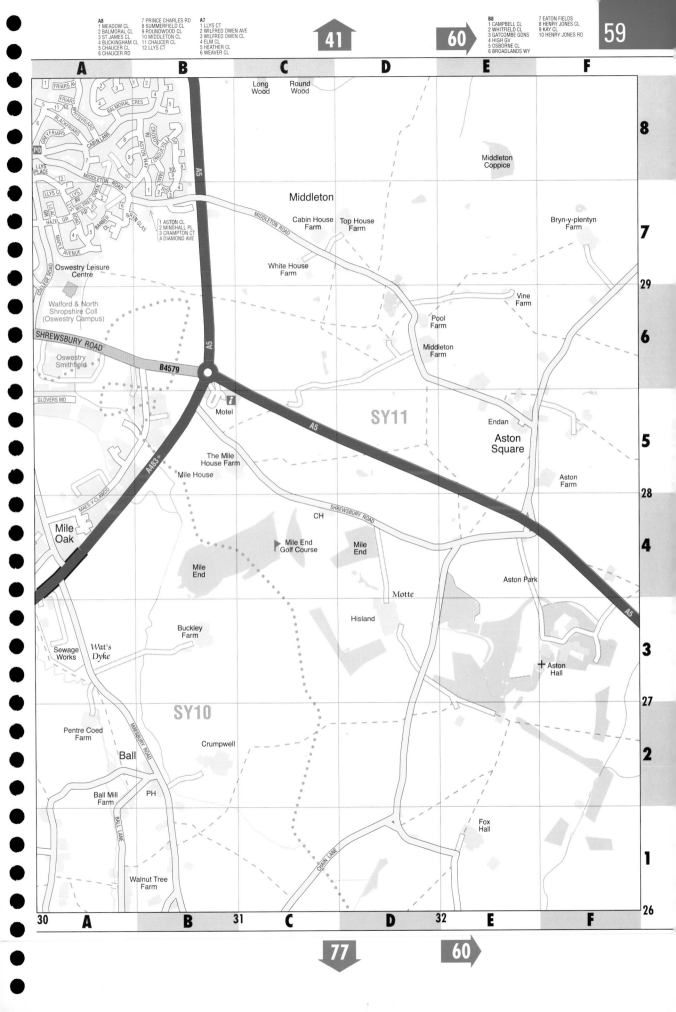

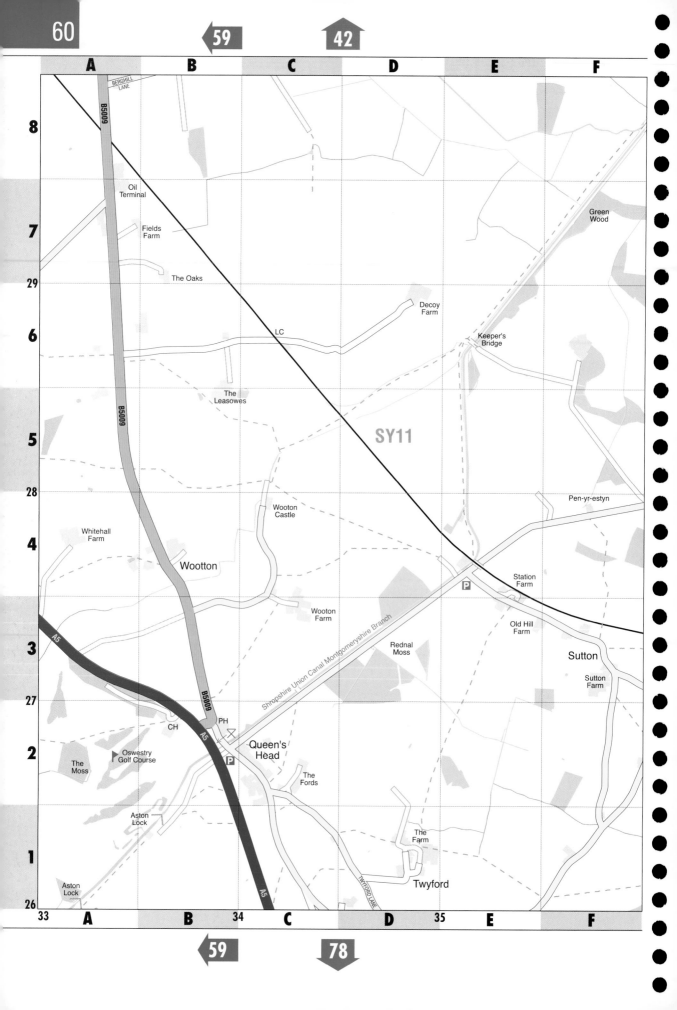

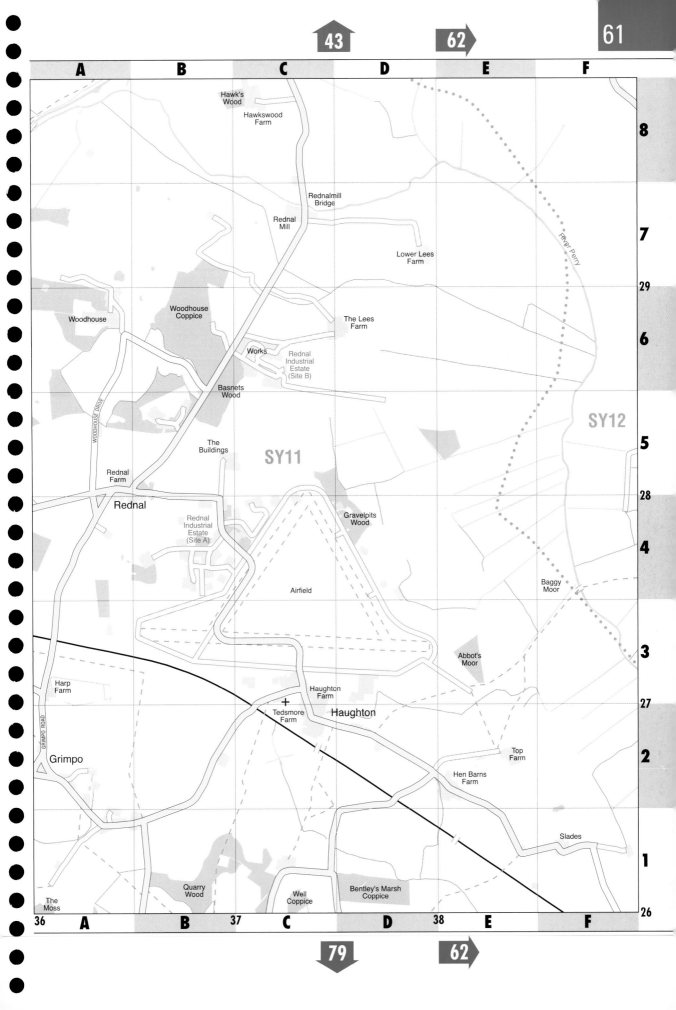

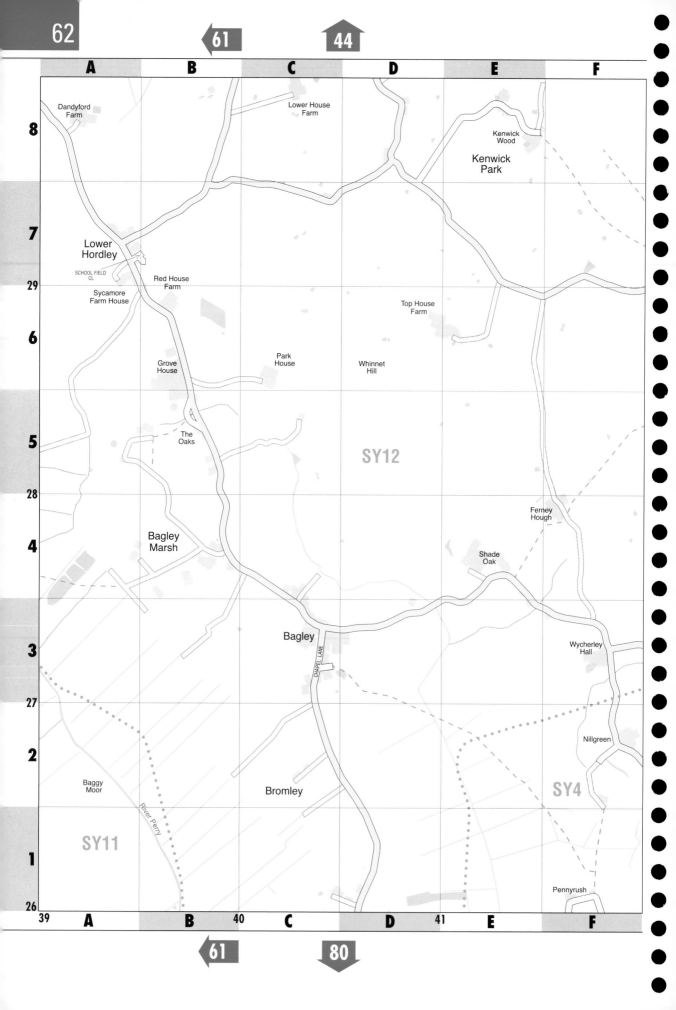

A B C D E F

8

7

29

6

5

28

4

3

27

2

1

26

Dandyford Farm

Lower House Farm

Kenwick Wood

Kenwick Park

Lower Hordley

SCHOOL FIELD CL

Red House Farm

Sycamore Farm House

Top House Farm

Grove House

Park House

Whinnet Hill

The Oaks

SY12

Ferney Hough

Bagley Marsh

Shade Oak

Bagley

Wycherley Hall

CHAPEL LANE

Nillgreen

Baggy Moor

Bromley

SY4

River Perry

SY11

Pennyrush

39 A B 40 C D 41 E F

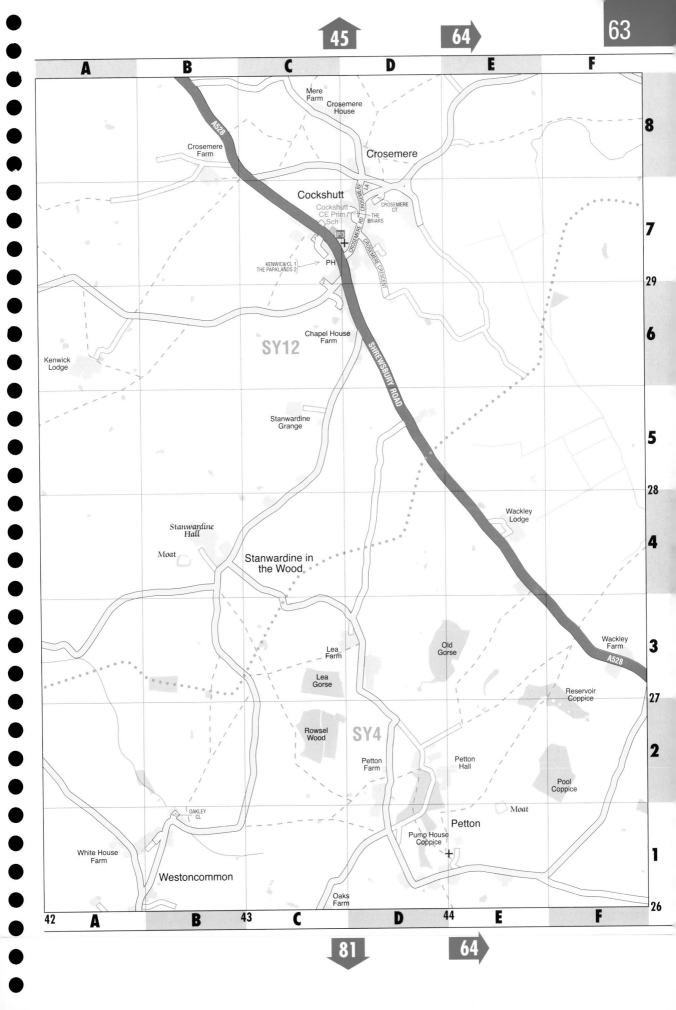

A B C D E F

8

Mere Farm
Crosemere House
Crosemere
Crosemere Farm
A528
Cockshutt
Cockshutt CE Prim Sch
THE BRIARS
CROSEMERE CT
CROSEMERE LA
CROSEMERE RD
PO
7
29
KENWICK CL 1
THE PARKLANDS 2
PH
Kenwick Lodge
SY12
Chapel House Farm
CROSEMERE CRESCEN
6
SHREWSBURY ROAD
Stanwardine Grange
5
28
Wackley Lodge
Stanwardine Hall
4
Moat
Stanwardine in the Wood
Wackley Farm
A528
3
27
Lea Farm
Old Gorse
Reservoir Coppice
Lea Gorse
Rowsel Wood
SY4
2
Petton Farm
Petton Hall
Pool Coppice
Moat
OAKLEY CL
Petton
Pump House Coppice
1
White House Farm
Westoncommon
Oaks Farm
26

63
46

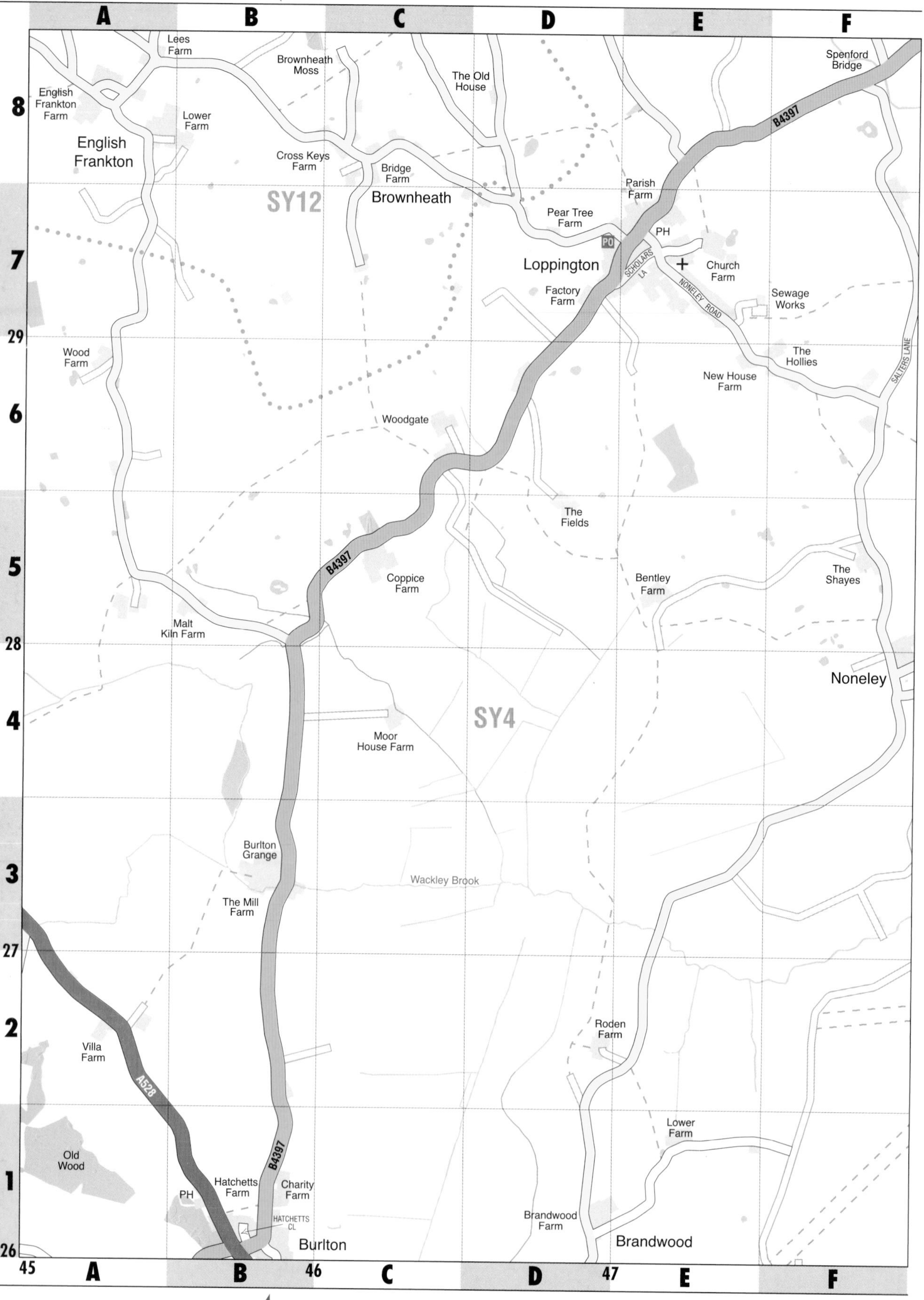

A   B   C   D   E   F

8

Lees Farm
Brownheath Moss
The Old House
Spenford Bridge
English Frankton Farm
English Frankton
Lower Farm
Cross Keys Farm
Bridge Farm
Brownheath
Parish Farm
B4397

SY12

7

Pear Tree Farm
PO
PH
Loppington
Church Farm
SCHOLARS LA.
NONELEY ROAD
Factory Farm
Sewage Works

29

Wood Farm
The Hollies
New House Farm

SALTERS LANE

6

Woodgate
The Fields

5

B4397
Coppice Farm
Bentley Farm
The Shayes

28

Malt Kiln Farm
Noneley

4

SY4
Moor House Farm

3

Burlton Grange
Wackley Brook

The Mill Farm

27

Villa Farm
A528
Roden Farm

2

Lower Farm

1

Old Wood
PH
Hatchetts Farm
B4397
Charity Farm
HATCHETTS CL.
Brandwood Farm
Brandwood

26

45   A   B   46   C   D   47   E   F

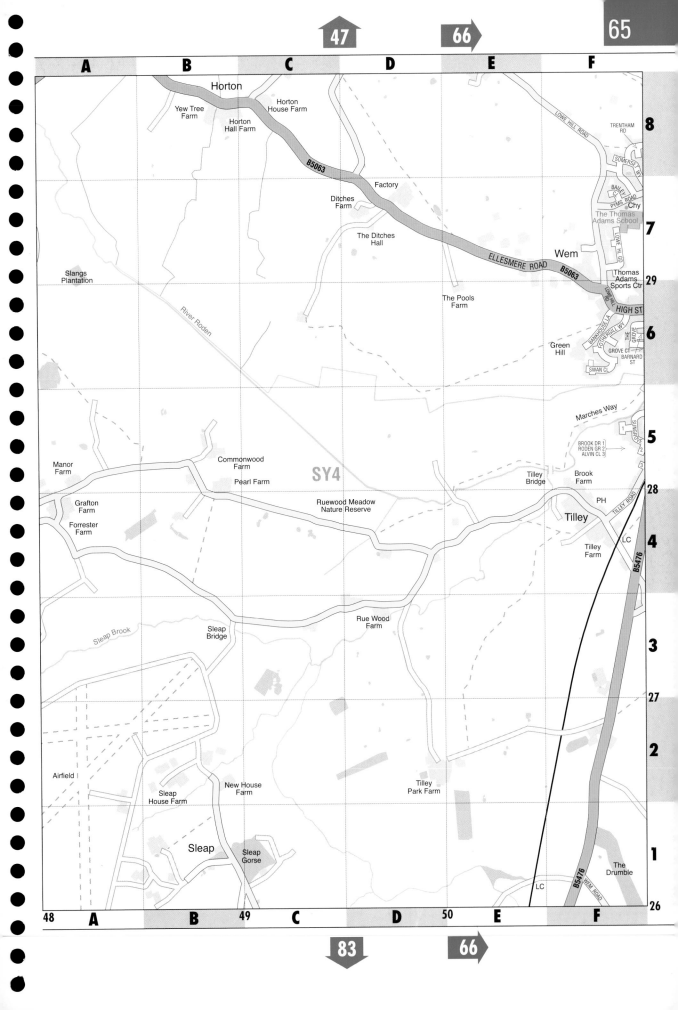

A   B   C   D   E   F

Horton

Yew Tree
Farm

Horton House Farm

Horton
Hall Farm

B5063

Factory

Ditches
Farm

The Ditches
Hall

ELLESMERE ROAD   B5063

Wem

LOWE HILL ROAD

TRENTHAM
RD

SOMERSET WY

BAILEY
C
PYMS ROAD   Chy

The Thomas
Adams School

LOWE HILL GD

Thomas
Adams
Sports Ctr

8

7

29

Slangs
Plantation

River Roden

The Pools
Farm

Green
Hill

LOWE HILL

HIGH ST

BANKHOUSE LA

FOTHERGILL WY

THE GROVE

GROVE CT
BARNARD
ST

SWAN CL

6

Marches Way

STINGHTS

BROOK DR 1
RODEN GR 2
ALVIN CL 3

1

2

3

5

Manor
Farm

Commonwood
Farm

Pearl Farm

SY4

Ruewood Meadow
Nature Reserve

Tilley
Bridge

Brook
Farm

PH

Tilley

Tilley
Farm

LC

TILLEY ROAD

B5476

28

4

Grafton
Farm

Forrester
Farm

Sleap Brook

Sleap
Bridge

Rue Wood
Farm

3

27

2

Airfield

Sleap
House Farm

New House
Farm

Tilley
Park Farm

B5476

WEM ROAD

The
Drumble

Sleap

Sleap
Gorse

LC

1

26

48   A   B   49   C   D   50   E   F

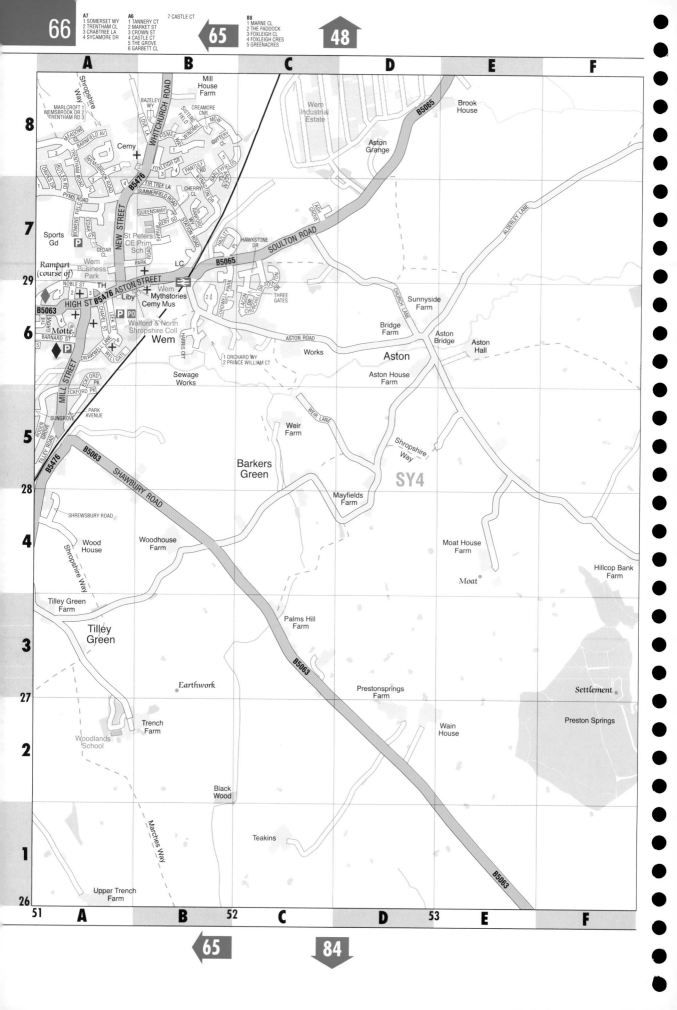

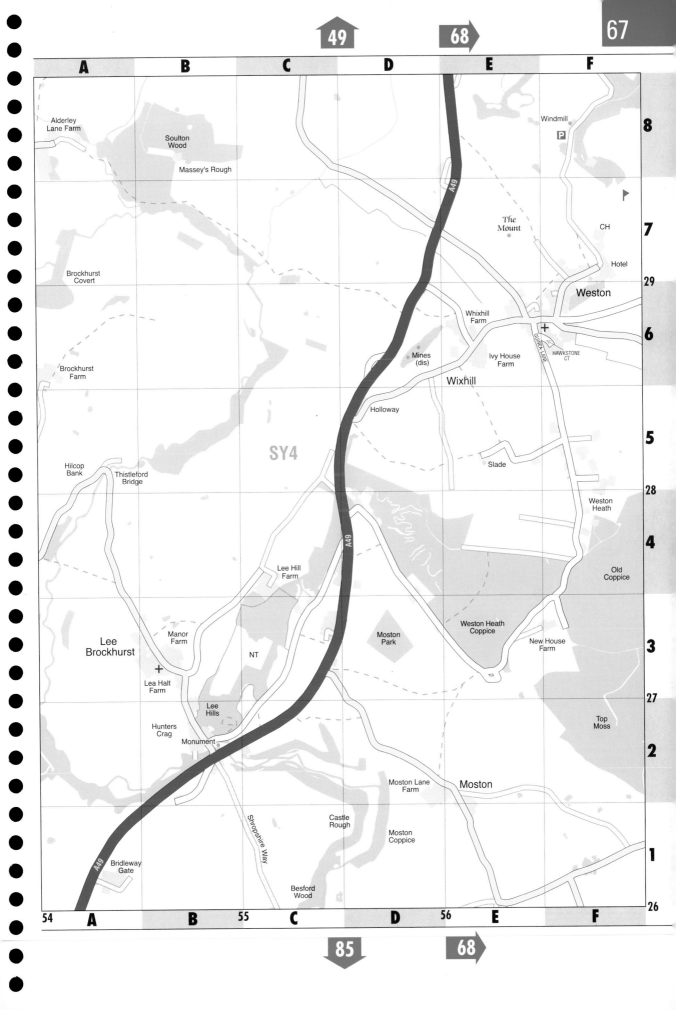

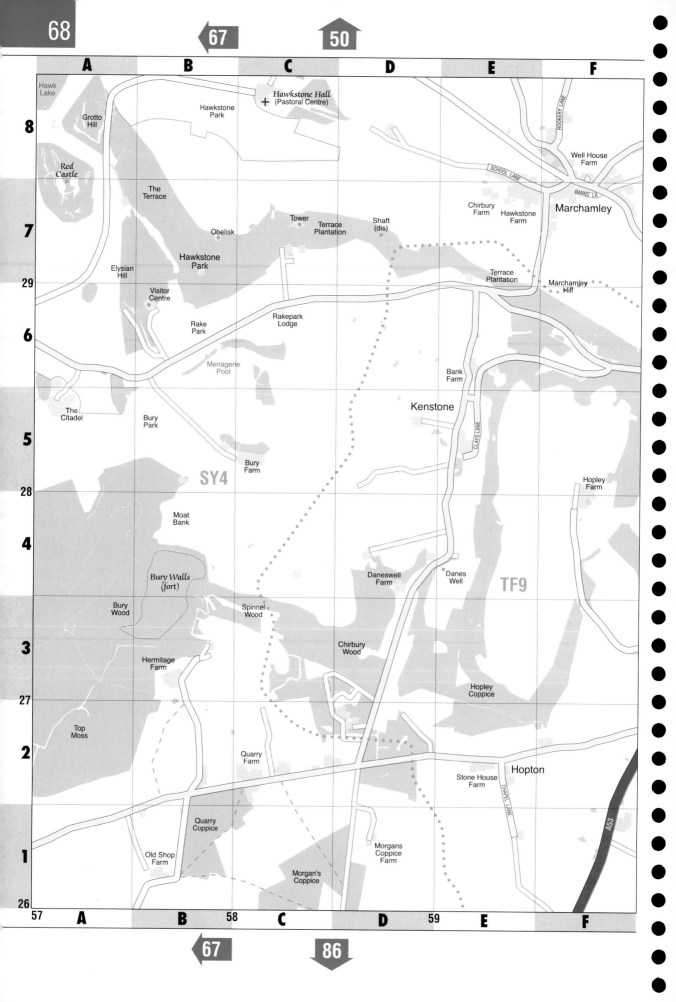

67
50

A   B   C   D   E   F

Hawk
Lake

8

Grotto
Hill

Hawkstone
Park

✠ Hawkstone Hall
(Pastoral Centre)

ROOKERY LANE

Well House
Farm

SCHOOL LANE

BARNS LA.

Red
Castle

The
Terrace

Chirbury
Farm

Hawkstone
Farm

Marchamley

7

Obelisk

Tower

Terrace
Plantation

Shaft
(dis)

Hawkstone
Park

Elysian
Hill

Terrace
Plantation

Marchamley
Hill

29

Visitor
Centre

Rakepark
Lodge

6

Rake
Park

Menagerie
Pool

Bank
Farm

The
Citadel

Bury
Park

Kenstone

CLAY'S LANE

Hopley
Farm

5

Bury
Farm

SY4

28

Moat
Bank

4

Bury Walls
(fort)

Daneswell
Farm

Danes
Well

TF9

Bury
Wood

Spinnel
Wood

3

Hermitage
Farm

Chirbury
Wood

Hopley
Coppice

27

Top
Moss

Quarry
Farm

2

Stone House
Farm

Hopton

CHAPEL LANE

A53

1

Quarry
Coppice

Old Shop
Farm

Morgan's
Coppice

Morgans
Coppice
Farm

26

57   A   B   58   C   D   59   E   F

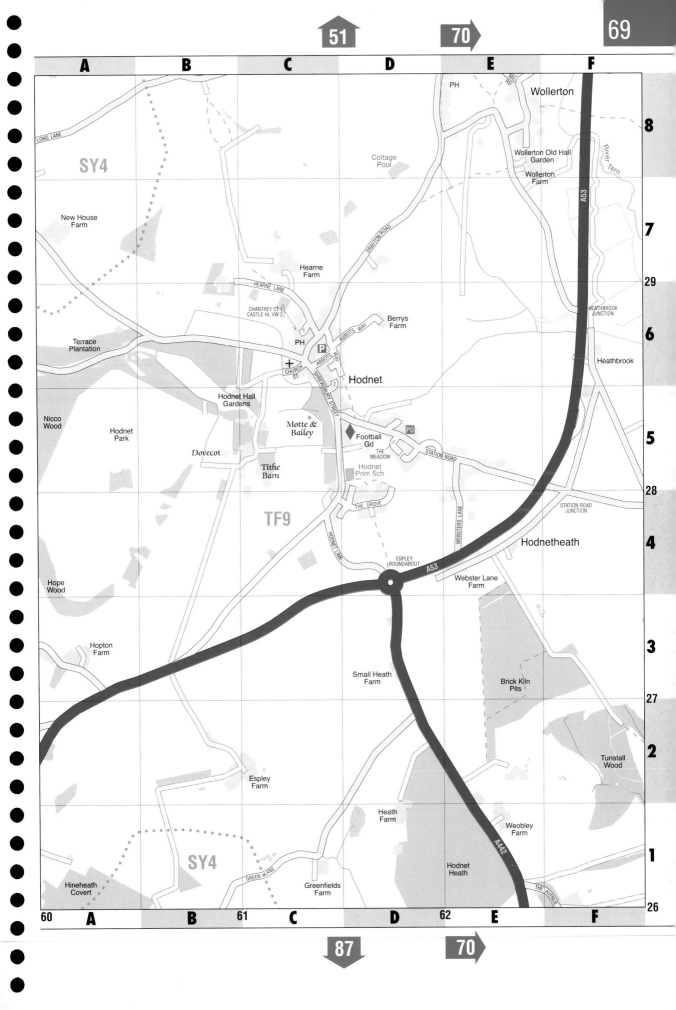

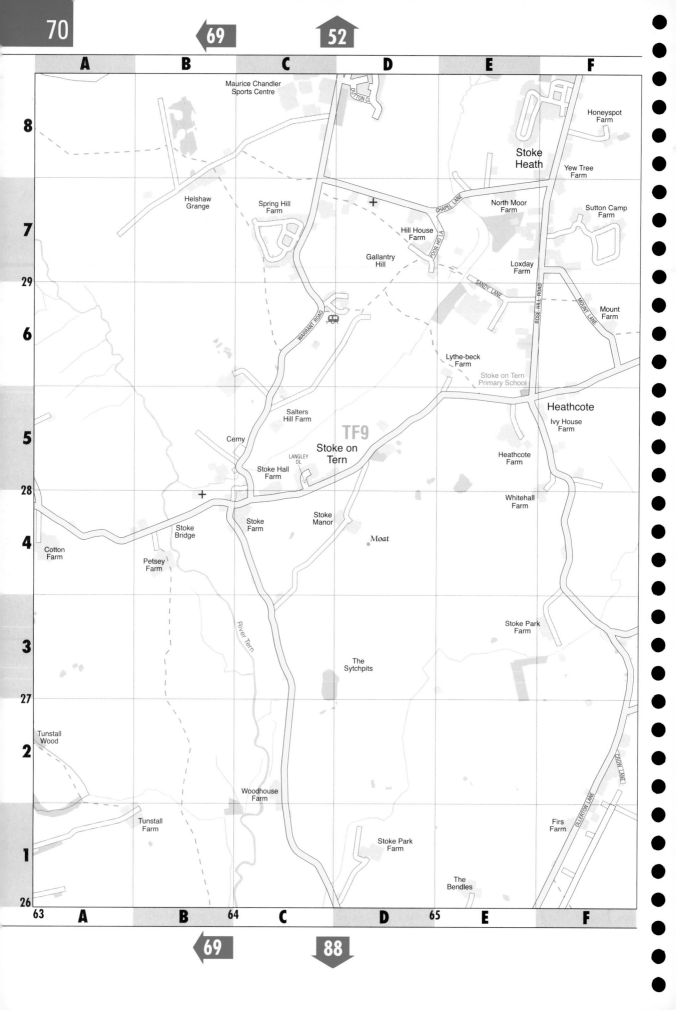

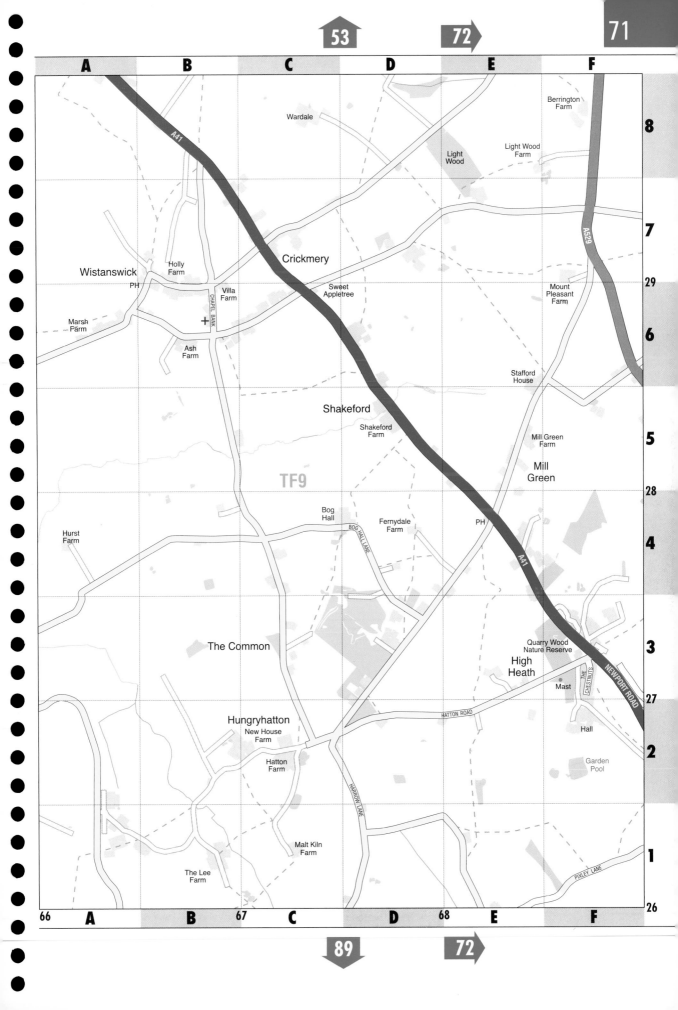

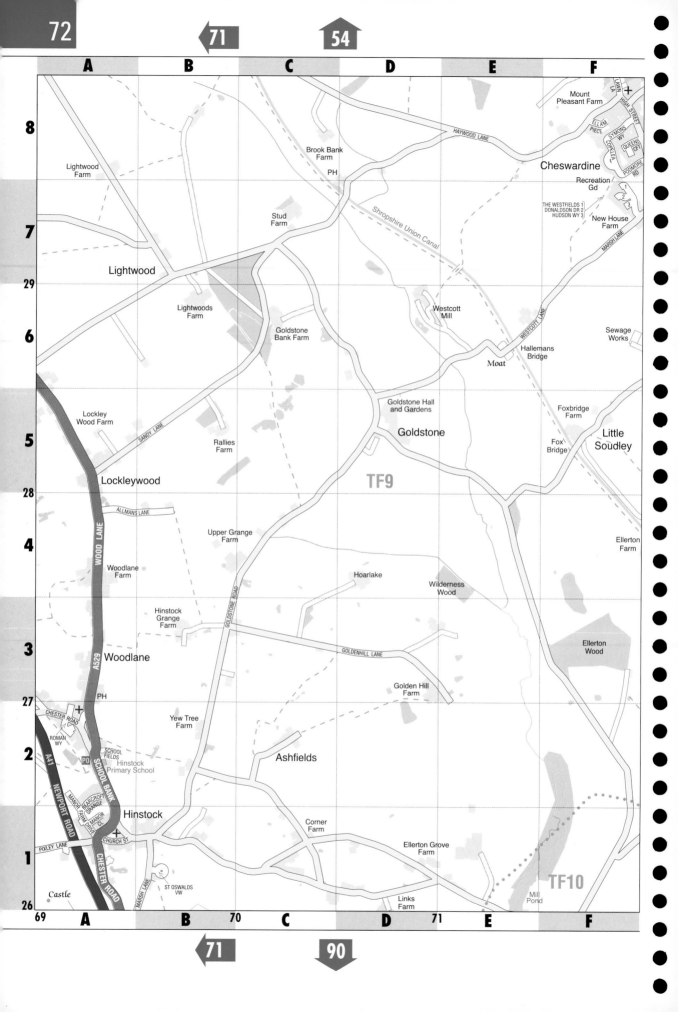

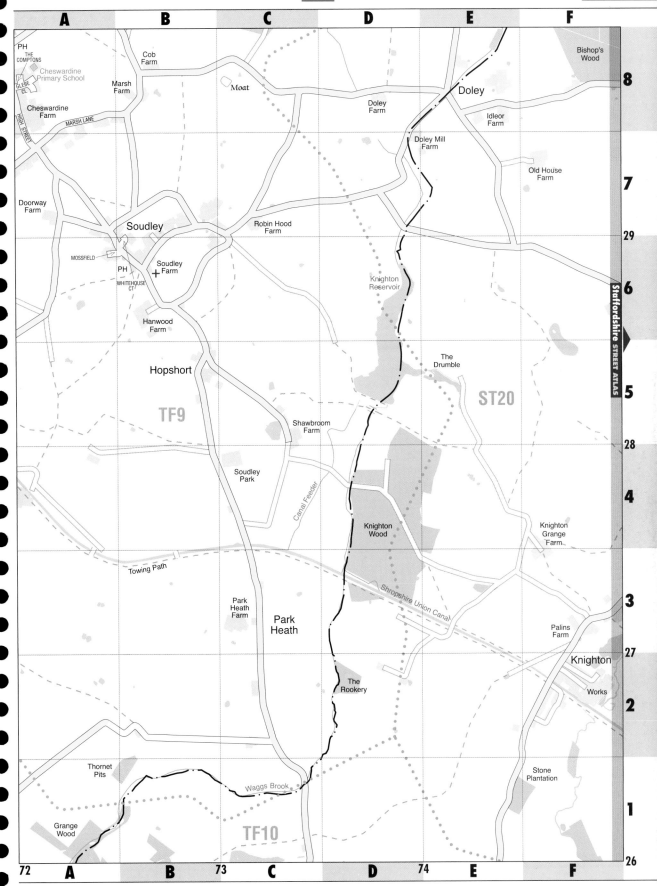

A B C D E F

8

PH
THE COMPTONS
Cheswardine Primary School
GLEBE CL
Cheswardine Farm
MARSH LANE
HIGH STREET

Cob Farm

Marsh Farm

Moat

Doley Farm

Doley

Bishop's Wood

Idleor Farm

Doley Mill Farm

Old House Farm

7

Doorway Farm

Soudley

Robin Hood Farm

29

MOSSFIELD

PH

WHITEHOUSE CT

Soudley Farm

Knighton Reservoir

6

Staffordshire STREET ATLAS

Hanwood Farm

The Drumble

Hopshort

TF9

ST20

5

Shawbroom Farm

28

Soudley Park

Canal Feeder

Knighton Wood

Knighton Grange Farm

4

Towing Path

Shropshire Union Canal

3

Park Heath Farm

Park Heath

Palins Farm

27

Knighton

The Rookery

Works

2

Thornet Pits

Stone Plantation

Waggs Brook

1

Grange Wood

TF10

26

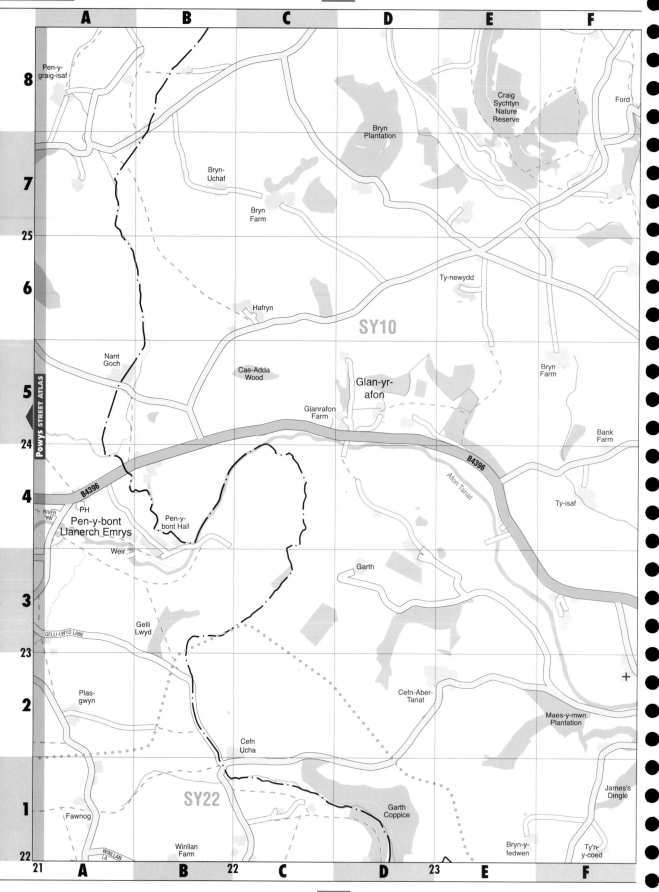

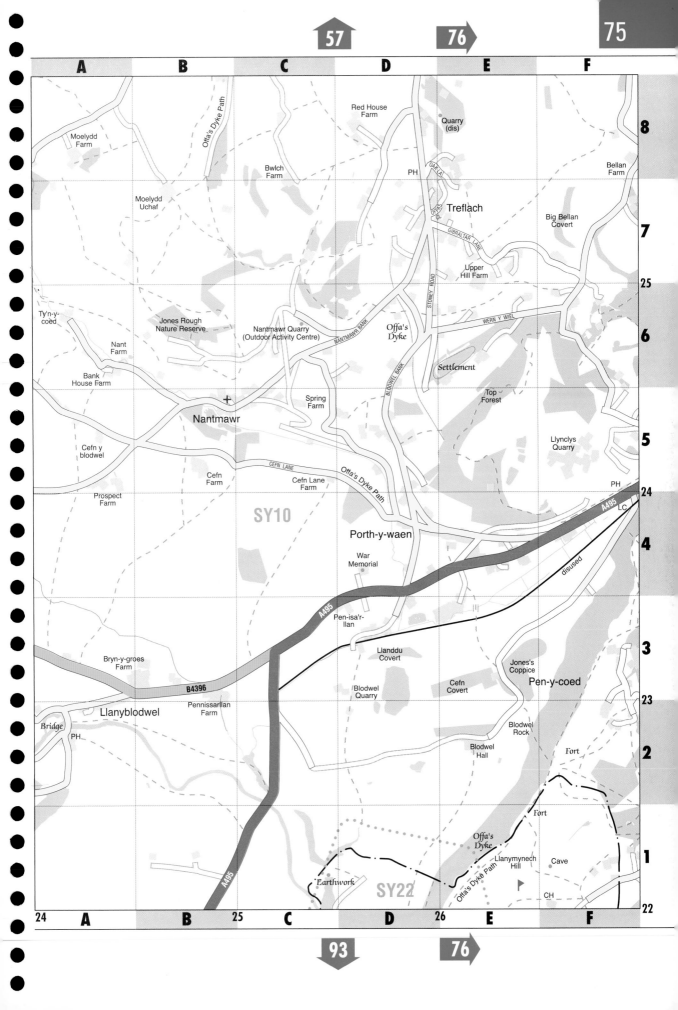

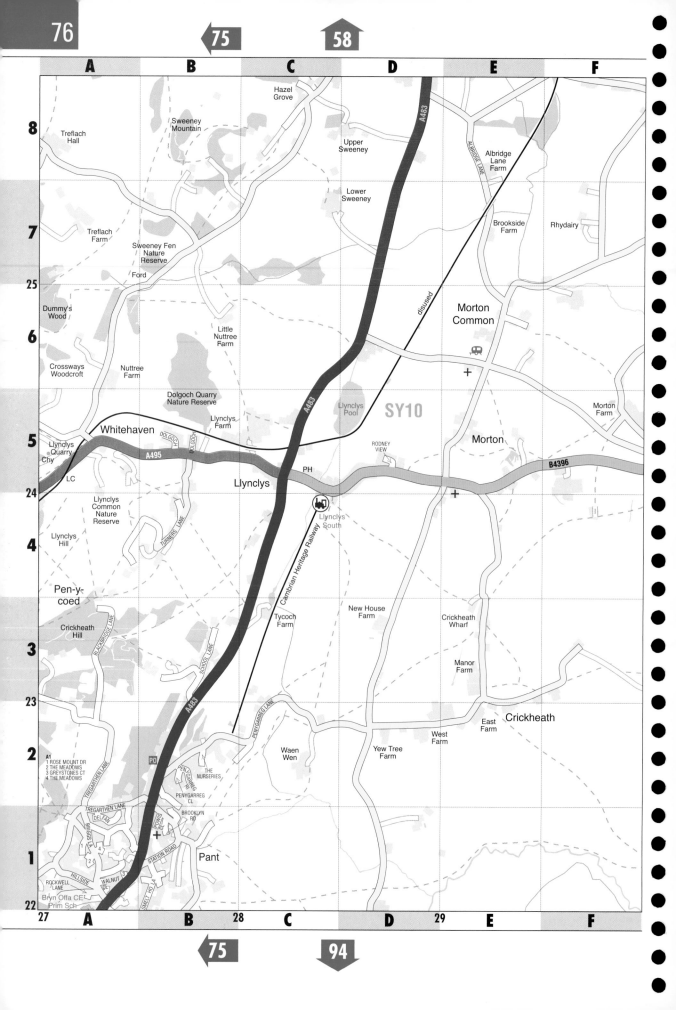

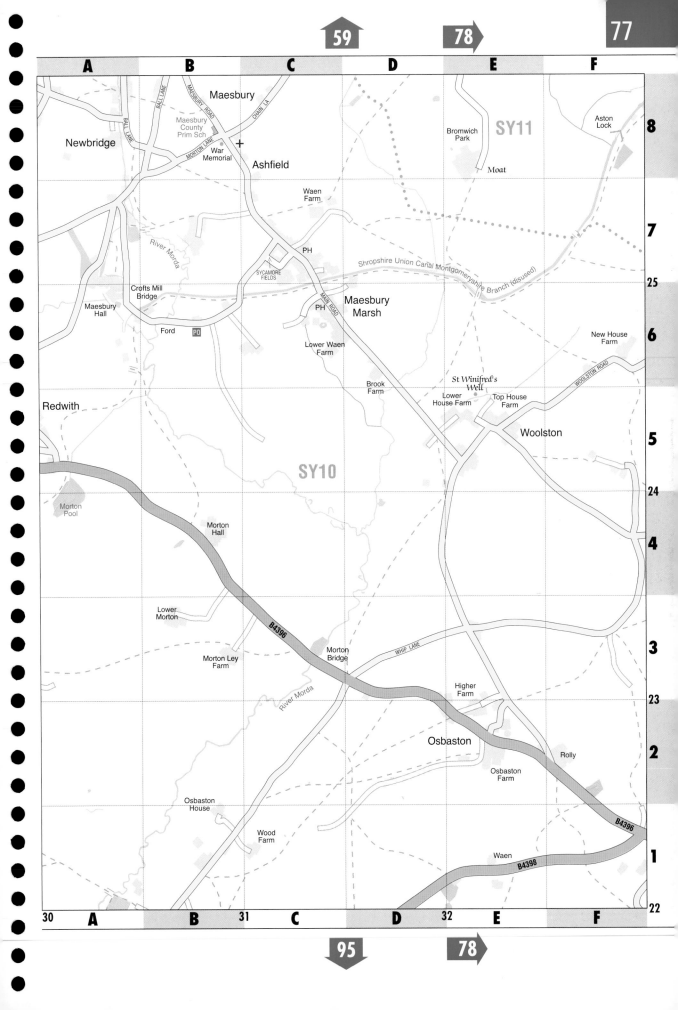

59
78

A B C D E F

Maesbury

Newbridge

BALL LANE
MAESBURY ROAD
CHAIN LA
MORTON LANE

Maesbury County Prim Sch

War Memorial

Ashfield

Waen Farm

Bromwich Park

Moat

Aston Lock

SY11

8

PH

River Morda

SYCAMORE FIELDS

Shropshire Union Canal Montgomeryshire Branch (disused)

7

25

Crofts Mill Bridge

Maesbury Hall

Ford   PO

PH

Maesbury Marsh

Lower Waen Farm

New House Farm

6

WOOLSTON ROAD

Brook Farm

St Winifred's Well

Lower House Farm

Top House Farm

Redwith

SY10

Woolston

5

24

Morton Pool

Morton Hall

4

Lower Morton

B4396

Morton Bridge

WHIP LANE

Higher Farm

3

Morton Ley Farm

River Morda

Osbaston

23

Rolly

2

Osbaston Farm

Osbaston House

B4396

Wood Farm

Waen   B4398

1

30   A   B   31   C   D   32   E   F   22

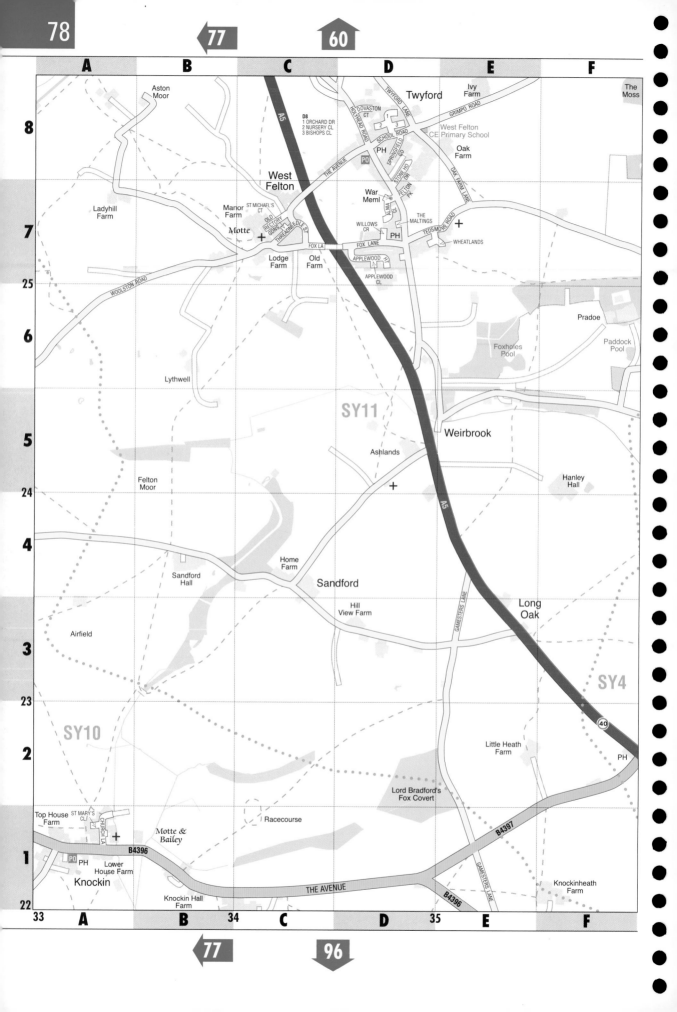

A   B   C   D   E   F

8

7

25

6

5

24

4

3

23

2

1

22

33   A   B   34   C   D   35   E   F

Aston Moor

The Moss

Twyford

Ivy Farm

GRIMPO ROAD

West Felton CE Primary School

D8
1 ORCHARD DR
2 NURSERY CL
3 BISHOPS CL

TWYFORD LANE

HOLYHEAD ROAD

DOVASTON CT

SCHOOL ROAD

PH

PO

SPRINGFIELD

STONE HO DR

FELTON PK

Oak Farm

OAK FARM LANE

West Felton

THE AVENUE

A5

War Meml

ALMA CT

WILLOWS CR

THE MALTINGS

PH

TEDSMORE ROAD

WHEATLANDS

Ladyhill Farm

Manor Farm

ST MICHAEL'S CT

OLD RECTORY GDNS

THREAPNEEDLE ST

Motte

Lodge Farm

Old Farm

FOX LA

FOX LANE

APPLEWOOD CT

APPLEWOOD CL

WOOLSTON ROAD

Pradoe

Paddock Pool

Foxholes Pool

Lythwell

SY11

Weirbrook

Felton Moor

Ashlands

Hanley Hall

A5

Airfield

Home Farm

Sandford Hall

Sandford

Hill View Farm

GAMESTERS LANE

Long Oak

SY4

SY10

Little Heath Farm

40

PH

Lord Bradford's Fox Covert

Top House Farm

ST MARY'S CL

CHURCH LA

Motte & Bailey

Racecourse

B4397

GAMESTERS LANE

Knockinheath Farm

PO   PH

B4396

Lower House Farm

Knockin

THE AVENUE

Knockin Hall Farm

B4396

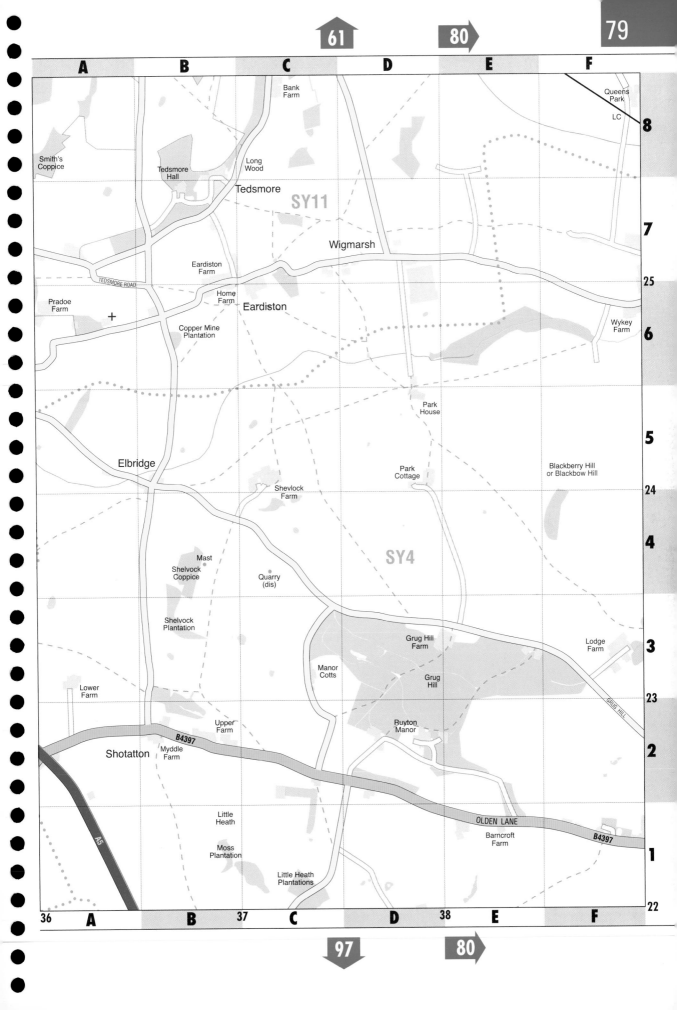

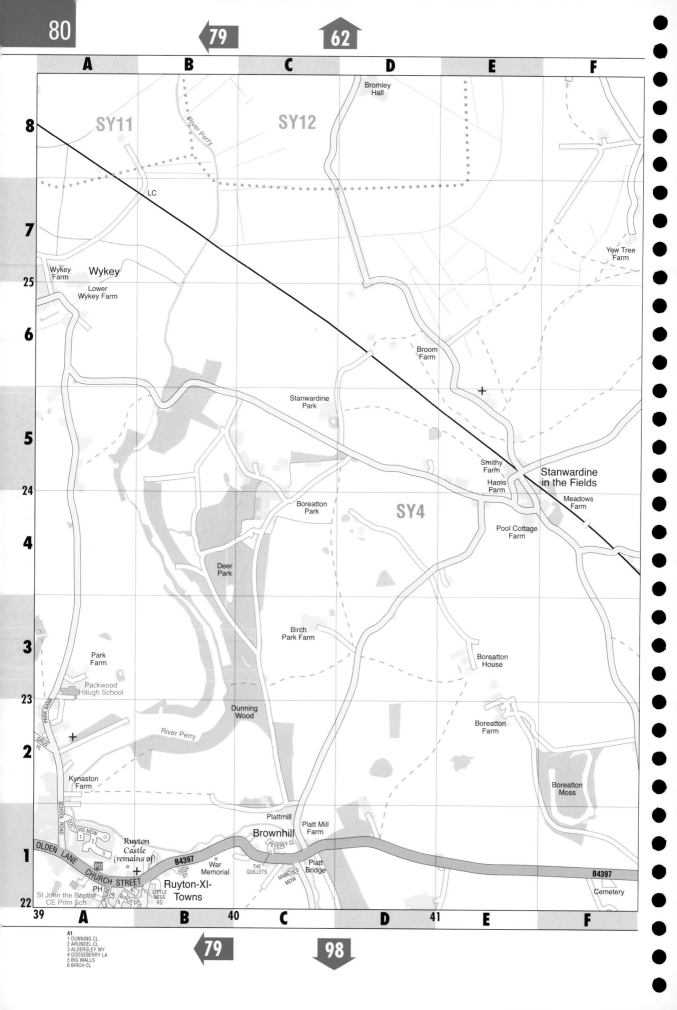

A   B   C   D   E   F

8

SY11

River Perry

SY12

Bromley
Hall

LC

7

25

Wykey
Farm

Wykey

Lower
Wykey Farm

Yew Tree
Farm

6

Broom
Farm

Stanwardine
Park

5

Smithy
Farm

Stanwardine
in the Fields

24

Boreatton
Park

Harris
Farm

SY4

Meadows
Farm

4

Pool Cottage
Farm

Deer
Park

Birch
Park Farm

Boreatton
House

3

Park
Farm

Packwood
Haugh School

Boreatton
Farm

23

Dunning
Wood

River Perry

2

Kynaston
Farm

PARK BANK

GRUG HL

Boreatton
Moss

Plattmill

Platt Mill
Farm

SCHOOL ROAD

TUTORS MDW

Brownhill

PEVEREY CL

Ruyton
Castle
(remains of)

1

OLDEN LANE

PO

CHURCH STREET

B4397

HIGH ST

War
Memorial

THE
QUILLETS

MARCHES MDW

Platt
Bridge

B4397

St John the Baptist
CE Prim Sch

PH

Ruyton-XI-
Towns

LITTLE NESS RD

Cemetery

22

39   A   B   40   C   D   41   E   F

A1
1 DUNNING CL
2 ARUNDEL CL
3 ALDERSLEY WY
4 GOOSEBERRY LA
5 BIG WALLS
6 BIRCH CL

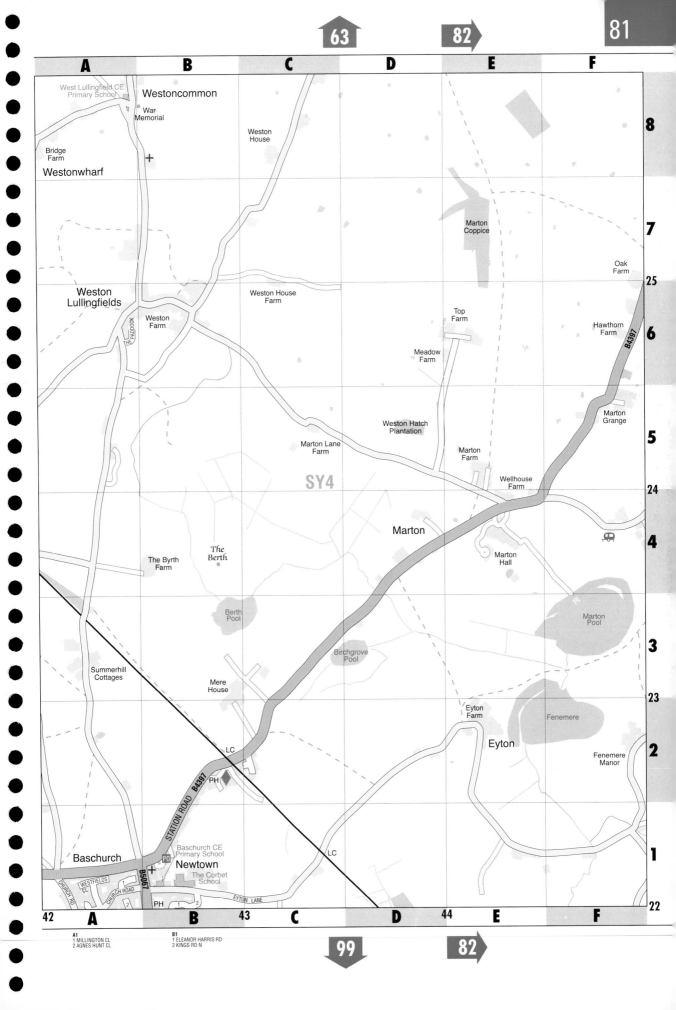

A1
1 MILLINGTON CL
2 AGNES HUNT CL

B1
1 ELEANOR HARRIS RD
2 KINGS RD N

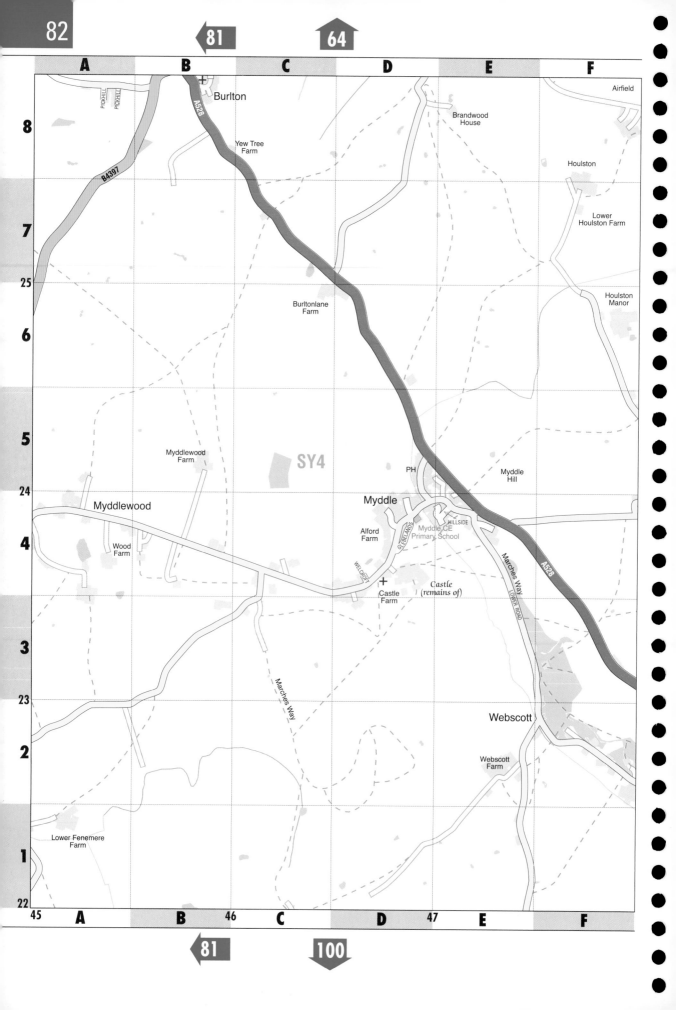

81
64

A   B   C   D   E   F

8

Burlton

Yew Tree
Farm

B4397

A528

PICKHILL

Brandwood
House

Airfield

Houlston

7

Lower
Houlston Farm

25

Burltonlane
Farm

Houlston
Manor

6

5

SY4

Myddlewood
Farm

PH

Myddle
Hill

24

Myddlewood

Myddle

HILLSIDE

Wood
Farm

Alford
Farm

GLEBELANDS

Myddle CE
Primary School

WELCROFT

4

Marches Way

A528

LOWER ROAD

Castle
Farm

Castle
(remains of)

3

23

Marches Way

Webscott

2

Webscott
Farm

Lower Fenemere
Farm

1

22

45   A   B   46   C   D   47   E   F

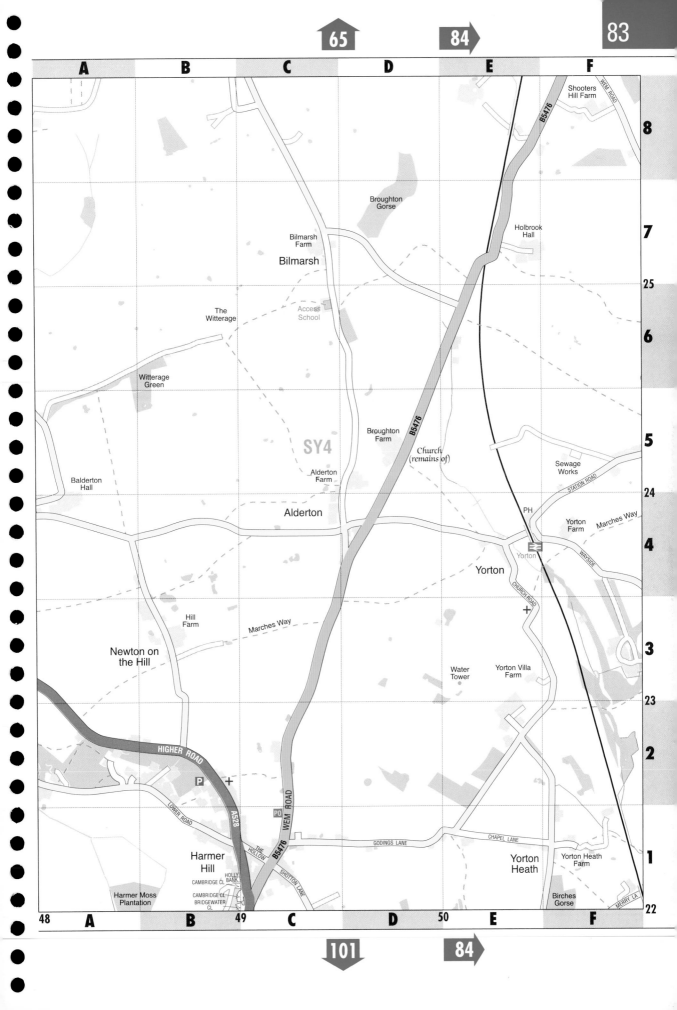

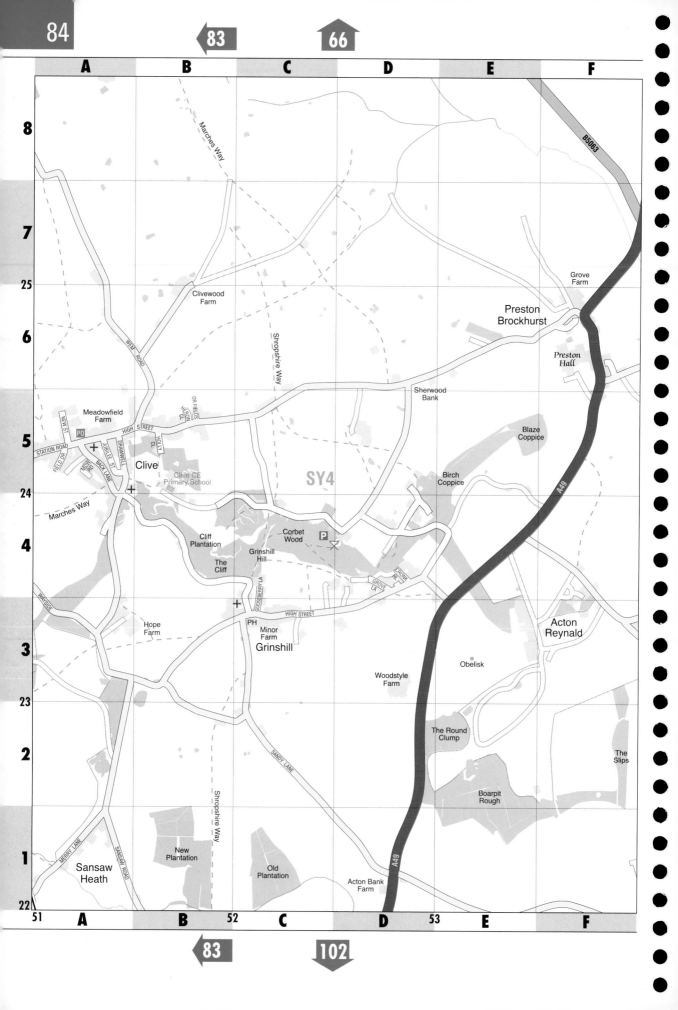

83
66

A B C D E F

8

7

25

Marches Way

6

Clivewood
Farm

Shropshire Way

Preston
Brockhurst

Grove
Farm

B5063

WEM ROAD

Sherwood
Bank

Preston
Hall

Meadowfield
Farm

OR FIELDS

HESON
CL

Blaze
Coppice

5

NEW ST

PO

HIGH STREET

HOLLY

CL

Clive

STATION ROAD

FIELD DR

MINOR
RD

JUBILEE ST

DRAWWELL

BACK LANE

SY4

Birch
Coppice

24

Clive CE
Primary School

A49

Marches Way

Cliff
Plantation

Corbet
Wood

P

4

The
Cliff

Grinshill
Hill

GOOSEBERRY LA

CROWN
PL

GROVE
LA

Acton
Reynald

WAYSIDE

Hope
Farm

HIGH STREET

PH

Minor
Farm

Grinshill

Obelisk

3

Woodstyle
Farm

23

The Round
Clump

SANDY LANE

2

The
Slips

Shropshire Way

1

MERRY LANE

SANSAW ROAD

Sansaw
Heath

New
Plantation

Old
Plantation

Acton Bank
Farm

A49

Boarpit
Rough

22

83
102

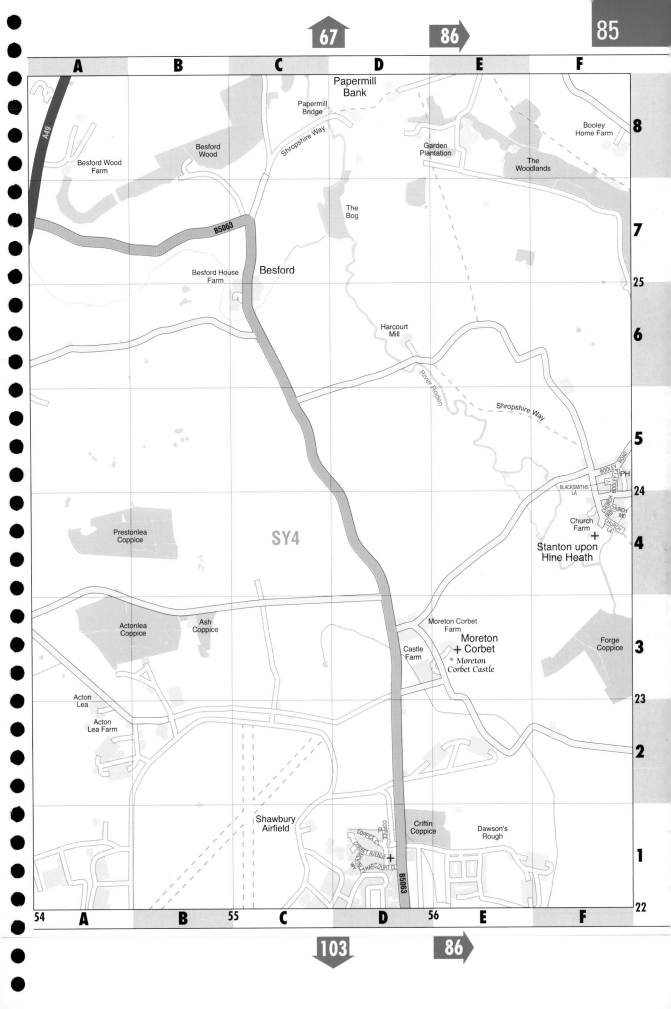

85
68

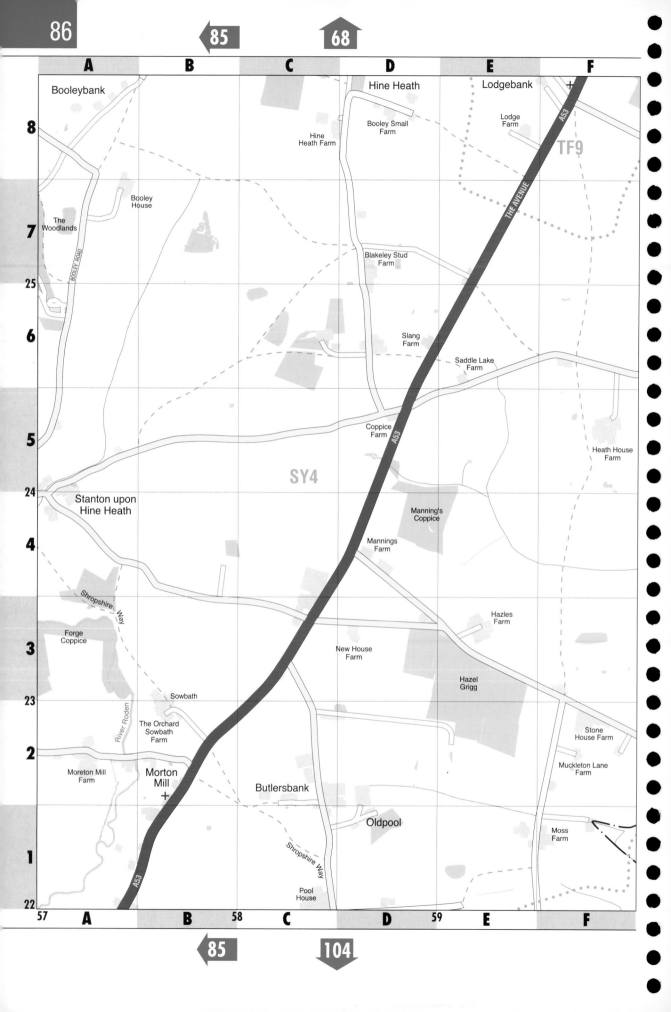

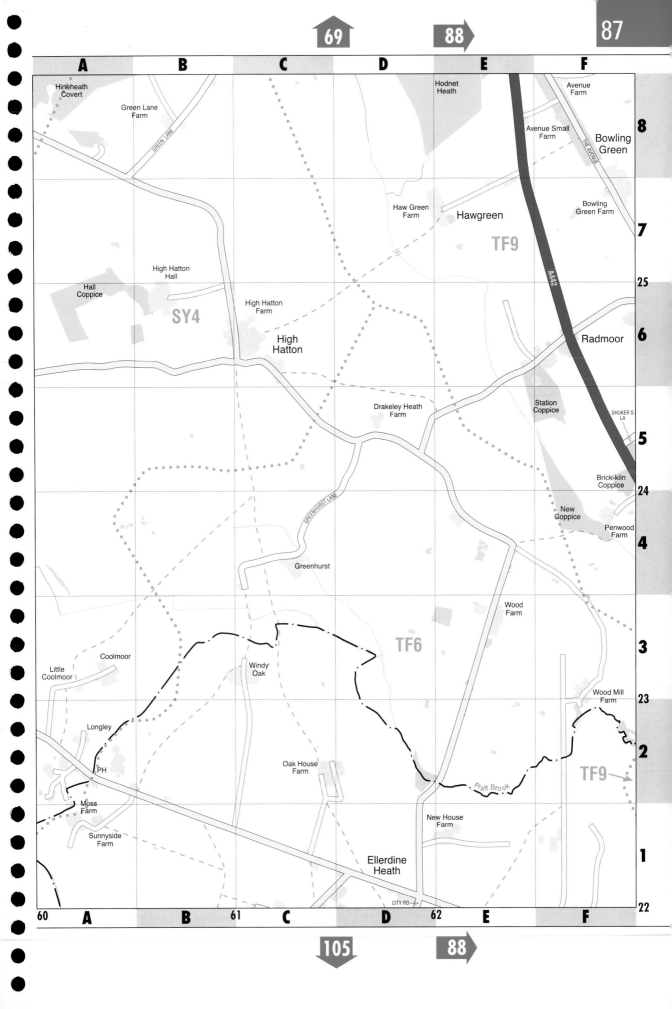

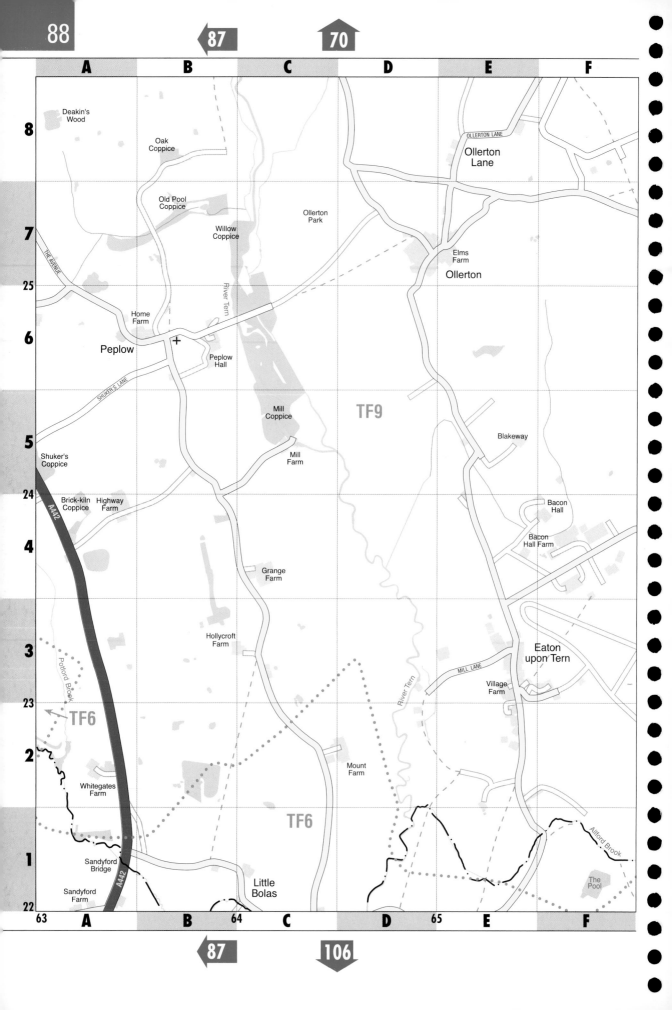

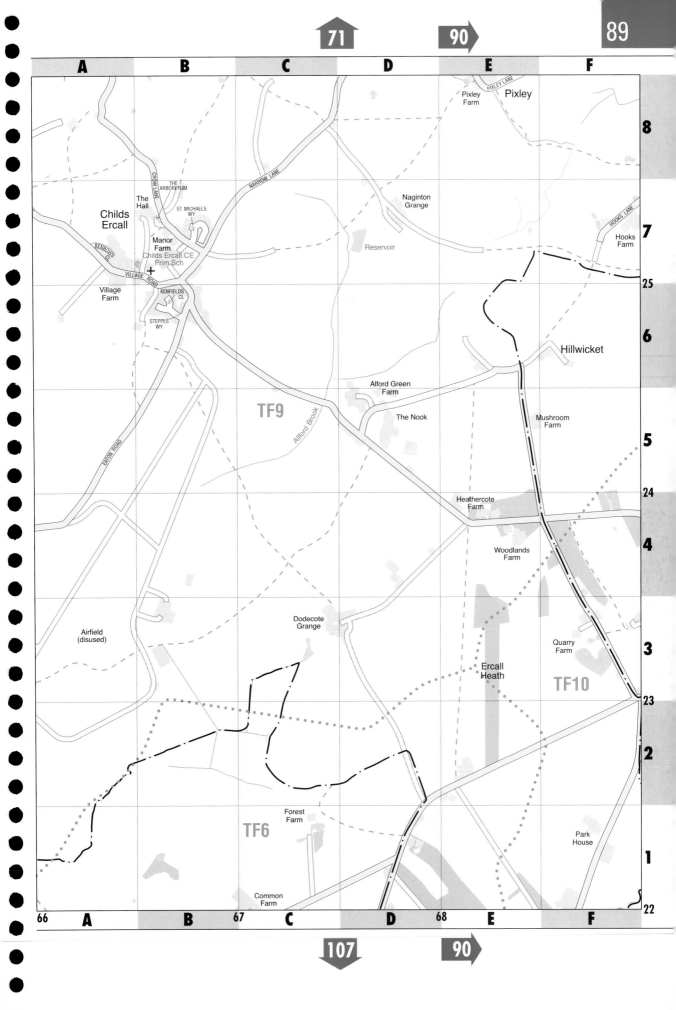

A   B   C   D   E   F

8
7
25
6
5
24
4
3
23
2
1
22

Pixley Farm
Pixley
PIXLEY LANE

Naginton Grange

HOOKS LANE
Hooks Farm

THE ARBORETUM
CROW LANE
The Hall
Childs Ercall
ST MICHAELS WY
NARROW LANE

Manor Farm
Childs Ercall CE Prim Sch
Reservoir

BENBOWS CL
VILLAGE ROAD
Village Farm
KENFIELDS CL
STEPPES WY

Hillwicket

Alford Green Farm

TF9
The Nook

Mushroom Farm

Alford Brook

EATON ROAD

Heathercote Farm

Woodlands Farm

Airfield (disused)

Dodecote Grange

Ercall Heath

Quarry Farm

TF10

TF6

Forest Farm

Park House

Common Farm

66   A   B   67   C   D   68   E   F   22

89 72

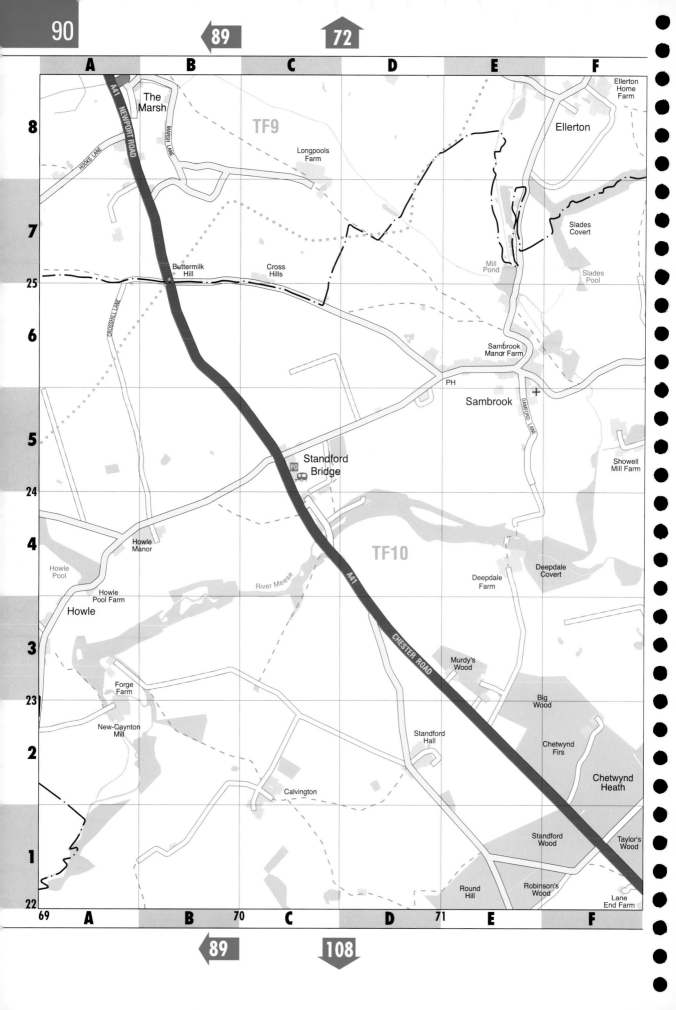

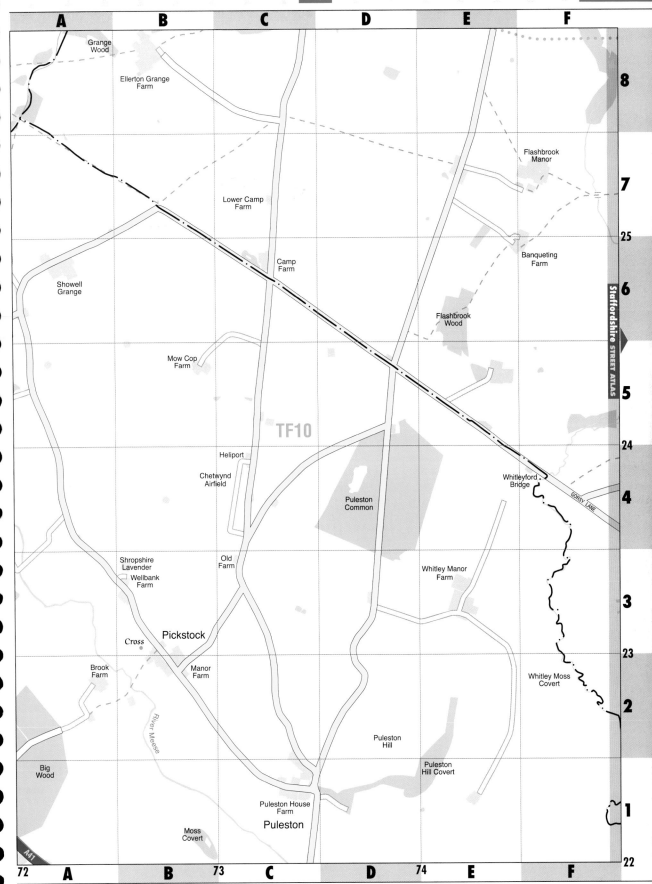

A · B · C · D · E · F

8

Grange Wood

Ellerton Grange Farm

Flashbrook Manor

7

25

Lower Camp Farm

Camp Farm

Banqueting Farm

6

Showell Grange

Flashbrook Wood

Staffordshire STREET ATLAS

Mow Cop Farm

5

TF10

24

Heliport

Chetwynd Airfield

Puleston Common

Whitleyford Bridge

GORSY LANE

4

Shropshire Lavender
Wellbank Farm

Old Farm

Whitley Manor Farm

3

Pickstock

Cross

23

Brook Farm

Manor Farm

Whitley Moss Covert

2

River Meese

Puleston Hill

Big Wood

Puleston Hill Covert

Puleston House Farm

Puleston

1

A41

Moss Covert

22

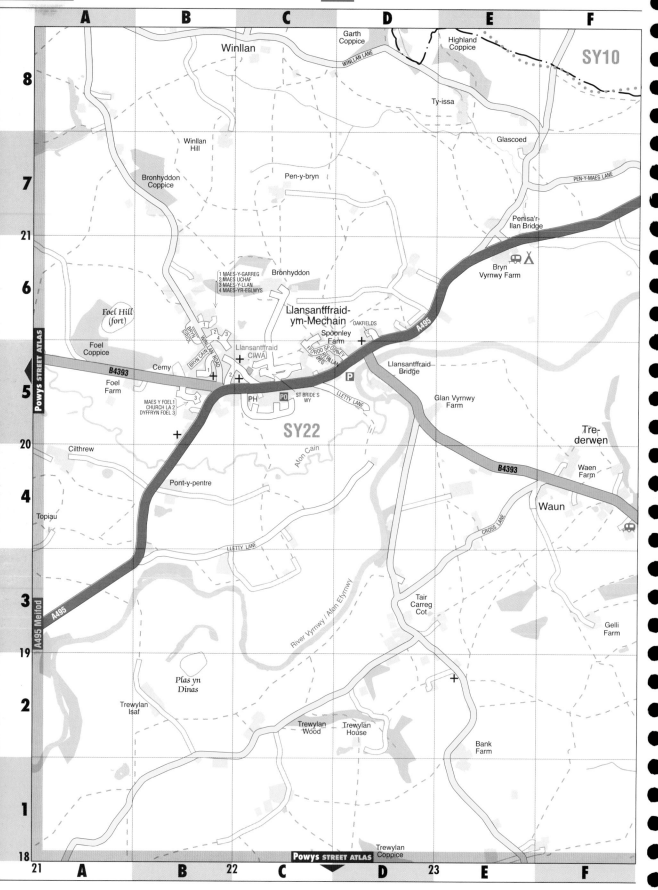

F6
1 BARLEY MDWS
2 MAES Y BERLLAN
3 ASHFIELD DR
4 HAFOD CL
5 TAN-Y-FOEL DR

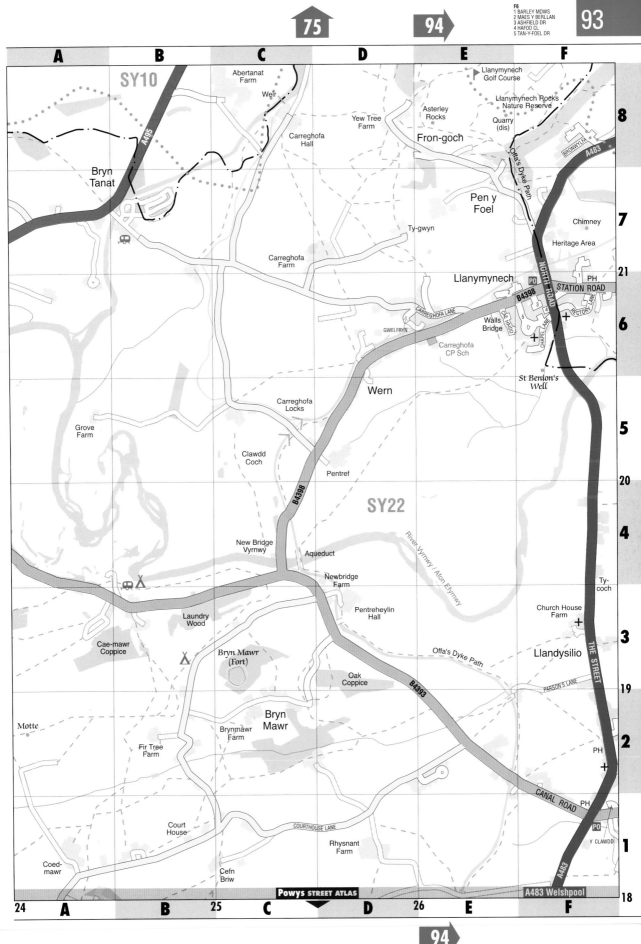

SY10

Abertanat Farm

Weir

Llanymynech Golf Course

Asterley Rocks

Llanymynech Rocks Nature Reserve

Quarry (dis)

Yew Tree Farm

Carreghofa Hall

Fron-goch

Bryn Tanat

A495

Ty-gwyn

Pen y Foel

Chimney

Heritage Area

Carreghofa Farm

Llanymynech

21

Carreghofa Lane

GWELFRYN

Walls Bridge

STATION ROAD

PH

PO

B4398

NORTH ROAD

CHAPEL LANE

CAE HAFOD

RECTORY LANE

Carreghofa CP Sch

Wern

St Benion's Well

Grove Farm

Carreghofa Locks

Clawdd Coch

Pentref

B4398

SY22

20

New Bridge Vyrnwy

Aqueduct

River Vyrnwy / Afon Efyrnwy

Ty-coch

Newbridge Farm

Laundry Wood

Pentreheylin Hall

Offa's Dyke Path

Church House Farm

Llandysilio

THE STREET

Cae-mawr Coppice

Oak Coppice

Bryn Mawr (Fort)

Offa's Dyke Path

PARSON'S LANE

19

Motte

Bryn Mawr

B4393

Brynmawr Farm

Fir Tree Farm

PH

Court House

COURTHOUSE LANE

Rhysnant Farm

CANAL ROAD

PH

PO

Y CLAWDD

Coed-mawr

Cefn Briw

A483

8

7

6

5

4

3

2

1

A   B   C   D   E   F

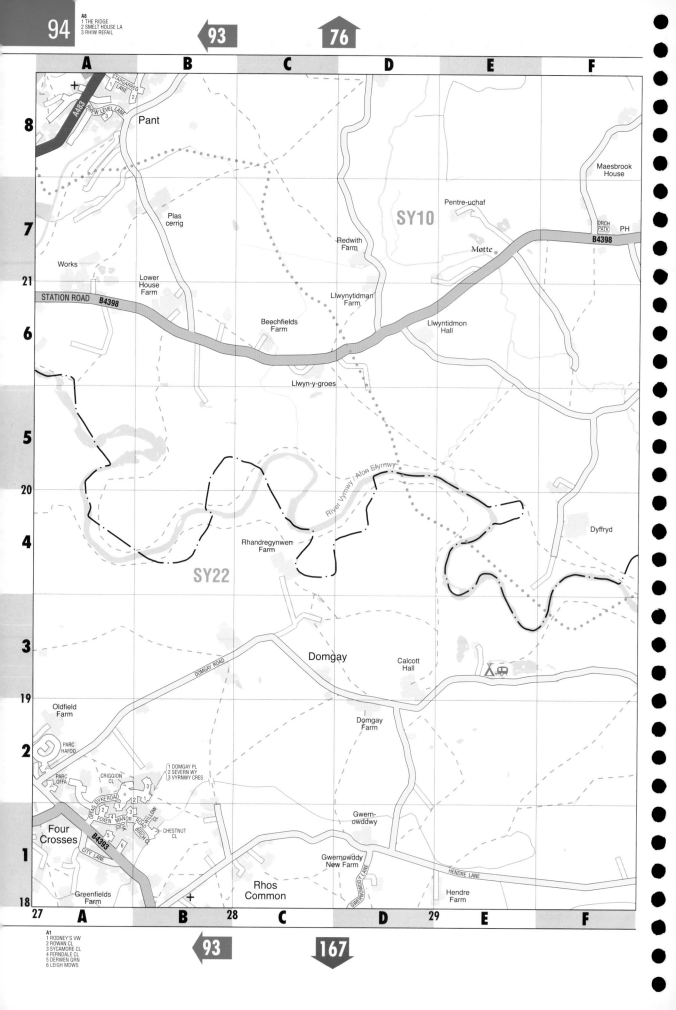

93
76

A B C D E F

Pant

STARGARREG LANE

A483

RHIW LEVEL LANE

Plas cerrig

Maesbrook House

Pentre-uchaf

ORCH PATK

B4398 PH

Redwith Farm

Motte

SY10

Works

Lower House Farm

Llwynytidman Farm

STATION ROAD B4398

Beechfields Farm

Llwyntidmon Hall

Llwyn-y-groes

River Vyrnwy / Afon Efyrnwy

Rhandregynwen Farm

SY22

Dyffryd

Domgay

Calcott Hall

Oldfield Farm

Domgay Farm

PARC HAFOD

DOMGAY ROAD

PARC OFFA

1 DOMGAY PL
2 SEVERN WY
3 VYRNWY CRES

CRIGGION CL

OFFAS DYKE ROAD

FOXEN

MANOR ROAD

BIRCH CL

WILLOW CL

CHESTNUT CL

Gwern-owddwy

Four Crosses

B4393

CITY LANE

Greenfields Farm

Rhos Common

Gwernowddy New Farm

GWERNDDY LANE

HENDRE LANE

Hendre Farm

27 A B 28 C D 29 E F

93
167

A1
1 RODNEY'S VW
2 ROWAN CL
3 SYCAMORE CL
4 FERNDALE CL
5 DERWEN GRN
6 LEIGH MDWS

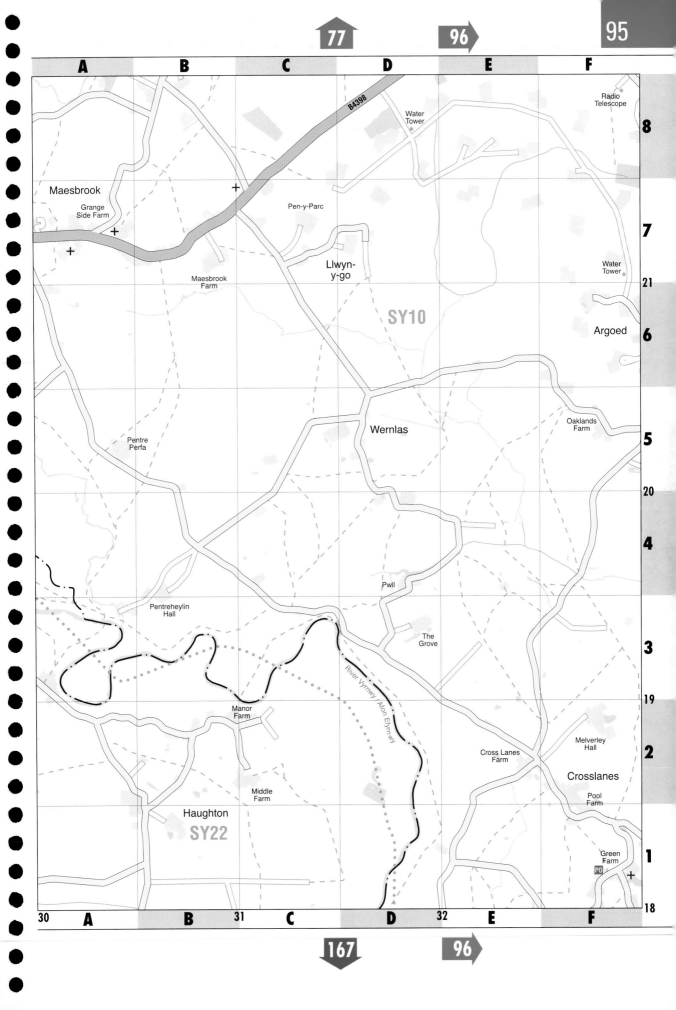

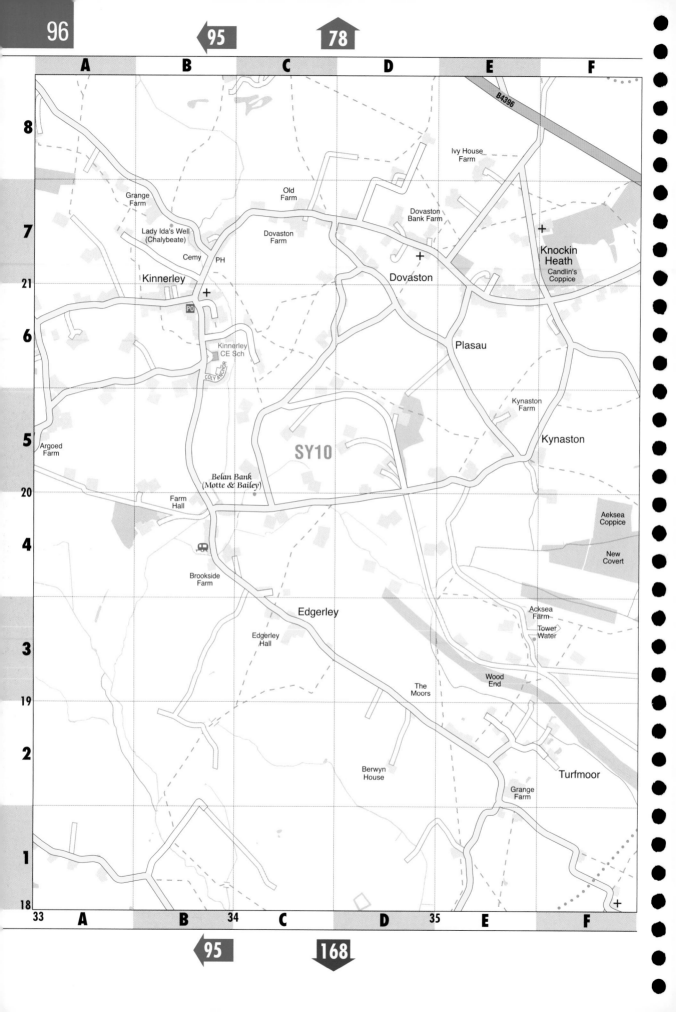

A B C D E F

B4396

8

Grange
Farm

7

Lady Ida's Well
(Chalybeate)

Old
Farm

Ivy House
Farm

Dovaston
Bank Farm

Knockin
Heath

Candlin's
Coppice

Cemy
PH

21

Kinnerley

Dovaston
Farm

Dovaston

PO

6

Kinnerley
CE Sch

Plasau

COLY ANCHOR

Kynaston
Farm

5

Argoed
Farm

SY10

Kynaston

Belan Bank
(Motte & Bailey)

20

Farm
Hall

Aeksea
Coppice

4

New
Covert

Brookside
Farm

 Acksea
Farm

Edgerley

Tower
Water

3

Edgerley
Hall

Wood
End

19

The
Moors

2

Berwyn
House

Turfmoor

Grange
Farm

1

18

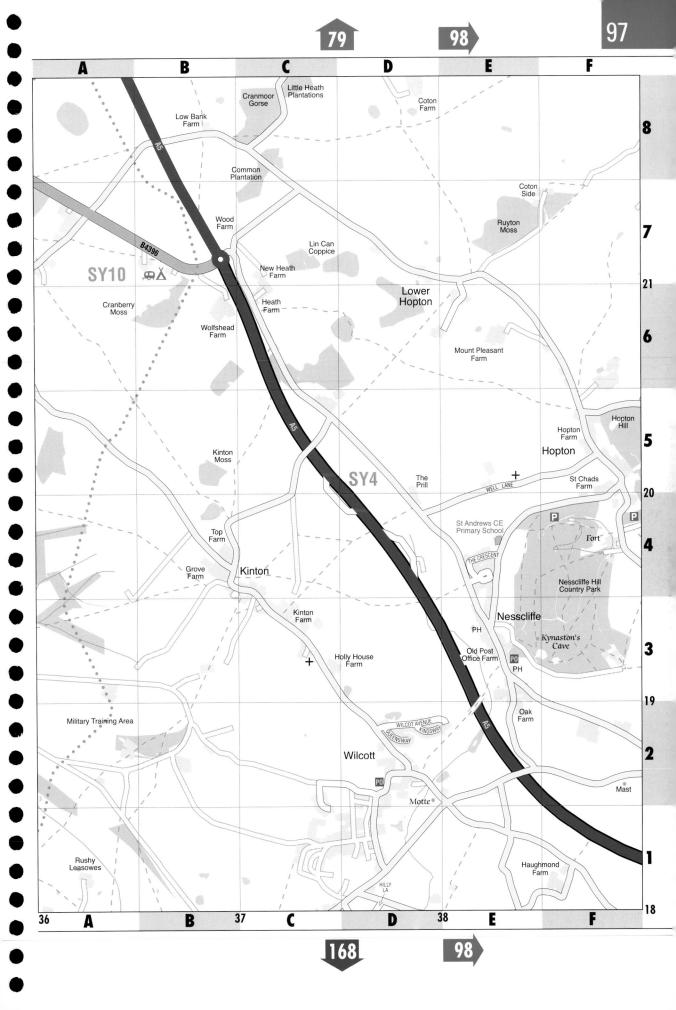

A B C D E F

8
7
21
6
5
20
4
19
3
2
1
18

SY10

SY4

Little Heath Plantations

Cranmoor Gorse

Coton Farm

Low Bank Farm

Common Plantation

Coton Side

Ruyton Moss

Wood Farm

Lin Can Coppice

New Heath Farm

Lower Hopton

Cranberry Moss

Heath Farm

Wolfshead Farm

Mount Pleasant Farm

Hopton Hill

Hopton Farm

Hopton

Kinton Moss

The Prill

St Chads Farm

WELL LANE

St Andrews CE Primary School

Top Farm

THE CRESCENT

Fort

Grove Farm

Kinton

Nesscliffe Hill Country Park

Nesscliffe

Kinton Farm

Kynaston's Cave

PH

Holly House Farm

Old Post Office Farm

PO

PH

Military Training Area

Oak Farm

WILCOT AVENUE

KINGSWAY

QUEENSWAY

Wilcott

PO

Mast

Motte

Rushy Leasowes

HILLY LA

Haughmond Farm

A5

B4396

36 37 38

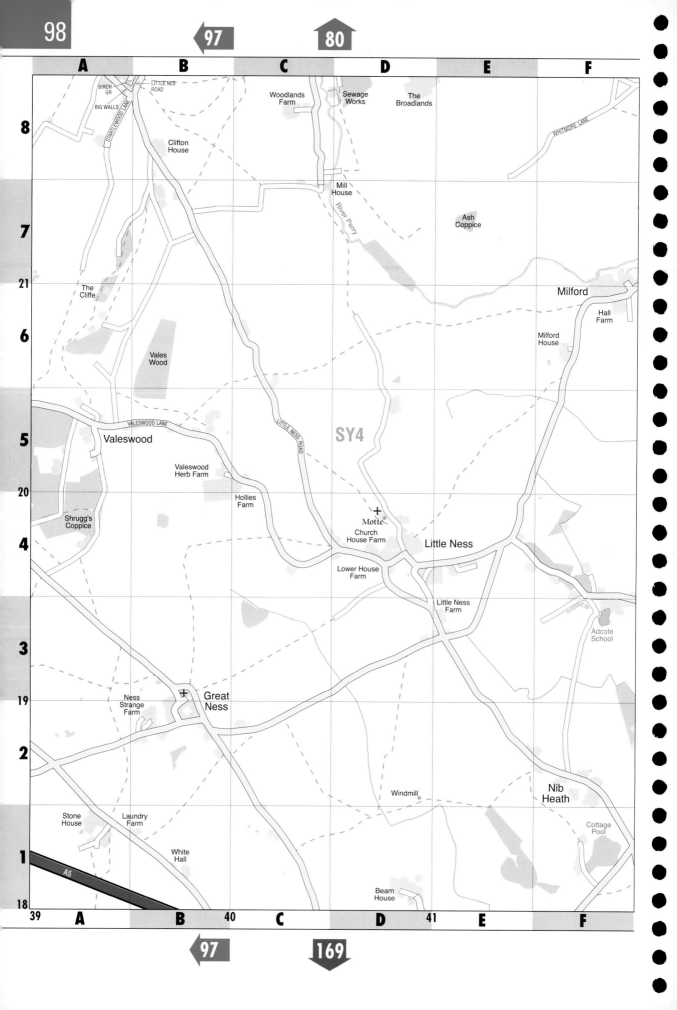

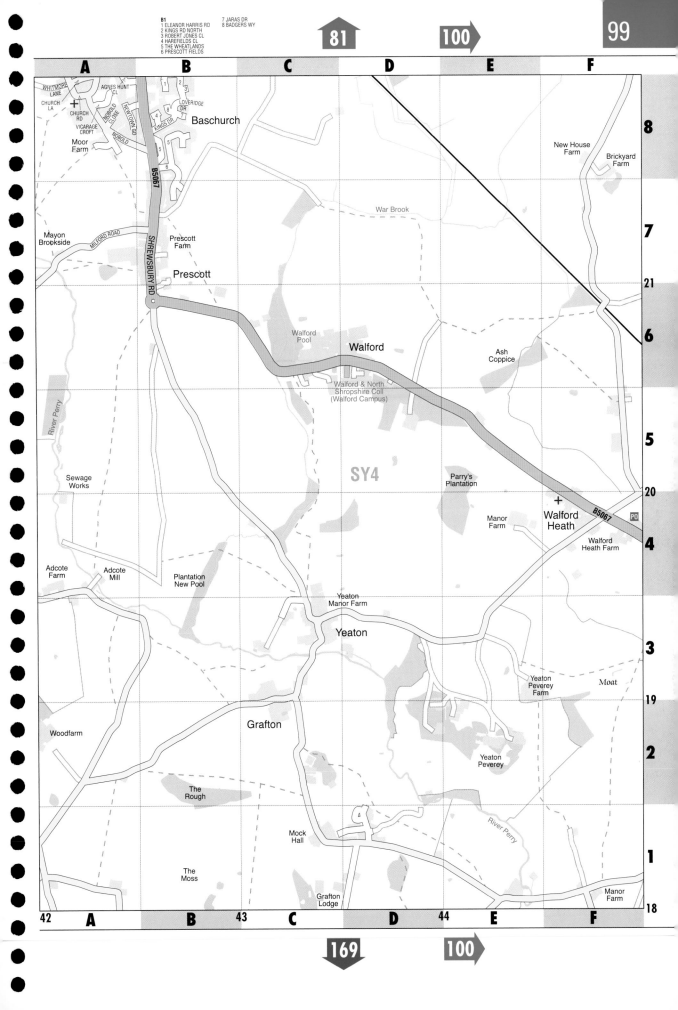

B1
1 ELEANOR HARRIS RD
2 KINGS RD NORTH
3 ROBERT JONES CL
4 HAREFIELDS CL
5 THE WHEATLANDS
6 PRESCOTT FIELDS
7 JARAS DR
8 BADGERS WY

A B C D E F

8
21
7
6
5
20
4
3
19
2
1
18

WHITMORE LANE
AGNES HUNT CL
CHURCH LA
CHURCH RD
VICARAGE CROFT
Moor Farm
NOBOLD CLOSE
NEWTOWN RD
KINGS DR
LOVERIDGE DR
Baschurch
B5067
SHREWSBURY RD
Mayon Brookside
MILFORD ROAD
Prescott Farm
Prescott
War Brook
New House Farm
Brickyard Farm
Walford Pool
Walford
Ash Coppice
Walford & North Shropshire Coll (Walford Campus)
River Perry
Sewage Works
SY4
Parry's Plantation
Manor Farm
Walford Heath
B5067
PO
Walford Heath Farm
Adcote Farm
Adcote Mill
Plantation New Pool
Yeaton Manor Farm
Yeaton
Yeaton Peverey Farm
Moat
Woodfarm
Grafton
Yeaton Peverey
The Rough
River Perry
Mock Hall
The Moss
Grafton Lodge
Manor Farm

42 A B 43 C D 44 E F 18

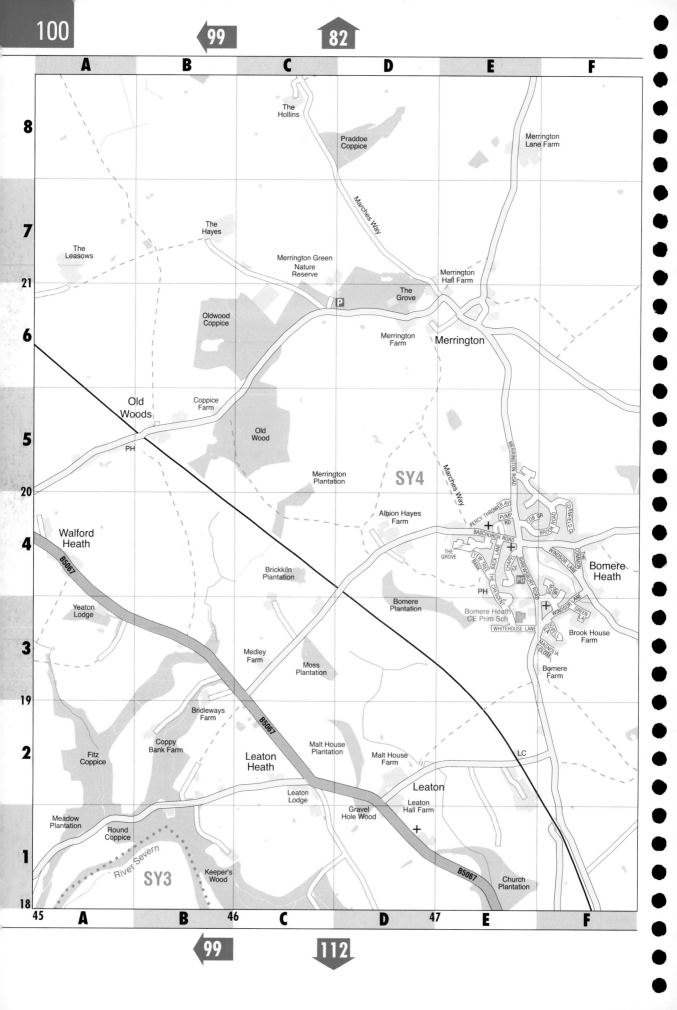

A   B   C   D   E   F

8

7

21

6

5

20

4

3

19

2

1

18

45   A   B   46   C   D   47   E   F

The Hollins

Praddoe Coppice

Merrington Lane Farm

Marches Way

The Leasows

The Hayes

Merrington Green Nature Reserve

Merrington Hall Farm

The Grove

Merrington

P

Oldwood Coppice

Merrington Farm

Old Woods

Coppice Farm

Old Wood

PH

Merrington Plantation

SY4

Marches Way

MERRINGTON ROAD

Walford Heath

B5067

Albion Hayes Farm

PERCY THROWER AVE

PUMP RD

COB GR

CORNFIELD CL

BROW

THE GROVE

BASCHURCH ROAD

Yeaton Lodge

Brickkiln Plantation

YEW TREE CL

BACK LANE

CHAPEL

THE CRESCENT

BANK

SHREWSBURY ROAD

WINDSOR LANE

THE COMMON

Bomere Heath

Bomere Plantation

PO

BOW WAY

WINDSOR GREEN LA

Brook House Farm

Medley Farm

PH

Bomere Heath CE Prim Sch

WHITEHOUSE LANE

DOBELL CL

MAGNOLIA CLOSE

Bomere Farm

Moss Plantation

Fitz Coppice

Coppy Bank Farm

Bridleways Farm

B5067

Malt House Plantation

Malt House Farm

LC

Leaton Heath

Leaton

Meadow Plantation

Round Coppice

Leaton Lodge

Gravel Hole Wood

Leaton Hall Farm

River Severn

SY3

Keeper's Wood

B5067

Church Plantation

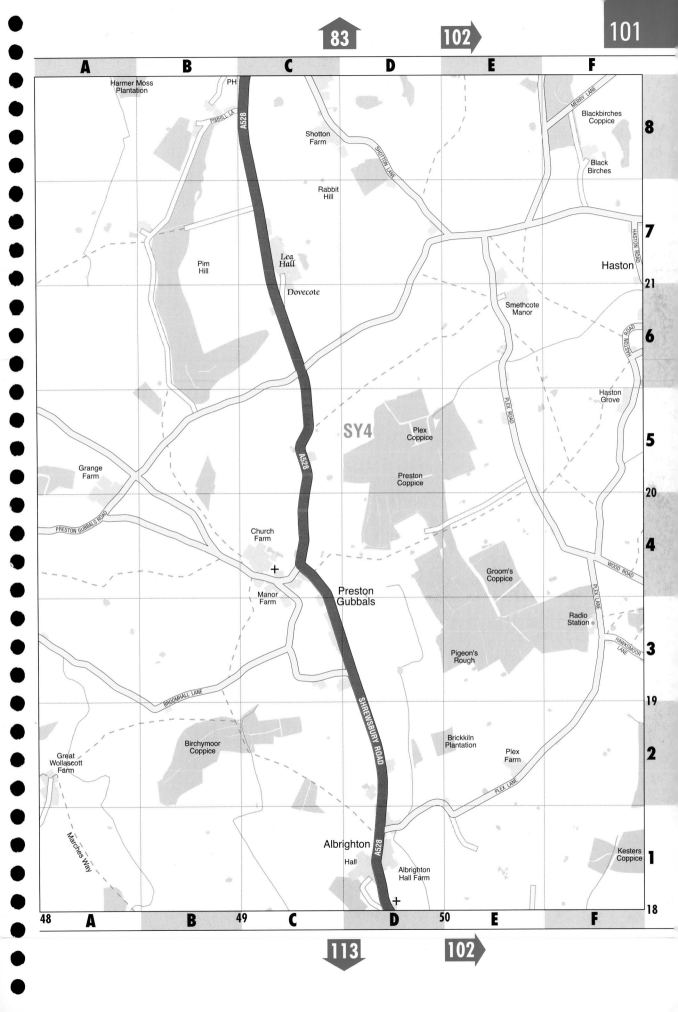

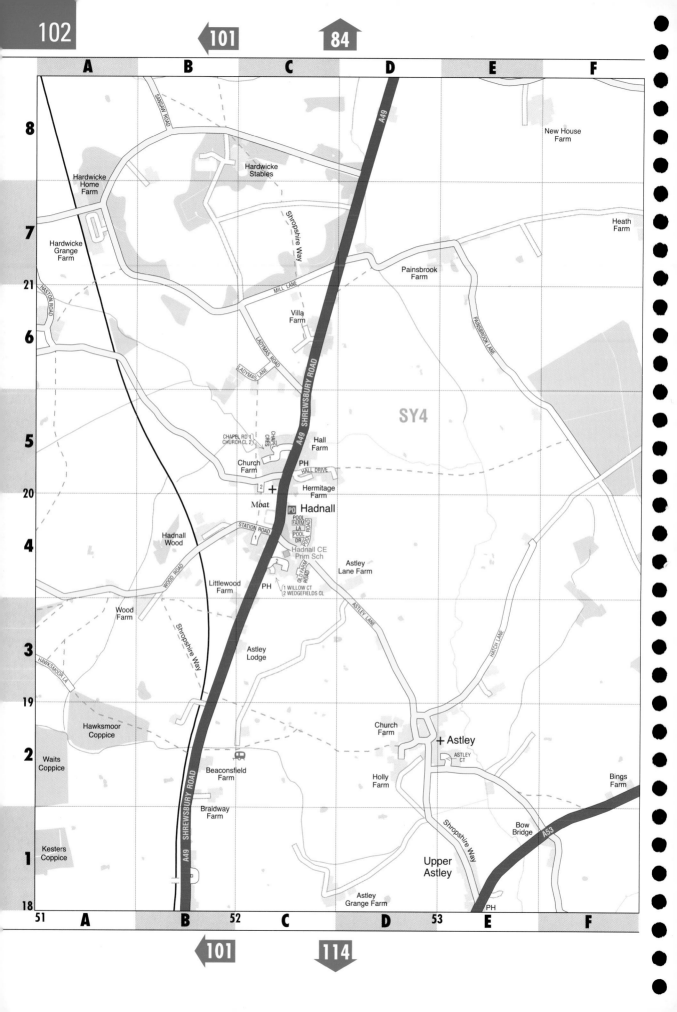

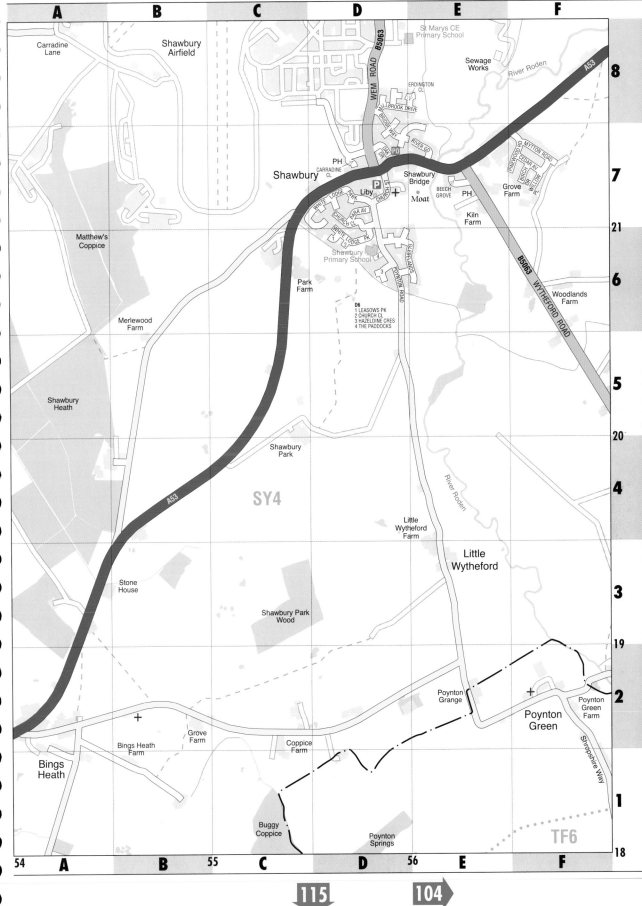

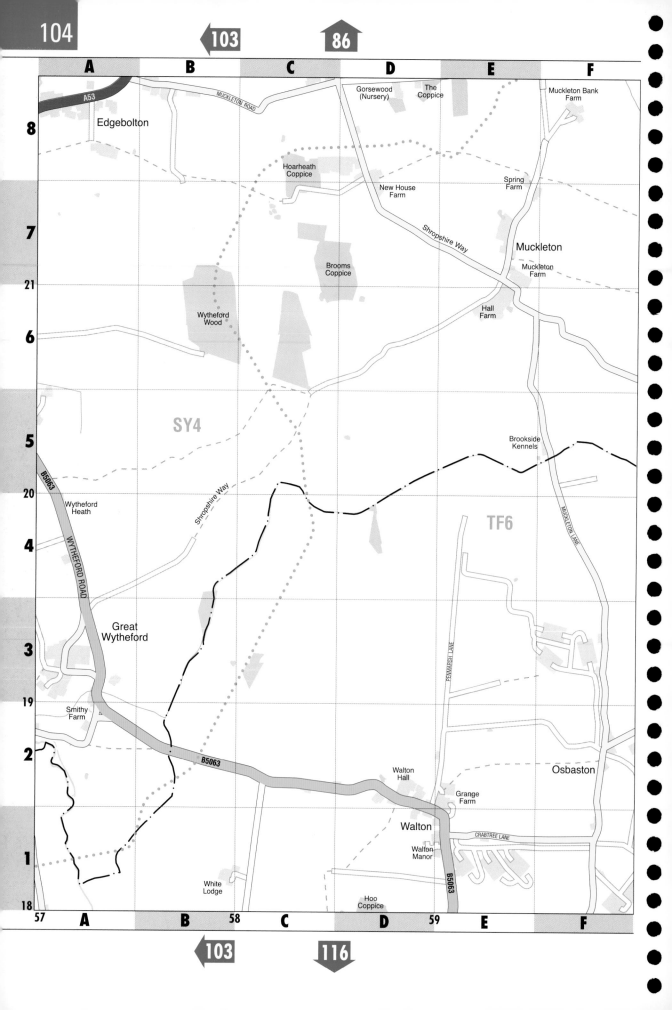

A53

MUCKLETON ROAD

Edgebolton

Gorsewood
(Nursery)

The
Coppice

Muckleton Bank
Farm

Hoarheath
Coppice

New House
Farm

Spring
Farm

Shropshire Way

Muckleton

Muckleton
Farm

Brooms
Coppice

Wytheford
Wood

Hall
Farm

SY4

Brookside
Kennels

Shropshire Way

B5063

Wytheford
Heath

TF6

MUCKLETON LANE

WYTHEFORD ROAD

Great
Wytheford

PENHMARSH LANE

Smithy
Farm

Osbaston

B5063

Walton
Hall

Grange
Farm

Walton

CRABTREE LANE

Walton
Manor

B5063

White
Lodge

Hoo
Coppice

57   A   B   58   C   D   59   E   F

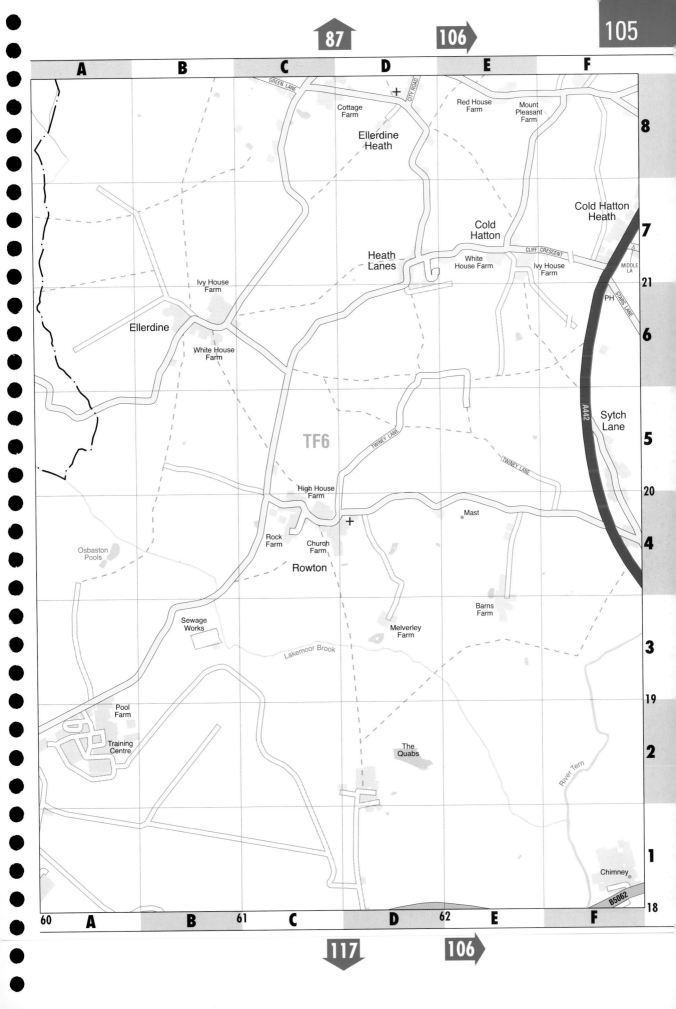

A B C D E F

8

Ellerdine Heath

Cold Hatton Heath

Red House Farm
Mount Pleasant Farm
Cottage Farm

Cold Hatton

7

White House Farm

Heath Lanes

CLIFF CRESCENT

Ivy House Farm

MIDDLE LA

21

PH

STARS LANE

Ivy House Farm

6

Ellerdine

White House Farm

A442

Sytch Lane

5

TF6

TWINEY LANE

TWINEY LANE

20

High House Farm

Mast

4

Rock Farm

Church Farm

Barns Farm

Osbaston Pools

Rowton

Melverley Farm

Sewage Works

Lakemoor Brook

3

19

Pool Farm

The Quabs

2

Training Centre

River Tern

1

Chimney

B5062

18

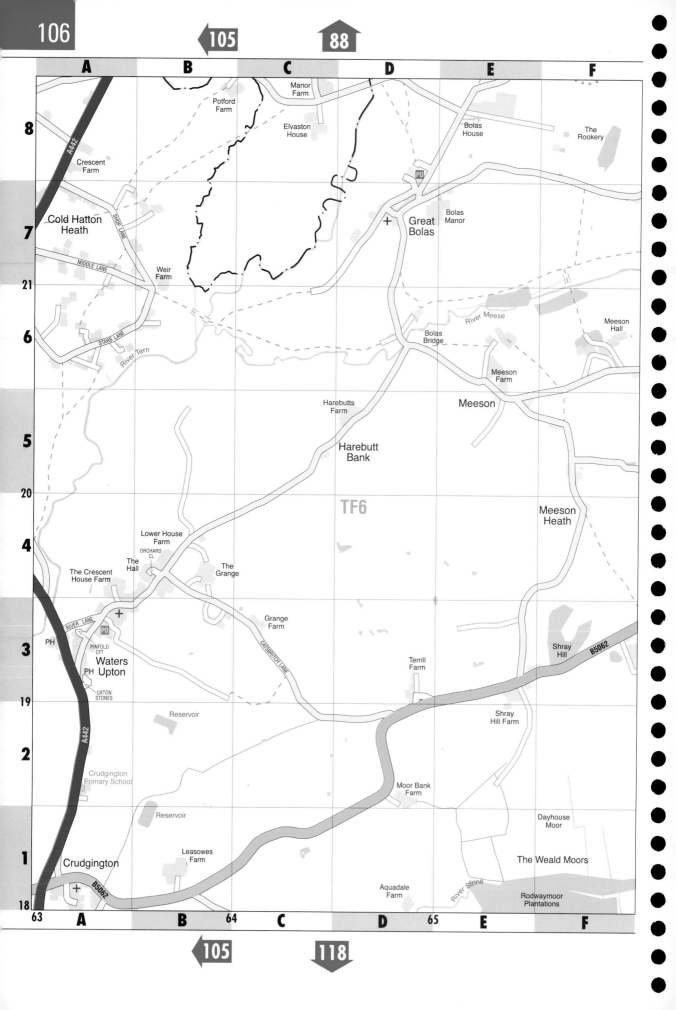

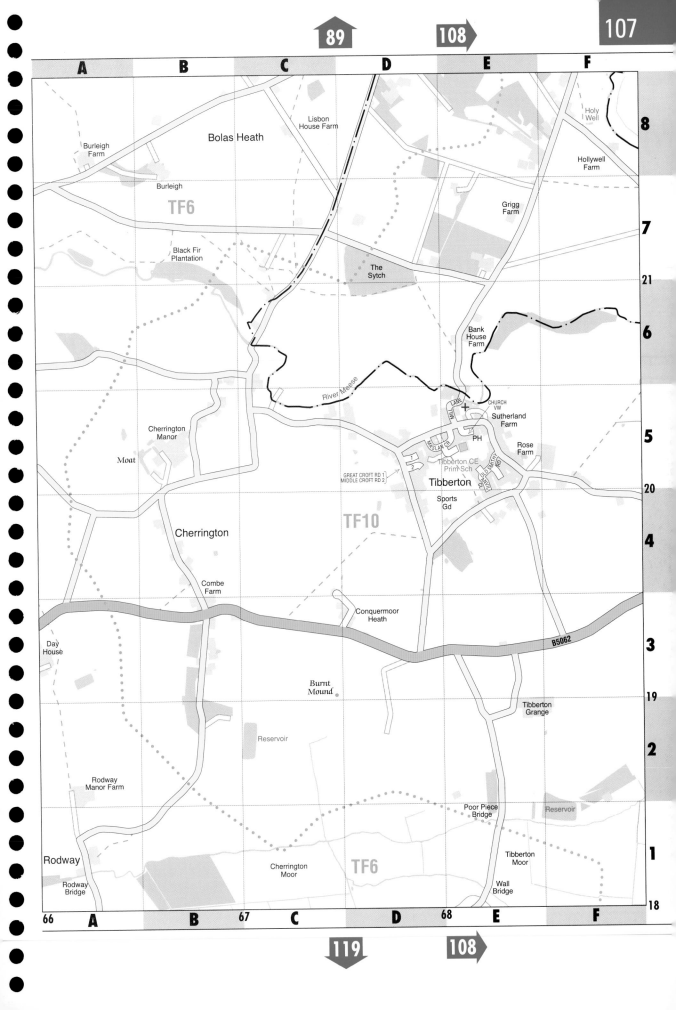

89

108

A   B   C   D   E   F

8

Holy
Well

Burleigh
Farm

Bolas Heath

Lisbon
House Farm

Hollywell
Farm

Burleigh

TF6

Grigg
Farm

7

Black Fir
Plantation

21

The
Sytch

Bank
House
Farm

6

River Meese

CHURCH
VW

Cherrington
Manor

TWL LANE

Sutherland
Farm

Moat

MASLAN CR

PH

Rose
Farm

5

1
2

Tibberton CE
Prim Sch

OLD SMITHY RD

CLINTN

GREAT CROFT RD 1
MIDDLE CROFT RD 2

Tibberton

20

Sports
Gd

Cherrington

TF10

4

Combe
Farm

Conquermoor
Heath

B5062

3

Day
House

Burnt
Mound

Tibberton
Grange

19

Reservoir

2

Reservoir

Rodway
Manor Farm

Poor Piece
Bridge

Rodway

Tibberton
Moor

1

Rodway
Bridge

Cherrington
Moor

TF6

Wall
Bridge

18

66   A   B   67   C   D   68   E   F

119

108

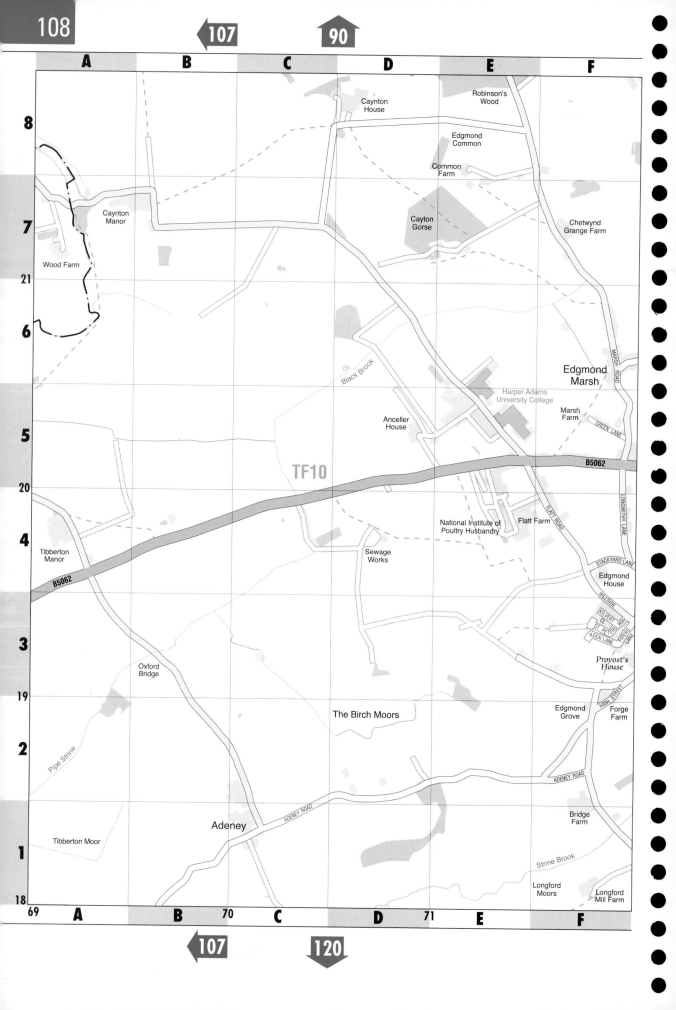

A   B   C   D   E   F

8

7

21

6

Edgmond
Marsh

5

20

TF10

4

3

19

2

1

18

69   A   B   70   C   D   71   E   F

Caynton
House

Robinson's
Wood

Edgmond
Common

Common
Farm

Caynton
Manor

Cayton
Gorse

Chetwynd
Grange Farm

Wood Farm

MARSH ROAD

Harper Adams
University College

Marsh
Farm

GREEN LANE

Black Brook

Anceller
House

B5062

LONGWITHY LANE

Tibberton Manor

National Institute of
Poultry Husbandry

Flatt Farm

FLATT ROAD

B5062

Sewage
Works

STACKYARD LANE

Edgmond
House

HILLSIDE

KILVERT CL
ST. PETERS WAY
RIVERS LANE
ROCK LANE

Oxford
Bridge

Provost's
House

The Birch Moors

Edgmond
Grove

HIGH STREET

Forge
Farm

Pipe Strine

ADENEY ROAD

Adeney

ADENEY ROAD

Bridge
Farm

Tibberton Moor

Strine Brook

Longford
Moors

Longford
Mill Farm

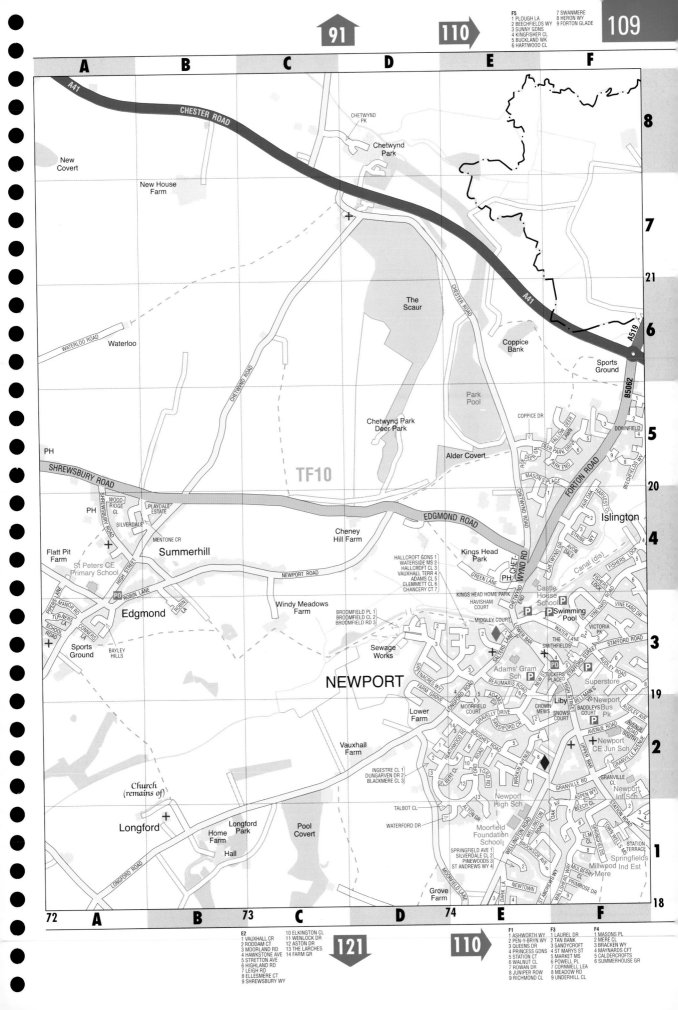

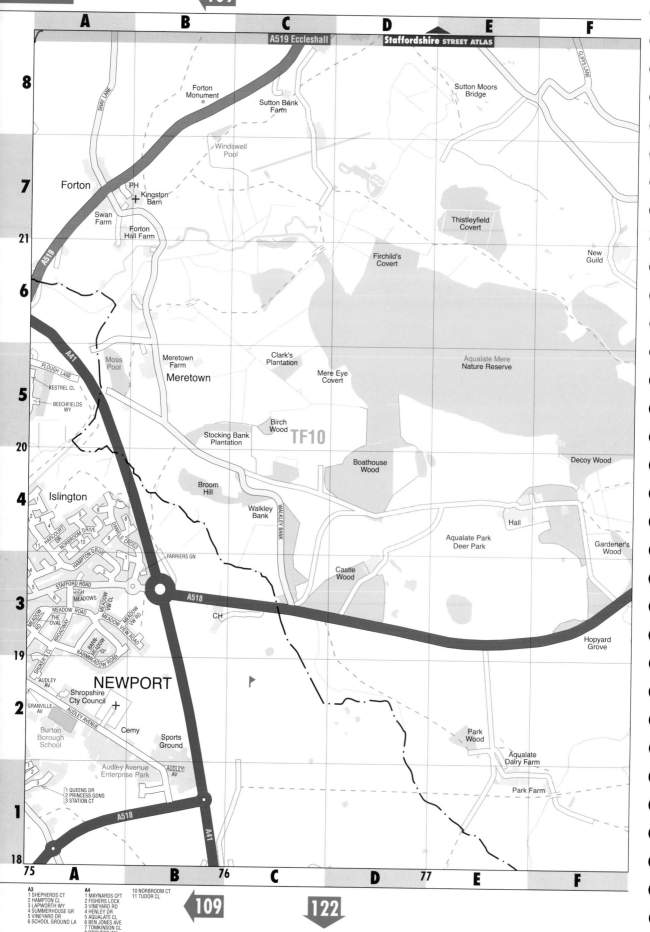

A519 Eccleshall

Staffordshire STREET ATLAS

8

Forton
Monument

Sutton Moors
Bridge

Sutton Bank
Farm

Windswell
Pool

7

Forton

PH

Kingston
Barn

Thistleyfield
Covert

21

Swan
Farm

Forton
Hall Farm

Firchild's
Covert

New
Guild

6

A519

A41

Meretown
Farm

Clark's
Plantation

Aqualate Mere
Nature Reserve

PLOUGH LANE

Moss
Pool

Meretown

Mere Eye
Covert

KESTREL CL

5

BEECHFIELDS
WY

Birch
Wood

TF10

Stocking Bank
Plantation

20

Boathouse
Wood

Decoy Wood

Islington

4

Broom
Hill

Hall

Walkley
Bank

WALKLEY BANK

Aqualate Park
Deer Park

Gardener's
Wood

HARCOURT
DR

DANIELS CROSS

NORBROOM DRIVE

HAMPTON DRIVE

FARRIERS GN

Castle
Wood

STAFFORD ROAD

3

HIGH
MEADOWS

A518

MEADOW VW CL

MEADOW
ROAD

THE
OVAL

BROADWAY

MEADOW VIEW ROAD

MEADOW
VW RD

CH

Hopyard
Grove

19

SHUKER CL

BARN
MEADOW
CL

BARNMEADOW ROAD

AUDLEY
AV

NEWPORT

Shropshire
Cty Council

GRANVILLE
AV

2

AUDLEY AVENUE

Cemy

Sports
Ground

Park
Wood

Burton
Borough
School

Aqualate
Dairy Farm

Audley Avenue
Enterprise Park

AUDLEY
AV

Park Farm

1

1 QUEENS DR
2 PRINCESS GDNS
3 STATION CT

A518

A41

18

75 A B 76 C D 77 E F

A3
1 SHEPHERDS CT
2 HAMPTON CL
3 LAPWORTH WY
4 SUMMERHOUSE GR
5 VINEYARD DR
6 SCHOOL GROUND LA

A4
1 MAYNARDS CFT
2 FISHERS LOCK
3 VINEYARD RD
4 HENLEY DR
5 AQUALATE CL
6 BEN JONES AVE
7 TOMKINSON CL
8 DROVERS WY
9 PLOUGHMANS CFT

10 NORBROOM CT
11 TUDOR CL

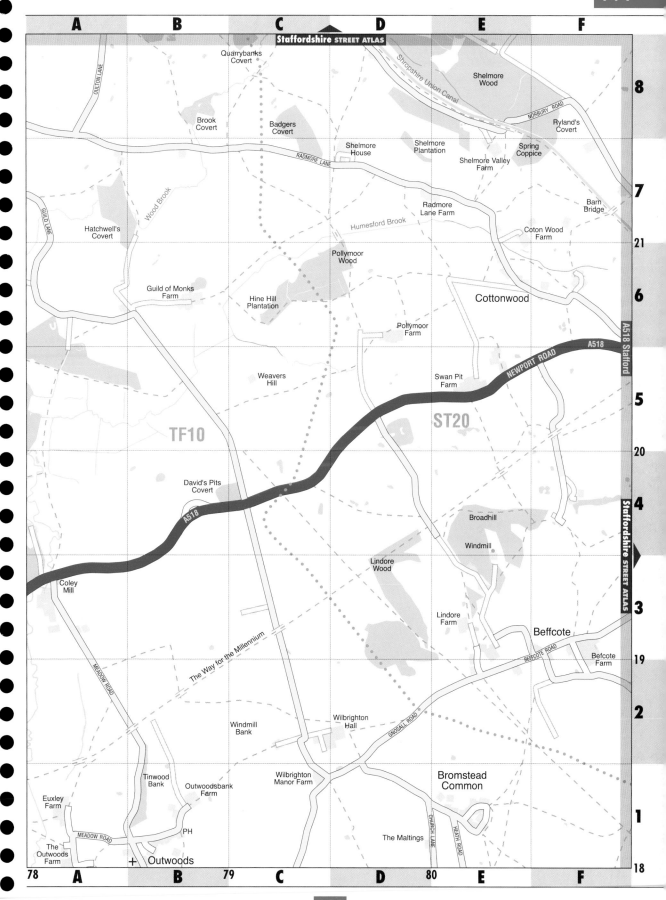

169
100

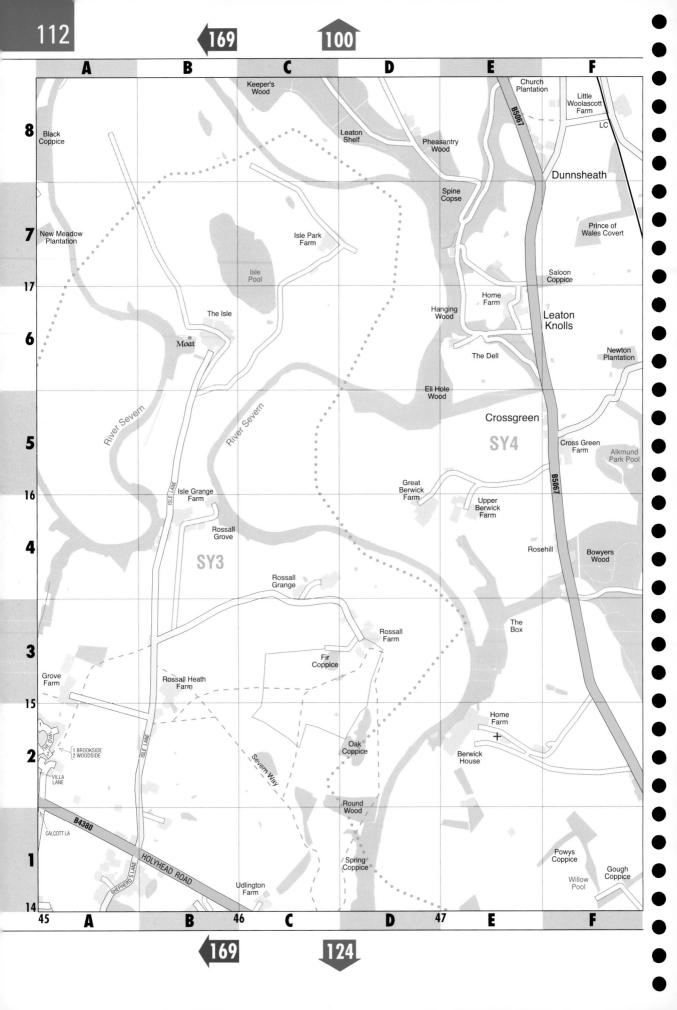

169
124

D5	E5	7 WILLINGTON CL	
1 OUTWOOD	1 WAYHILL	8 FRESHFIELDS	
2 OVERSTONE	2 DERWENT AVE		
3 LITTLEOVER AVE	3 LITTLE HARLESCOTT LA		113
4 BAKEWELL CL	4 WAINCOTT		
5 HODGKINSON WLK	5 CHATWOOD CT		
6 DUNBAR	6 ALLESTREE CL		

101 **114**

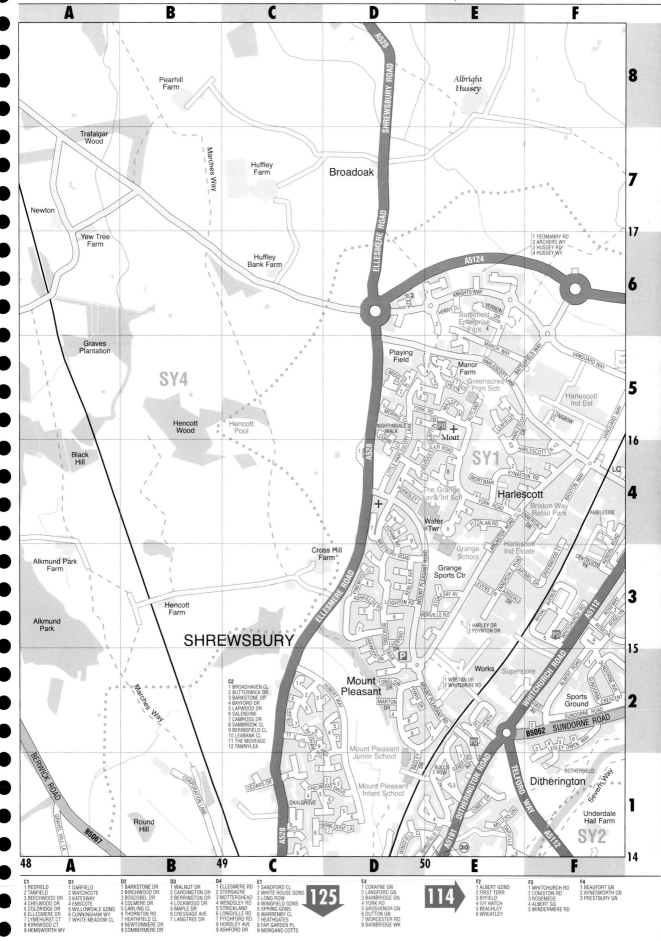

C2
1 BROADHAVEN CL
2 BUTTERWICK DR
3 BARKSTONE DR
4 BAYFORD DR
5 LAPWOOD DR
6 SALENDINE
7 CAMROSS DR
8 SAMBROOK CL
9 BERINSFIELD CL
10 LEABANK CL
11 THE MOVEAGE
12 TAWNYLEA

17
6
5
16
4
3
15
2
1
14

8
7

C1
1 REDFIELD
2 TANFIELD
3 BEECHWOOD DR
4 CHELWOOD DR
5 COLDRIDGE DR
6 ELLESMERE DR
7 LYMEHURST CT
8 KIRKWOOD CT
9 HEMSWORTH WY

D1
1 DARFIELD
2 WATCHCOTE
3 KATESWAY
4 EMSCOTE
5 WILLOWDALE GDNS
6 CUNNINGHAM WY
7 WHITE MEADOW CL

D2
1 BARKSTONE DR
2 BIRCHWOOD DR
3 BOSCOBEL DR
4 BERRINGTON DR
5 CARLING CL
6 THORNTON RD
7 HEATHFIELD CL
8 NEWTONMERE CL
9 COMBERMERE DR

D3
1 WALNUT DR
2 CARDINGTON DR
3 LOCKWOOD DR
4 MAPLE DR
5 CRESSAGE AVE
6 LANGTREE DR

D4
1 ELLESMERE RD
2 STERSACRE
3 MOTTERSHEAD
4 WENDSLEY RD
5 STRICKLAND
6 LONGVILLE RD
7 PITCHFORD RD
8 HORDLEY AVE
9 ASHFORD DR

E1
1 SANDFORD CL
2 WHITE HOUSE GDNS
3 LONG ROW
4 WINGFIELD GDNS
5 SPRING GDNS
6 WARRENBY CL
7 HEATHGATES
8 FAR GARDEN PL
9 MORGANS COTTS

125

E4
1 COKAYNE GN
2 LANGFORD GN
3 BAINBRIDGE GN
4 YORK RD
5 GROSVENOR GN
6 DUTTON GN
7 WORCESTER RD
8 BAINBRIDGE WK

114

F2
1 ALBERT GDNS
2 FIRST TERR
3 BYFIELD
4 IVY HATCH
5 BEACHLEY
6 WHEATLEY

F3
1 WHITCHURCH RD
2 CONISTON RD
3 ROSEMEDE
4 ALBERT SQ
5 WINDERMERE RD

F4
1 BEAUFORT GN
2 AYNESWORTH GN
3 PRESTBURY GN

A B C D E F

8

Upper Battlefield

Battlefield Farm

Ball's Coppice

SHREWSBURY ROAD

A49

7

17

ROBERT JONES WY

A53

6

A5124

A5112

Wheatley Farm

Shropshire Way

Albrightlee Villa Farm

Kendricks Rough

Sunderton Farm

PH

Battlefield

5

VANGUARD WY

Chy

BATTLEFIELD ROAD

BATTLEFIELD CT

SHILLINGSTONE DRIVE

HOLT END

Sunderton Pool

Albrightlee Hall Farm

Colins Rough

SY4

Sunderton Farm

New

16

P&R

Superstore

Sundorne Retail Park

ARLINGTON WY

ARLINGTON WY

HALLAM DR

LATCHFORD LANE

FARRAN GR

A49

B4
1 GREATFORD GN
2 LAWSON GDNS
3 TRALLAM DR
4 PEACEHAVEN
5 GOWAN CT
6 RAMSEY MDWS
7 MALLARD CL
8 SWALLOW DR
9 WOODPECKER CL
10 KESTREL DR

The Dell Farm

A5112

WHITCHURCH ROAD

HARLESCOTT LANE

Works

Harlescott

SY1

Superstore

SWIFT DR

HERON DR

LONG JACK

PARTRIDGE CL

ROBIN CL

Sundorne Farm

4

ROSELYN

MEADOW FARM DRIVE

FEATHERBED LANE

BROUGHTON ROAD

FIELD CRESCENT

STANTON DR

FIELD CR

MOSTON DR

ALLERTON RD

THE ARNS

LINNET

ALBURY DRIVE

GOLDCREST DRI

C3
1 WREN CL
2 KESTREL DR
3 CURLEW CL
4 CHAFFINCH WY
5 WOODLARK CL
6 KINGFISHER CL
7 QUATFORD CL
8 NORTHSIDE CL

Sundorne Castle Farm

Abbey Farm

Hillside Farm

3

Harlescott Junior School

CORNDON CRESCENT

Sundorne Sec Sch

Sundorne Inf Sch

Liby

EAST CRESCENT

EBURY AVENUE

CAVERLEY CR

CAVERLEY RD

ALLERTON ROAD

1 WHITTINGTON CL
2 HOLDGATE DR
3 OVERTON CL
4 FARMOOR

Meadows Farm

B5062

15

Sundorne Road

2

B5062

SUNDORNE ROAD

P P

FERNDALE RD
HOPTON DR

TA Centre

Sports Pitches

Sundorne Road Education Centre

Welti Tennis Club

Sports Ground

Sundorne Pool

Shrewsbury Sports Village

SHREWSBURY

Pimley Manor

1

Severn Way

Shropshire Way

SY2

Gables Farm

Shropshire Way

The Hollies

14

CHURCH RD

A49

51 A B 52 C D 53 E F

A2
1 SUNDORNE CR
2 CORNDON CL
3 CORNDON ROAD
4 MEADOW CL
5 MONTGOMERY WY
6 WELLINGTON CL
7 MARLBOROUGH CT

A3
1 DOUNTON CL
2 HARLESCOTT CL
3 HAUGHMOND AVE
4 ROSEWAY
5 CORNDON DR
6 MOSTON GN
7 ROSEDALE

A4
1 WHITCHURCH RD
2 HAWKESTONE RD

B3
1 THE BRADLEYS
2 THE SPRINGS
3 THE HIG
4 THE HASSACKS
5 CRAIG CL
6 ALLERTON RD

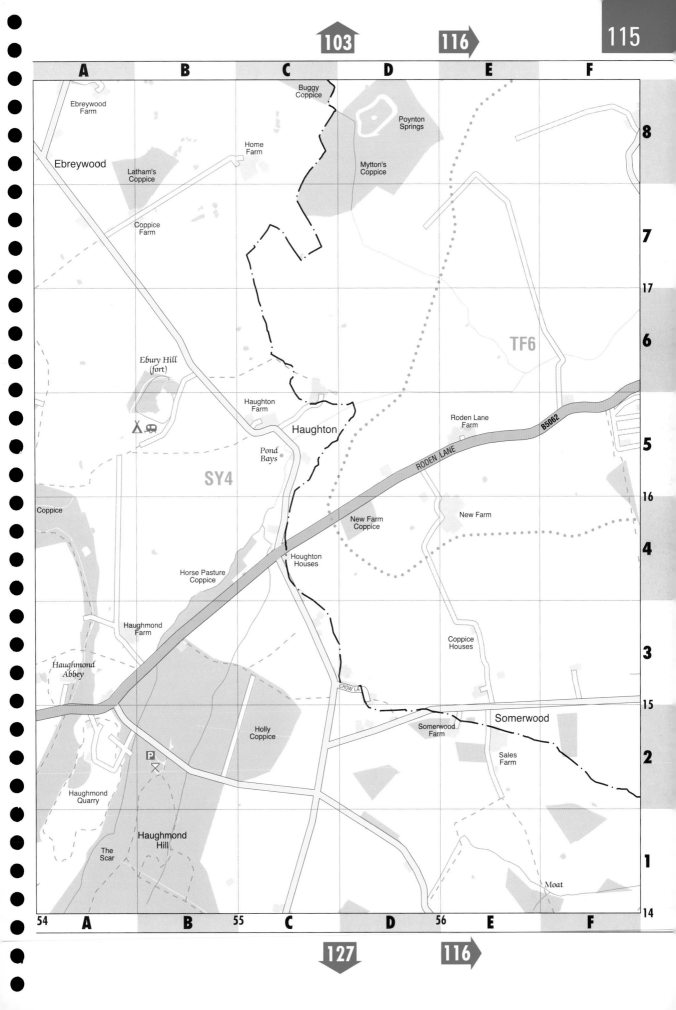

115
104

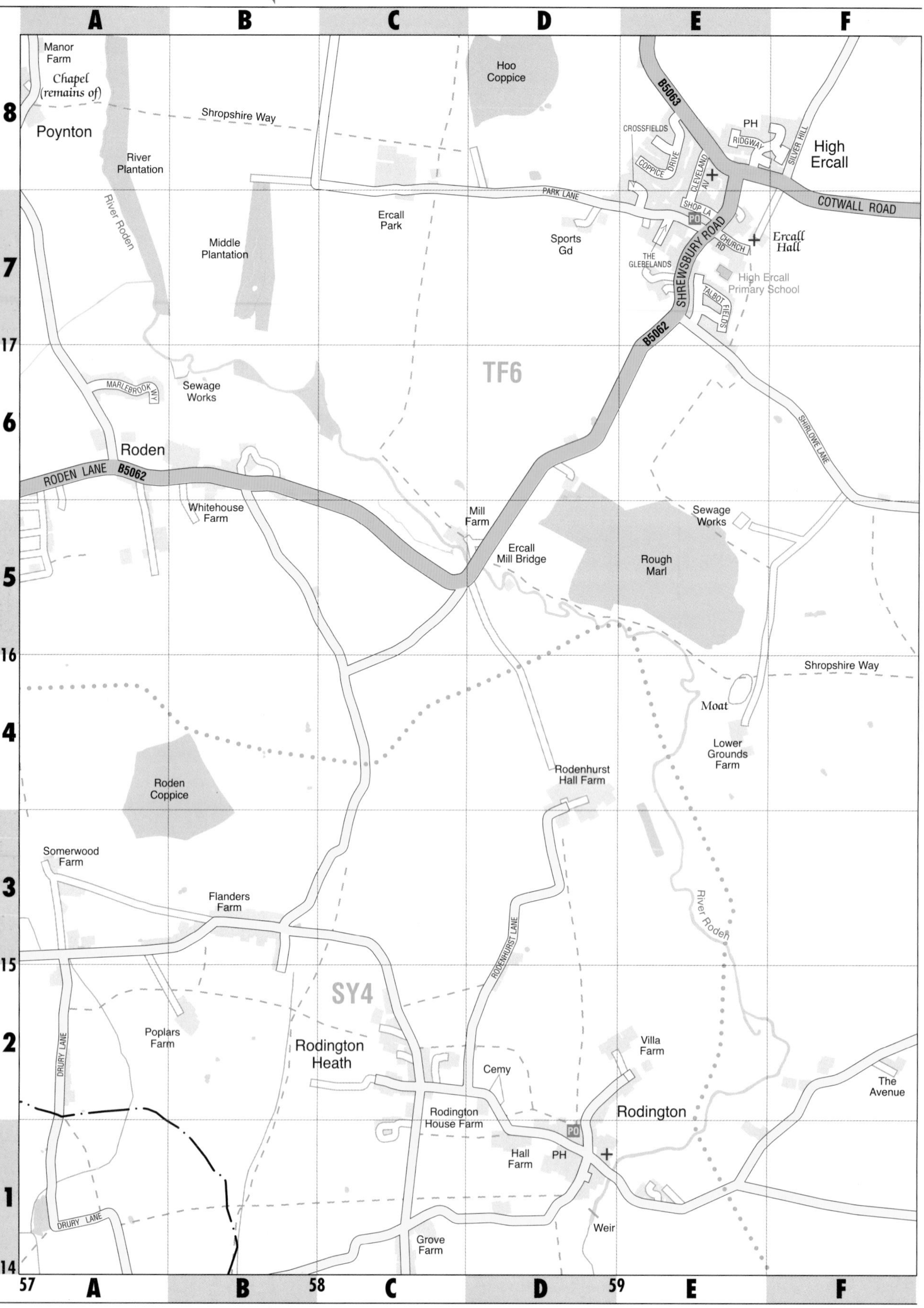

A B C D E F

8

Manor Farm
Chapel (remains of)
Poynton
River Plantation
Shropshire Way
Hoo Coppice

B5063
CROSSFIELDS
PH
RIDGWAY
CLEVELAND DRIVE
COPPICE
SILVER HILL
High Ercall
COTWALL ROAD

7

Middle Plantation
Ercall Park
PARK LANE
Sports Gd
THE GLEBELANDS
SHOP LA
PO
SHREWSBURY ROAD
CHURCH RD
Ercall Hall
High Ercall Primary School
TALBOT FIELDS

17

MARLEBROOK WAY
Sewage Works
TF6
B5062

6

Roden
RODEN LANE   B5062
Whitehouse Farm
SHIRLOWE LANE
Sewage Works

5

Mill Farm
Ercall Mill Bridge
Rough Marl
River Roden

16

Shropshire Way
Moat

4

Roden Coppice
Rodenhurst Hall Farm
Lower Grounds Farm

3

Somerwood Farm
Flanders Farm
RODENHURST LANE
River Roden

15

DRURY LANE
SY4

2

Poplars Farm
Rodington Heath
Cemy
Villa Farm
The Avenue

Rodington House Farm
PO
Rodington
PH

1

DRURY LANE
Hall Farm
Weir

14

57   A   B   58   C   D   59   E   F

Grove Farm

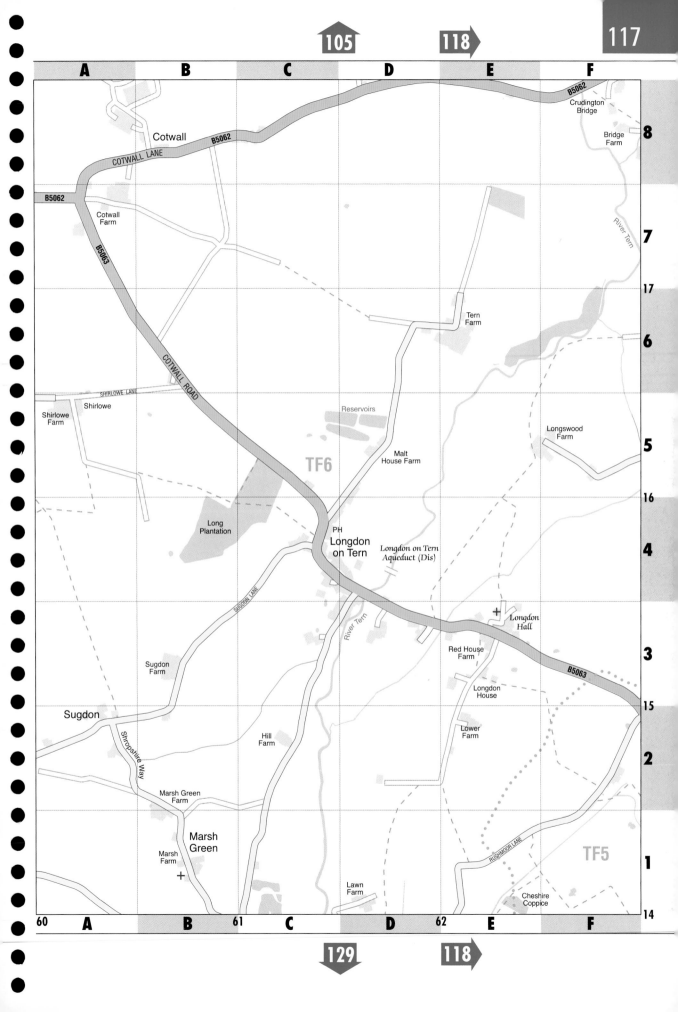

A   B   C   D   E   F

B5062

Crudington
Bridge

Cotwall   B5062

8

COTWALL LANE

Bridge
Farm

B5062

River Tern

7

Cotwall
Farm

B5063

17

COTWALL ROAD

6

Tern
Farm

SHIRLOWE LANE

Shirlowe

Reservoirs

Longswood
Farm

5

Shirlowe
Farm

Shirlowe

Malt
House Farm

TF6

16

Long
Plantation

PH
Longdon
on Tern

Longdon on Tern
Aqueduct (Dis)

4

Longdon
Hall

River Tern

Red House
Farm

3

SUGDON LANE

Sugdon
Farm

B5063

Longdon
House

Sugdon

15

Shropshire Way

Hill
Farm

Lower
Farm

2

Marsh Green
Farm

Marsh
Green

RUSHMOOR LANE

TF5

1

Marsh
Farm

Lawn
Farm

Cheshire
Coppice

14

60   A   B   61   C   D   62   E   F

A   **B**   **C**   **D**   **E**   **F**

Crudgington

Greenacres
Farm

Holly
Farm

Crudgington
Green

Crudgington
Moor

Rodwaymoor
Plantations

Sleap
Moor Farm

Rodway
Moor

8

A442

Crudgingtongreen
Plantation

7

Sleap
Moor

Sidney
Plantation

17

Sleap
Farm

Sidney
Moor

6

The Weald Moors

Woodfield
Farm

THE DUKE'S DRIVE

Sidney
Cottages

5

New House
Farm

TF6

Wrockwardine
Moor

Sleapford
Farm

16

Old
Rookery

Reservoir

Eyton
Moor

Sleapford

4

Canal (dis)   PH

Long Lane

The
Farm

Long
Lane
Farm

Weir

Fresh
Winds Farm

Weir

3

Weir

15

RUSHMOOR
LA

Eyton House
Farm

✚

Eyton upon the
Weald Moors

Mantle
Covert

2

Wheelwright
Covert

Eyton
Hall

B5063

TF5

A442

Bratton
Park Farm

Park
Covert

1

SHERWOOD CL 1
HARRINGTON HEATH 2
FOREST CL 3
ARROW RD 4

Longpit
Coppice

Wappenshall
Farm

PH   SILKIN
WY

Bratton
Farm

HOPKINS HEATH

GLADE WAY

14

63   **A**   **B**   **64**   **C**   **D**   **65**   **E**   **F**

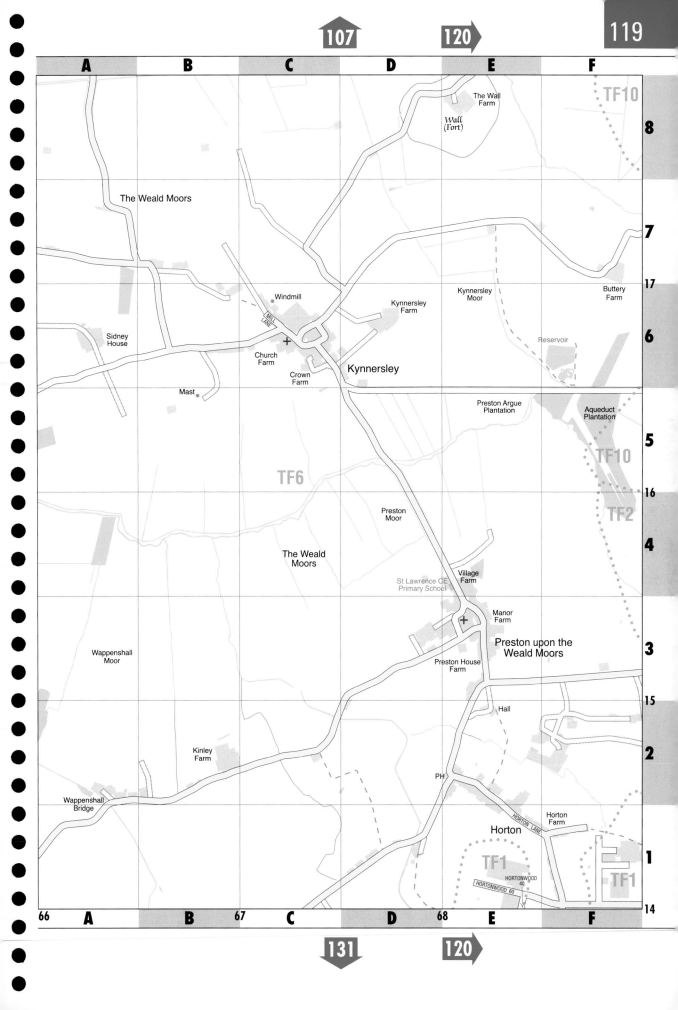

A B C D E F

8
7
17
6
5
16
4
3
15
2
1
14

The Wall Farm

Wall (Fort)

TF10

The Weald Moors

Windmill

MILL LANE

Sidney House

Church Farm

Crown Farm

Mast

Kynnersley Farm

Kynnersley

Kynnersley Moor

Preston Argue Plantation

Buttery Farm

Reservoir

Aqueduct Plantation

TF10

TF6

TF2

Preston Moor

The Weald Moors

St Lawrence CE Primary School

Village Farm

Manor Farm

Preston upon the Weald Moors

Preston House Farm

Wappenshall Moor

Hall

Kinley Farm

PH

Wappenshall Bridge

HORTON LANE

Horton Farm

Horton

TF1

HORTONWOOD 40
HORTONWOOD 60

TF1

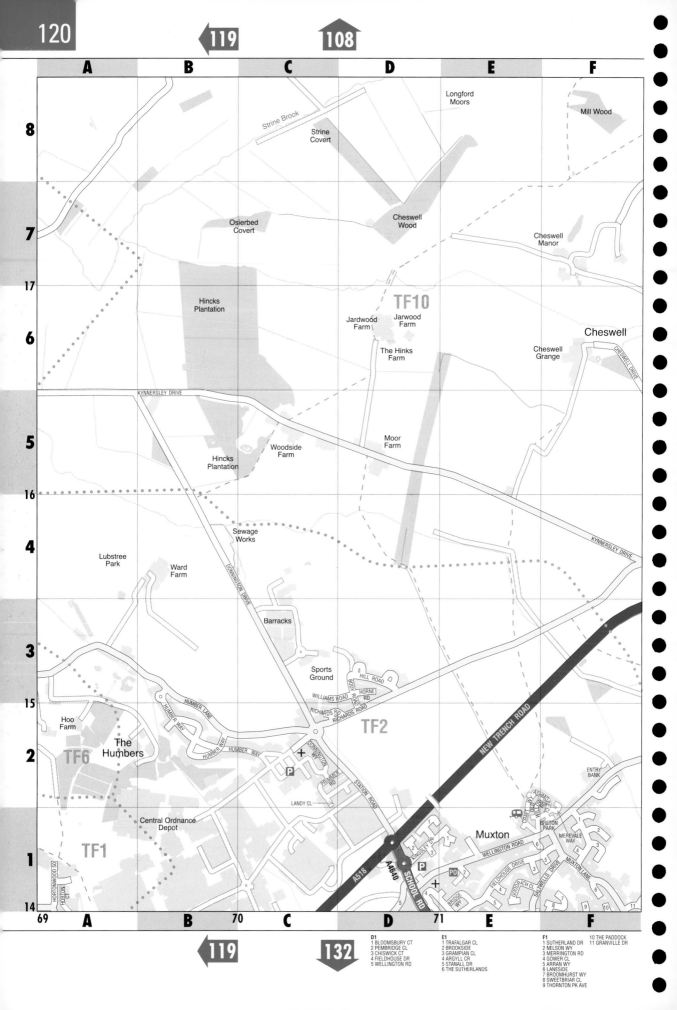

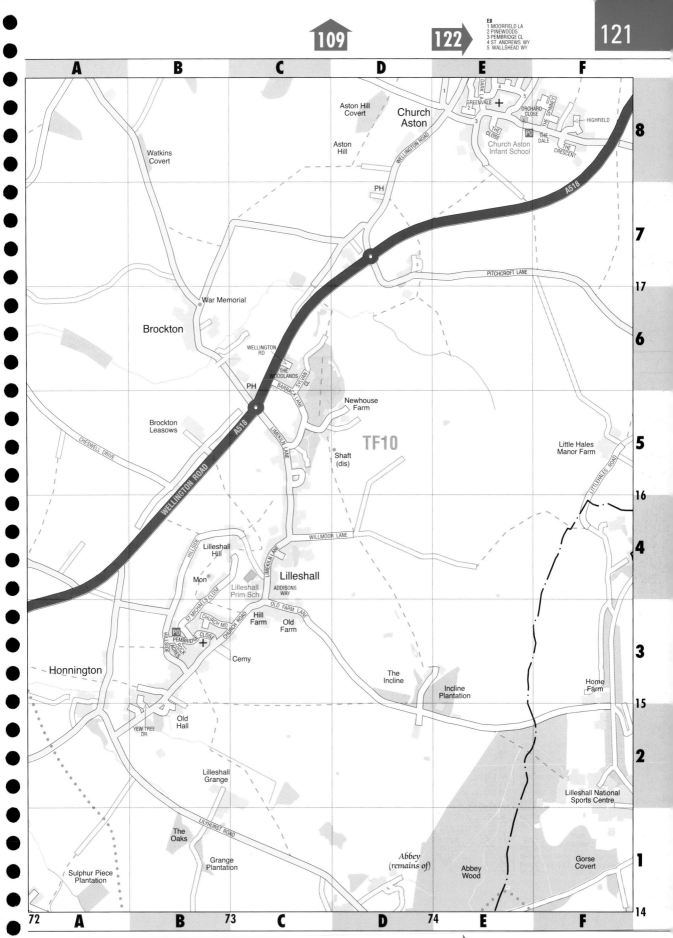

109
122
E8
1 MOORFIELD LA
2 PINEWOODS
3 PEMBRIDGE CL
4 ST ANDREWS WY
5 WALLSHEAD WY
121

A   B   C   D   E   F

8
7
17
6
5
16
4
3
15
2
1
14

Aston Hill
Covert

Church
Aston

GREENVALE

THE SPINNEY

DARK LA

ORCHARD
CLOSE

HIGHFIELD

THE
CLOSE

PO

THE
DALE

THE
CRESCENT

Church Aston
Infant School

Aston
Hill

A518

PH

PITCHCROFT LANE

Watkins
Covert

War Memorial

Brockton

WELLINGTON
RD

THE
WOODLANDS

SYLVAN
CL

Newhouse
Farm

PH

Little Hales
Manor Farm

BARRACK LANE

Brockton
Leasows

A518

LIMEKILN
LANE

TF10

Shaft
(dis)

LITTLEHALES ROAD

CHESWELL DRIVE

WELLINGTON ROAD

WILLMOOR LANE

HILLSIDE

Lilleshall
Hill

LIMEKILN LANE

Lilleshall

Mon

Lilleshall
Prim Sch

ADDISONS
WAY

OLD FARM LANE

Hill
Farm

Old
Farm

Home
Farm

ST MICHAEL'S CLOSE

CHURCH MD

CHURCH ROAD

PO

Pembridge

CLOSE

Honnington

HILLSIDE

BLOCK
ADNEYS

Cemy

The
Incline

Incline
Plantation

YEW TREE
DR

Old
Hall

Lilleshall
Grange

LILYHURST ROAD

Lilleshall National
Sports Centre

The
Oaks

Grange
Plantation

Abbey
(remains of)

Abbey
Wood

Gorse
Covert

Sulphur Piece
Plantation

72   A   B   73   C   D   74   E   F

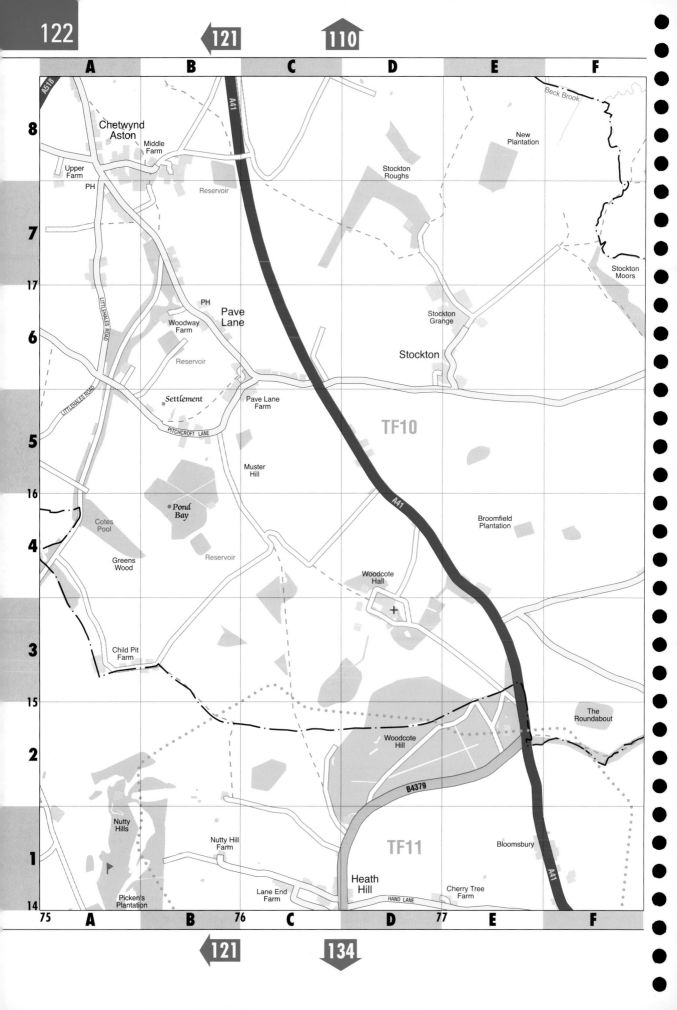

A518

Chetwynd
Aston

Middle
Farm

Upper
Farm

PH

A41

Reservoir

Beck Brook

New
Plantation

Stockton
Roughs

LITTLEHALES ROAD

PH

Pave
Lane

Woodway
Farm

Stockton
Grange

Stockton

LITTLEHALES ROAD

Reservoir

Settlement

Pave Lane
Farm

PITCHCROFT LANE

TF10

Muster
Hill

Pond
Bay

Cotes
Pool

Reservoir

A41

Broomfield
Plantation

Greens
Wood

Woodcote
Hall

✛

Child Pit
Farm

The
Roundabout

Woodcote
Hill

Nutty
Hills

B4379

Nutty Hill
Farm

TF11

Bloomsbury

Heath
Hill

Lane End
Farm

HAND LANE

Cherry Tree
Farm

A41

Picken's
Plantation

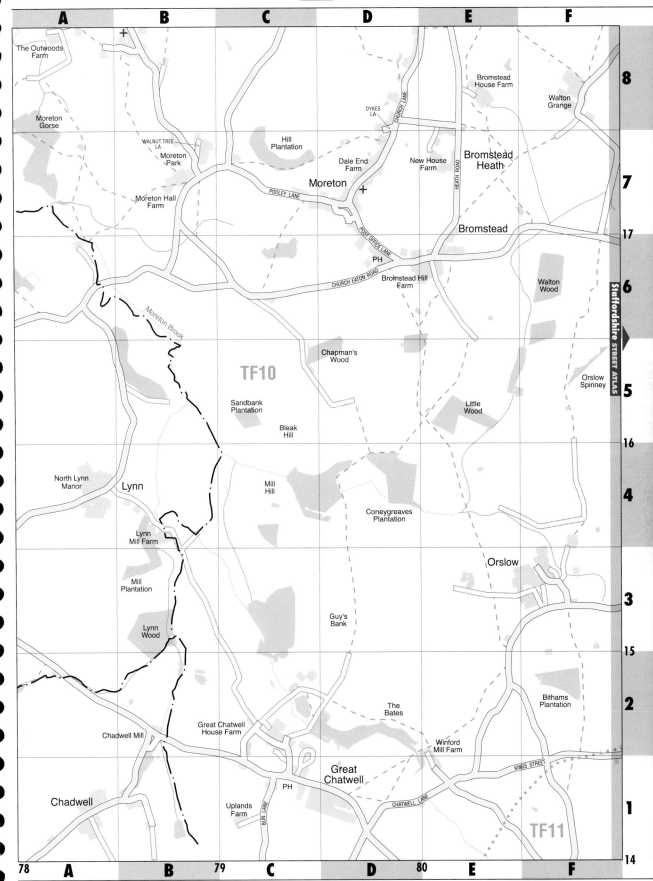

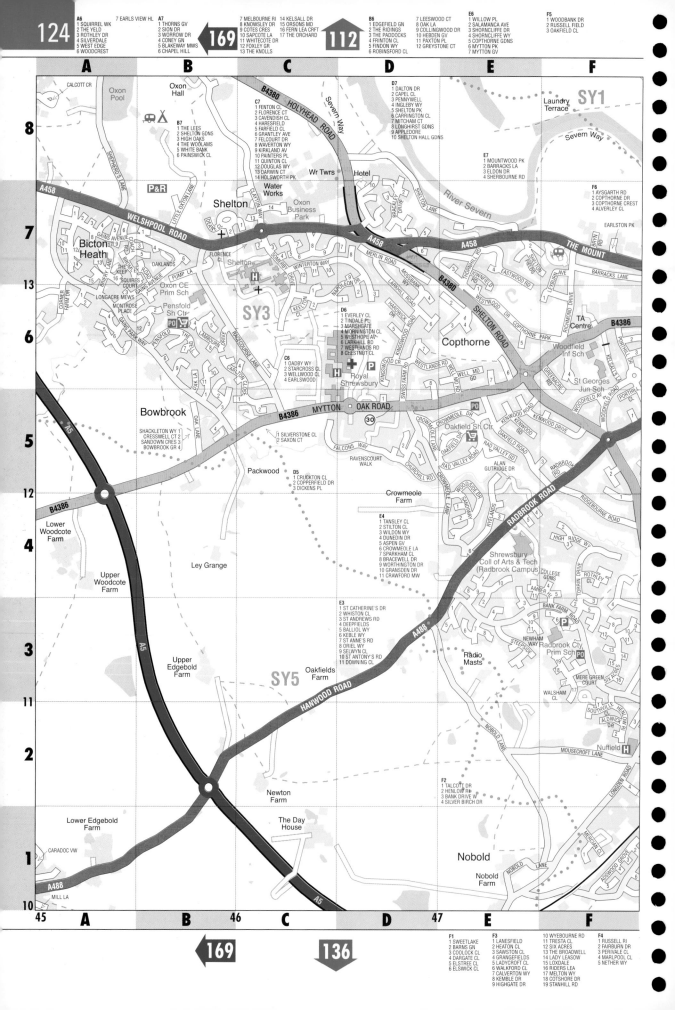

A6
1 SQUIRREL WK
2 THE YELD
3 ROTHLEY DR
4 SILVERDALE
5 WEST EDGE
6 WOODCREST

7 EARLS VIEW HL

A7
1 THORNS GV
2 SION DR
3 WORROW DR
4 CONEY GN
5 BLAKEWAY MWS
6 CHAPEL HILL

7 MELBOURNE RI
8 KNOWSLEY DR
9 COTES CRES
10 SAPCOTE LA
11 WHITECOTE DR
12 FOXLEY GR
13 THE KNOLLS

14 KELSALL DR
15 ORSONS MD
16 FERN LEA CRFT
17 THE ORCHARD

B6
1 EDGEFIELD GN
2 THE RIDINGS
3 THE PADDOCKS
4 FRINTON CL
5 FINDON WY
6 ROBINSFORD CL

7 LEESWOOD CT
8 OAK LA
9 COLLINGWOOD DR
10 HEBDEN GV
11 PAXTON PL
12 GREYSTONE CT

E6
1 WILLOW PL
2 SALAMANCA AVE
3 SHORNCLIFFE DR
4 SHORNCLIFFE WY
5 COPTHORNE GDNS
6 MYTTON PK
7 MYTTON GV

F5
1 WOODBANK DR
2 RUSSELL FIELD
3 OAKFIELD CL

F1
1 SWEETLAKE
2 BARNS GN
3 COOLOCK CL
4 DARGATE CL
5 ELSTREE CL
6 ELSWICK CL

F3
1 LANESFIELD
2 HEATON CL
3 SAWSTON CL
4 GRANGEFIELDS
5 LADYCROFT CL
6 WALKFORD CL
7 CALVERTON WY
8 KEMBLE DR
9 HIGHGATE DR

10 WYEBOURNE RD
11 TRESTA CL
12 SIX ACRES
13 THE BROADWELL
14 LADY LEASOW
15 LOXDALE
16 RIDERS LEA
17 MELTON WY
18 COTSHORE DR
19 STANHILL RD

F4
1 RUSSELL RI
2 FAIRBURN DR
3 PERIVALE CL
4 MARLPOOL CL
5 NETHER WY

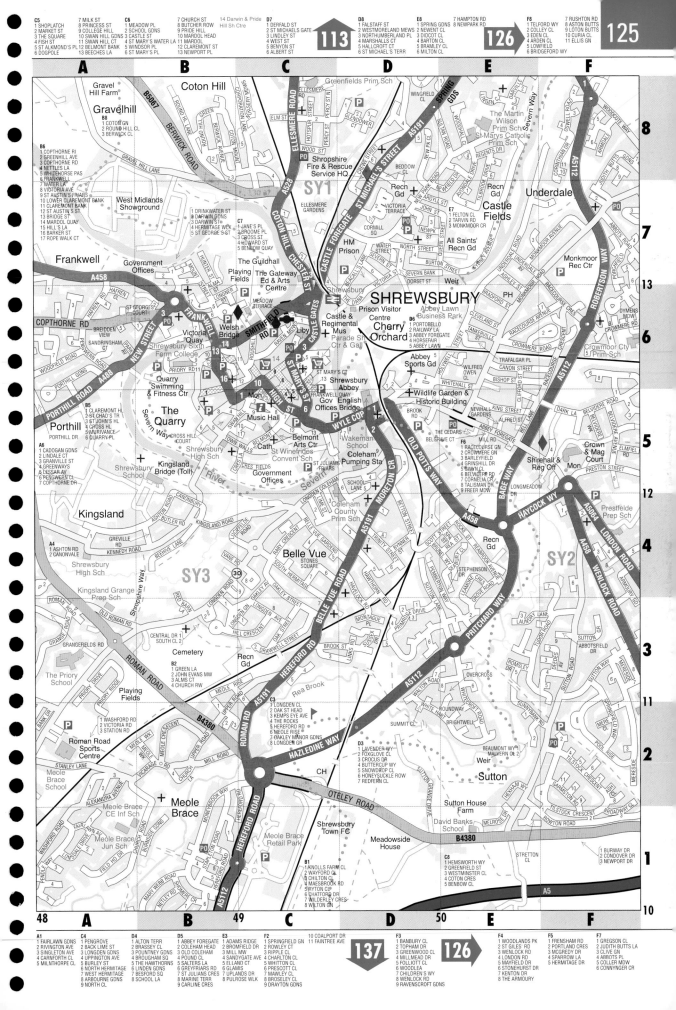

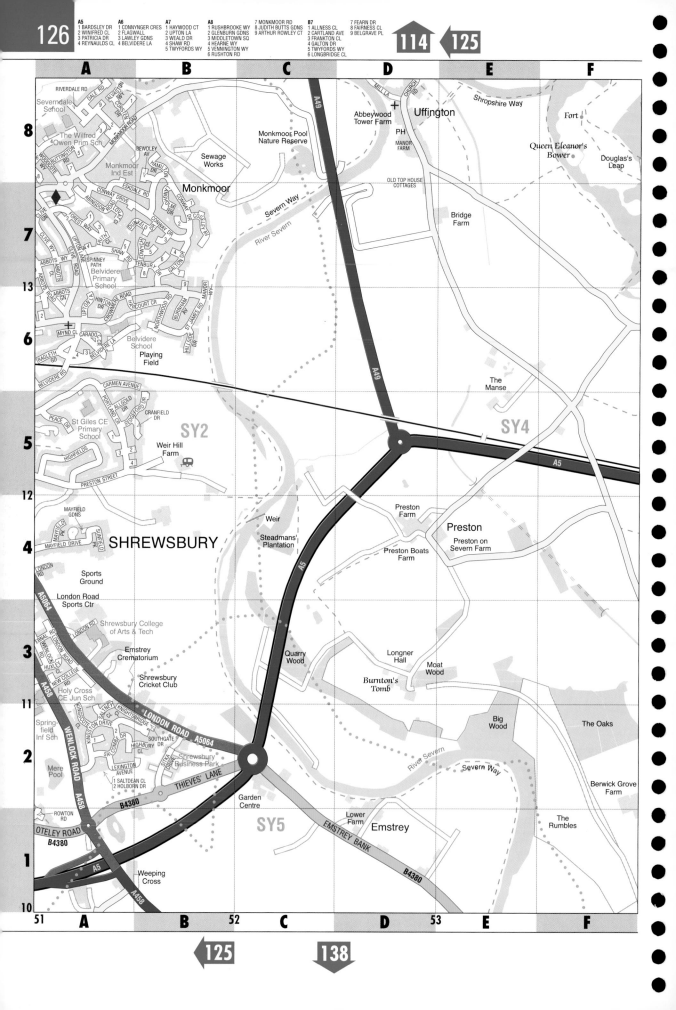

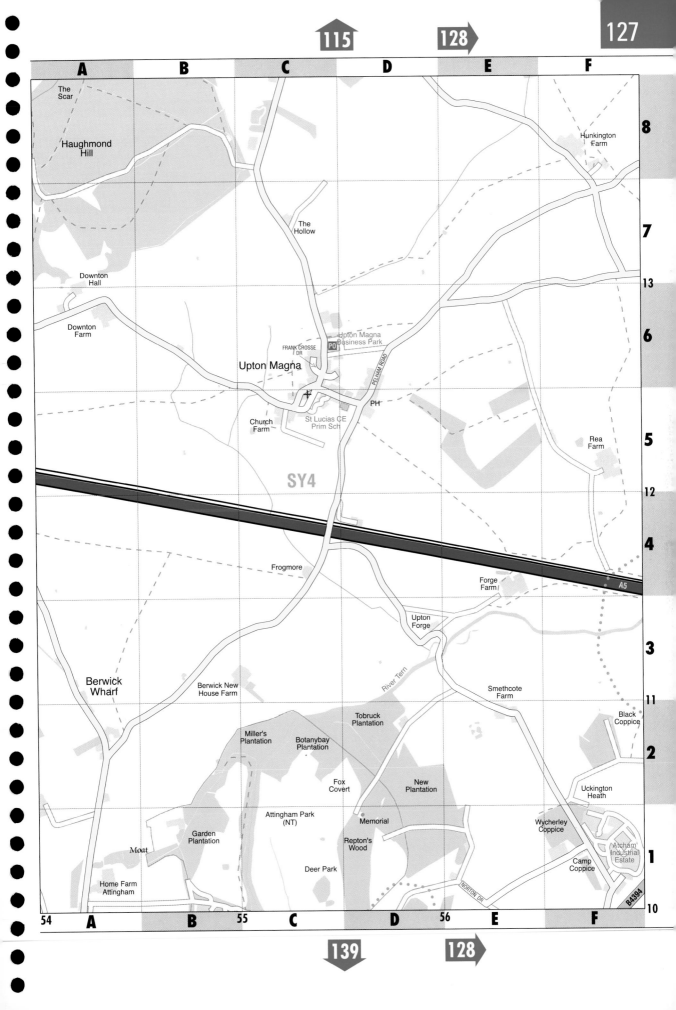

A B C D E F

The Scar

Haughmond Hill

8

Downton Hall

The Hollow

7

13

Downton Farm

Upton Magna Business Park

PO

6

FRANK CROSSE DR

Upton Magna

Church Farm

PH

St Lucias CE Prim Sch

Rea Farm

5

SY4

12

4

Frogmore

Forge Farm

A5

Upton Forge

3

Berwick Wharf

Berwick New House Farm

River Tern

Smethcote Farm

11

Black Coppice

Tobruck Plantation

Miller's Plantation

Botanybay Plantation

2

Fox Covert

New Plantation

Uckington Heath

Wycherley Coppice

'Atcham' Industrial Estate

Attingham Park (NT)

Memorial

Garden Plantation

Repton's Wood

Moat

Camp Coppice

Deer Park

Home Farm Attingham

NORTON DR

B4394

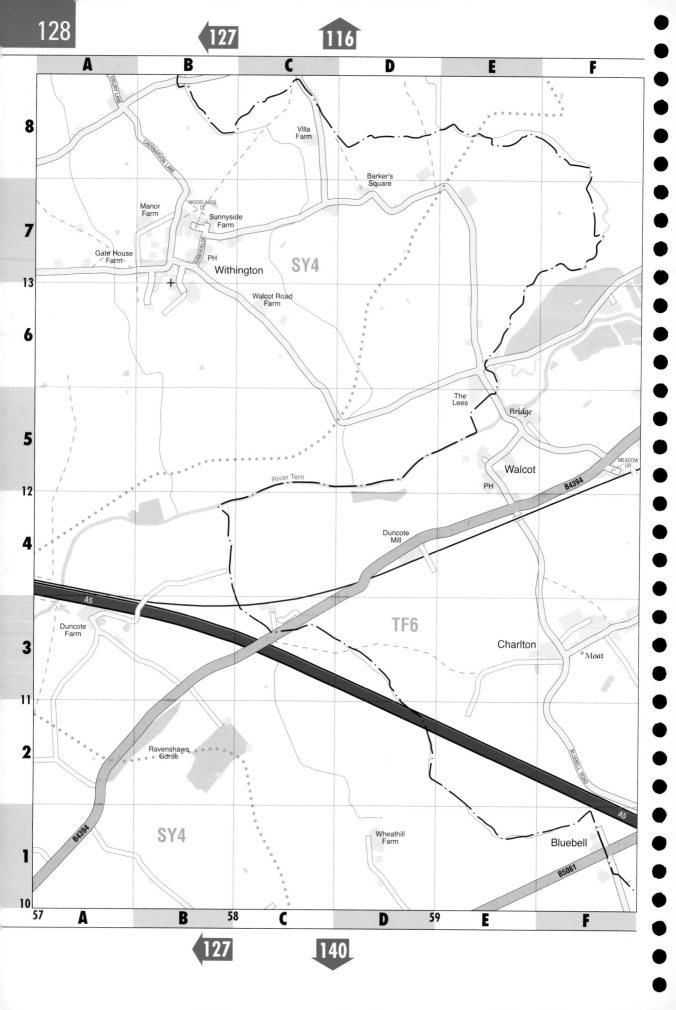

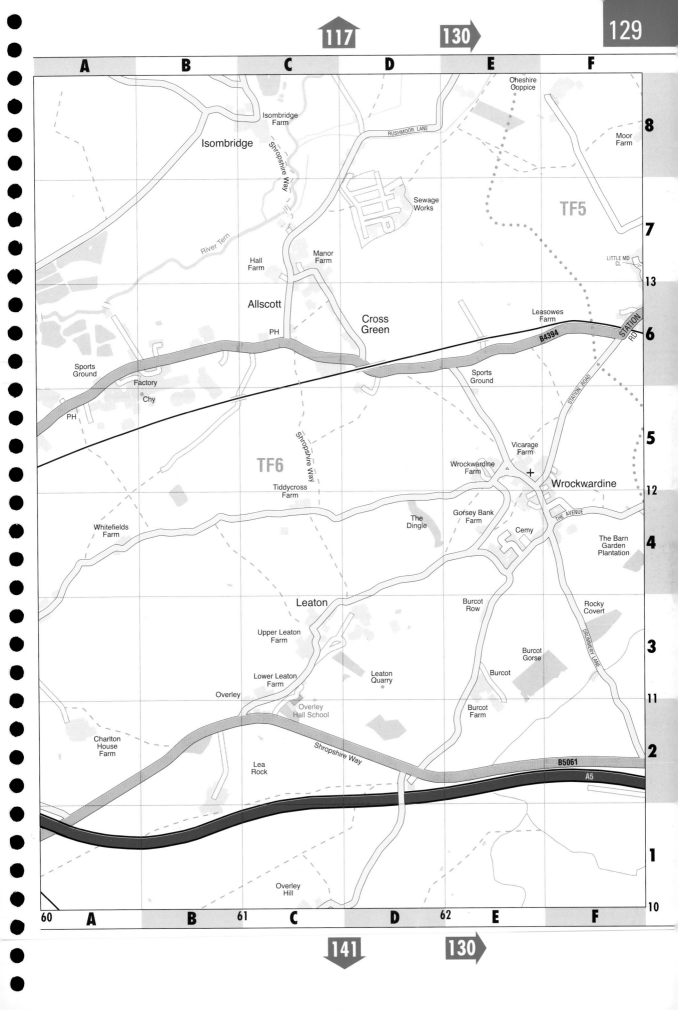

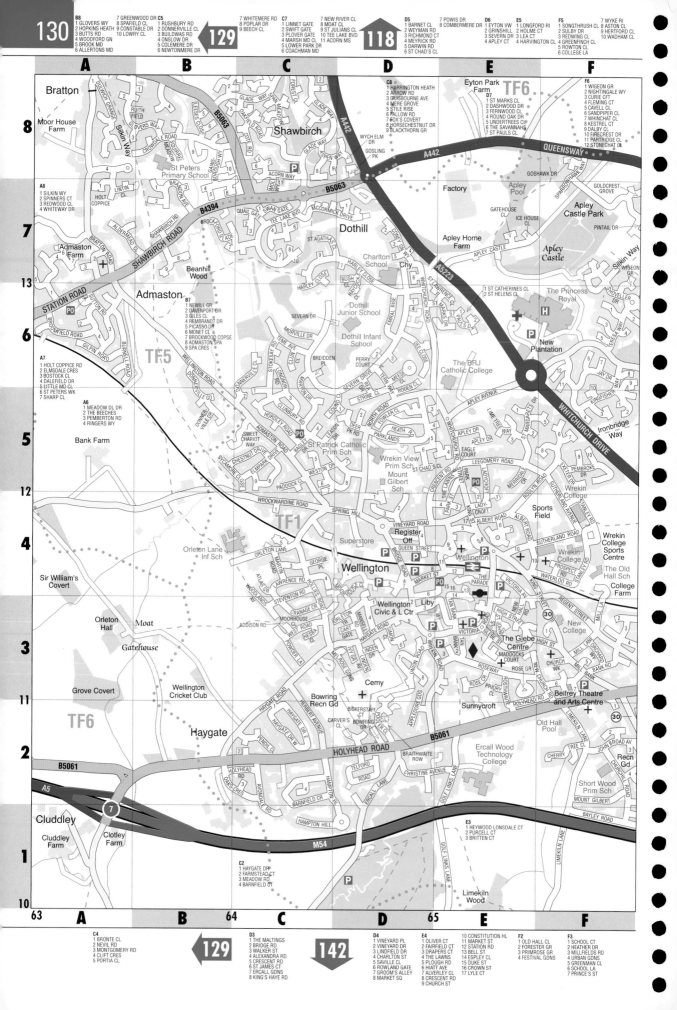

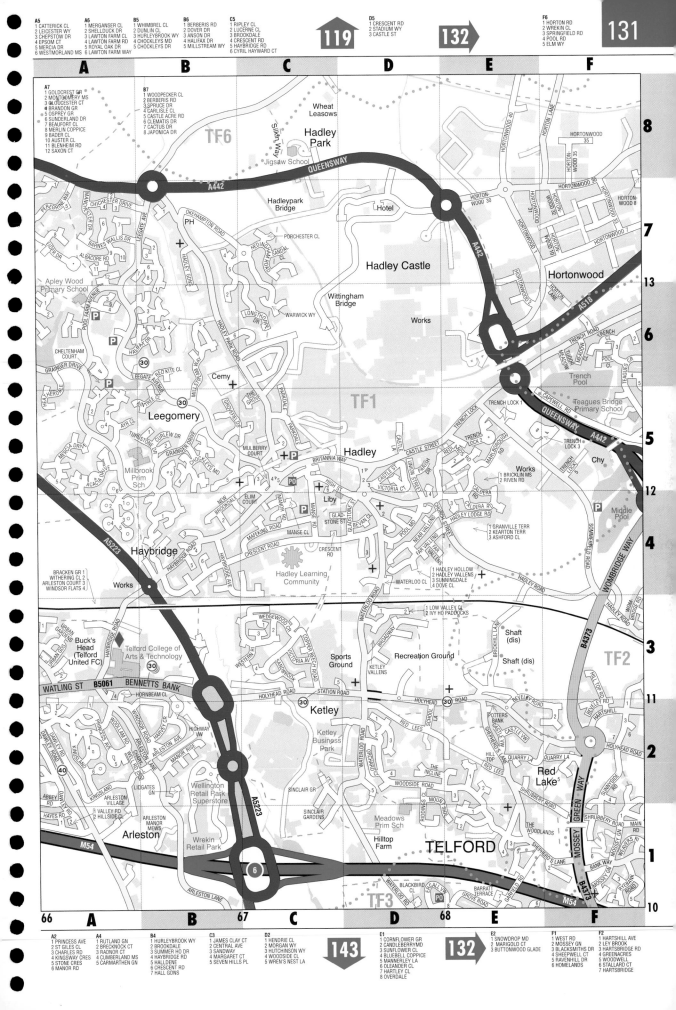

119   132
143   132

Map labels include: Wheat Leasows, Hadley Park, TF6, Hadleypark Bridge, Hotel, Hadley Castle, Hortonwood, Hortonwood 40/35/30 etc., Queensway A442, Horton Lane, A518, Trench Road, Trench Pool, Teagues Bridge Primary School, Apley Wood Primary School, Cheltenham Court, Grainger Drive, Leegomery, Cemy, TF1, Hadley, Castle Street, Union Street, Trench Lock, Works, Middle Pool, Haybridge, A5223, Hadley Learning Community, Waterloo Cl, Sports Ground, Recreation Ground, Ketley Vallens, Buck's Head (Telford United FC), Telford College of Arts & Technology, Watling St, Bennetts Bank B5061, Ketley, Ketley Business Park, Wellington Retail Park Superstore, Wrekin Retail Park, A5223, Arleston, Hilltop Farm, Meadows Prim Sch, TELFORD, Red Lake, TF2, Mossey Green Way, Holyhead Road, M54, TF3, Wombridge Way, B4373.

Hortonwood

TF1

Donnington

Muxton

Muxton County Primary School

Donnington Wood

Granville Country Park

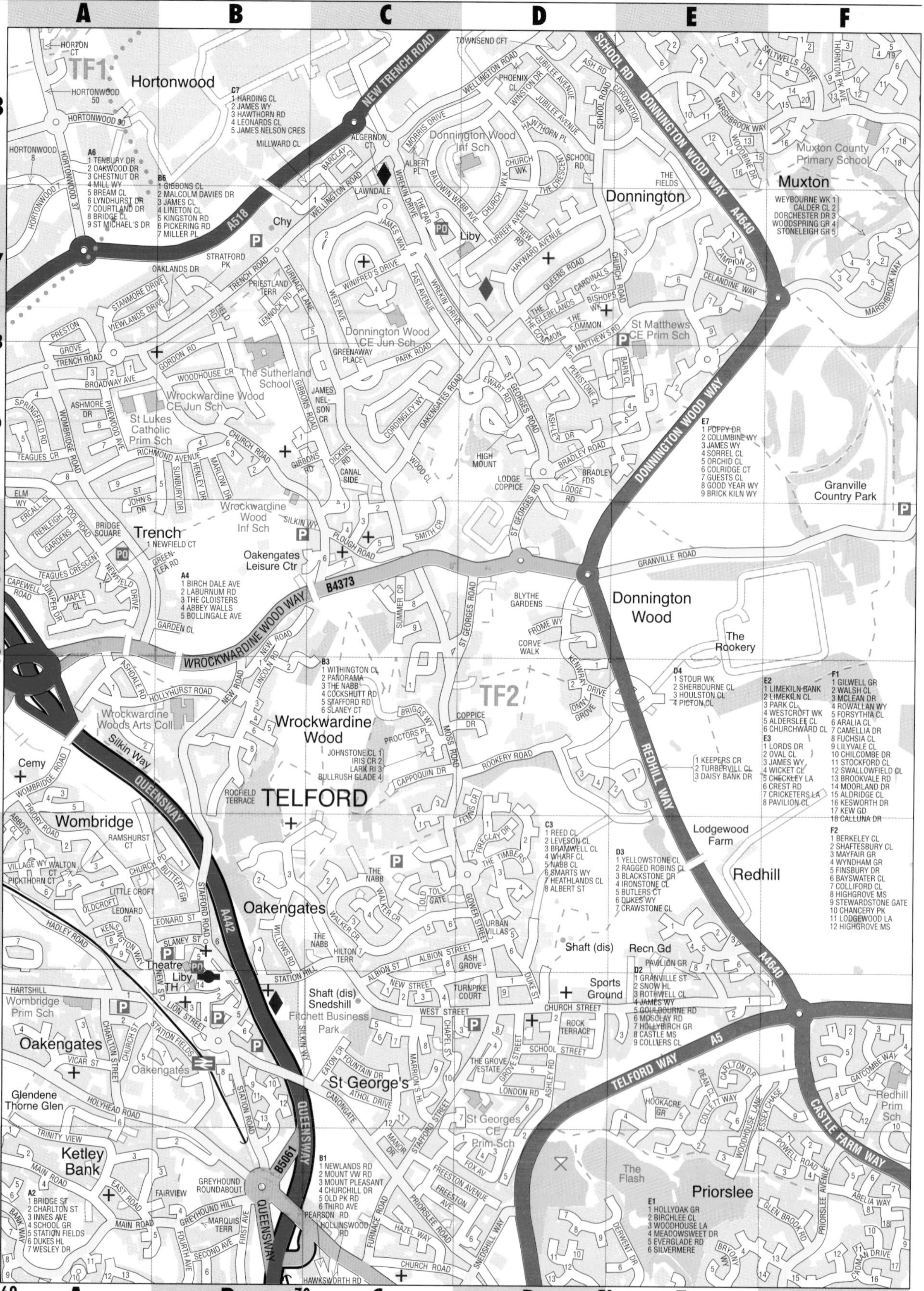

Trench

Wrockwardine Wood

TELFORD

TF2

Wombridge

Oakengates

Lodgewood Farm

Redhill

St George's

Ketley Bank

Priorslee

The Flash

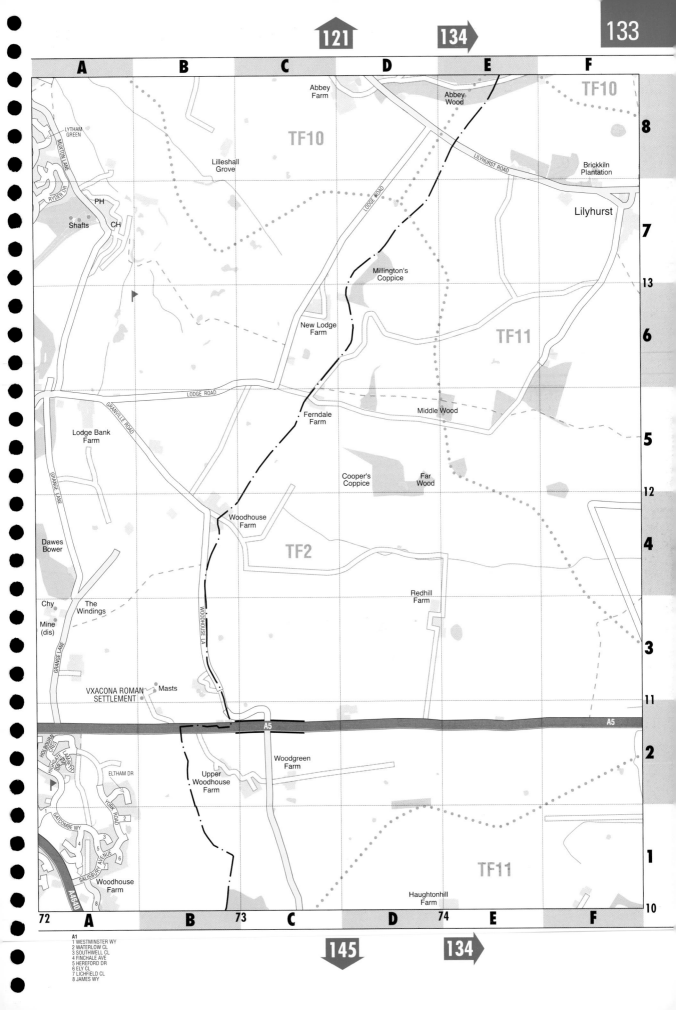

A · B · C · D · E · F

8
7
13
6
5
12
4
3
11
2
1
10

TF10

Abbey
Farm

Abbey
Wood

TF10

Lytham
Green

Lilleshall
Grove

LILYHURST ROAD

Brickkiln
Plantation

Lilyhurst

MUXTON LANE

RYDER DR

PH

CH

Shafts

LODGE ROAD

Millington's
Coppice

New Lodge
Farm

TF11

GRANVILLE ROAD

LODGE ROAD

Ferndale
Farm

Middle Wood

Lodge Bank
Farm

GRANGE LANE

Cooper's
Coppice

Far
Wood

Woodhouse
Farm

TF2

Dawes
Bower

Chy

The
Windings

Mine
(dis)

Redhill
Farm

WOODHOUSE LA.

GRANGE LANE

VXACONA ROMAN
SETTLEMENT

Masts

A5

A5

HOLBOURN CRES

HIGHGATE

RYDER DR

LAMBETH

ELTHAM DR

Woodgreen
Farm

Upper
Woodhouse
Farm

GATCOMBE WY

YORK ROAD

1
2
3
4
5
6

SALISBURY AVENUE

A4640

Woodhouse
Farm

TF11

Haughtonhill
Farm

72 · A · B · 73 · C · D · 74 · E · F

A1
1 WESTMINSTER WY
2 WATERLOW CL
3 SOUTHWELL CL
4 FINCHALE AVE
5 HEREFORD DR
6 ELY CL
7 LICHFIELD CL
8 JAMES WY

A | **B** | **C** | **D** | **E** | **F**

Playing Field

Lilleshall Golf Course

CH

TF10

Picken's Plantation

Heath Hill Farm

Cross

New House Farm

B4379

Weston Heath

PH

DAMSON LANE

A41

Woodside Farm

STUMP LANE

Weston Heath Farm

LILYHURST ROAD

KING'S STREET

Corner Farm

SHERIFFHALES DRIVE

Hilton Farm

Attwell Park Farm

Hunger Hill Plantation

JAMES CL

LARKRISE FIELDS

Kingstreet Grange

Village Farm

THE CRESCENT

SHAW CROFT

KETTLEMORE LANE

Hunger Hill Farm

HALES CT

PINFOLD

PO

Sheriffhales Common

Middle Farm

CHURCH LANE

Sherriffhales

Sherriffhales Manor

THE EVERGREENS

TF11

Common Farm

THE ROCK

Sheriffhales Primary School

Marsh Farm

Burlington Wood

MARSH ROAD

Works

MARSH LANE

Crackleybank Plantation

BACK ROAD

Burlington Farm

Ford

TF2

Crackley Village Farm

Yew Tree Farm

A5

A5

Crackleybank

PH

Crackley Bank Farm

LIZARD LANE

Brewers Oak Farm

Dog Wood

Upper Gallops

B4379

NANNY MURPHY'S LANE

Middle Gallops

Lizard Wood

75 | **A** | **B** | 76 | **C** | **D** | 77 | **E** | **F**

8
7
13
6
5
12
4
3
11
2
1
10

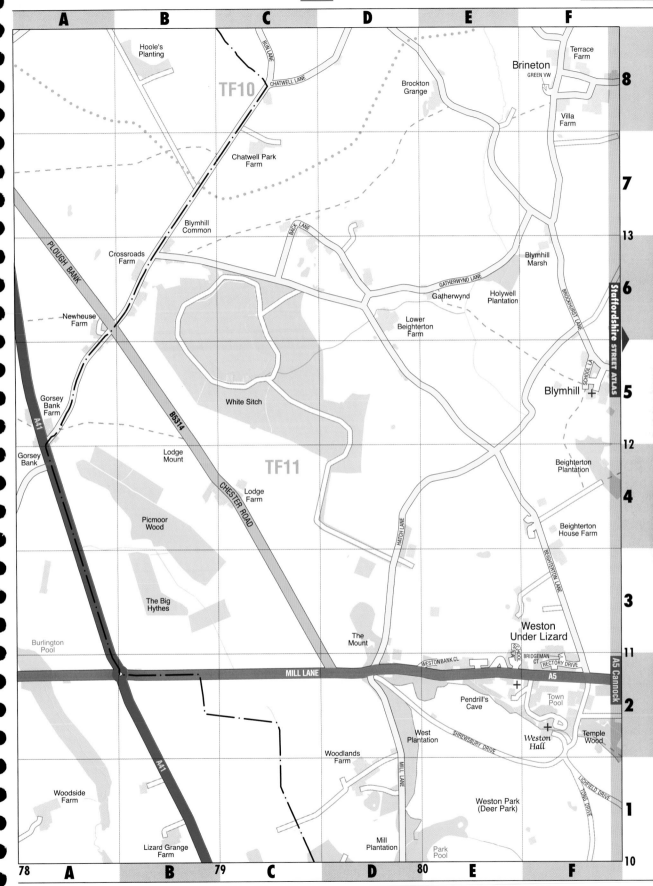

Hoole's Planting

TF10

Chatwell Lane

BUN LANE

Brockton Grange

Brineton

Terrace Farm

GREEN VW

Villa Farm

8

Chatwell Park Farm

7

Blymhill Common

BACK LANE

13

Blymhill Marsh

Crossroads Farm

PLOUGH BANK

GATHERWYND LANE

Gatherwynd

Holywell Plantation

BROOKHURST LANE

6

Newhouse Farm

Lower Beighterton Farm

Blymhill

5

TOOKS LA

Gorsey Bank Farm

B5314

White Sitch

A41

12

Gorsey Bank

Lodge Mount

TF11

Beighterton Plantation

CHESTER ROAD

Lodge Farm

4

Picmoor Wood

Beighterton House Farm

BEIGHTERTON LANE

The Big Hythes

3

Weston Under Lizard

Burlington Pool

The Mount

WESTON BANK CL

SCHOOL LA

BRIDGEMAN CT

RECTORY DRIVE

A5

11

MILL LANE

A5 Cannock

Pendrill's Cave

Town Pool

2

West Plantation

SHREWSBURY DRIVE

Weston Hall

Temple Wood

MILL LANE

Woodlands Farm

LICHFIELD DRIVE

A41

Woodside Farm

Weston Park (Deer Park)

TONG DRIVE

1

Lizard Grange Farm

Mill Plantation

Park Pool

10

78

A

B

79

C

D

80

E

F

Staffordshire STREET ATLAS

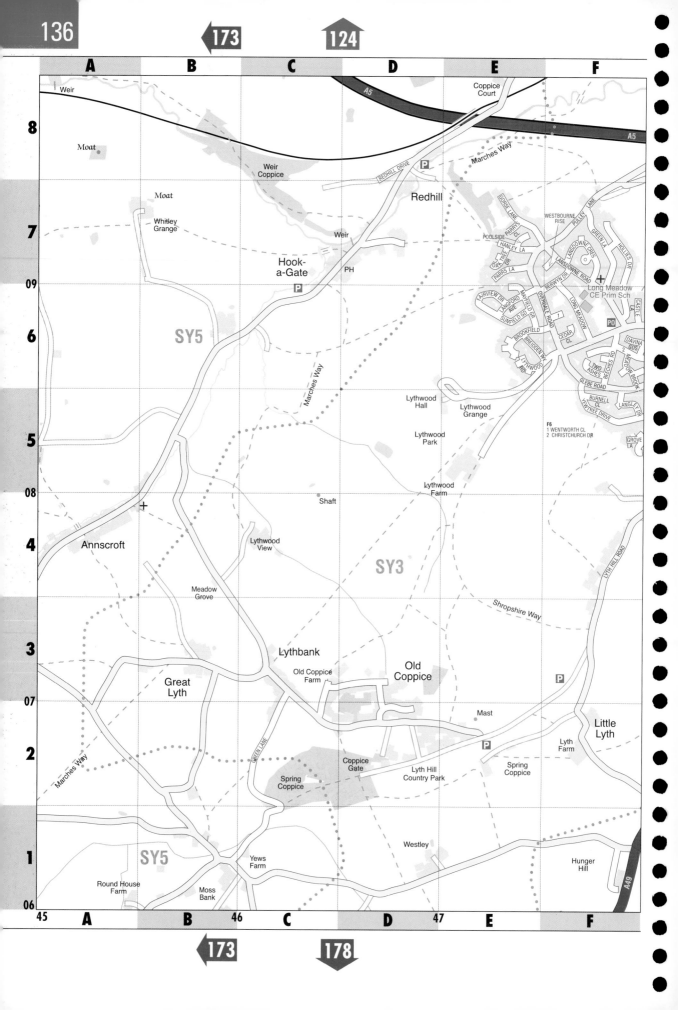

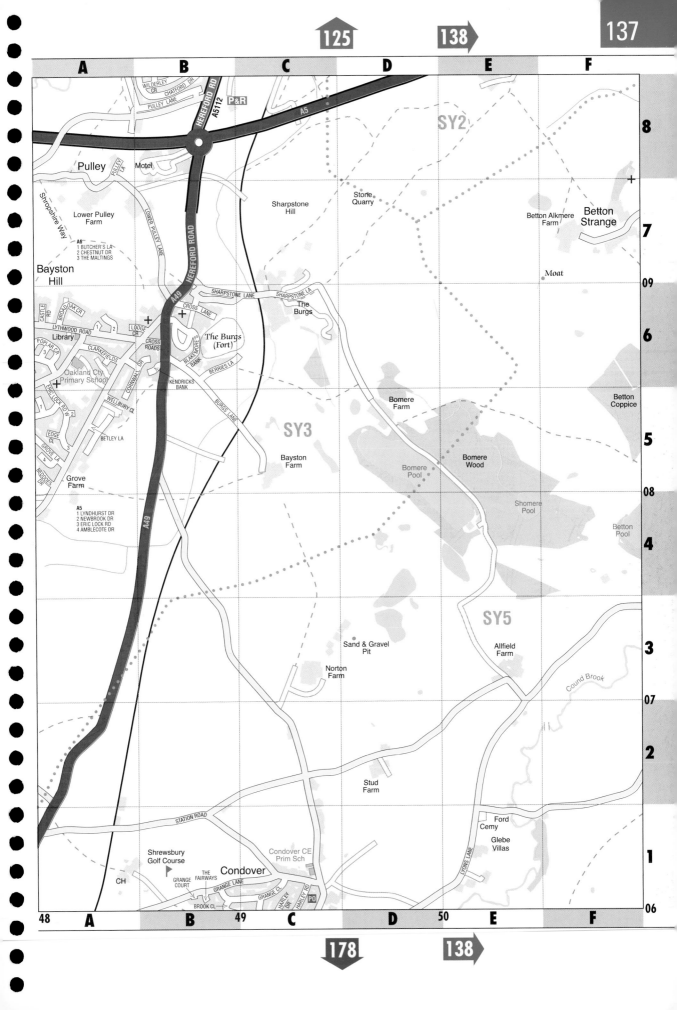

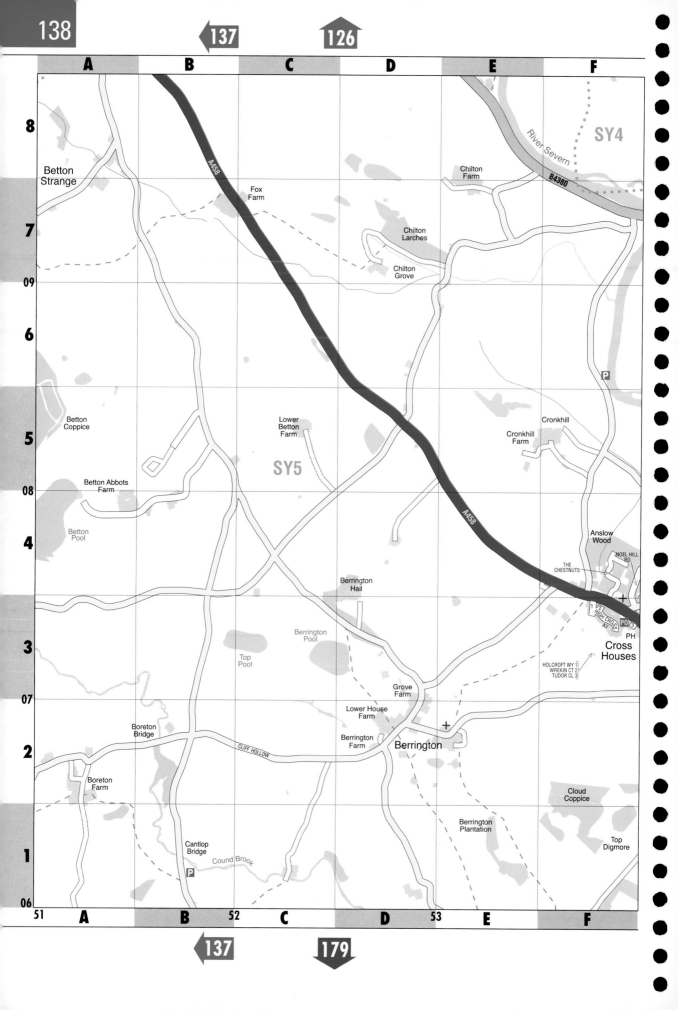

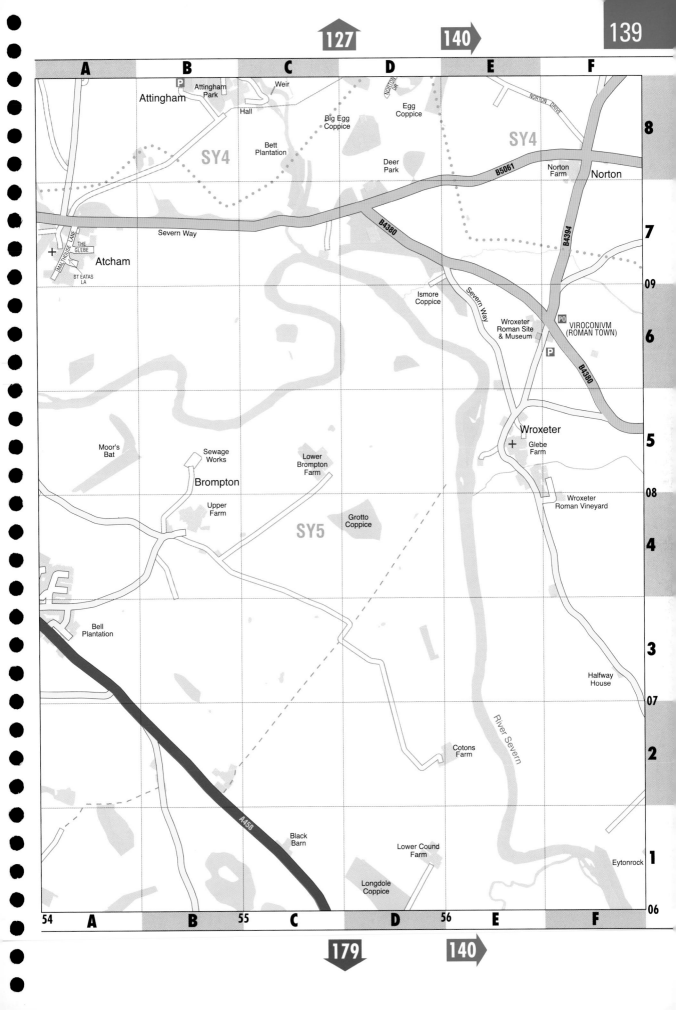

A B C D E F

8

Attingham Park
Attingham
Hall
Weir
NORTON LA
Egg Coppice
Big Egg Coppice
SY4
Bett Plantation
Deer Park
NORTON DRIVE
SY4
B5061
Norton Farm
Norton
B4394

7 Severn Way
B4380
THE GLEBE
MALTHOUSE LANE
Atcham
ST EATAS LA
Severn Way

09

Ismore Coppice
Wroxeter Roman Site & Museum
PO VIROCONIVM (ROMAN TOWN)
6
P
B4380

5
Wroxeter
Glebe Farm

Moor's Bat
Sewage Works
Lower Brompton Farm
Brompton
Upper Farm
SY5
Grotto Coppice
08
Wroxeter Roman Vineyard

4

Bell Plantation
3
Halfway House
07

River Severn
Cotons Farm
2

A458
Black Barn
Lower Cound Farm
Eytonrock
1

Longdole Coppice

06

54 A B 55 C D 56 E F

139
128

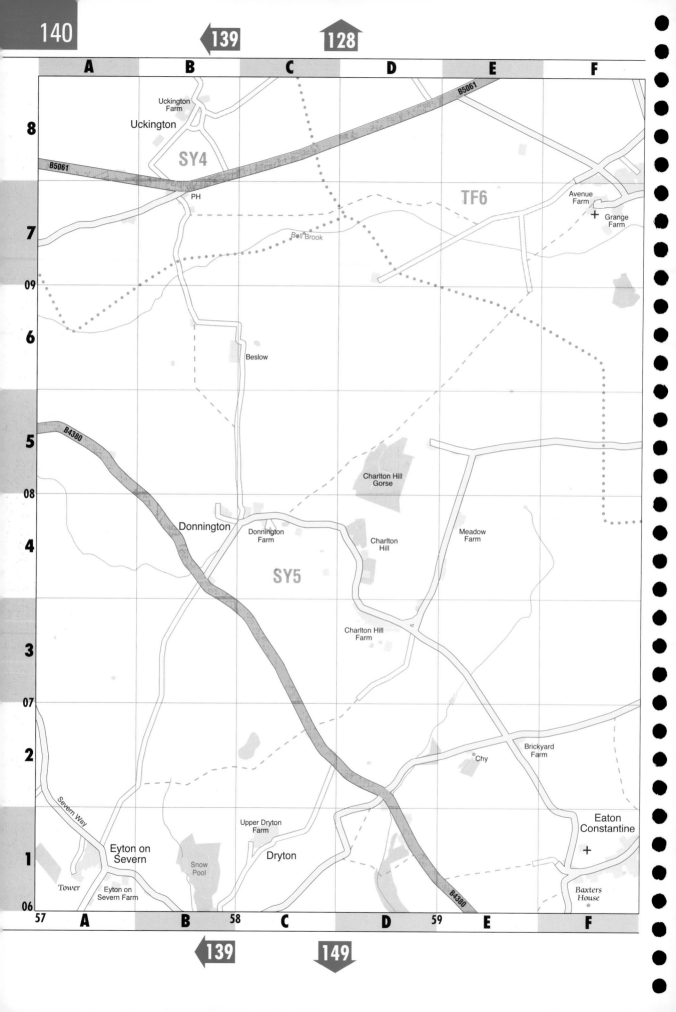

A B C D E F

8

B5061

Uckington
Farm

Uckington

SY4

B5061

PH

TF6

Avenue
Farm

Grange
Farm

7

Bell Brook

09

6

Beslow

5

B4380

Charlton Hill
Gorse

08

Donnington

Donnington
Farm

SY5

Charlton
Hill

Meadow
Farm

4

Charlton Hill
Farm

3

07

Brickyard
Farm

2

Chy

Eaton
Constantine

Severn Way

Upper Dryton
Farm

1

Eyton on
Severn

Snow
Pool

Dryton

Tower

Eyton on
Severn Farm

Baxters
House

B4380

06

57 A B 58 C D 59 E F

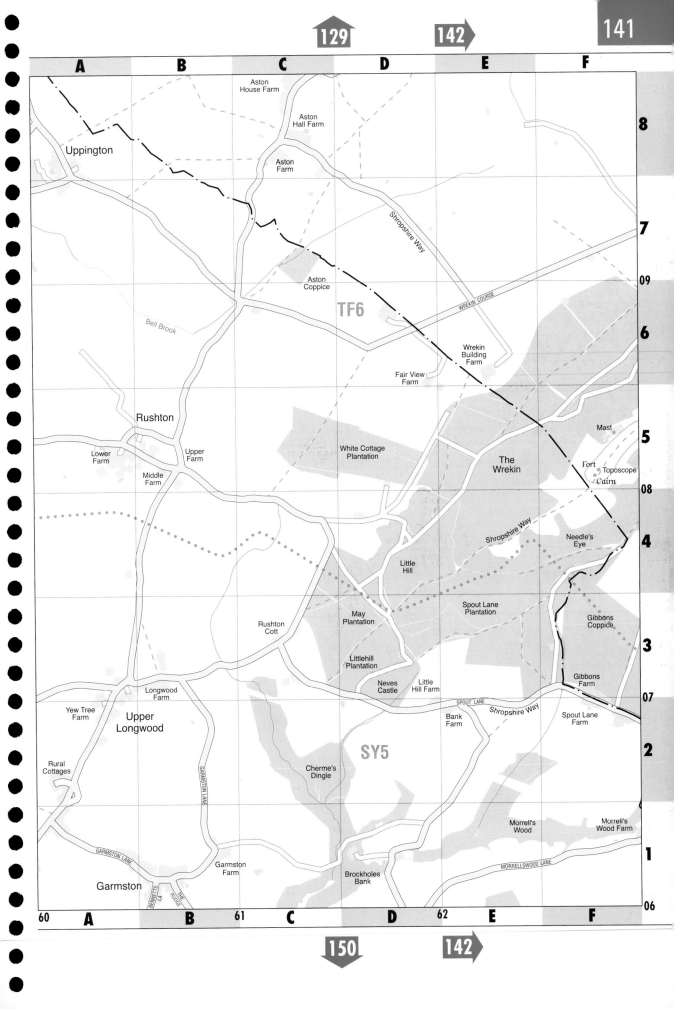

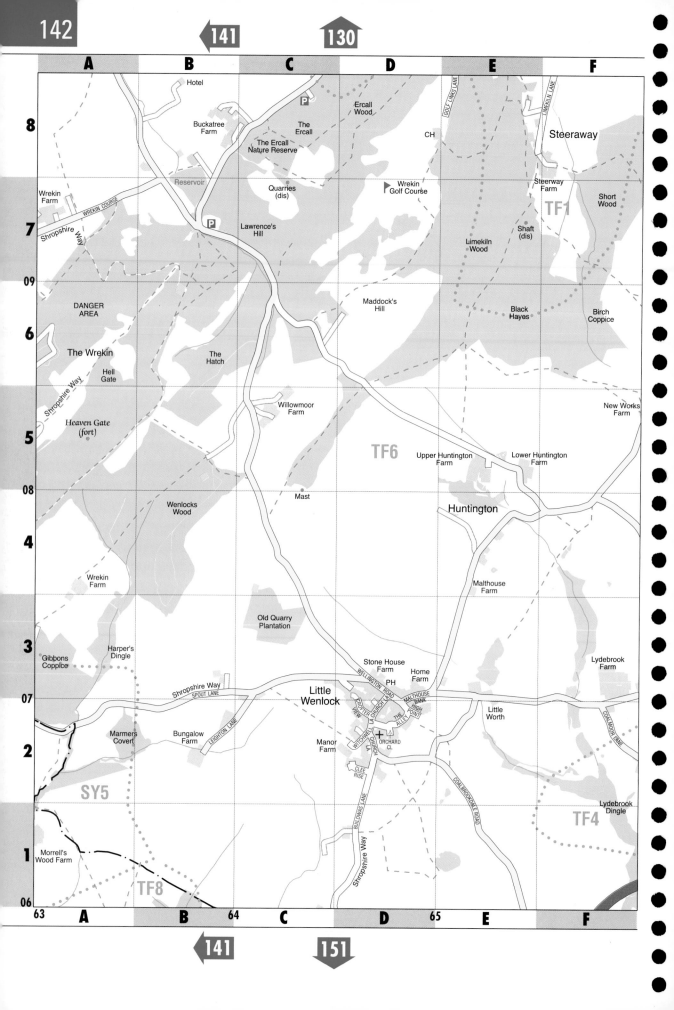

141 130

8

Hotel

Buckatree
Farm

The Ercall
Nature Reserve

Reservoir

The
Ercall

Ercall
Wood

CH

Steeraway

Wrekin
Farm

WREKIN COURSE

Quarries
(dis)

Wrekin
Golf Course

Steerway
Farm

Short
Wood

TF1

7

Shropshire Way

Lawrence's
Hill

Shaft
(dis)

09

Limekiln
Wood

Black
Hayes

Birch
Coppice

DANGER
AREA

Maddock's
Hill

6

The Wrekin

The
Hatch

Hell
Gate

Shropshire Way

Willowmoor
Farm

New Works
Farm

Heaven Gate
(fort)

TF6

Upper Huntington
Farm

Lower Huntington
Farm

5

08

Wenlocks
Wood

Mast

Huntington

4

Wrekin
Farm

Malthouse
Farm

Old Quarry
Plantation

Lydebrook
Farm

3

Gibbons
Coppice

Harper's
Dingle

Stone House
Farm

PH

Home
Farm

Shropshire Way

SPOUT LANE

Little
Wenlock

MALTHOUSE BANK

Little
Worth

COALMOOR LANE

07

Marmers
Covert

Bungalow
Farm

LEIGHTON LANE

WELLINGTON ROAD

CHURCH LANE

THE ALLEY

HIGH POINT

Manor
Farm

WITCHWELL

CROFTER ROAD

VIEW

ORCHARD
CL

CLEE
RISE

CHURCH

2

SY5

COALBROOKDALE ROAD

Lydebrook
Dingle

TF4

1

Morrell's
Wood Farm

BUILDWAS LANE

Shropshire Way

TF8

06

63   **A**   **B**   64   **C**   **D**   65   **E**   **F**

141 151

A B C D E F

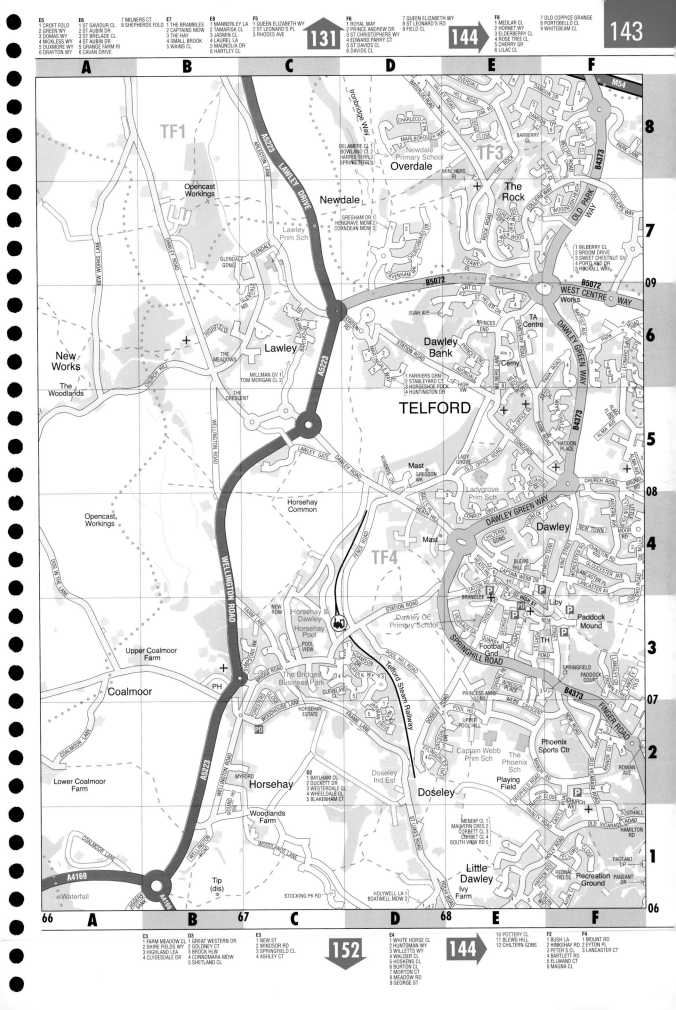

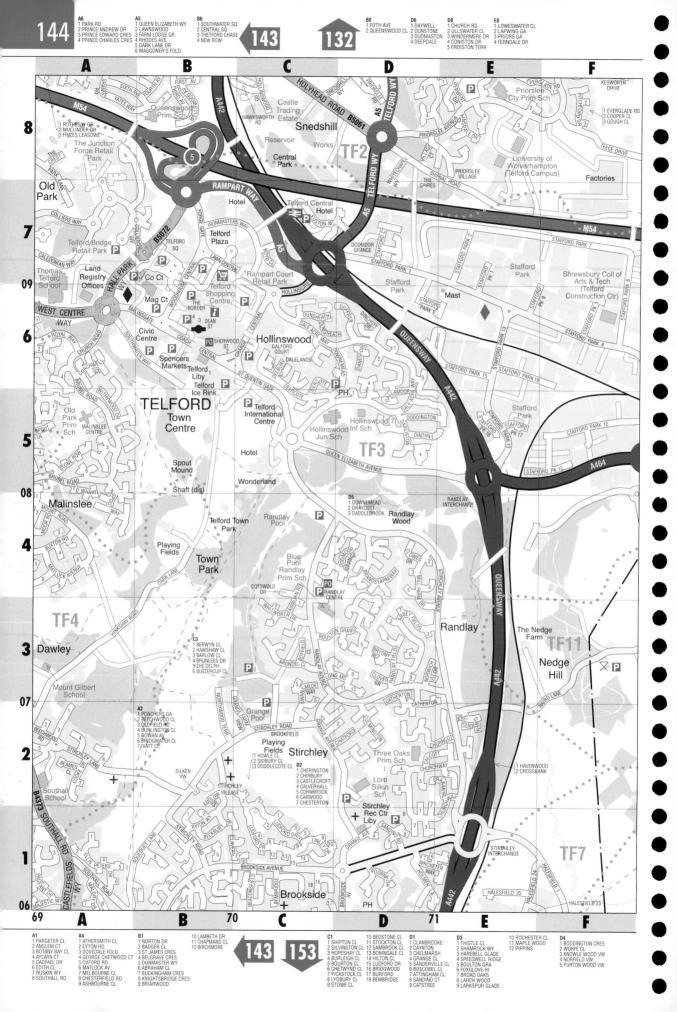

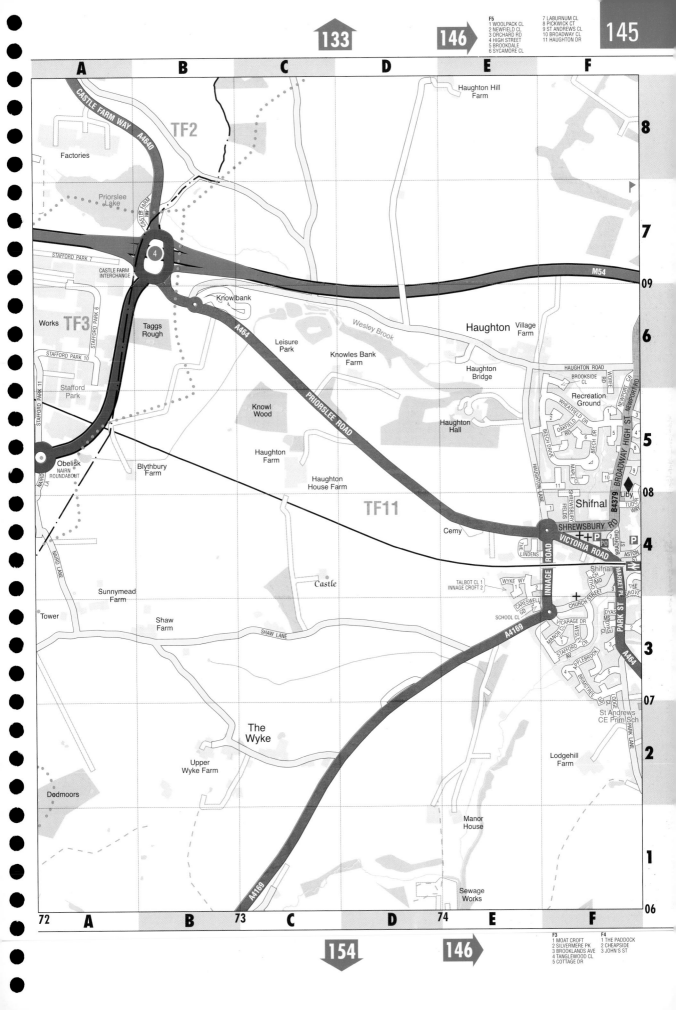

A B C D E F

Haughton Hill Farm

CASTLE FARM WAY A4640

TF2

8

Factories

Priorslee Lake

7

STAFFORD PARK 7

M54

09

CASTLE FARM INTERCHANGE

Knowlbank

Haughton

Village Farm

6

Works TF3

STAFFORD PARK 6

Taggs Rough

A464

Leisure Park

Wesley Brook

HAUGHTON ROAD

BROOKSIDE CL

NEWPORT RD

WYRLE

STAFFORD PARK 10

Knowles Bank Farm

Haughton Bridge

Recreation Ground

Wheatfield

BEECH DRIVE

OAKFIELD RD

BEECH

5

Stafford Park

Knowl Wood

PRIORSLEE ROAD

Haughton Hall

MAPLE CL

BROADWAY HIGH ST

Liby

08

Obelisk

NAIRN ROUNDABOUT

Blythbury Farm

Haughton Farm

SHREWSBURY FIELDS

Shifnal

B4379

TUDOR WAY

NAIRN LA

TF11

Haughton House Farm

Cemy

SHREWSBURY RD

SHREWSBURY ROAD

VICTORIA ROAD

P PO

ASTON ST

P

4

THE LINDENS

Shifnal Sch

MARKET PL

PARK ST

Sunnymead Farm

Castle

TALBOT CL 1
INNAGE CROFT 2

WYKE WY

INNAGE ROAD

CHURCH STREET

THE GROVE

CARESWELL GD

VICARAGE DR

A464

Tower

Shaw Farm

SHAW LANE

SCHOOL CL

MANOR RD

WESLEY

STAFFORD AV

DYAS MS

3

A4169

APPLEBROOK

BRIMSTREE

LODGE

07

St Andrews CE Prim Sch

PARK LANE

The Wyke

Lodgehill Farm

2

Upper Wyke Farm

Dodmoors

Manor House

1

A4169

Sewage Works

06

72 A B 73 C D 74 E F

145
134

A
B
C
D
E
F
8
7
09
6
5
08
4
3
07
2
1
06
75
76
77
NANNY MURPHY'S LANE
WOODCOCK CORNER
Drayton Lodge Farm
CH
Drayton Lodge
Lizard Wood
Shifnal Golf Course
B4379
Coppice Green
Cramp Pool Farm
M54
NEWPORT ROAD
Coppice Green
Cramp Pools
Lizard Farm
MEADOW DR
ADMIRALS CL
BALFOUR RD
ADMIRALS WAY
DRAYTON RD
LOVELL CL
A6
1 MOUNTBATTEN CL
2 NELSON CT
3 COPPICE RD
4 BEATTY CL
5 JELLICOE CRES
6 RODNEY CL
7 COLLINGWOOD CT
Idsall School
Football Ground
Idsall Sp Ctr
Aston Coppice
BARN RD
ORCHARD RD
BOTFIELD RD
BARN RD
A5
1 IDSALL CR
2 BARRINGTON CT
3 GRENVILLE CT
4 CORNWALLIS DR
TF11
M54
Lizard House Farm
Shifnal Prim Sch
GREENFIELDS CR
CURRIERS LANE
Aston Hall
Hill Wood
GROSVENOR GD
Shifnal
Stantonhill Farm
Stanton Hill Wood
ASTON ROAD
ASTON ST
Works
STANTON ROAD
STANTON ROAD
STANTON ROAD
Timlet Bridge
A4
1 GREENFIELDS
2 BLUEGATE
3 ASTON DL
4 THE GROVE
THE GR
MEAD WY
MERE CL
STAFFORD PL
SILVERMERE PK
Stanton
Shifnal Ind Est
Timlet Covert
LAMLEDGE LANE
Park Farm
Young Options College
St Andrews CE Prim Sch
Loam Wood
Monk's Wood
Monarch's Way
Windmill
Ruckley Pool
Big Wood
Ruckley Grange
A464
Bonemill Bridge
The Terrace
Upton Farm
Lower Upton Farm
Ruckley Sidings Farm
Slaney's Covert
Reservoir

145
155

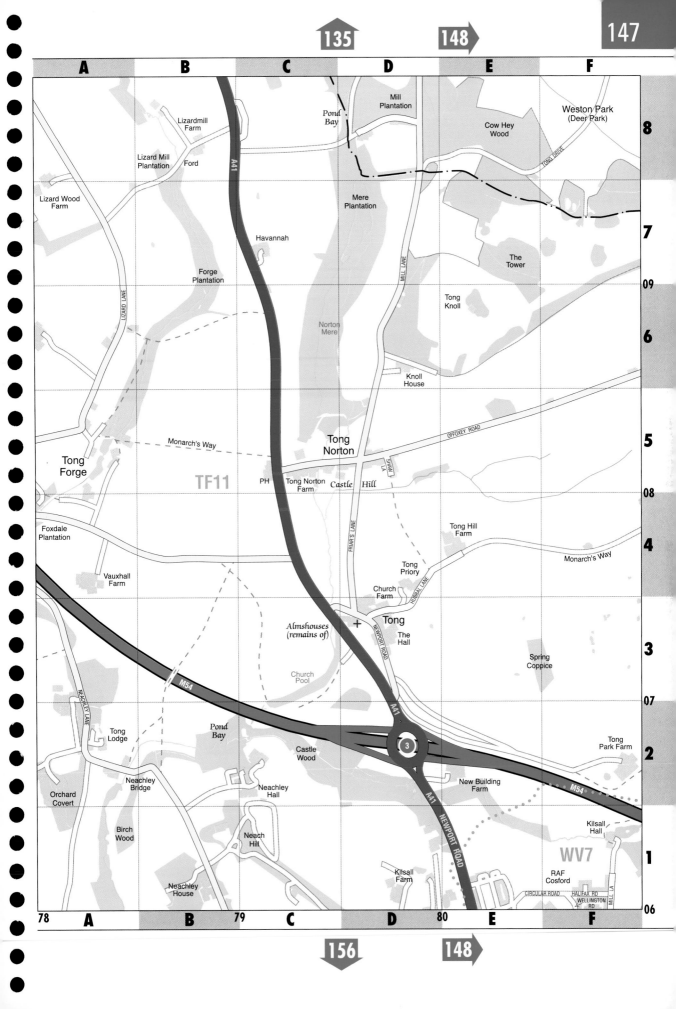

135
148

A B C D E F

8

Weston Park
(Deer Park)

Lizardmill
Farm

Mill
Plantation

Cow Hey
Wood

Pond
Bay

Lizard Mill
Plantation

Ford

Lizard Wood
Farm

A41

Mere
Plantation

7

Havannah

The
Tower

09

Forge
Plantation

Tong
Knoll

MILL LANE

6

Norton
Mere

Knoll
House

Monarch's Way

OFFOXEY ROAD

Tong
Norton

5

Tong
Forge

TF11

PH

Tong Norton
Farm

Castle Hill

SHAW LA

08

Tong Hill
Farm

Foxdale
Plantation

Monarch's Way

4

FRIAR'S LANE

Tong
Priory

Vauxhall
Farm

HUBBAL LANE

Church
Farm

Tong

Almshouses
(remains of)

✚

The
Hall

Spring
Coppice

3

NEWPORT ROAD

Church
Pool

07

M54

NEACHLEY LANE

Tong
Lodge

Pond
Bay

Castle
Wood

A41

Tong
Park
Farm

2

M54

Neachley
Bridge

Neachley
Hall

New Building
Farm

Orchard
Covert

Kilsall
Hall

Birch
Wood

Neach
Hill

WV7

1

Kilsall
Farm

RAF
Cosford

NEWPORT ROAD

Neachley
House

CIRCULAR ROAD

HALIFAX RD

MILL LA

WELLINGTON RD

06

78 A B 79 C D 80 E F

156
148

147

E8
1 THE FIRSWAY
2 BROOKSIDE GDNS
3 OAKAPPLE CL
4 ROYAL OAK DR
5 WESTON CL
6 SPRING LA

Staffordshire STREET ATLAS

Staffordshire STREET ATLAS

Weston Park
(Deer Park)

Obelisk

Newport
Plantation

Moat

Bishops
Wood

WHITEGATES DR

TONG CL

OLD WESTON ROAD

IVETSEY BANK ROAD

Church
Farm

Park Oak
Farm

St Johns
CE First
Sch

BEACON
PK

OLD COACH ROAD

Scilly
Grove

Offoxey
Plantation

Tong Road

White
Oak Farm

OFFOXEY ROAD

Tong
Rough

ST19

Hawkshead
Pool

Offoxey
Farm

The
Holt

Boscobel
Dingle

Boscobel
House

Meashill
Farm

TF11

Monarch's Way

Monarch's Way

White Ladies
Priory
(rems of)

Royal Oak
Wood

White Ladies
Plantation

Spring
Coppice

WV8

Monarch's Way

White Ladies
Farm

The
Wood
House

Renshaw Wood Lane

WV7

Donington Lane

Old Shackerley Lane

Shackerley Lane

Shackerley

Wigmore
Wood

M54

147
157

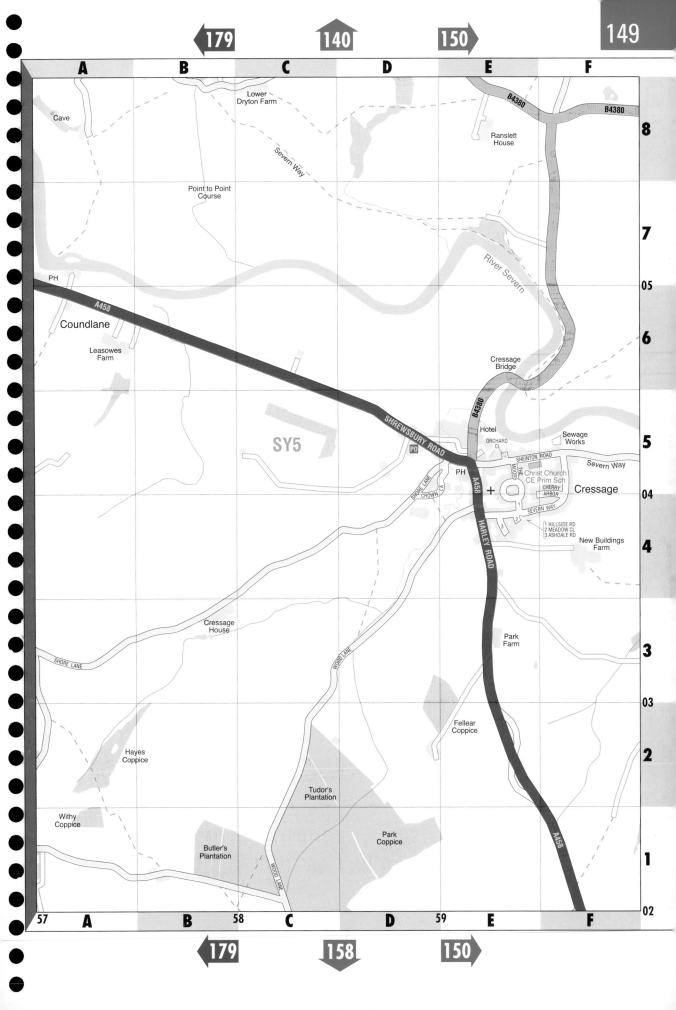

A   B   C   D   E   F

Cave

Lower
Dryton Farm

Severn Way

Point to Point
Course

Ranslett
House

B4380

B4380

River Severn

PH

A458

Coundlane

Leasowes
Farm

Cressage
Bridge

B4380

SY5

SHREWSBURY ROAD

PO

Hotel

ORCHARD
CL

Sewage
Works

SHEINTON ROAD

Severn Way

PH

SHORE LANE

CROWN LA

A458

THE MOORS

Christ Church
CE Prim Sch

CHERRY
ARBOR

Cressage

SEVERN WAY

1 HILLSIDE RD
2 MEADOW CL
3 ASHDALE RD

New Buildings
Farm

Cressage
House

HARLEY ROAD

Park
Farm

SHORE LANE

WOOD LANE

Fellear
Coppice

Hayes
Coppice

Tudor's
Plantation

Park
Coppice

A458

Withy
Coppice

Butler's
Plantation

WOOD LANE

8
7
05
6
5
04
4
3
03
2
1
02

57   58   59

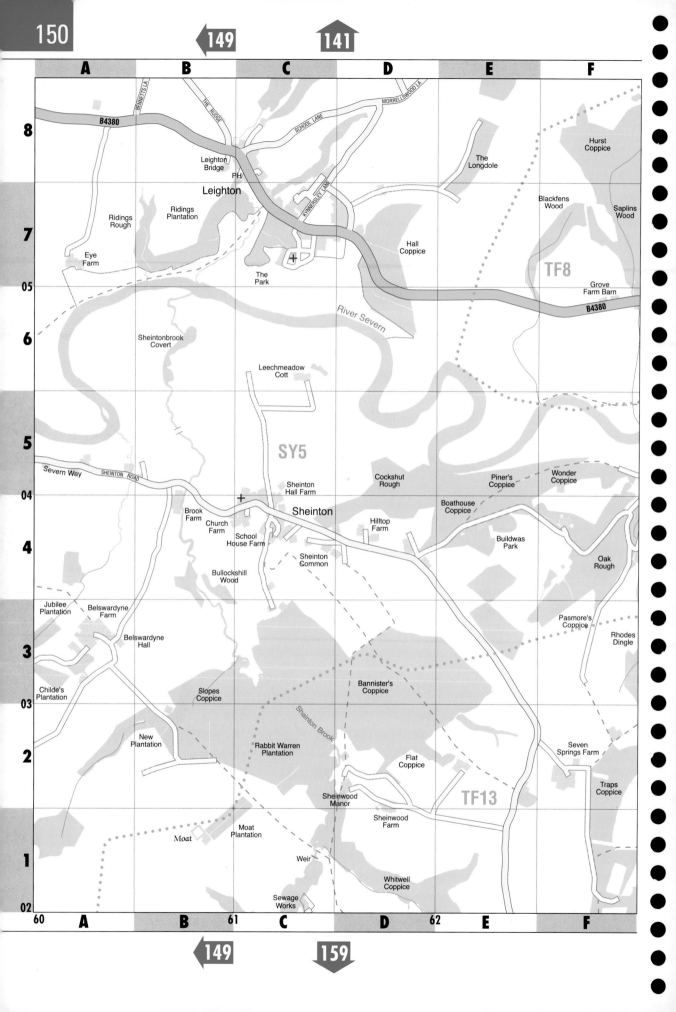

A B C D E F

8

7

05

6

5

04

4

3

03

2

1

02

60 A B 61 C D 62 E F

B4380

BENNETTS LA
THE RUDGE
SCHOOL LANE
MORRELLSWOOD LA
KYNNERSLEY LANE

Leighton
Bridge
PH

Leighton

Ridings
Rough

Ridings
Plantation

Eye
Farm

The
Longdole

Blackfens
Wood

Hurst
Coppice

Saplins
Wood

Hall
Coppice

The Park

TF8

Grove
Farm Barn

River Severn

B4380

Sheintonbrook
Covert

Leechmeadow
Cott

SY5

Severn Way

SHEINTON ROAD

Sheinton
Hall Farm

Sheinton

Cockshut
Rough

Piner's
Coppice

Wonder
Coppice

Boathouse
Coppice

Brook
Farm

Church
Farm

School
House Farm

Hilltop
Farm

Buildwas
Park

Oak
Rough

Bullockshill
Wood

Sheinton
Common

Jubilee
Plantation

Belswardyne
Farm

Pasmore's
Coppice

Rhodes
Dingle

Belswardyne
Hall

Childe's
Plantation

Slopes
Coppice

Bannister's
Coppice

New
Plantation

Sheinton Brook

Rabbit Warren
Plantation

Flat
Coppice

Seven
Springs Farm

Traps
Coppice

TF13

Sheinwood
Manor

Sheinwood
Farm

Moat

Moat
Plantation

Weir

Whitwell
Coppice

Sewage
Works

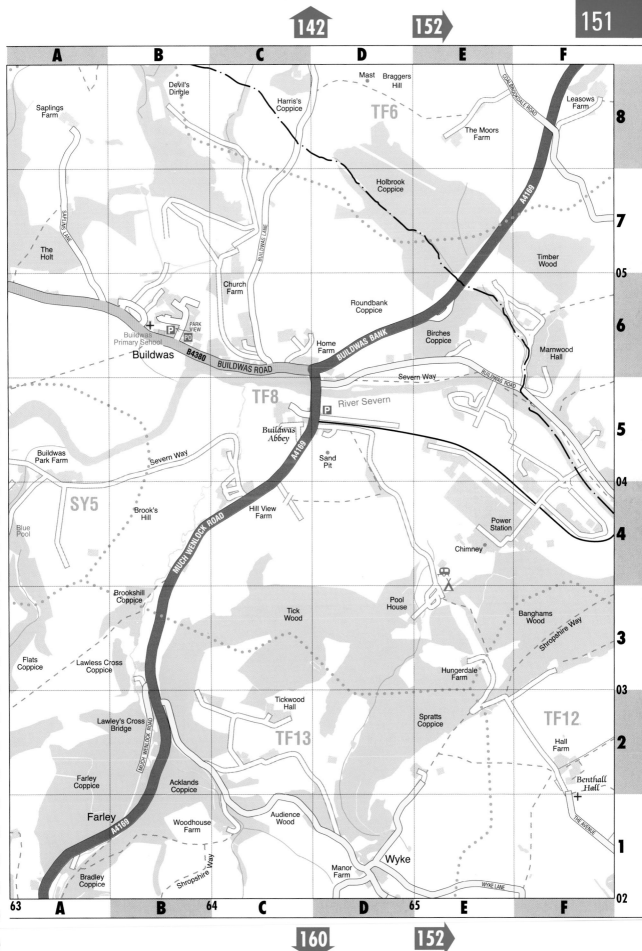

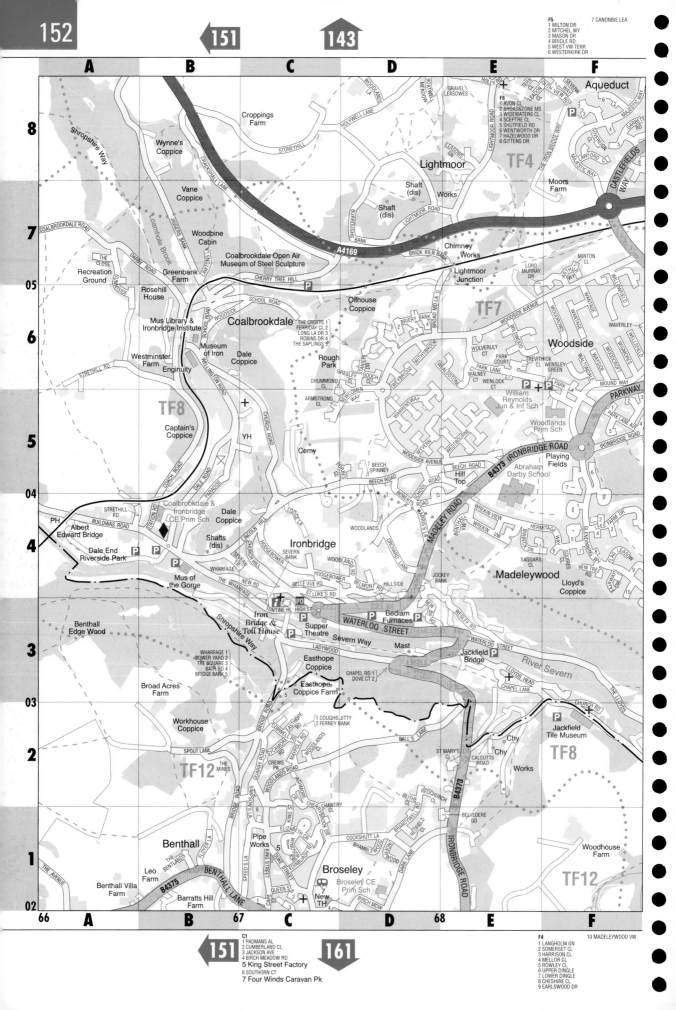

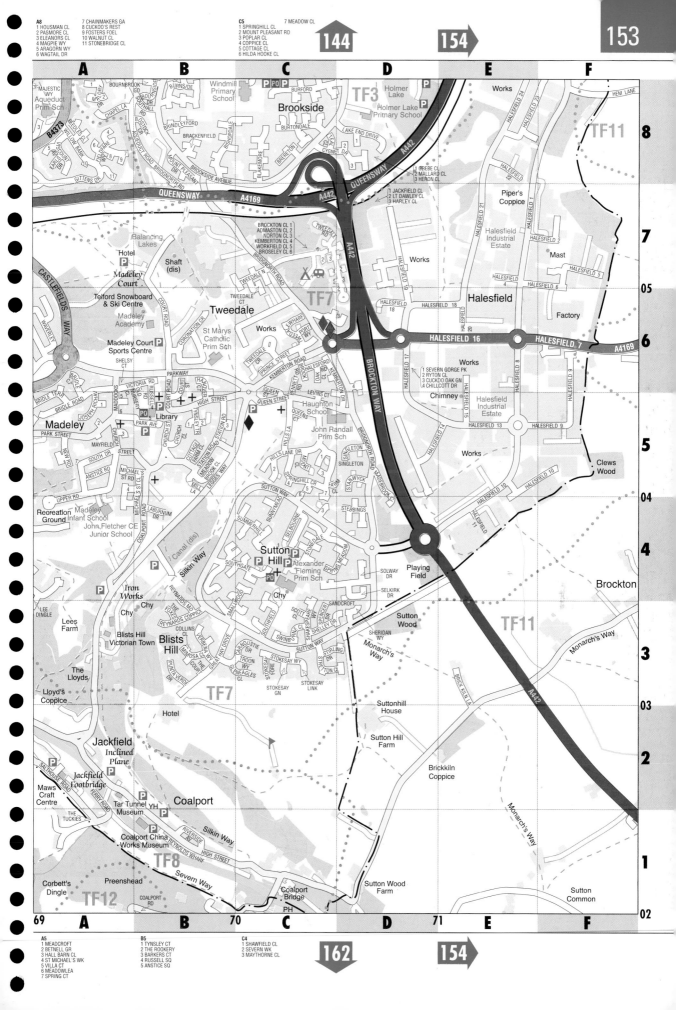

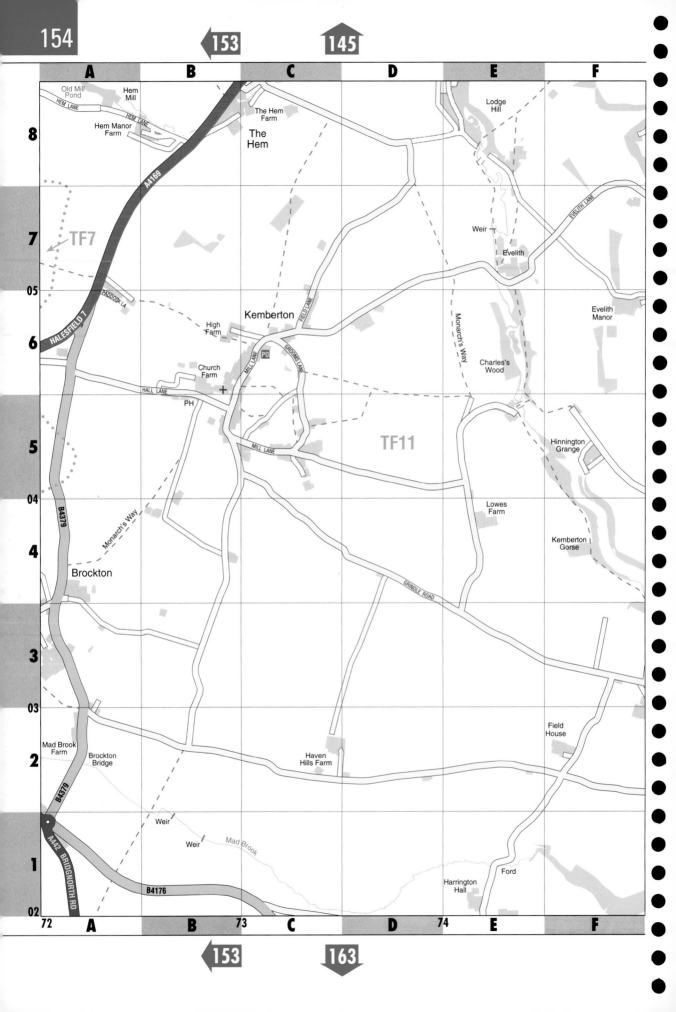

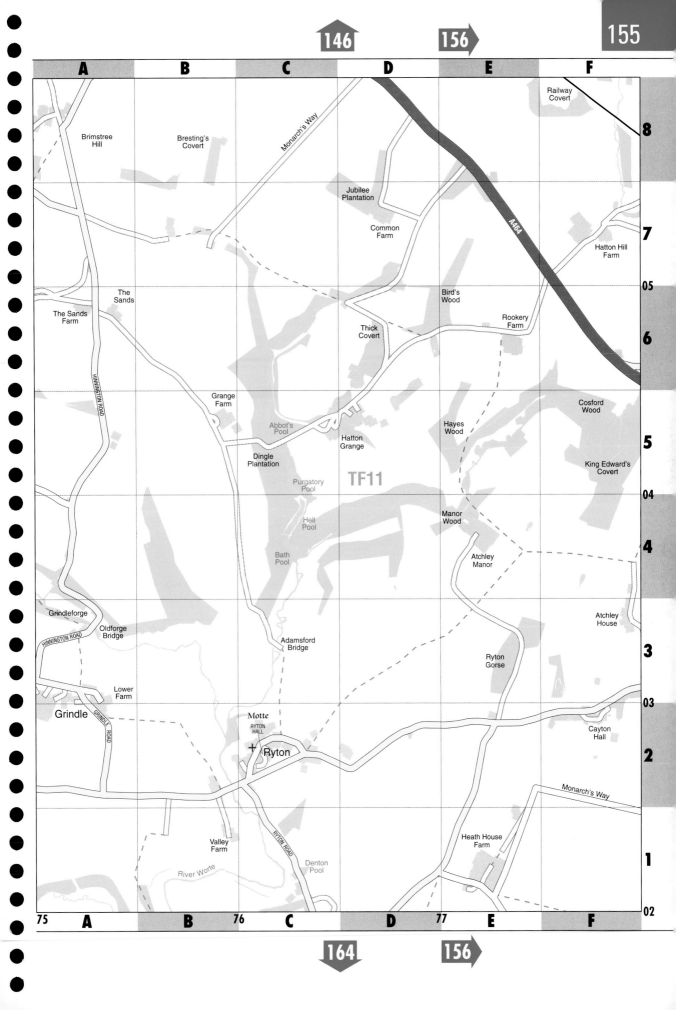

Railway Covert

8

Brimstree Hill

Bresting's Covert

Monarch's Way

Jubilee Plantation

Common Farm

7

Hatton Hill Farm

The Sands

05

Bird's Wood

The Sands Farm

Thick Covert

Rookery Farm

6

HINNINGTON ROAD

Grange Farm

Cosford Wood

Abbot's Pool

Hatton Grange

Hayes Wood

5

Dingle Plantation

King Edward's Covert

Purgatory Pool

TF11

04

Hell Pool

Manor Wood

Bath Pool

Atchley Manor

4

Grindleforge

Atchley House

Oldforge Bridge

HINNINGTON ROAD

Adamsford Bridge

Ryton Gorse

3

Lower Farm

03

Grindle

GRINDLE ROAD

Motte

RYTON HALL

Cayton Hall

+ Ryton

2

RYTON ROAD

Monarch's Way

Valley Farm

Denton Pool

Heath House Farm

1

River Worfe

02

75
76
77

A464

E7
1 NEWTON CL
2 VICTORIA RD
3 VALENCIA RD
4 VICTOR CL

F8
1 BLENHEIM CRES
2 HEREFORD CL
3 ABINGDON RD

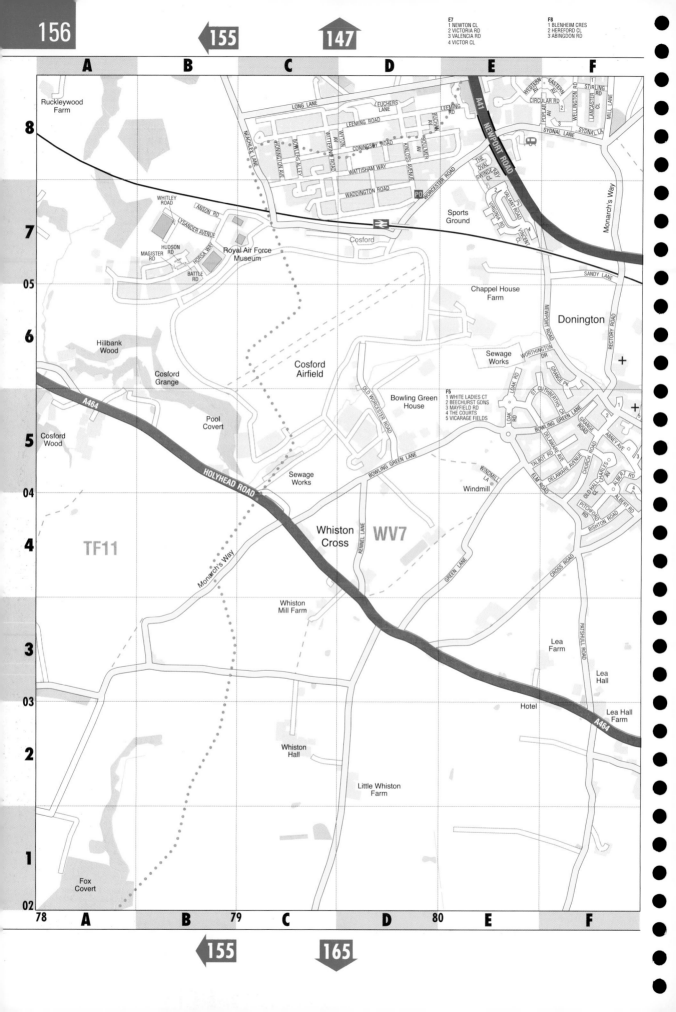

A B C D E F

8

7

05

6

5

04

4

3

03

2

1

02

Ruckleywood Farm

Long Lane
FEUCHERS LANE
Leeming Road
LEEMING RD
WYTON AV
BUCHAN AV
Coningsby Road
KIRLOSS AVENUE
BOULMER
Wattisham Way
Waddington Road
WORCESTER ROAD
PO

WHITLEY ROAD
ANSON RD
LYSANDER AVENUE
HUDSON RD
MAGISTER RD
HORSA WAY
BATTLE RD
Royal Air Force Museum

NEACHLE LANE
DONINGTON AVE
BOWLERS ALLEY
WITTERING ROAD

Cosford

Sports Ground

A41
NEWPORT ROAD
WESTERN AV
EASTERN AV
CIRCULAR RD
POPLAR AV
STIRLING AV
WELLINGTON RD
LANCASTER RD
MILL LANE
SYDNAL LANE
SYDNA LA
THE SWINDELEY
VALIANT ROAD
VIRGINIA RD
VINCENT CL

Monarch's Way

SANDY LANE

Chappel House Farm

Donington

NEWPORT ROAD
RECTORY ROAD

Hillbank Wood

Cosford Grange

Cosford Wood
A464 HOLYHEAD ROAD

Pool Covert

Cosford Airfield

Sewage Works

OLD WORCESTER ROAD

Bowling Green House

F5
1 WHITE LADIES CT
2 BEECHURST GDNS
3 MAYFIELD RD
4 THE COURTS
5 VICARAGE FIELDS

Sewage Works
WORTHINGTON DR
GRANGE PK
LOAK RD
ST CUTHBERTS CR
BOWLING GREEN LANE
GRANGE ROAD
DELAWARE AVE
TALBOT RD
ABNEY AVE
CHURCH ROAD
CHARLES AV
ALBERT RD
ELM ROAD
PITCHFORD RD
OLD HALL CL
BISHTON ROAD
ALBERT RD

Bowling Green Lane

Windmill
WINDMILL LA

TF11

Monarch's Way

Whiston Cross

WV7

KENNEL LANE

GREEN LANE

CROSS ROAD

Lea Farm

PATSHULL ROAD

Lea Hall

Whiston Mill Farm

Whiston Hall

Little Whiston Farm

Hotel

Lea Hall Farm
A464

Fox Covert

78 A B 79 C D 80 E F

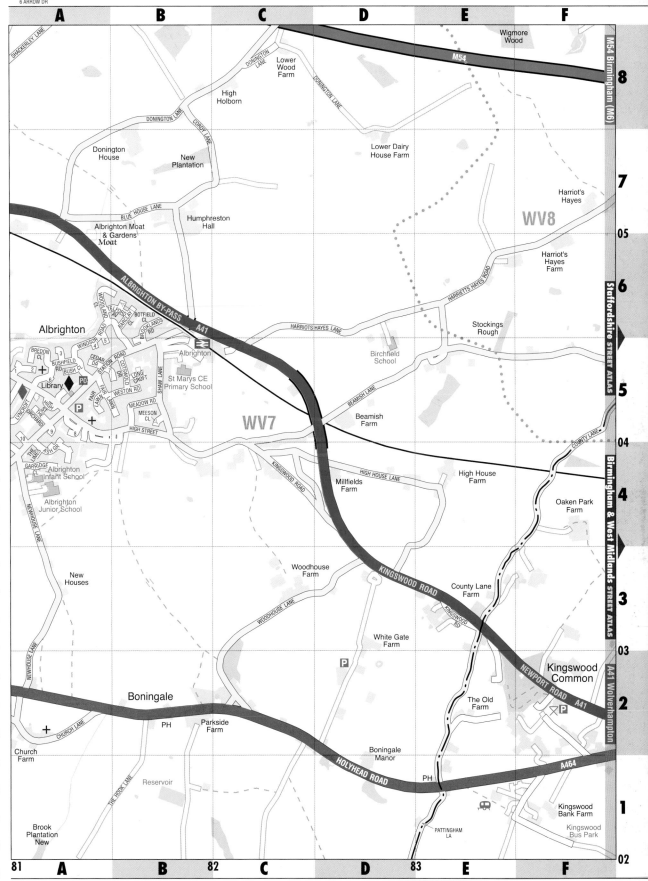

A5
1 ST MARY'S CL
2 THE GLEBE
3 BARRINGTON CL
4 MAYFAIR CL
5 BRINDLEY CL
6 ARROW DR
7 REDFORD DR
8 WOLVERLEY CT
9 MANOR GDNS
10 WHISTON CL

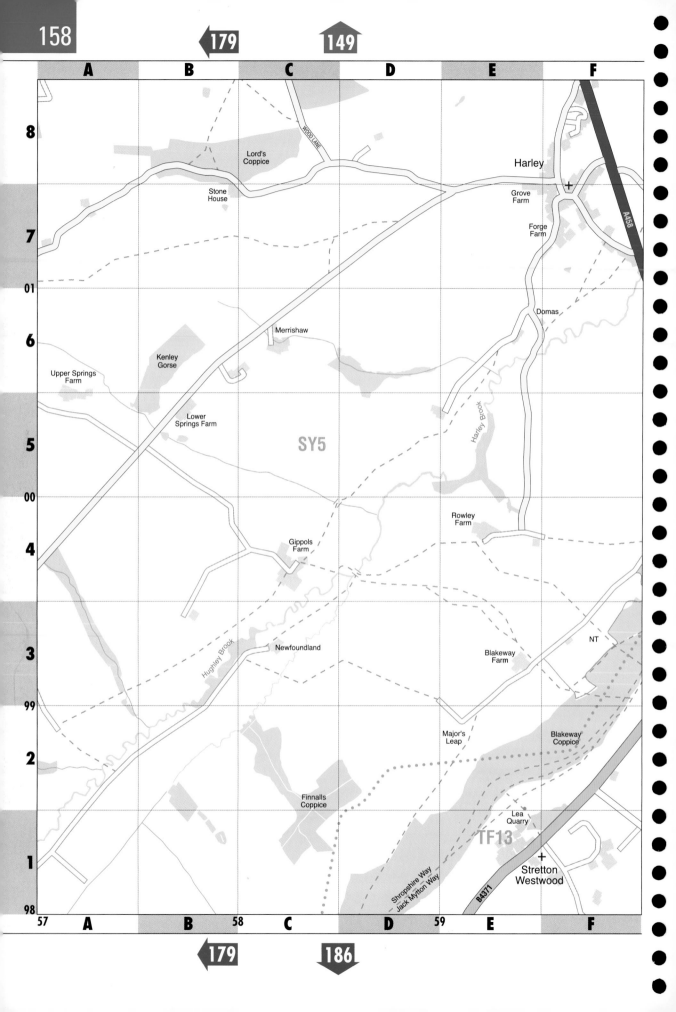

A   B   C   D   E   F

8

Lord's Coppice

WOOD LANE

Harley

Stone House

Grove Farm

7

Forge Farm

A458

01

Domas

Merrishaw

6

Kenley Gorse

Upper Springs Farm

Harley Brook

Lower Springs Farm

SY5

5

00

Rowley Farm

4

Gippols Farm

NT

Hughley Brook

3

Newfoundland

Blakeway Farm

99

Major's Leap

Blakeway Coppice

2

Finnalls Coppice

Lea Quarry

TF13

Shropshire Way
Jack Myton Way

1

B4371

Stretton Westwood

98

57   A   B   58   C   D   59   E   F

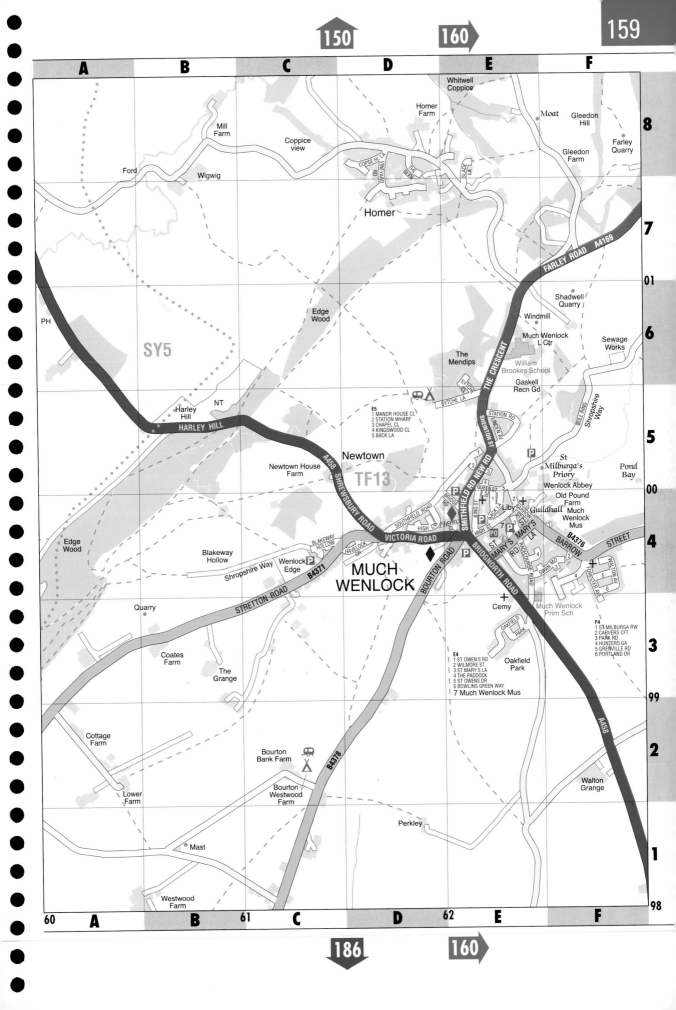

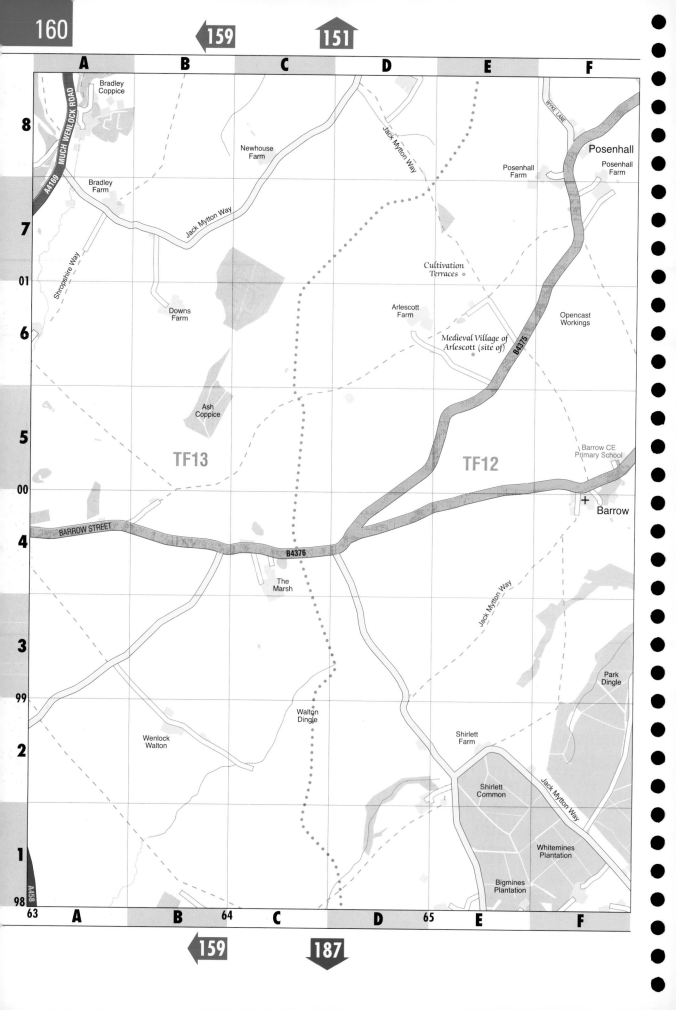

159
151

A B C D E F

8

7

01

6

5

00

4

3

99

2

1

98

Bradley
Coppice

MUCH WENLOCK ROAD

A4169

Bradley
Farm

Newhouse
Farm

Jack Mytton Way

Jack Mytton Way

Posenhall

Posenhall
Farm

Posenhall
Farm

WYKE LANE

Shropshire Way

Downs
Farm

Cultivation
Terraces

Arlescott
Farm

Medieval Village of
Arlescott (site of)

Opencast
Workings

B4375

Ash
Coppice

TF13

TF12

Barrow CE
Primary School

Barrow

BARROW STREET

B4376

The
Marsh

Jack Mytton Way

Walton
Dingle

Park
Dingle

Wenlock
Walton

Shirlett
Farm

Shirlett
Common

Jack Mytton Way

Whitemines
Plantation

Bigmines
Plantation

A458

63 A B 64 C D 65 E F

159
187

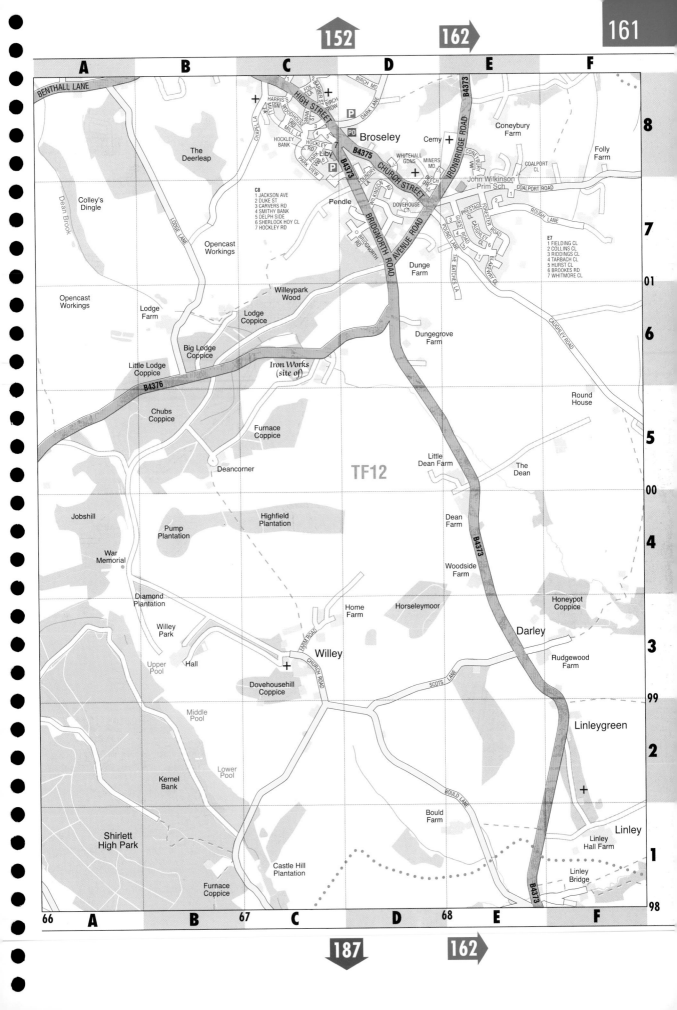

A B C D E F

8
7
01
6
5
00
4
3
99
2
1
98

BENTHALL LANE

The Deerleap

Colley's Dingle

Dean Brook

LODGE LANE

Opencast Workings

Opencast Workings

Lodge Farm

Lodge Coppice

Big Lodge Coppice

Little Lodge Coppice

B4376

Chubs Coppice

Furnace Coppice

Deancorner

Willeypark Wood

Iron Works (site of)

HIGH STREET

CHAPEL LA

HARRIS'S MEWS
WOODHOUSE LA
MILL LA
MILL LA

HOCKLEY BANK

FOX LA
BARBER'S ROW
BIRCH ROW

PARK VIEW

HOCKLEY RD

1
2
3
4
5
6
7

P
PO
Liby
P

B4375
B4373

Broseley

DARK LANE

BIRCH MD

Cemy

WHITEHALL GDNS

MINERS MD

BEECH DR

CHURCH STREET

BRIDGNORTH ROAD

AVENUE ROAD

WILKINSON AV

FOUNDRY LA

DOVEHOUSE CT

Pendle

C8
1 JACKSON AVE
2 DUKE ST
3 CARVERS RD
4 SMITHY BANK
5 DELPH SIDE
6 SHERLOCK HOY CL
7 HOCKLEY RD

IRONBRIDGE ROAD
B4373

CONEYBURY VW

John Wilkinson Prim Sch

Coneybury Farm

Folly Farm

COALPORT CL

COALPORT ROAD

ROUGH LANE

PRESTAGE
GUEST ROAD
FORESTER ROAD
CAUGHLEY CL
BLAKEWAY CL

1
2
3
4
5
6

E7
1 FIELDING CL
2 COLLINS CL
3 RIDDINGS CL
4 TARBACH CL
5 HURST CL
6 BROOKES RD
7 WHITMORE CL

THE BATCHES LA
POUND LANE

Dunge Farm

Dungegrove Farm

CAUGHLEY ROAD

Round House

TF12

Little Dean Farm

The Dean

Jobshill

Pump Plantation

Highfield Plantation

Dean Farm

B4373

War Memorial

Woodside Farm

Honeypot Coppice

Diamond Plantation

Home Farm

Horseleymoor

Willey Park

Hall

Upper Pool

FARM ROAD

Willey

CHURCH ROAD

Darley

Rudgewood Farm

Dovehousehill Coppice

Middle Pool

SCOTS LANE

Linleygreen

Kernel Bank

Lower Pool

BOULD LANE

Bould Farm

Linley

Shirlett High Park

Castle Hill Plantation

Linley Hall Farm

Linley Bridge

B4373

Furnace Coppice

66 A 67 B C 67 D 68 E F

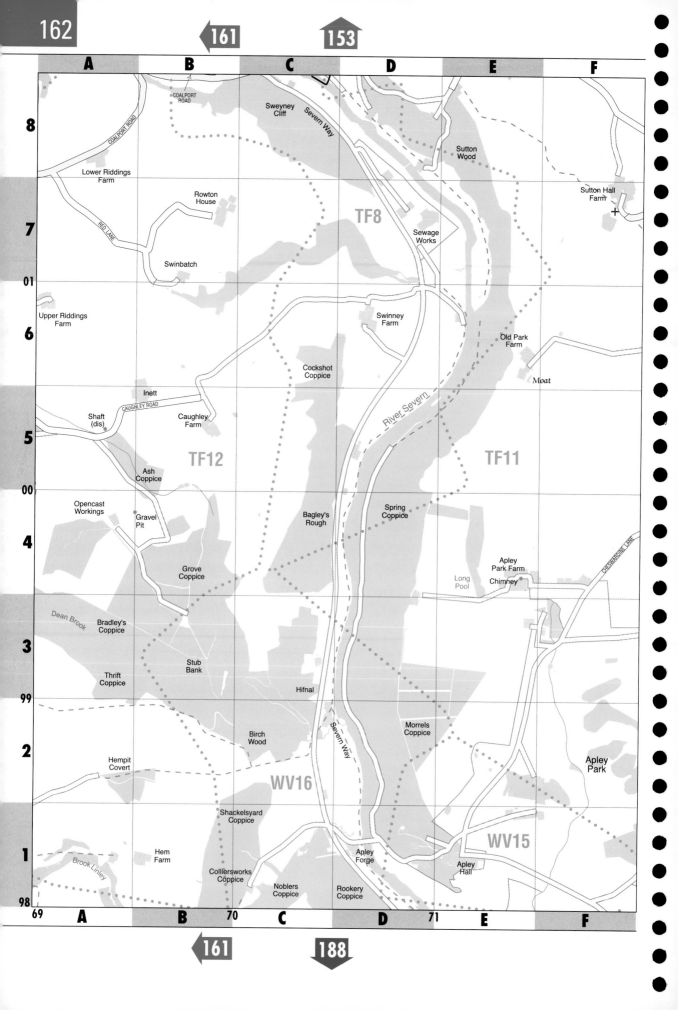

A   B   C   D   E   F

8

COALPORT ROAD

COALPORT ROAD

Sweyney Cliff

Severn Way

Sutton Wood

Lower Riddings Farm

Rowton House

TF8

Sutton Hall Farm

7

RED LANE

Swinbatch

Sewage Works

01

Swinney Farm

Old Park Farm

6

Upper Riddings Farm

Cockshot Coppice

Moat

Inett

CAUGHLEY ROAD

River Severn

Shaft (dis)

Caughley Farm

5

TF12

TF11

Ash Coppice

00

Opencast Workings

Gravel Pit

Bagley's Rough

Spring Coppice

Apley Park Farm

4

Grove Coppice

Long Pool

Chimney

Dean Brook

Bradley's Coppice

3

Stub Bank

Thrift Coppice

Hifnal

99

Morrels Coppice

Birch Wood

Severn Way

2

Hempit Covert

WV16

Apley Park

Shackelyard Coppice

WV15

1

Hem Farm

Brook Linley

Colliersworks Coppice

Apley Forge

Apley Hall

Noblers Coppice

Rookery Coppice

98

69   A   B   70   C   D   71   E   F

CHESWARDINE LANE

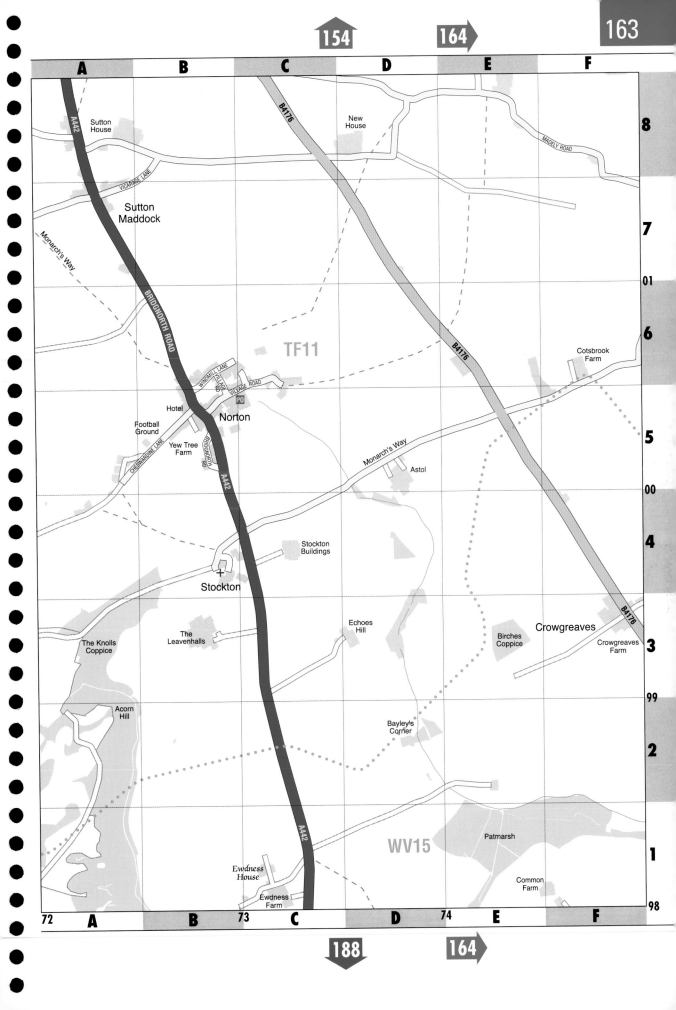

163
155

A B C D E F

8

7

01

6

5

00

4

3

99

2

1

98

75 A B 76 C D 77 E F

Fox Covert

Ryton Road

Beckbury Farm

Lawton Cl

Caynton Road

Monarch's Way

Beckbury

Badger Lane

PH

Dingle Dr

Madely Road

Brook Farm

Sewage Works

Higford Lane

Beckbury CE Prim Sch

Monarch's Way

TF11

Big Wood Farm

Snowdon Lane

Snowdon Farm

New Options Coll

Elslow Coppice

Higford Farm

Riddens Coppice

Badger Farm

Spring Coppice

New Pool

WV6

Badger

Town Pool

Badger Heath Farm

Newton's Wood

Upper Pool

Badger Dingle

River Worfe

Lower Pool

WV15

Sewage Works

The Tyte Farm

PH

Stableford Bridge

Stableford

Stableford Road

Ackleton

Rosemount Gdns

Back Lane

Hall

Royal Pool

Stableford Farm

Jays Farm

Maltings Cl

Foley Road

B4176

Haden Hill

Broad Bridge

Weir

A B C D E F

WV7

New Brook
Plantation

8

Rous's
Covert

RUSHEY LANE

Bishton
Manor

FARM ROAD

Home
Farm

HOME FARM ROAD

Monkey
Bridge

Bickley's
Rough

7

Snowdon
Pool

Wilderness
Hill

01

Monkeybridge
Plantation

Bennetts
Wood

Moat

Patshull
Hall

6

Lower
Snowdon

SNOWDON ROAD

PH

Bath
Plantation

Burnhill
Green

Decoy
Wood

Church
Pool

Thorn
Plantation

Old
Park

Middle
Ley

Boathouse
Plantation

Half Moon
Plantation

Shepherds
Buildings

5

Cut
Spinney

Eel Stew
Plantation

00

Shepherds
Plantation

Green's
Coppice

Far Ley

The Great
Pool

Jubilee
Plantation

WV6

Brewers Lodge
Plantation

4

Mill
Ponds

Bridgnorth
Plantation

CH Hotel

Pasford

3

Stanlow
Farm

99

Stanlow

Kingslow
Farm

2

Kingslow
Hall

Nun Brook

1

Birchley
Farm

98

78 A B 79 C D 80 E F

New Brook Plantation

Upper Pepperhill Farm

Simmonds's Wood

WV7

Wrottesley Lodge Farm

Bickley's Rough

Scott's Bank Plantation

Hawk's Well

Birch Coppice

01

Black Maria Plantation

Wrottesley Old Park

High Park

Park Plantation

The Butts Spinney

Spring Coppice

Upper Westbeech Farm

Mere Oak

Rifle Range Plantation

Westbeech Road

The Meadleys

Westbeech

The Hollies

00

Nurton Hill

Slangs Plantation

Nurton Farm

WV6

Grange Farm

Nurton

Wolverhampton Road

Nurton Hall Farm

New Buildings Cottages

Patshull Road

College Farm

Highgate Farm

St Chads CE Prim Sch

Newgate

Tuters Hill

Pattingham

Copley Lane

PH

Damson Pk

99

PO

Orchard Cl

Letchmere Rd

Broadwell La

High Street

Beech Cl

Hall End Lane

Hall La

Letchmere La

Yew Tree Rd

Copley Farm

Beech House Farm

Sewage Works

Marlbrook Lane

Fenway Gd

Sandringham Rd

Clive Road

The Elms Paddock

Moor Lane Farm

Great Moor Farm

Chesterton Road

Rudge Road

Moor Lane

Hall End Farm

Westfield Farm

Little Moor

Bennett's Lane

Great Moor Road

Hamley Park

Madame's Coppice

98

81   82   83

Birmingham & West Midlands STREET ATLAS

C2
1 BEECH CFT
2 THE GREENWAY
3 GREEN CL
4 DARTMOUTH AVE
5 HALL END CL
6 WINDSOR RD
7 BRAEMAR RD
8 ST CHADS CL

C3
1 COLLEGE FARM CL
2 MERCHANT CL
3 OLD SMITHY CL
4 THE RETREAT GDNS

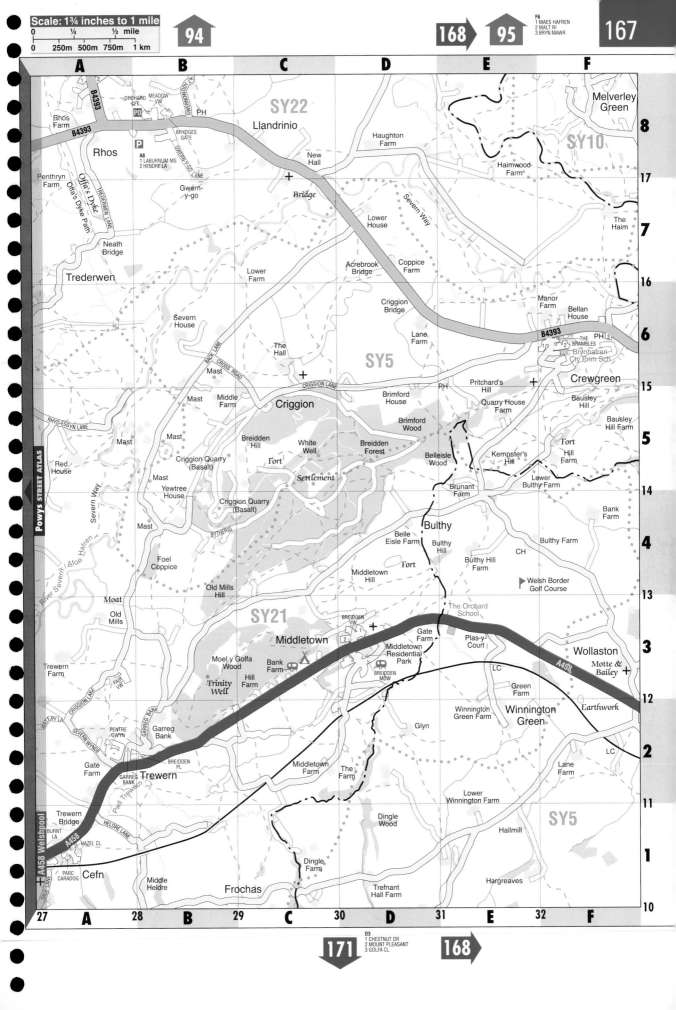

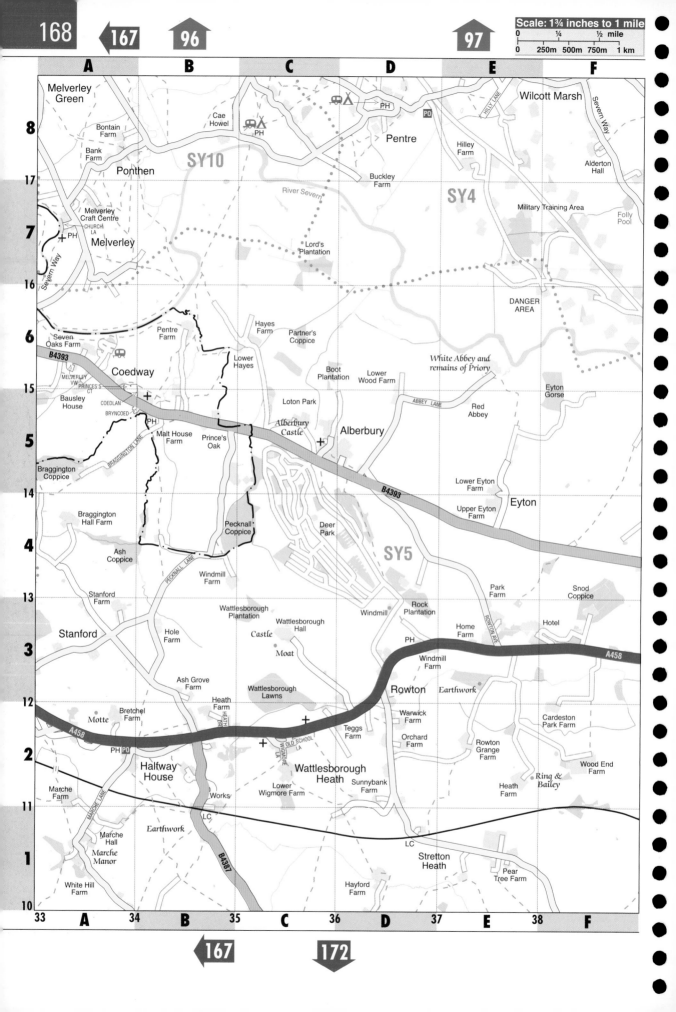

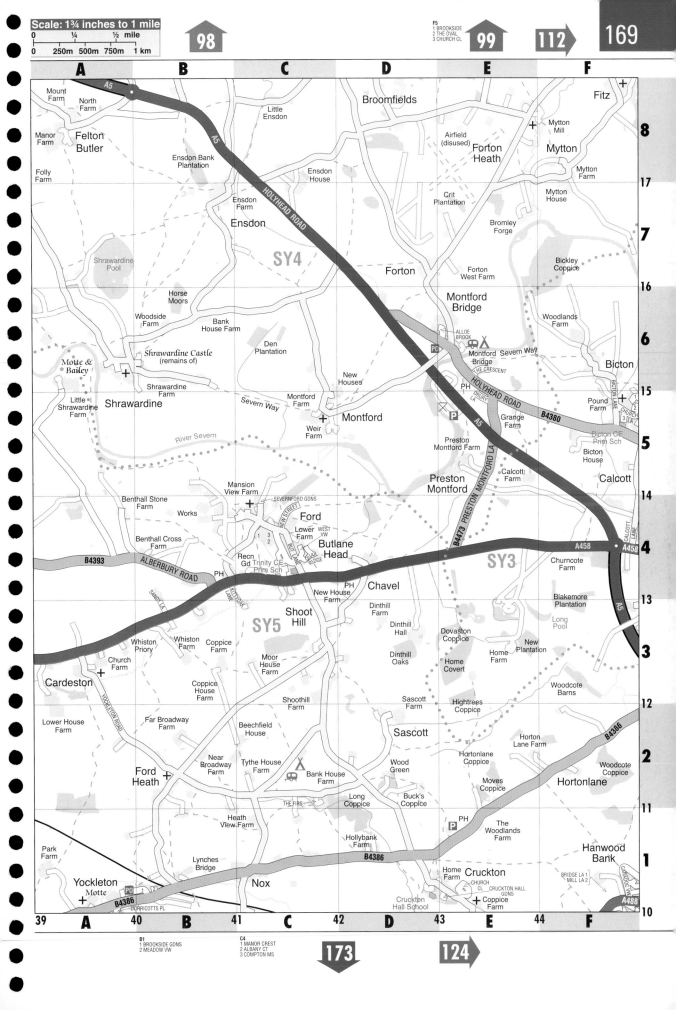

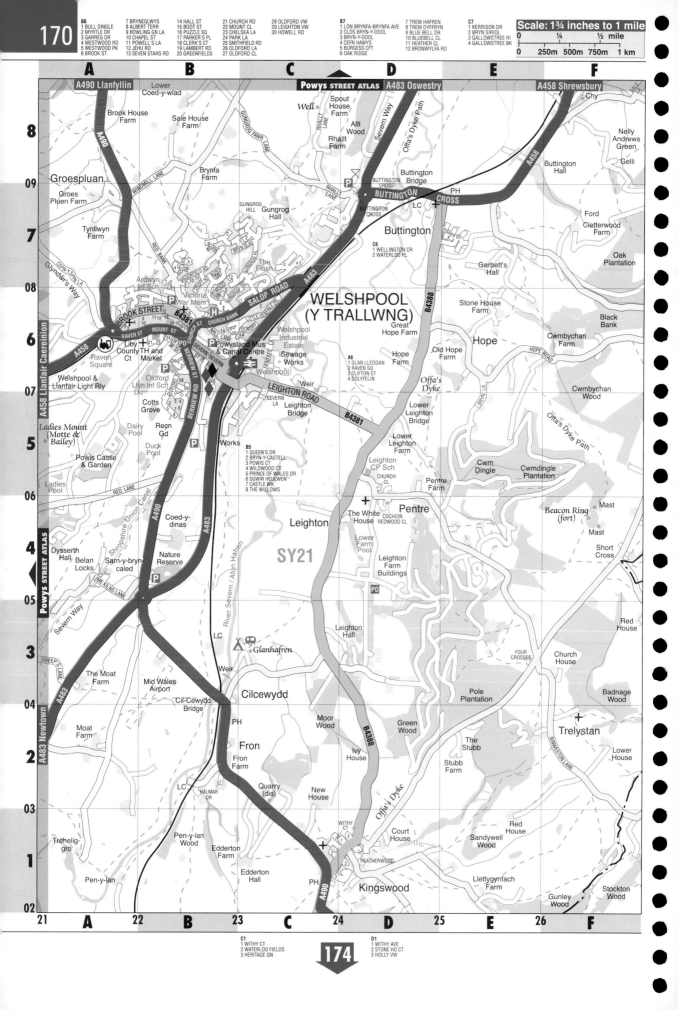

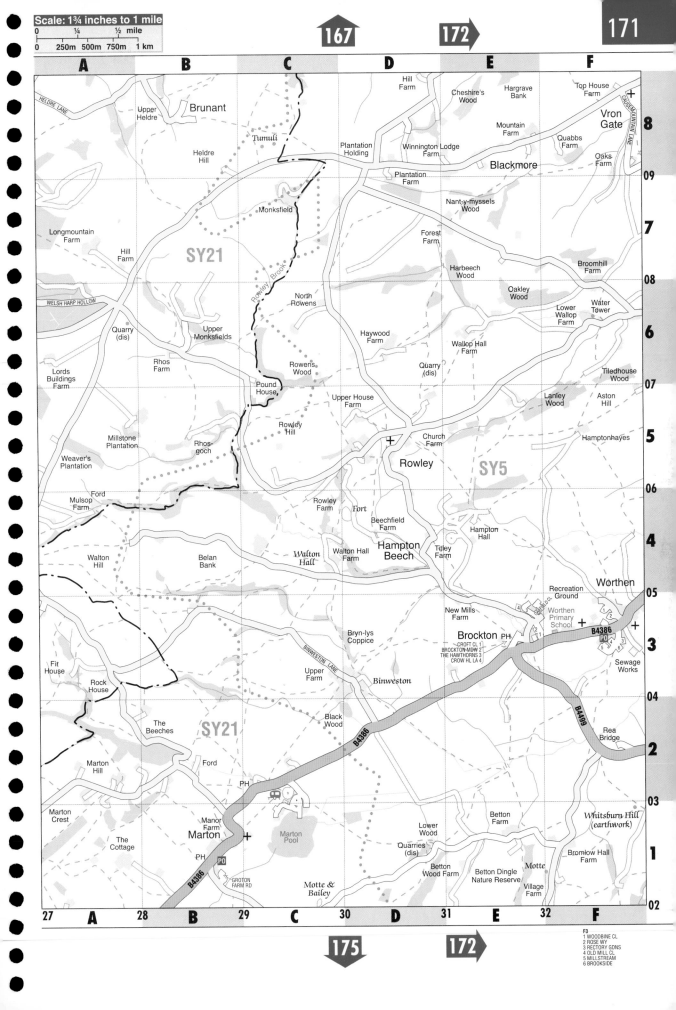

A   B   C   D   E   F

8

Heldre Lane

Upper Heldre   Brunant

Hill Farm   Cheshire's Wood   Hargrave Bank   Top House Farm   Vron Gate

Tumuli   Mountain Farm   Quabbs Farm   Oaks Farm

Heldre Hill   Plantation Holding   Winnington Lodge Farm   Blackmore

09

Monksfield   Plantation Farm

Nant-y-myssels Wood

7

Longmountain Farm   SY21   Forest Farm   Broomhill Farm

Hill Farm   Rowley Brook   Harbeech Wood   08

North Rowens   Oakley Wood   Lower Wallop Farm   Water Tower

Welsh Harp Hollow   6

Quarry (dis)   Upper Monksfields   Haywood Farm   Wallop Hall Farm   Tiledhouse Wood

Rhos Farm   Rowens Wood   Quarry (dis)   Lanley Wood   07   Aston Hill

Lords Buildings Farm   Pound House   Upper House Farm   Hamptonhayes

5

Millstone Plantation   Rhos-goch   Rowley Hill   Church Farm   SY5

Weaver's Plantation   Rowley   06

Ford   Rowley Farm   Fort   Hampton Hall

Mulsop Farm   Beechfield Farm   4

Walton Hill   Belan Bank   Walton Hall   Walton Hall Farm   Hampton Beech   Titley Farm   Worthen

05

New Mills Farm   Recreation Ground   Worthen Primary School

Fit House   Brockton   PH   B4386   PO

Rock House   Bryn-lys Coppice   Sewage Works   3

SY21   Upper Farm   Binweston   CROFT CL 1 BROCKTON-MDW 2 THE HAWTHORNS 3 CROW HL LA 4

The Beeches   Black Wood   04

Marton Hill   Ford   B4386   B4499   Rea Bridge   2

Marton Crest   Whitsburn Hill (earthwork)

The Cottage   Manor Farm   Marton   Marton Pool   Betton Farm   03

PH   PO   Lower Wood   Betton Dingle Nature Reserve   Motte   Bromlow Hall Farm   1

B4386   GROTON FARM RD   Quarries (dis)   Motte & Bailey   Betton Wood Farm   Village Farm   02

27   A   28   B   29   C   30   D   31   E   32   F

F3
1 WOODBINE CL
2 ROSE WY
3 RECTORY GDNS
4 OLD MILL CL
5 MILLSTREAM
6 BROOKSIDE

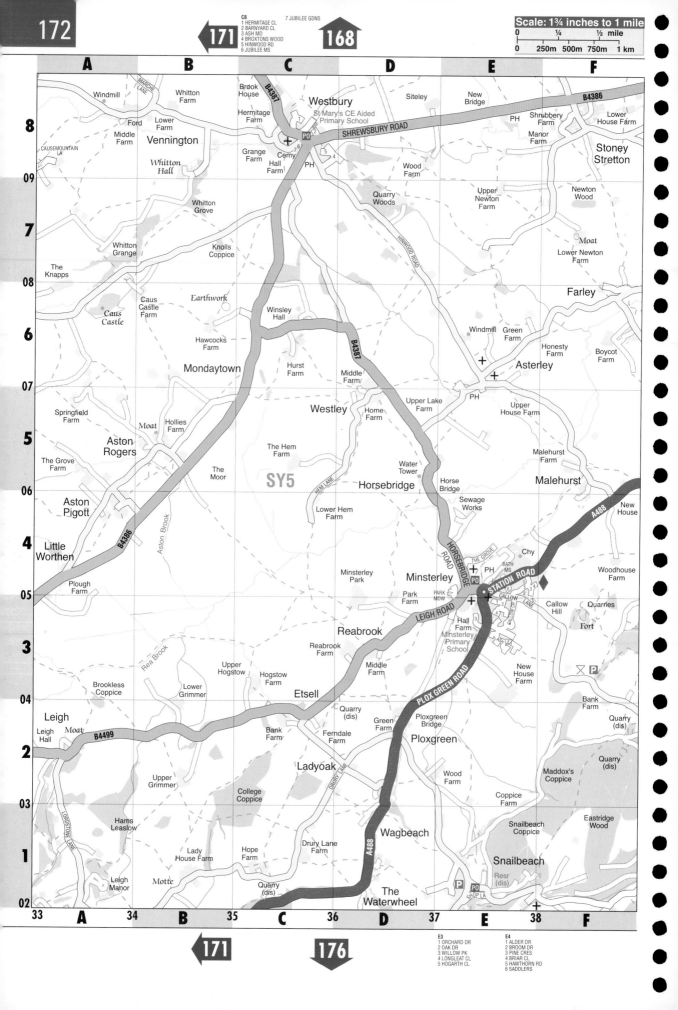

171
168

C8
1 HERMITAGE CL
2 BARNYARD CL
3 ASH MD
4 BROXTONS WOOD
5 HINWOOD RD
6 JUBILEE MS

7 JUBILEE GDNS

Scale: 1¾ inches to 1 mile

0   ¼   ½   mile
0   250m 500m 750m 1 km

A   B   C   D   E   F

Windmill
Whitton Farm
Brook House
Westbury
St Mary's CE Aided Primary School
Siteley
New Bridge
B4386
Shrubbery Farm
Lower House Farm

Ford
Lower Farm
Hermitage Farm
PO
SHREWSBURY ROAD
PH
Manor Farm
Stoney Stretton

Middle Farm
MARCHE LANE
Vennington
Grange Farm
Cemy
Hall Farm
PH
Wood Farm
Upper Newton Farm
Newton Wood

CAUSEMOUNTAIN LA
Whitton Hall
Quarry Woods
HINWOOD ROAD
Moat
Lower Newton Farm

Whitton Grove
Knolls Coppice
Farley

The Knapps
Whitton Grange
Winsley Hall
Windmill
Green Farm
Honesty Farm
Boycot Farm

Earthwork
Caus Castle Farm
B4387
Asterley

Caus Castle
Hawcocks Farm
Hurst Farm
Middle Farm
PH
Upper House Farm

Mondaytown
Upper Lake Farm
Malehurst Farm
Malehurst

Springfield Farm
Westley
Home Farm

Aston Rogers
Moat
Hollies Farm
The Hem Farm
Water Tower
Horse Bridge
Sewage Works

The Grove Farm
The Moor
HEM LANE
Horsebridge
A488
New House

Aston Pigott
Lower Hem Farm
Minsterley Park
Horse Bridge
THE GROVE
Chy
Woodhouse Farm

Little Worthen
B4386
Aston Brook
SY5
Minsterley
HORSEBRIDGE ROAD
BATH MS
PO
PH
STATION ROAD
CALLOW
Callow Hill
Quarries

Plough Farm
Park Farm
PARK MDW
Hall Farm
Minsterley Primary School
New House Farm
Callow Hill
Fort

Reabrook
LEIGH ROAD
ASH LEA
Bank Farm

Rea Brook
Upper Hogstow
Reabrook Farm
Middle Farm
PLOX GREEN ROAD
Quarry (dis)

Brookless Coppice
Hogstow Farm
Etsell
Quarry (dis)
Green Farm
Ploxgreen Bridge
Ploxgreen
Quarry (dis)

Lower Grimmer
Bank Farm
Ferndale Farm
Ploxgreen
Maddox's Coppice

Leigh
Moat
B4499
Ladyoak
DRURY LANE
Wood Farm
Coppice Farm
Quarry (dis)

Leigh Hall
Upper Grimmer
College Coppice
Drury Lane Farm
Wagbeach
Snailbeach Coppice
Eastridge Wood

LORDSTONE LANE
Hams Leaslow
Lady House Farm
Hope Farm
A488
Snailbeach
Resr (dis)

Leigh Manor
Motte
Quarry (dis)
The Waterwheel
PO
SHOP LA

171
176

E3
1 ORCHARD DR
2 OAK DR
3 WILLOW PK
4 LONGLEAT CL
5 HOGARTH CL

E4
1 ALDER DR
2 BROOM DR
3 PINE CRES
4 BRIAR CL
5 HAWTHORN RD
6 SADDLERS

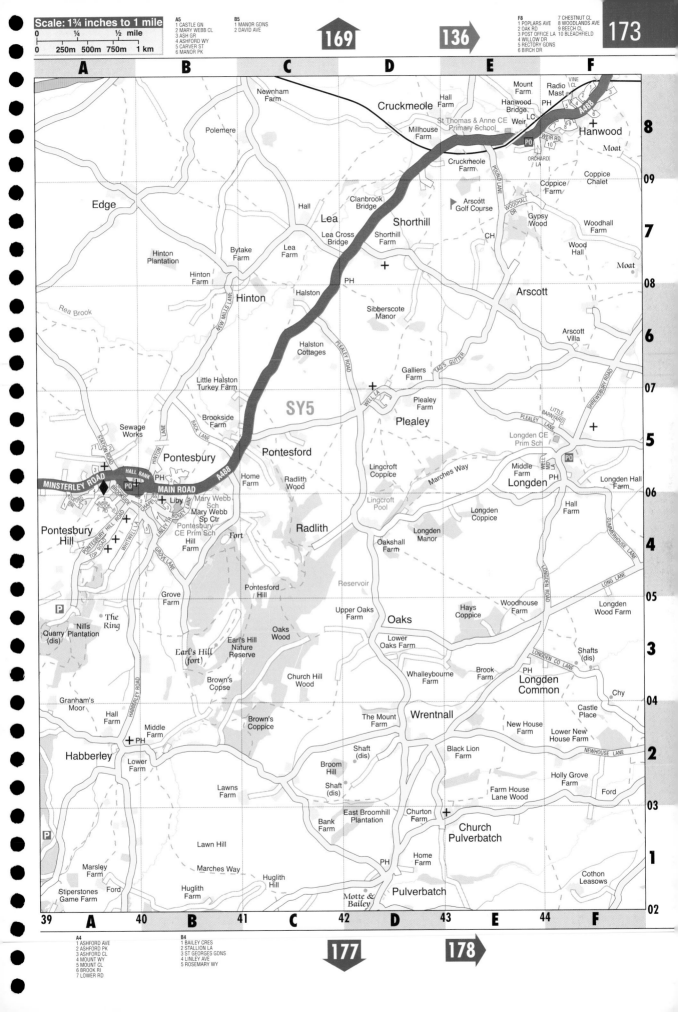

Scale: 1¾ inches to 1 mile
0   ¼   ½ mile
0   250m 500m 750m 1 km

A B C D E F

8
01
7
00
6
99
5
98
4
97
3
96
2
95
1
94

21 A 22 B 23 C 24 D 25 E 26 F

The Grove
Pen-y-lan
Lower Munlyn
Church Farm
Forden Cin W Prim Sch
Offa's Dyke Path
Motte & Bailey
Kingswood Farm
Ackley Farm
Gunley Wood
Stockton
Gunley Hall
Forden (Ffodun)
SY21
Nantcribbau Farm
Rhyd-y-groes
Camlad
Cwm Farm
LC
PH
PO
Camlad
Keith Davis Farm
Great Hem Farm
Upper Hem Farm
Lower Hem Farm
Quarry (dis)
[CAMLAD DR 1] [MAES-Y-FELIN 2]
Hem Moor
Pit (dis)
Salt Bridge
Shiregrove Bridge
Walcot Farm
B4386
Stalloe
Quarry
Earthwork
Chirbury CE Primary School
PH
PO
CAMLAD CTS
HORSESHOE RD
Hendomen
Rownal
Crankwell Farm
Winsbury Farm
Chirbury
LC
Motte & Bailey
Hendomen Farm
B4386
A490
B4385
Sewage Works
Dudston
Motte
Lower Lane
STATION RD
FORDEN ROAD
NEW ROAD
[1 VERLON CL] [2 ARTHURS GATE]
County Boundary Bridge
Great Moat Farm
Moat
Timberth
Ffridd Wood
POOL RD
CHIRBURY ROAD
Ffridd Faldwyn (fort)
Castle
The Old Bell Mus
TH PO
Upper Pool
Timberth Wood
Sidnal Farm
MONTGOMERY (TREFDLDWYN)
PRINCES ST
Hendomen Dr
Lymore Park
SY15
Broad Street Farm
KERRY GATE
Lower Pool
Boardyhall Wood
Whitley Wood
Rockley Wood
Caeprior
Hill Top Farm
BISHOP'S CASTLE STREET
War Memorial
Llwynobin
New Covert
Gwarthlow
Motte
Rhiston
Offa's Dyke Path
Pant-y-maen Wood
Weston Madoc
Rockley Farm
Rockley
Coed Farm
Upper Pentre
Pen-y-bryn Hall
B4385
Little Brompton Farm
COED LANE
CAE GWYN
Churchstoke
A489

B3
1 GAOL RD
2 CHIRBURY GATE
3 SCHOOL BANK
4 ARTHUR ST
5 LYMORE VIEW
6 LIONS BANK
7 TAN Y MUR
8 CHURCH BANK
9 BROAD ST
10 KERRY ST
11 BACK LA
12 MALDWYN WY
13 CORNDON DR
14 WELL ST
15 KERRY RD
16 CASTLE WALK

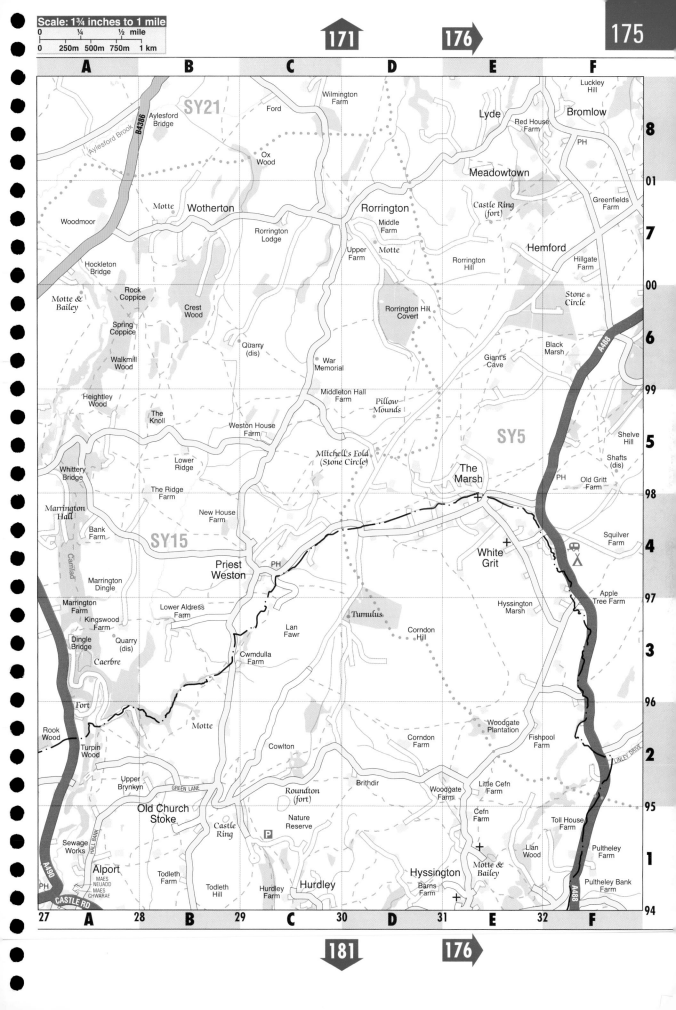

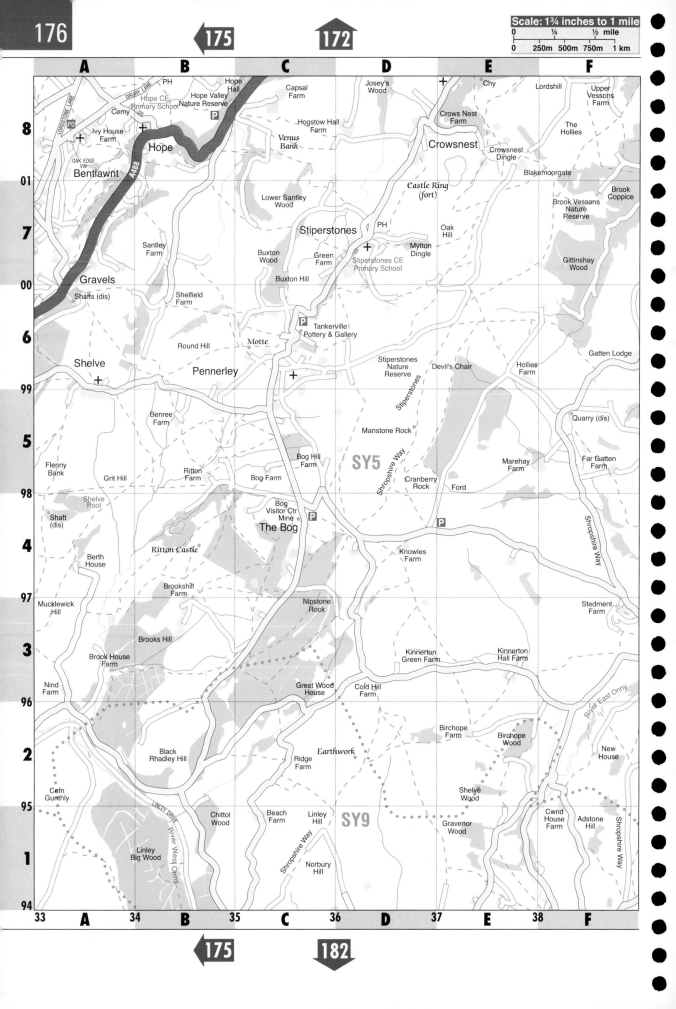

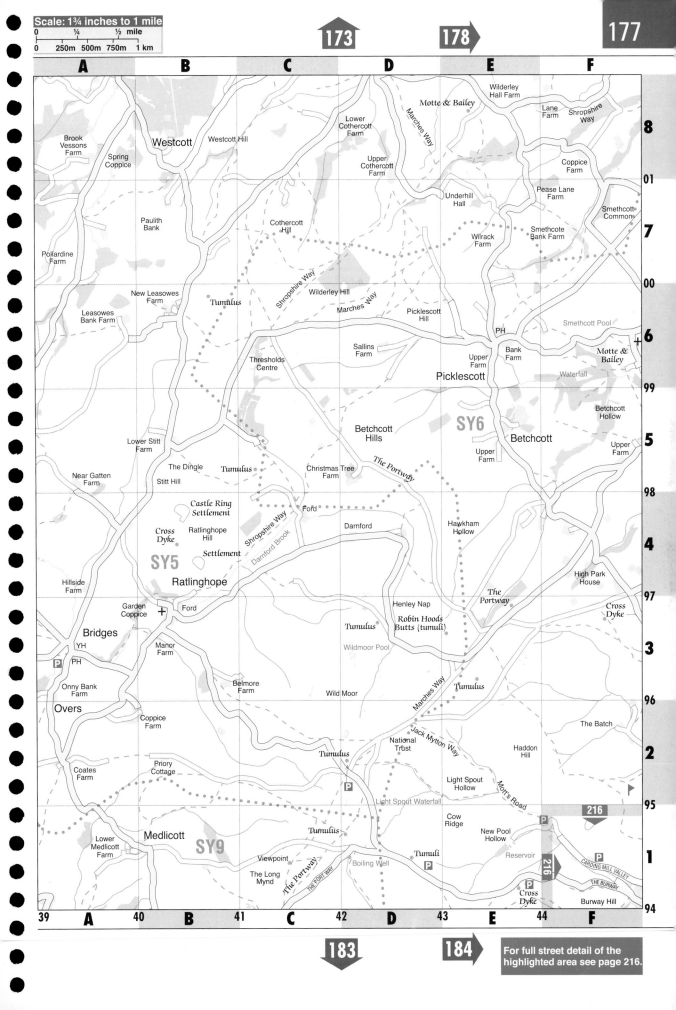

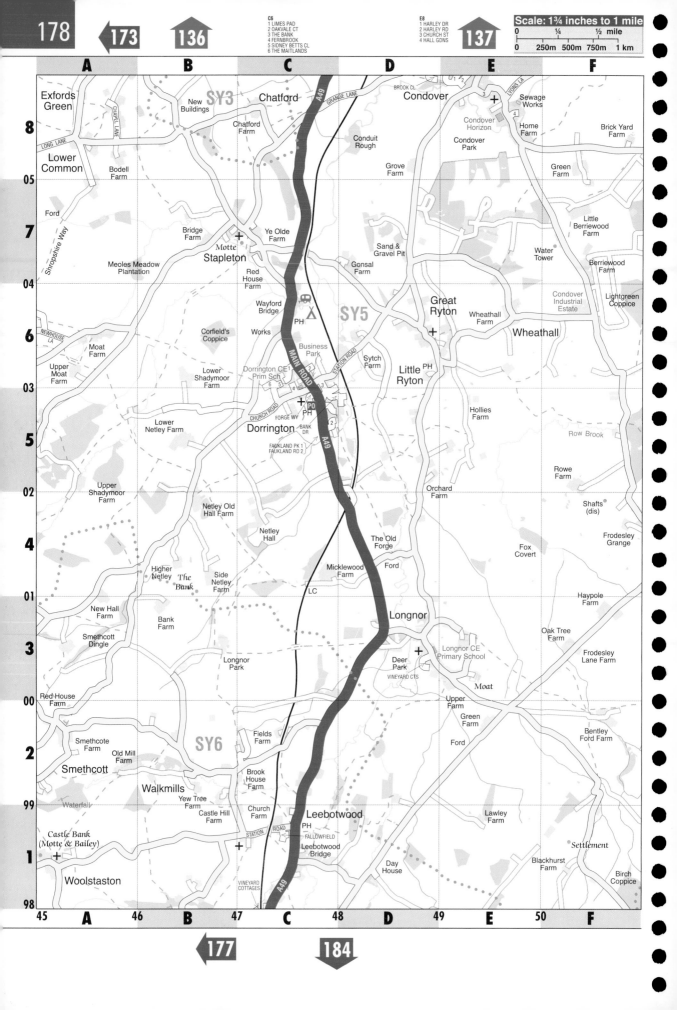

C6
1 LIMES PAD
2 OAKVALE CT
3 THE BANK
4 FERNBROOK
5 SIDNEY BETTS CL
6 THE MAITLANDS

E8
1 HARLEY DR
2 HARLEY RD
3 CHURCH ST
4 HALL GDNS

Exfords Green
New Buildings
SY3
Chatford
GRANGE LANE
BROOK CL
Condover
Sewage Works
LYONS LA

Lower Common
Chatford Farm
Condover Horizon
Home Farm
Brick Yard Farm

Bodell Farm
Conduit Rough
Condover Park
Green Farm

Ford
Shropshire Way
Bridge Farm
Ye Olde Farm
Grove Farm
Little Berriewood Farm

Motte Stapleton
Sand & Gravel Pit
Water Tower
Berriewood Farm

Meoles Meadow Plantation
Red House Farm
Gonsal Farm
Great Ryton
Wheathall Farm
Condover Industrial Estate
Lightgreen Coppice

NEWHOUSE LA
Wayford Bridge
PH
Works
SY5
Wheathall

Moat Farm
Corfield's Coppice
Business Park
Sytch Farm
Little Ryton
PH

Upper Moat Farm
Lower Shadymoor Farm
Dorrington CE Prim Sch
STATION ROAD
Hollies Farm
Row Brook

Lower Netley Farm
CHURCH ROAD
Dorrington
PO PH
FORGE WY
BANK DR
MAIN ROAD
Rowe Farm

Upper Shadymoor Farm
FAUKLAND PK 1
FAUKLAND RD 2
A49
Orchard Farm
Shafts (dis)

Netley Old Hall Farm
Frodesley Grange

Netley Hall
The Old Forge
Fox Covert

Higher Netley
The Bank
Side Netley Farm
Micklewood Farm
Ford
Haypole Farm

New Hall Farm
LC
Longnor
Oak Tree Farm

Smethcott Dingle
Bank Farm
Deer Park
Longnor CE Primary School
Moat
Frodesley Lane Farm

Red House Farm
Longnor Park
VINEYARD CTS
Upper Farm

Smethcote Farm
Old Mill Farm
Fields Farm
Green Farm
Ford
Bentley Ford Farm

Smethcott
SY6
Brook House Farm
Lawley Farm

Walkmills
Yew Tree Farm
Church Farm
Leebotwood
PH

Waterfall
Castle Hill Farm
STATION
ROAD
FALLOWFIELD
Leebotwood Bridge
Day House
Settlement

Castle Bank (Motte & Bailey)
Blackhurst Farm
Birch Coppice

Woolstaston
VINEYARD COTTAGES
A49

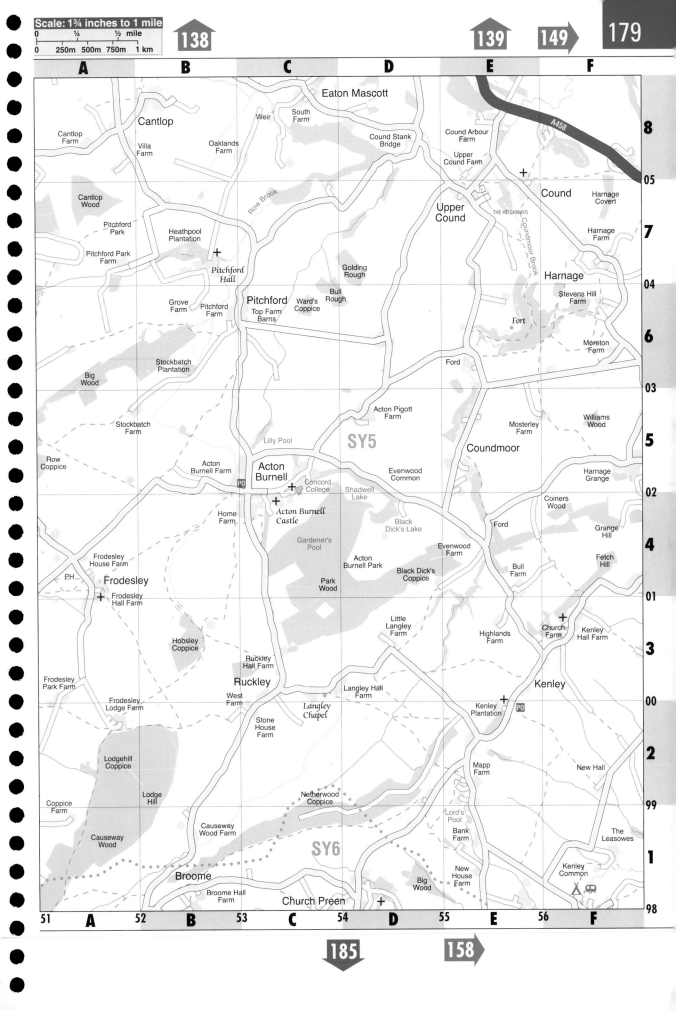

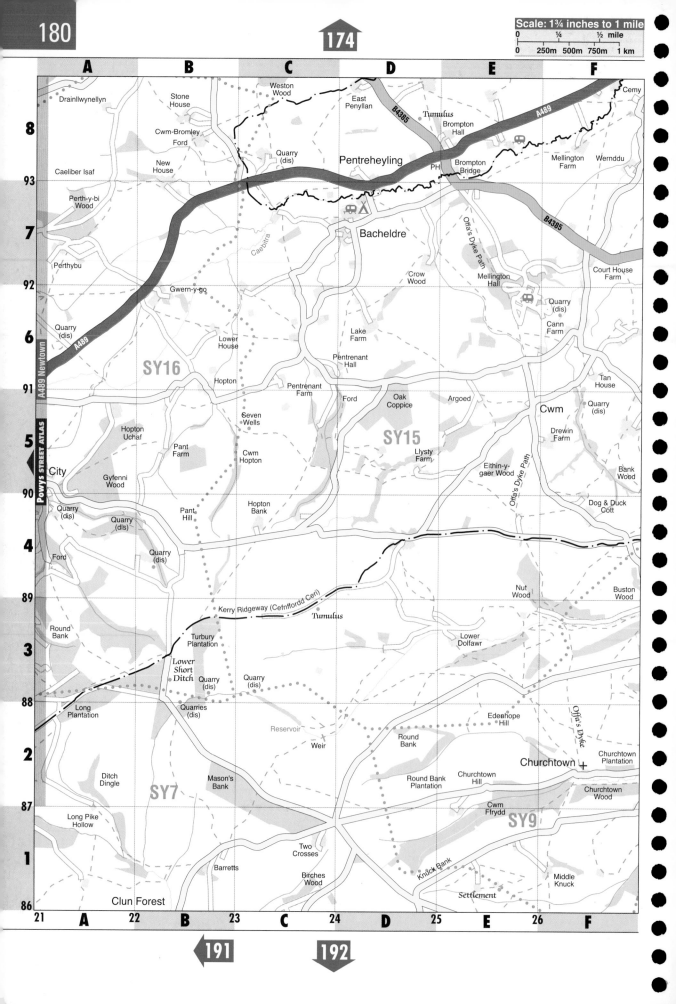

Drainllwynellyn

Stone House

Weston Wood

Weston Wood

East Penyllan

B4385

Tumulus

Brompton Hall

A489

Cemy

Cwm-Bromley Ford

Quarry (dis)

Pentreheyling

PH

Brompton Bridge

Mellington Farm

Wernddu

Caeliber Isaf

New House

Offa's Dyke Path

B4385

Perth-y-bi Wood

Bacheldre

Court House Farm

Perthybu

Caebitra

Crow Wood

Mellington Hall

Gwern-y-go

Quarry (dis)

Cann Farm

Quarry (dis)

A489

Lower House

Lake Farm

Pentrenant Hall

Tan House

SY16

Hopton

Pentrenant Farm

Ford

Oak Coppice

Argoed

Cwm

Quarry (dis)

Seven Wells

Drewin Farm

Hopton Uchaf

Pant Farm

Cwm Hopton

SY15

Llysty Farm

Eithin-y-gaer Wood

Offa's Dyke Path

Bank Wood

City

Gyfenni Wood

Pant Hill

Hopton Bank

Dog & Duck Cott

Quarry (dis)

Quarry (dis)

Ford

Quarry (dis)

Nut Wood

Buston Wood

Round Bank

Kerry Ridgeway (Cefnffordd Ceri)

Tumulus

Lower Dolfawr

Turbury Plantation

Lower Short Ditch

Quarry (dis)

Quarry (dis)

Edenhope Hill

Offa's Dyke

Long Plantation

Quarries (dis)

Reservoir

Weir

Round Bank

Churchtown

Churchtown Plantation

Ditch Dingle

Mason's Bank

Round Bank Plantation

Churchtown Hill

Churchtown Wood

SY7

Cwm Ffrydd

SY9

Long Pike Hollow

Two Crosses

Knuck Bank

Middle Knuck

Barretts

Birches Wood

Settlement

Clun Forest

Powys Street Atlas

A489 Newtown

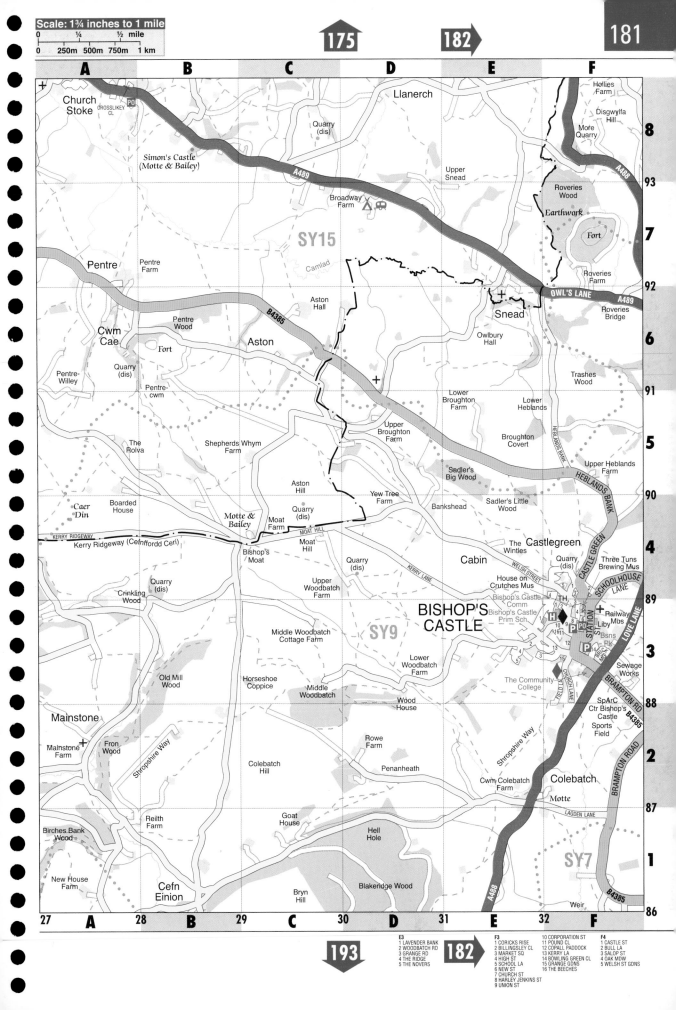

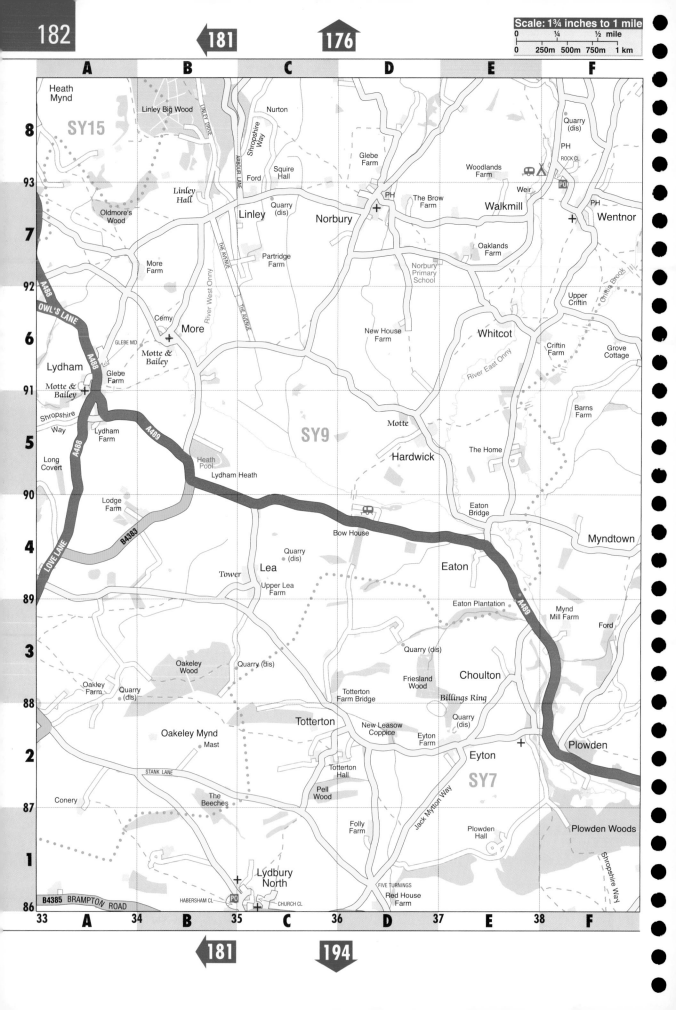

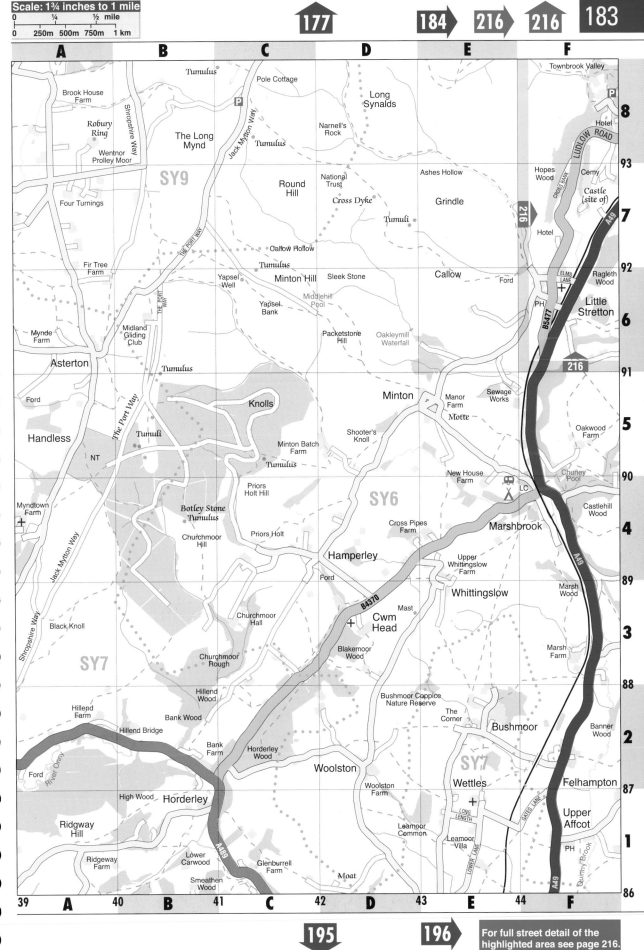

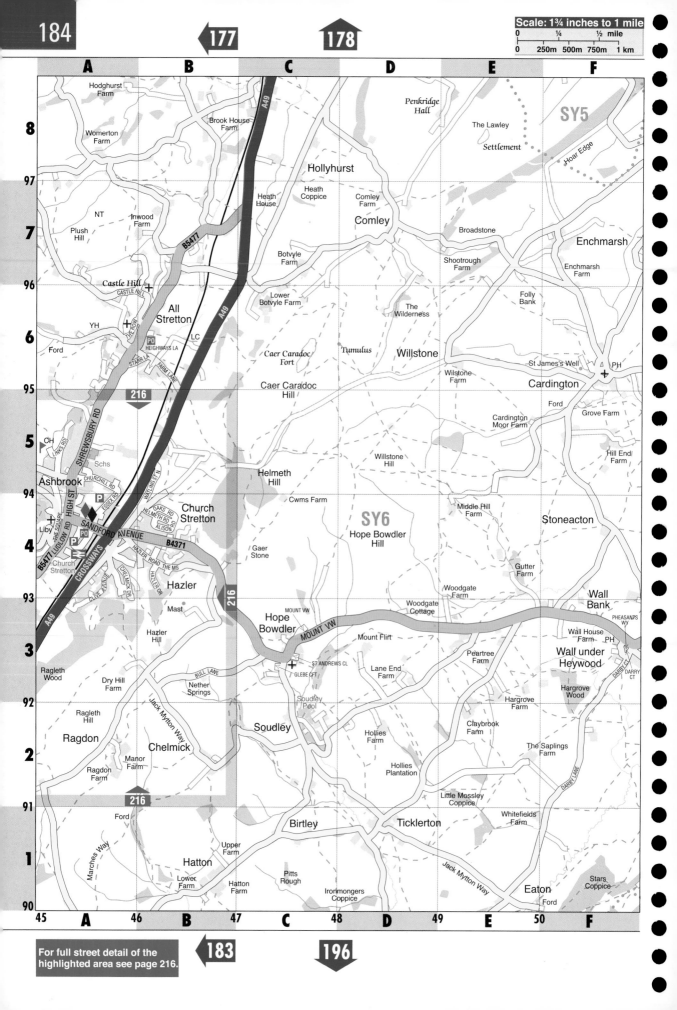

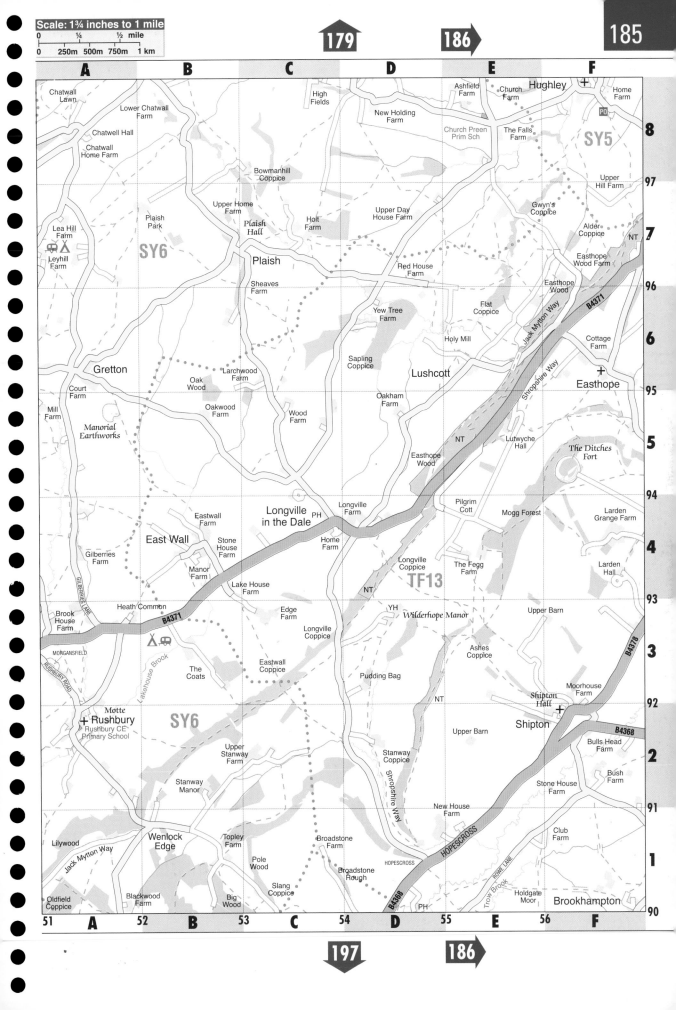

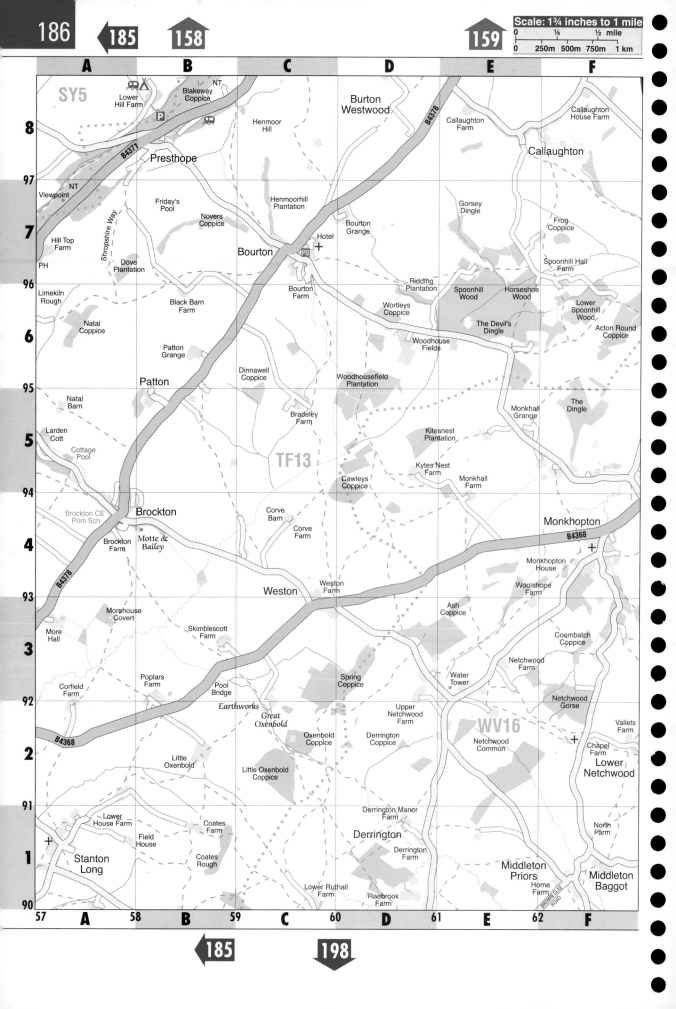

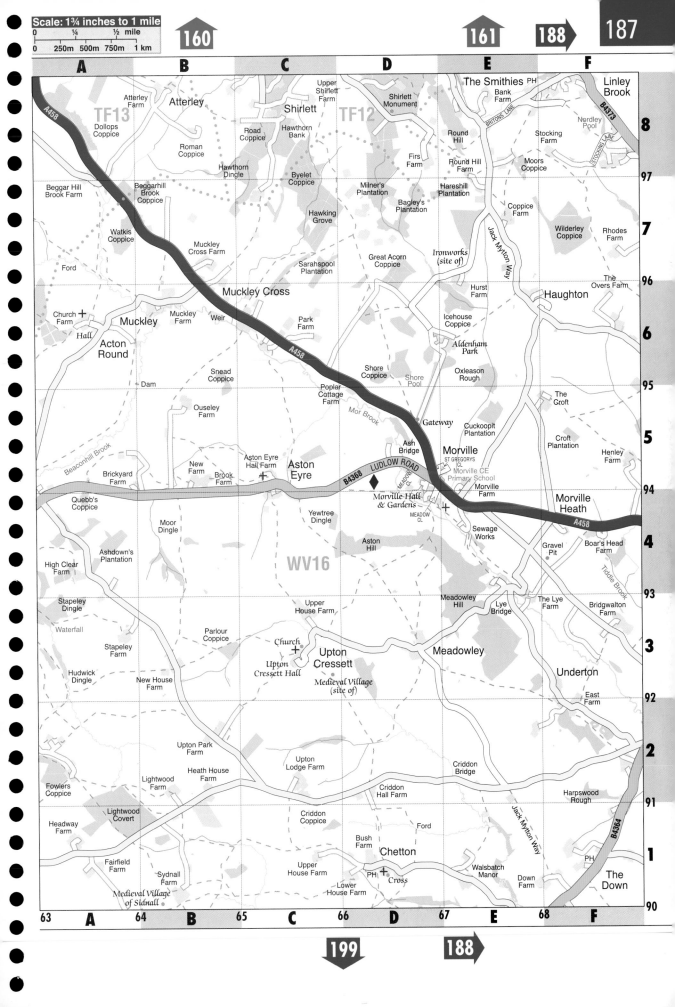

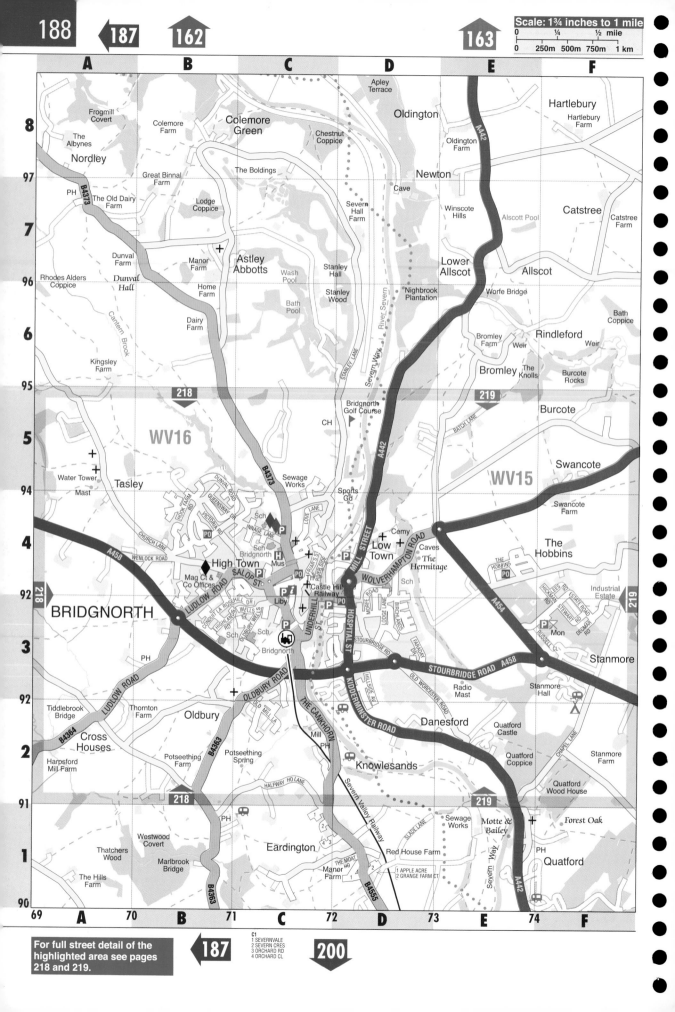

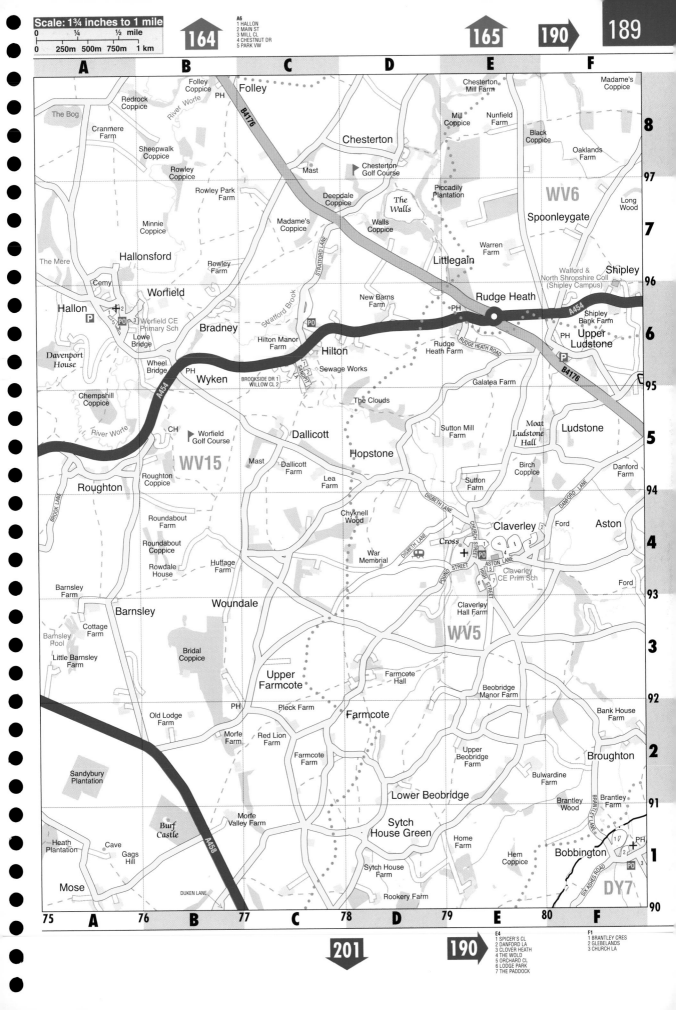

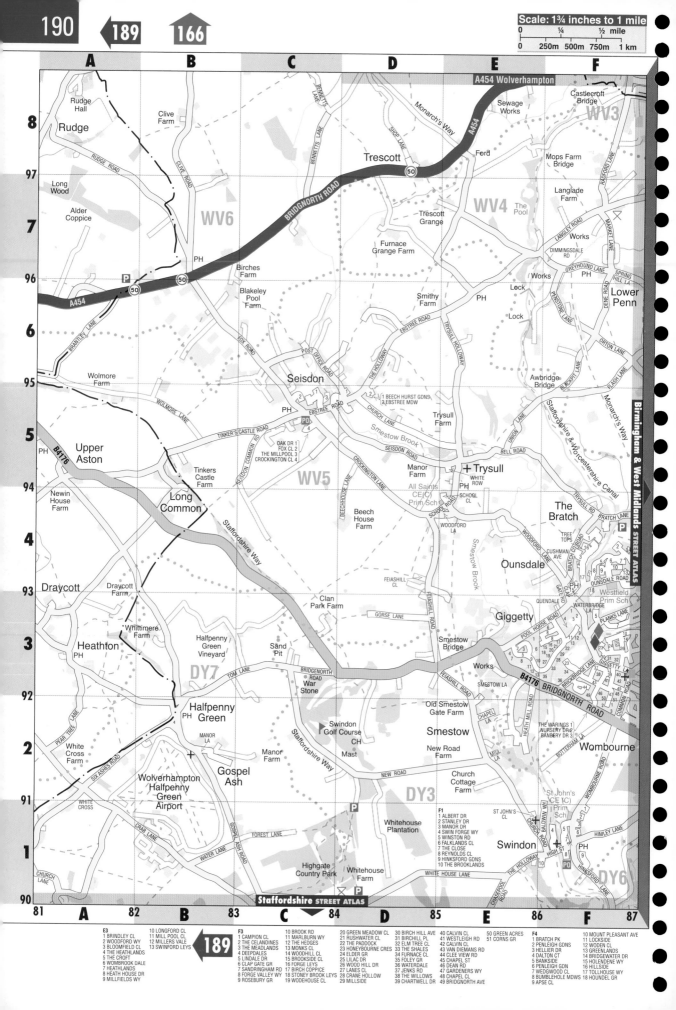

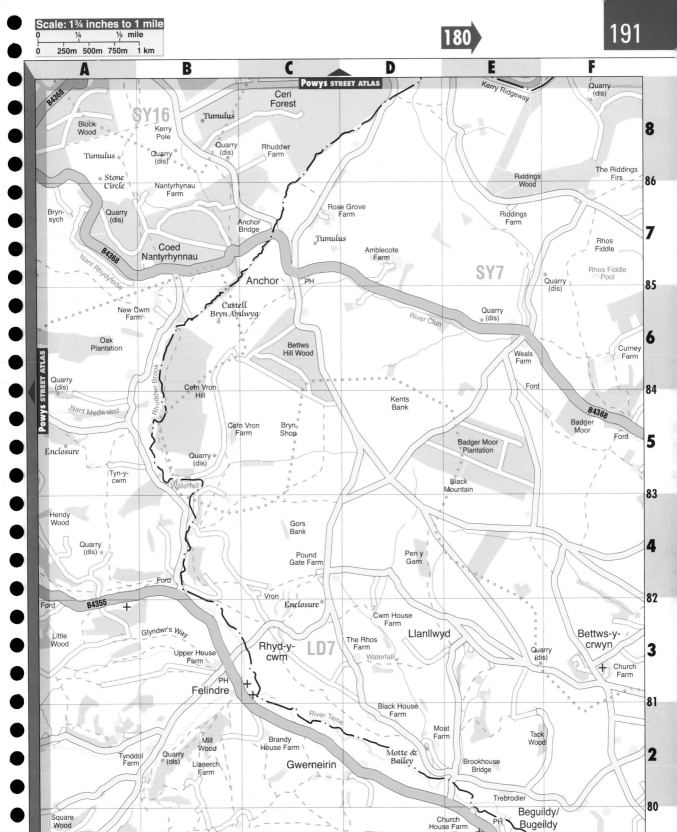

Scale: 1¾ inches to 1 mile
0   ¼   ½   mile
0   250m   500m   750m   1 km

A   B   C   D   E   F

Kerry Ridgeway

B4368

SY16

Block
Wood

Ceri
Forest

Tumulus

Quarry
(dis)

8

Kerry
Pole

Quarry
(dis)

Rhuddwr
Farm

Riddings
Wood

The Riddings
Firs

86

Tumulus

Quarry
(dis)

Nantyrhynnau
Farm

Stone
Circle

Rose Grove
Farm

Riddings
Farm

Rhos
Fiddle

7

Bryn-
sych

Anchor
Bridge

Tumulus

Amblecote
Farm

SY7

Rhos Fiddle
Pool

Quarry
(dis)

B4368

Coed
Nantyrhynnau

Anchor

PH

River Clun

Quarry
(dis)

85

Nant Rhydyfedw

Castell
Bryn Amlwyg

Quarry
(dis)

Curney
Farm

6

New Cwm
Farm

Weals
Farm

Oak
Plantation

Bettws
Hill Wood

Ford

B4368

Rhuddwr Brook

Cefn Vron
Hill

Kents
Bank

Badger
Moor

Ford

84

Quarry
(dis)

Nant Medwaled

Cefn Vron
Farm

Bryn
Shop

Badger Moor
Plantation

5

Enclosure

Quarry
(dis)

Black
Mountain

Tyn-y-
cwm

Waterfall

83

Hendy
Wood

Gors
Bank

Quarry
(dis)

Pound
Gate Farm

Pen y
Garn

4

Ford

Vron

Enclosure

82

Ford

B4355

Cwm House
Farm

Llanllwyd

Bettws-y-
crwyn

3

Little
Wood

Glyndwr's Way

The Rhos
Farm

LD7

Quarry
(dis)

Upper House
Farm

Rhyd-y-
cwm

Waterfall

Church
Farm

PH

Felindre

River Teme

Black House
Farm

81

Mill
Wood

Brandy
House Farm

Moat
Farm

Tack
Wood

2

Tynddol
Farm

Quarry
(dis)

Llanerch
Farm

Gwerneirin

Motte &
Bailey

Brookhouse
Bridge

Trebrodier

80

Square
Wood

Church
House Farm

PH

Beguildy/
Bugeildy

Hidmore

PO

1

Bailey
Wood

Glyndwr's Way

Church House
Wood

Weir

River Teme

B4355

Ford

Pantycaragle
Farm

Bwlch

Stone

79

15   A   16   B   17   C   18   D   19   E   20   F

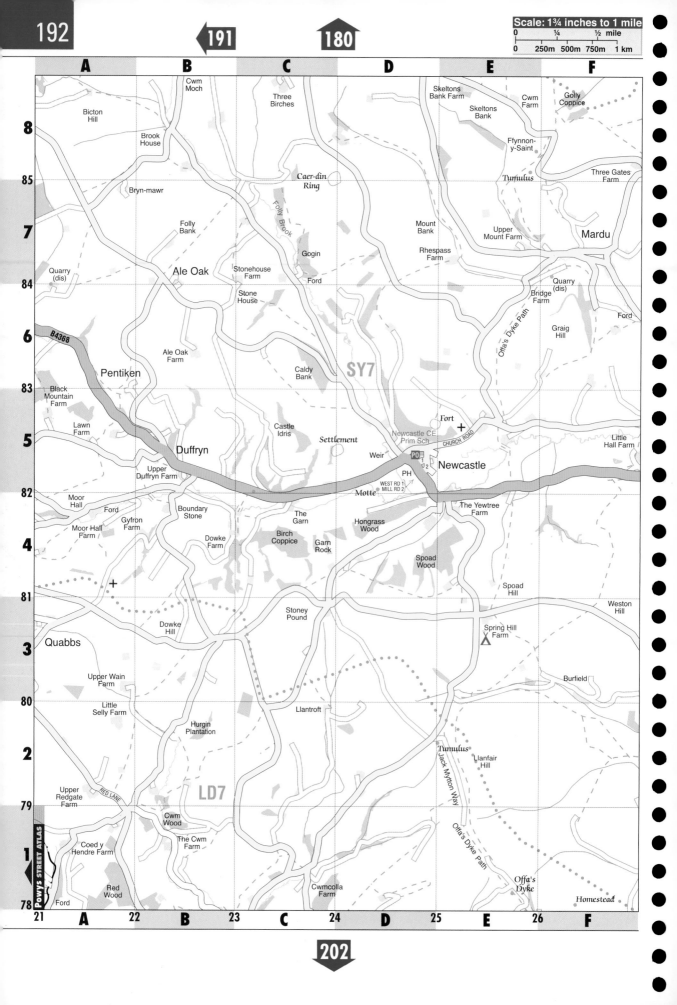

192

191

180

Scale: 1¾ inches to 1 mile

0   ¼   ½   mile
0   250m   500m   750m   1 km

A   B   C   D   E   F

8

Bicton Hill

Cwm Moch

Three Birches

Skeltons Bank Farm

Skeltons Bank

Cwm Farm

Golly Coppice

Brook House

85

Caer-din Ring

Ffynnon-y-Saint

Tumulus

Three Gates Farm

Bryn-mawr

7

Folly Bank

Mount Bank

Upper Mount Farm

Mardu

Folly Brook

Gogin

Rhespass Farm

Quarry (dis)

84

Ale Oak

Stonehouse Farm

Ford

Quarry (dis)

Bridge Farm

Ford

Stone House

6

B4368

Ale Oak Farm

Caldy Bank

SY7

Offa's Dyke Path

Graig Hill

Pentiken

83

Black Mountain Farm

Castle Idris

Settlement

Fort

Newcastle CE Prim Sch

CHURCH ROAD

Lawn Farm

5

Duffryn

Weir

PO

Newcastle

Little Hall Farm

Upper Duffryn Farm

PH

82

Moor Hall

Ford

Boundary Stone

Motte

WEST RD 1
MILL RD 2

The Yewtree Farm

Gyfron Farm

The Garn

Hongrass Wood

Moor Hall Farm

Dowke Farm

Birch Coppice

Garn Rock

Spoad Wood

4

Spoad Hill

81

Stoney Pound

Weston Hill

Dowke Hill

Spring Hill Farm

3

Quabbs

Burfield

Upper Wain Farm

Little Selly Farm

Llantroft

80

Hurgin Plantation

2

Tumulus

Llanfair Hill

Jack Mytton Way

LD7

79

Upper Redgate Farm

RED LANE

Cwm Wood

Offa's Dyke Path

1

Coed y Hendre Farm

The Cwm Farm

Offa's Dyke

Red Wood

Cwmcolla Farm

Homestead

Ford

78

21   A   22   B   23   C   24   D   25   E   26   F

POWYS STREET ATLAS

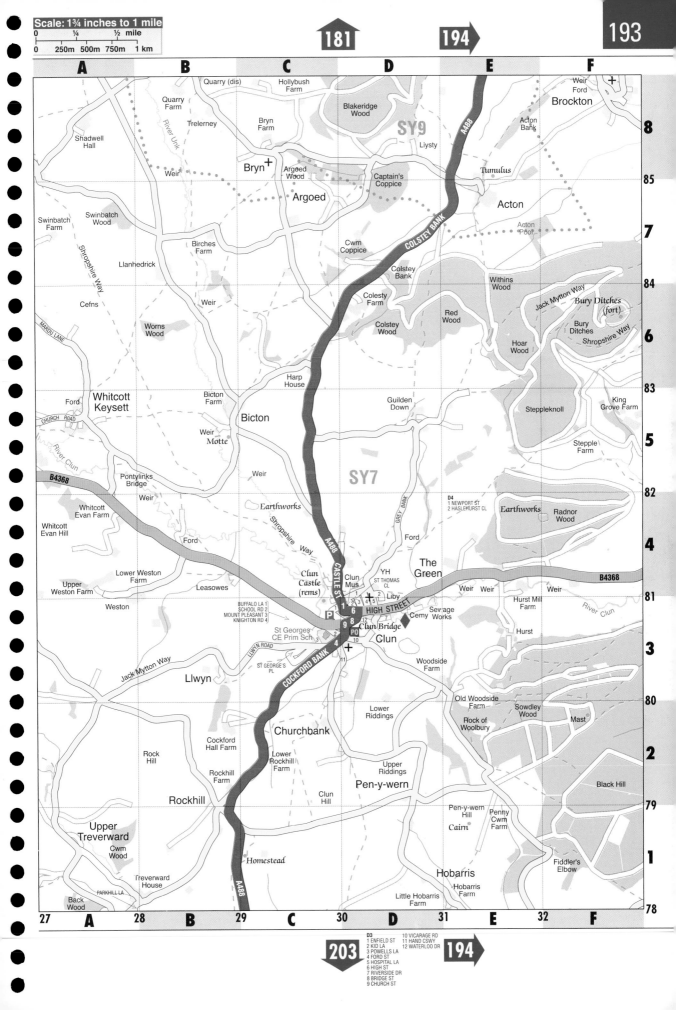

A   B   C   D   E   F

8
Quarry (dis)
Hollybush Farm
Weir Ford
Brockton
Quarry Farm
Blakeridge Wood
SY9
Acton Bank
Trelerney
Bryn Farm
A488
Shadwell Hall
River Unk
Liysty
Weir
Bryn +
Argoed Wood
Captain's Coppice
Tumulus

85
Argoed
Acton
COLSTEY BANK
Acton Pool

7
Swinbatch Farm
Swinbatch Wood
Birches Farm
Cwm Coppice
Withins Wood
Jack Mytton Way
Bury Ditches (fort)
Llanhedrick
Shropshire Way
Colstey Bank
Bury Ditches
Shropshire Way

84
Cefns
Worns Wood
Weir
Colesty Farm
Red Wood
Hoar Wood

6
Colstey Wood
MARDU LANE

Harp House
King Grove Farm

83
Whitcott Keysett
Ford
Bicton Farm
Guilden Down
Steppleknoll
CHURCH ROAD
Bicton
Weir Motte
Stepple Farm

5
River Clun
B4368
Weir
SY7
Earthworks
Radnor Wood

82
Whitcott Evan Farm
Pontylinks Bridge
Weir
Earthworks
D4
1 NEWPORT ST
2 HASLEHURST CL

Whitcott Evan Hill
Ford
Shropshire Way
A488
Ford

4
Upper Weston Farm
Lower Weston Farm
Leasowes
Clun Castle (rems)
Clun Mus
YH
ST THOMAS CL
The Green
B4368
Weston
Weir Weir Weir
Hurst Mill Farm
River Clun

81
BUFFALO LA 1
SCHOOL RD 2
MOUNT PLEASANT 3
KNIGHTON RD 4
1
5
Liby
CASTLE ST
Clun
HIGH STREET
Cemy
Sewage Works
Hurst

3
Jack Mytton Way
Llwyn
St Georges CE Prim Sch
St George's PL
LWYN ROAD
6
9
8
12
2
3
4
10
PO
Clun Bridge
Clun
11
COCKFORD BANK
Woodside Farm
Old Woodside Farm
Rock of Woolbury
Sowdley Wood
Mast

80
Rock Hill
Cockford Hall Farm
Churchbank
Lower Riddings

2
Rockhill Farm
Lower Rockhill Farm
Upper Riddings
Pen-y-wern
Black Hill
Rockhill
Clun Hill

79
Upper Treverward
Cwm Wood
Pen-y-wern Hill
Cairn
Penny Cwm Farm

1
Homestead
Fiddler's Elbow
Treverward House
A488
Hobarris
PARKHILL LA
Back Wood
Little Hobarris Farm
Hobarris Farm

27   28   29   30   31   32   78

A   B   C   D   E   F

D3
1 ENFIELD ST
2 KID LA
3 POWELLS LA
4 FORD ST
5 HOSPITAL LA
6 HIGH ST
7 RIVERSIDE DR
8 BRIDGE ST
9 CHURCH ST
10 VICARAGE RD
11 HAND CSWY
12 WATERLOO DR

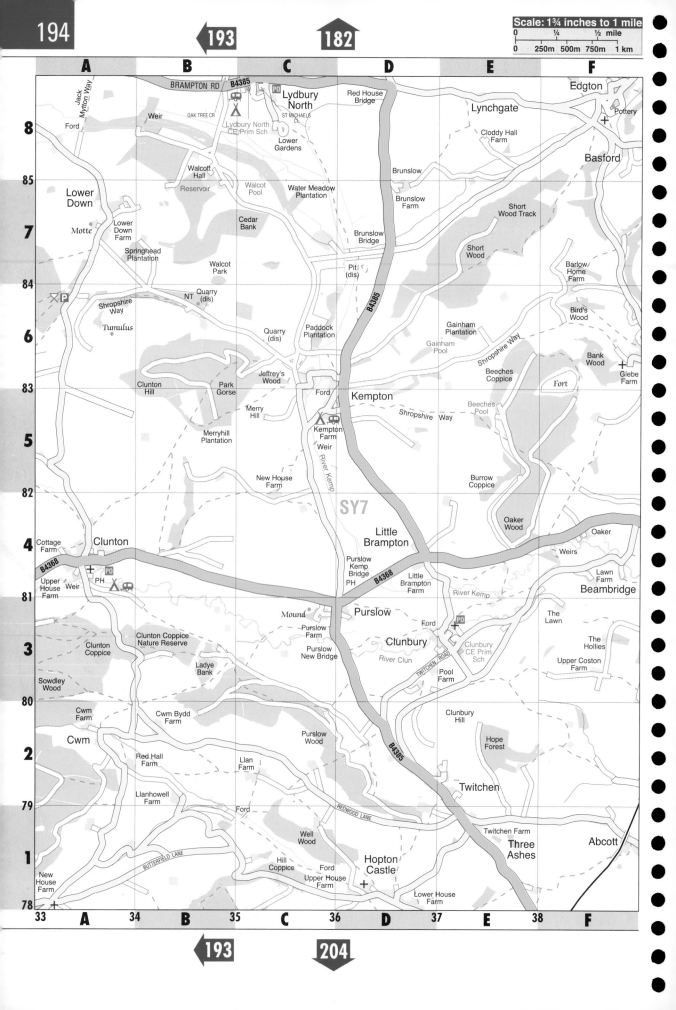

194

193

182

Scale: 1¾ inches to 1 mile

0   ¼   ½   mile

0   250m   500m   750m   1 km

A   B   C   D   E   F

8

85

7

84

6

83

5

82

4

81

3

80

2

79

1

78

Jack Mytton Way

BRAMPTON RD   B4385

Ford

Weir

OAK TREE CR

Walcott
Hall

Reservoir

Lower
Down

Motte

Lower
Down
Farm

Springhead
Plantation

Shropshire
Way

Tumulus

Lydbury North
CE Prim Sch

ST MICHAELS
CL

Lydbury
North

Lower
Gardens

Walcot
Pool

Cedar
Bank

Walcot
Park

NT   Quarry
(dis)

Quarry
(dis)

Water Meadow
Plantation

Red House
Bridge

Brunslow

Brunslow
Farm

Brunslow
Bridge

Lynchgate

Cloddy Hall
Farm

Edgton

Pottery

Basford

Short
Wood Track

Short
Wood

Barlow/
Home
Farm

Bird's
Wood

Bank
Wood

Glebe
Farm

Gainham
Plantation

Gainham
Pool

Shropshire Way

Beeches
Coppice

Fort

Pit
(dis)

B4385

P

Clunton
Hill

Park
Gorse

Jeffrey's
Wood

Merry
Hill

Merryhill
Plantation

Paddock
Plantation

Ford

Kempton

Shropshire   Way

Beeches
Pool

New House
Farm

Kempton
Farm

Weir

River Kemp

SY7

Burrow
Coppice

Oaker
Wood

Cottage
Farm

Clunton

B4368

Upper
House
Farm

Weir

PH   P

Little
Brampton

Purslow
Kemp
Bridge
PH

B4368

Little
Brampton
Farm

River Kemp

Oaker

Weirs

Lawn
Farm

Beambridge

Clunton Coppice
Nature Reserve

Clunton
Coppice

Ladye
Bank

Mound

Purslow
Farm

Purslow
New Bridge

Purslow

Clunbury

River Clun

Ford

Clunbury
CE Prim
Sch

Pool
Farm

PO

The
Lawn

The
Hollies

Upper Coston
Farm

Sowdley
Wood

Cwm
Farm

Cwm Bydd
Farm

Cwm

Red Hall
Farm

Llanhowell
Farm

Llan
Farm

Ford

Purslow
Wood

B4385

Clunbury
Hill

Hope
Forest

Twitchen

Twitchen Farm

Three
Ashes

Abcott

New
House
Farm

BUTTERFIELD LANE

Hill
Coppice

Well
Wood

Ford   Upper House
Farm

REDWOOD LANE

Hopton
Castle

Lower House
Farm

33   A   34   B   35   C   36   D   37   E   38   F

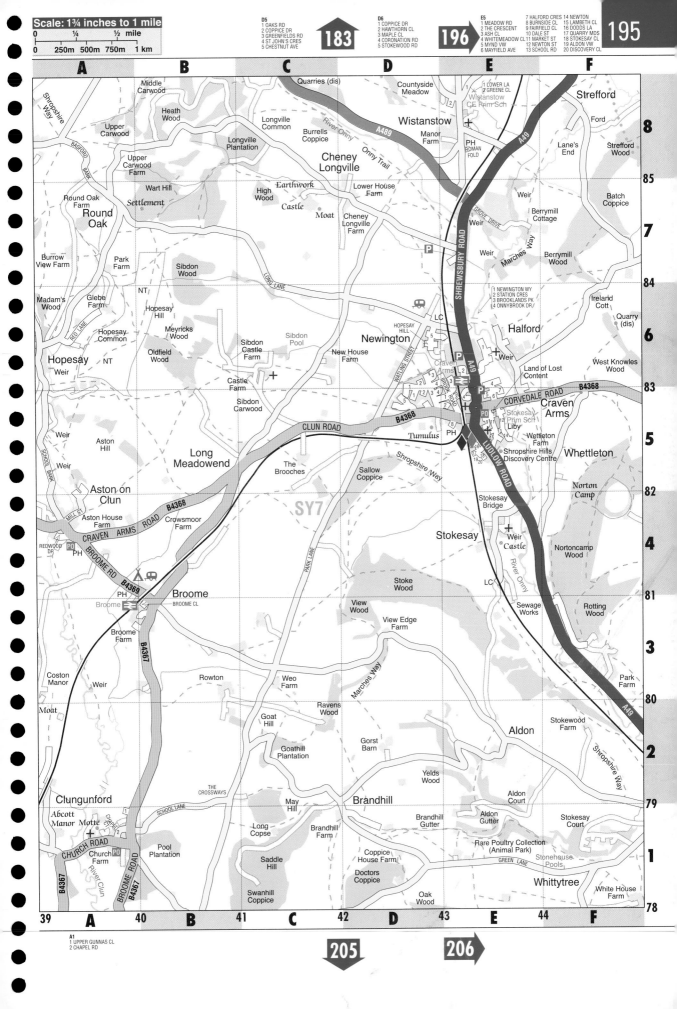

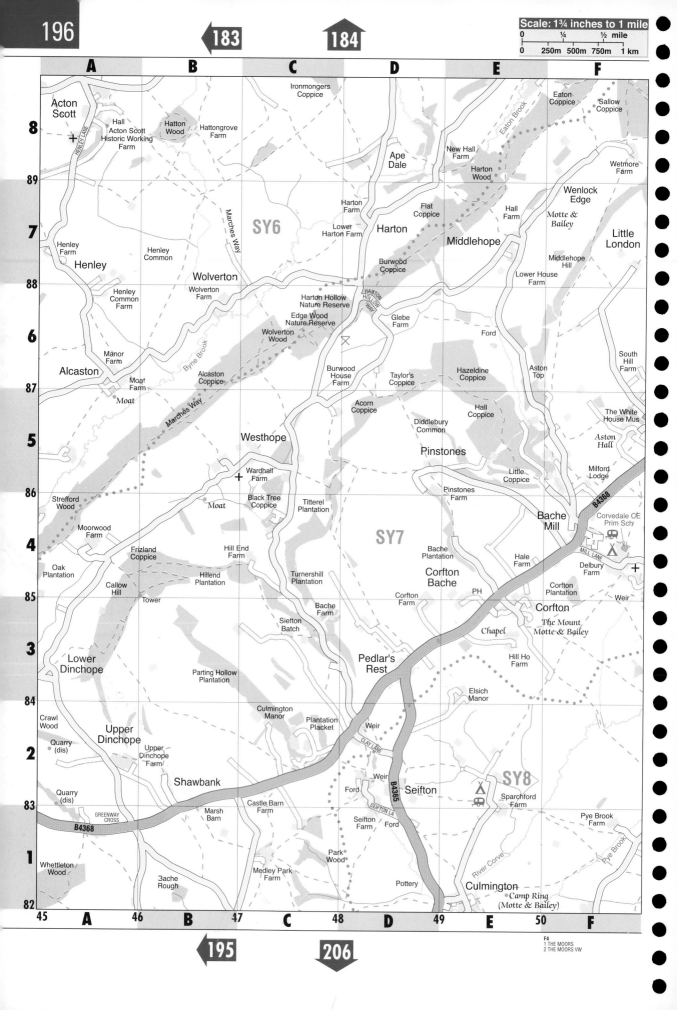

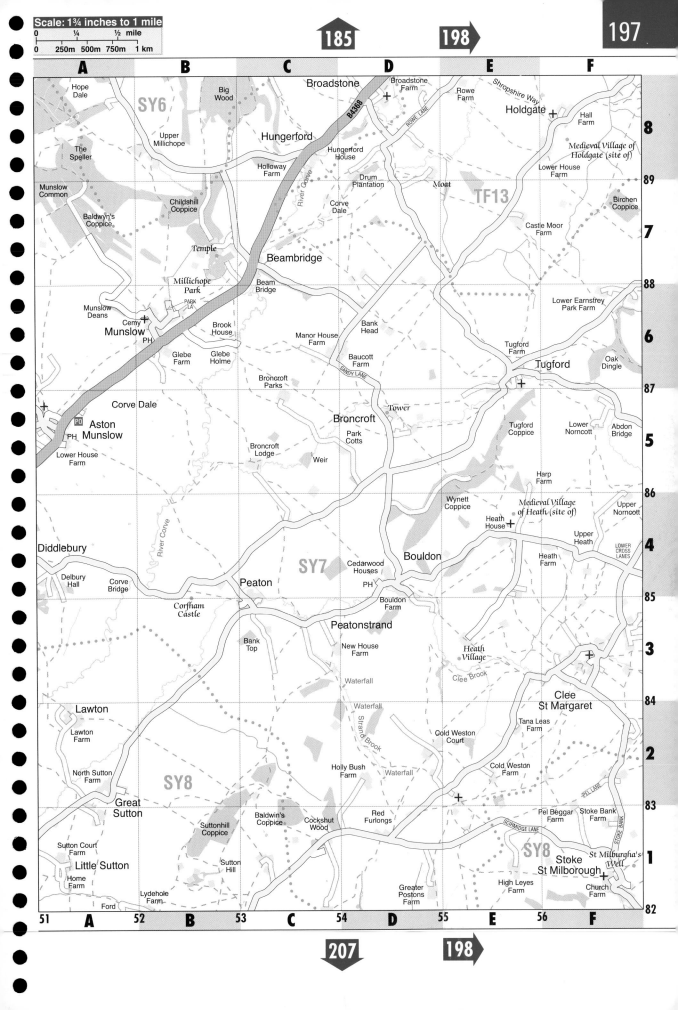

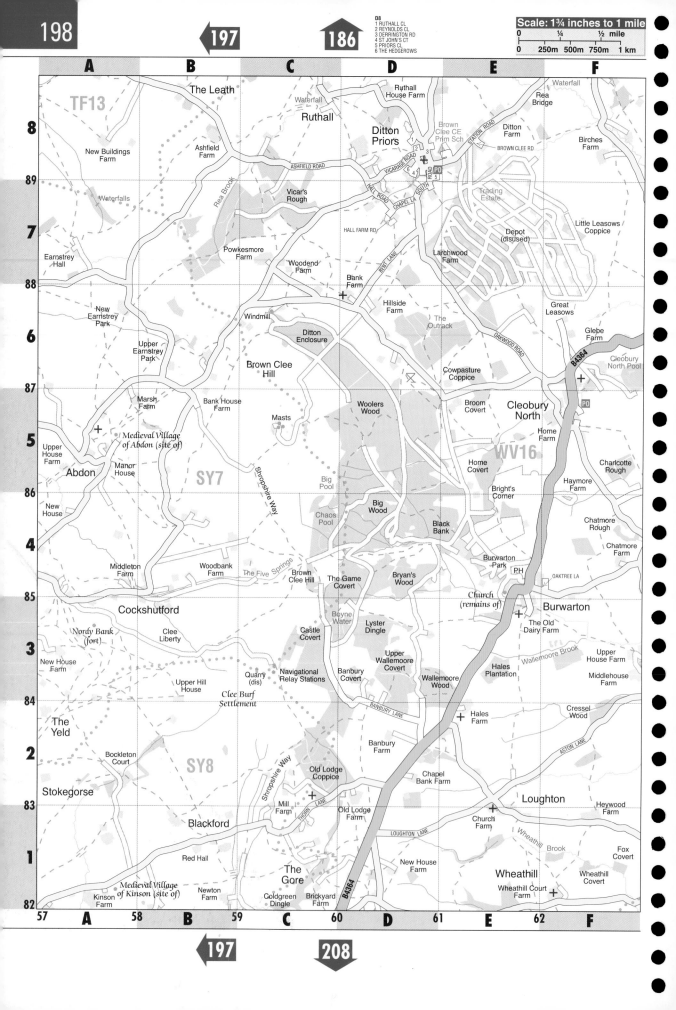

197
186

197
208

Scale: 1¾ inches to 1 mile
0   ¼   ½ mile
0   250m   500m   750m   1 km

D8
1 RUTHALL CL
2 REYNOLDS CL
3 DERRINGTON RD
4 ST JOHN'S CT
5 PRIORS CL
6 THE HEDGEROWS

TF13

The Leath

New Buildings Farm

Ashfield Farm

Waterfalls

Rea Brook

Ruthall

ASHFIELD ROAD

Vicar's Rough

Waterfall

Ruthall House Farm

Rea Bridge

Waterfall

Ditton Priors

Brown Clee CE Prim Sch

Ditton Farm

BROWN CLEE RD

Birches Farm

STATION ROAD

VICARAGE ROAD

PO

Trading Estate

Little Leasows Coppice

Earnstrey Hall

New Earnstrey Park

Upper Earnstrey Park

Powkesmore Farm

Windmill

Ditton Enclosure

Brown Clee Hill

Marsh Farm

Bank House Farm

Masts

Upper House Farm

Abdon

Medieval Village of Abdon (site of)

Manor House

New House

SY7

Shropshire Way

Big Pool

Chaos Pool

Middleton Farm

Woodbank Farm

The Five Springs

Brown Clee Hill

Cockshutford

Nordy Bank (fort)

Clee Liberty

New House Farm

Upper Hill House

Quarry (dis)

Clee Burf Settlement

The Yeld

Bockleton Court

SY8

Shropshire Way

Stokegorse

Blackford

Mill Farm

Old Lodge Coppice

Red Hall

Newton Farm

Medieval Village of Kinson (site of)

Kinson Farm

The Gore

Coldgreen Dingle

Brickyard Farm

B4364

Woodend Farm

Hall Farm Rd

HALL ROAD

CHAPEL LA

Bank Farm

BOAT LANE

Larchwood Farm

Hillside Farm

The Outrack

Depot (disused)

Great Leasows

OAKWOOD ROAD

Glebe Farm

B4364

Cleobury North Pool

Cowpasture Coppice

Woolers Wood

Broom Covert

Cleobury North

WV16

Home Farm

Charlcotte Rough

Home Covert

Bright's Corner

Haymore Farm

Big Wood

Black Bank

Chatmore Rough

Chatmore Farm

Bryan's Wood

Burwarton Park

PH

OAKTREE LA

The Game Covert

Boyne Water

Lyster Dingle

Church (remains of)

Burwarton

The Old Dairy Farm

Upper House Farm

Middlehouse Farm

Castle Covert

Upper Wallemoore Covert

Wallemoore Wood

Hales Plantation

Wallemoore Brook

Navigational Relay Stations

Banbury Covert

BANBURY LANE

Hales Farm

Cressel Wood

Banbury Farm

Chapel Bank Farm

ASTON LANE

New House Farm

THORN LANE

Old Lodge Farm

Church Farm

Loughton

Heywood Farm

LOUGHTON LANE

Wheathill Brook

Fox Covert

Wheathill

Wheathill Court Farm

Wheathill Covert

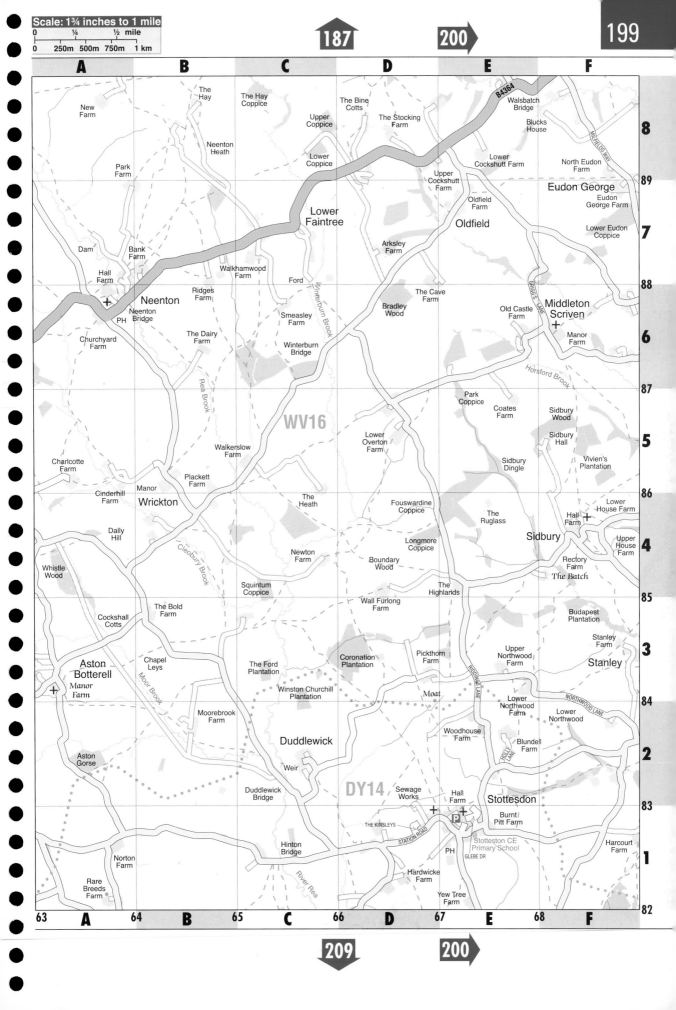

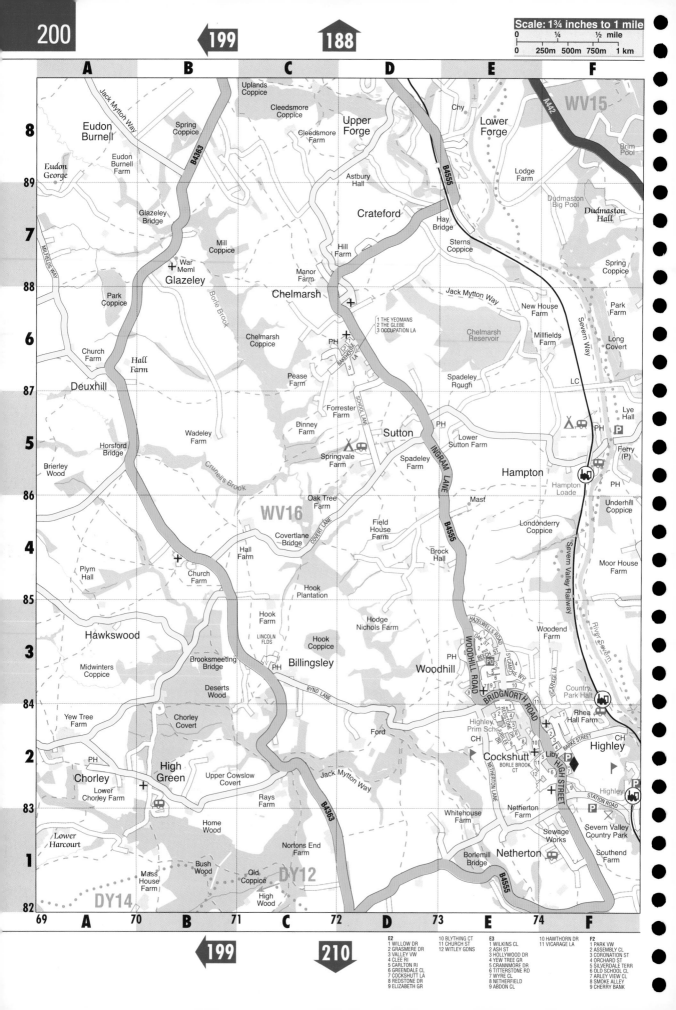

A   B   C   D   E   F

8
Comer Wood
DY7
Alder Farm
Rookery Farm
Gatacre Park Farm
Bobbington Hall
Works
Bine Farm
Broad Oak Wood
Gatacre Park
Wooton
Ford
PH
Broad Lanes
Broad Oak
College Farm

89
Seggy Pool
Wall Pool

7
PO Quatt Bridge
The Dower House School
Broad Lanes Farm
A458
Six Ashes
PH
Hay Farm
+ Quatt
Wooton Dingle
Tuckhill
New Plantation
Quatt Farm
Tuckhill Farm
Grove Farm
MERE LANE

88
Wallrea Coppice
Ridneyhill Wood
Kings Nordley Farm
+ Tuckhill Farm
Crump Hillocks Farm
Four Ashes
White Well
A458 Stourbridge

6
Long Covert
Birchen Coppice
The Lodge Farm
Bradbury's Farm
Coxgreen
BRADBURY LANE
MORFE LANE

Works
HOLLOW ASH LANE
Coton Farm
Keeper's Covert
Lindridge Farm
BATSELD LANE

87
Burntcroft Coppice
Coton Lane
Coton Hall
WV15
Lanegreen Farm
Beauty Bank Farm
DY7

5
Hampton Loade
Green House
Astley Farm
Astley
Chidleys Farm
Moat
The Hollies
HOLLIES LANE

86
Butter Cross
Lake House
Allum Bridge
Filletts
Leybrook Coppice
SHEEPWALKS LANE

4
Waterfall
PH
Birdsgreen
Perryhouse Dingle
Cains Coppice
No Man's Green
New Barns Farm
Turleygreen
PH
Bowhills Farm
Bowhills Dingle
Square Coppice
Top Gorse
HERONS GATE ROAD
NO MAN'S GN LA

85
Alveley Prim Sch
COOKSCROSS
BIRCH RD
DADDLEBROOK ROAD
BRIDGE RD

3
Alveley Industrial Estate
PH
PO
VICARAGE BANK
Alveley
Severn Valley Country Park
Moat
Fenn Green
Cross Farm
Hartsgreen
Hartsgreen Farm
Heath House Farm
Compton Park Farm

2
Visitor Centre
High House Farm
SHAM LANE
Ladypitt Farm
Lower House Farm
BEACON LANE
Hightrees Farm
BEACON LANE

84
Little London Coppice
May House Farm
Romsley
Tudor House
Brittle's Farm
Start's Green Farm

83
Stanley
Butts Farm
A442
LOWE LANE
Pool House Farm
PH
ROMSLEY LANE
Arley Wood
Reservoir
Goldridge Wood

1
Severn Way
Hextons Farm
Far Things
LOWE LANE
Lowe Farm
DY12
DY11

82

A   B   C   D   E   F
75   76   77   78   79   80

B3
1 MAPLE CRES
2 LIME CL
3 CEDAR CL
4 HONEYBOURNE RD
5 THE LEA
6 ROMSLEY VW
7 HOLME ORCH
8 HAZELGROVE
9 MALLARDS CL
10 GREEN LEYS CRES
11 ARDEN WY
12 MEADOWBROOK CL
13 CHURCH RD
14 WHITTAL CL
15 CHAPEL RD
16 SEABRIGHT WY
17 GOLDEN ACRES
18 CENTRE PL

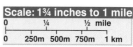

Scale: 1¾ inches to 1 mile

0   ¼   ½   mile
0   250m   500m   750m   1 km

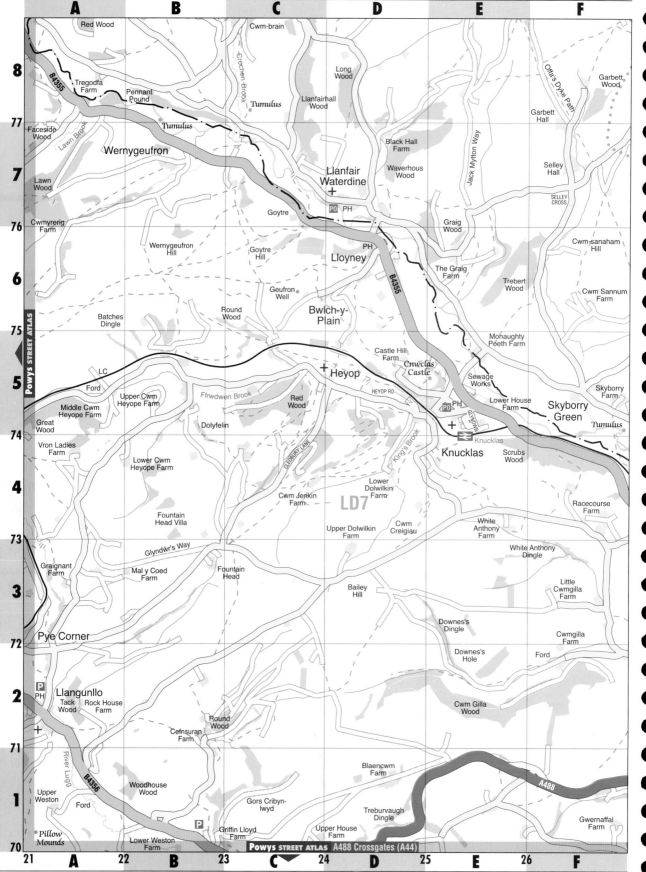

B4355
Red Wood
Tregodfa Farm
Pennant Pound
Faceside Wood
Lawn Brook
Wernygeufron
Tumulus
Cwmyrerig Farm
Lawn Wood
Wernygeufron Hill
Batches Dingle
Cwm-brain
Crochen Brook
Tumulus
Goytre Hill
Round Wood
Goytre
Long Wood
Llanfairhall Wood
Llanfair Waterdine
PO PH
Lloyney
Geufron Well
Bwlch-y-Plain
Black Hall Farm
Waverhous Wood
PH
B4355
Graig Wood
The Graig Farm
Jack Mytton Way
Garbett Hall
Selley Hall
SELLEY CROSS
Garbett Wood
Offa's Dyke Path
Cwm-sanaham Hill
Cwm Sannum Farm
Trebert Wood
Monaughty Poeth Farm
Castle Hill Farm
Cnwclas Castle
Sewage Works
Skyborry Farm
Skyborry Green
Tumulus
Heyop
HEYOP RD
PH
PO
Lower House Farm
Scrubs Wood
GT NEWP RD
Knucklas
Knucklas
Racecourse Farm

Powys STREET ATLAS

LC
Ford
Middle Cwm Heyope Farm
Upper Cwm Heyope Farm
Great Wood
Vron Ladies Farm
Lower Cwm Heyope Farm
Ffrwdwen Brook
Dolyfelin
Red Wood
Cwm Jenkin Farm
CLEOBURY LANE
King's Brook
Lower Dolwilkin Farm
LD7
Upper Dolwilkin Farm
Cwm Creigiau
White Anthony Farm
White Anthony Dingle
Little Cwmgilla Farm
Cwmgilla Farm
Ford

Fountain Head Villa
Glyndŵr's Way
Graignant Farm
Mal y Coed Farm
Fountain Head
Bailey Hill
Downes's Dingle
Downes's Hole
Pye Corner
P
PH
Llangunllo
Tack Wood
Rock House Farm
Cefnsuran Farm
Round Wood
Cwm Gilla Wood
River Lugg
B4356
Woodhouse Wood
Upper Weston
Ford
Pillow Mounds
Lower Weston Farm
P
Griffin Lloyd Farm
Gors Cribyn-lwyd
Treburvaugh Dingle
Upper House Farm
Blaencwm Farm
A488
Gwernaffal Farm

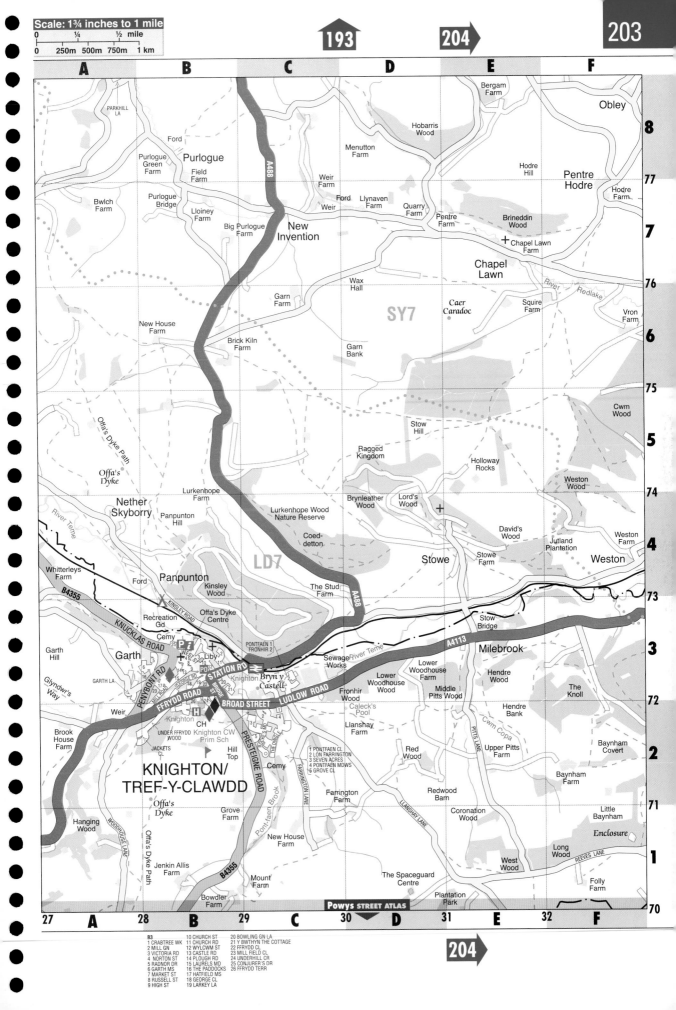

Scale: 1¾ inches to 1 mile

0   ¼   ½ mile
0 250m 500m 750m 1 km

A B C D E F

8
77
7
76
6
75
5
74
4
73
3
72
2
71
1
70

Obley

Bergam Farm

Hobarris Wood

Menutton Farm

Pentre Hodre

Hodre Hill

Hodre Farm

Weir Farm

Ford

Weir

Llynaven Farm

Quarry Farm

Pentre Farm

Brineddin Wood

Chapel Lawn Farm

Vron Farm

Wax Hall

Chapel Lawn

River Redlake

Garn Farm

SY7

Caer Caradoc

Squire Farm

Purlogue

Purlogue Green Farm

Field Farm

PARKHILL LA

Ford

Bwlch Farm

Purlogue Bridge

Lloiney Farm

Big Purlogue Farm

New Invention

A488

New House Farm

Brick Kiln Farm

Garn Bank

Stow Hill

Cwm Wood

Ragged Kingdom

Holloway Rocks

Weston Wood

Offa's Dyke Path

Offa's Dyke

Lurkenhope Farm

Brynleather Wood

Lord's Wood

David's Wood

Jutland Plantation

Weston Farm

Weston

Nether Skyborry

Panpunton Hill

Lurkenhope Wood Nature Reserve

Coed-detton

LD7

Stowe

Stowe Farm

River Teme

Whitterleys Farm

Panpunton

Kinsley Wood

The Stud Farm

A488

Stow Bridge

B4355

Ford

Weir

KINSLEY ROAD

Recreation Gd

Offa's Dyke Centre

PONTFAEN 1
FRONHIR 2

Sewage Works

River Teme

A4113

Milebrook

Lower Woodhouse Farm

Hendre Wood

The Knoll

Cemy

KNUCKLAS ROAD

Garth

Garth Hill

GARTH LA

Glyndwr's Way

PENYBONT RD

STATION RD

Knighton

Bryn y Castell

Ludlow Road

Fronhir Wood

Lower Woodhouse Wood

Middle Pitts Wood

Hendre Bank

BROAD STREET

FFRYDD ROAD

Knighton

CH

Caleck's Pool

Llanshay Farm

Cwm Copa

Hendre Bank

Upper Pitts Farm

Baynham Covert

UNDER FFRYDD WOOD

Knighton CW Prim Sch

JACKETS CL

Hill Top

Cemy

1 PONTFAEN CL
2 LON FARRINGTON
3 SEVEN ACRES
4 PONTFAEN MDWS
5 GROVE CL

Red Wood

Redwood Barn

Baynham Farm

PITTS LANE

KNIGHTON/
TREF-Y-CLAWDD

Offa's Dyke

Grove Farm

Farrington Farm

LLANSHAY LANE

Coronation Wood

Little Baynham

Hanging Wood

WOODHOUSE LANE

Offa's Dyke Path

New House Farm

West Wood

Long Wood

REEVES LANE

Enclosure

Brook House Farm

PRESTEIGNE ROAD

Pont-faen Brook

FARRINGTON LANE

Jenkin Allis Farm

B4355

Mount Farm

Bowdler Farm

The Spaceguard Centre

Plantation Park

Folly Farm

27 A 28 B 29 C 30 D 31 E 32 F

B3
1 CRABTREE WK
2 MILL GN
3 VICTORIA RD
4 NORTON ST
5 RADNOR DR
6 GARTH MS
7 MARKET ST
8 RUSSELL ST
9 HIGH ST
10 CHURCH ST
11 CHURCH RD
12 WYLCWM ST
13 CASTLE RD
14 PLOUGH RD
15 LAURELS MD
16 THE PADDOCKS
17 HATFIELD MS
18 GEORGE CL
19 LARKEY LA
20 BOWLING GN LA
21 Y BWTHYN THE COTTAGE
22 FFRYDD CL
23 MILL FIELD CL
24 UNDERHILL CR
25 CONJURER'S DR
26 FFRYDD TERR

C5
1 CHESTNUT MD
2 DOG KENNEL LA
3 OLD BEDSTONE RD
4 LADYWELL
5 REDLAKE MD

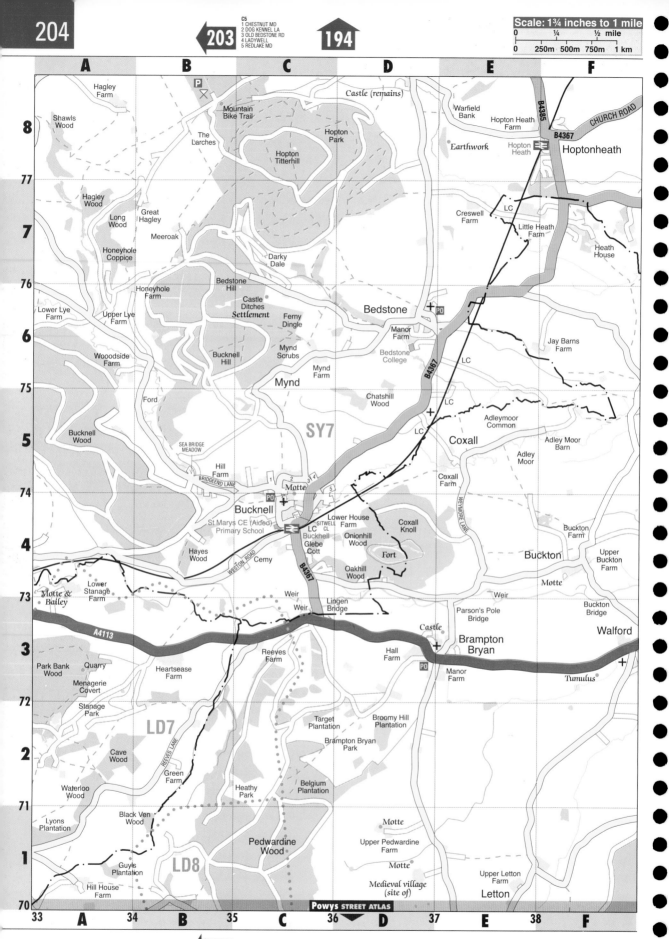

Shawls Wood
Hagley Farm
Hagley Wood
Long Wood
Great Hagley
Meeroak
Honeyhole Coppice
Lower Lye Farm
Upper Lye Farm
Honeyhole Farm
Wooodside Farm
Bucknell Wood
Ford
The Larches
Mountain Bike Trail
Hopton Titterhill
Hopton Park
Castle (remains)
Bedstone Hill
Castle Ditches
Settlement
Ferny Dingle
Mynd Scrubs
Mynd Farm
Bucknell Hill
Mynd
SY7
Hill Farm
SEA BRIDGE MEADOW
BRIDGEEND LANE
Motte
Bucknell
St Marys CE (Aided) Primary School
WESTON ROAD
Cemy
Hayes Wood
Bucknell Glebe Cott
Lower House Farm
Onionhill Wood
Coxall Knoll
Coxall Farm
Oakhill Wood
Fort
Lingen Bridge
Weir
Weir
Motte & Bailey
Lower Stanage Farm
A4113
Park Bank Wood
Quarry
Menagerie Covert
Heartsease Farm
Stanage Park
LD7
REEVES LANE
Cave Wood
Green Farm
Waterloo Wood
Lyons Plantation
Black Ven Wood
LD8
Guy's Plantation
Hill House Farm
Heathy Park
Pedwardine Wood
Reeves Farm
Target Plantation
Belgium Plantation
Brampton Bryan Park
Broomy Hill Plantation
Hall Farm
Manor Farm
Brampton Bryan
Castle
Parson's Pole Bridge
Weir
Buckton Bridge
Buckton
Motte
Buckton Farm
Upper Buckton Farm
Walford
WEYMORE LANE
Coxall
Adleymoor Common
Adley Moor
Adley Moor Barn
Warfield Bank
Earthwork
Hopton Heath Farm
Hopton Heath
Hoptonheath
B4385
B4367
CHURCH ROAD
Creswell Farm
Little Heath Farm
Heath House
Jay Barns Farm
Bedstone
Manor Farm
Bedstone College
Chatshill Wood
LC
LC
LC
LC
LC
B4367
Tumulus
Motte
Upper Pedwardine Farm
Motte
Medieval village (site of)
Upper Letton Farm
Letton

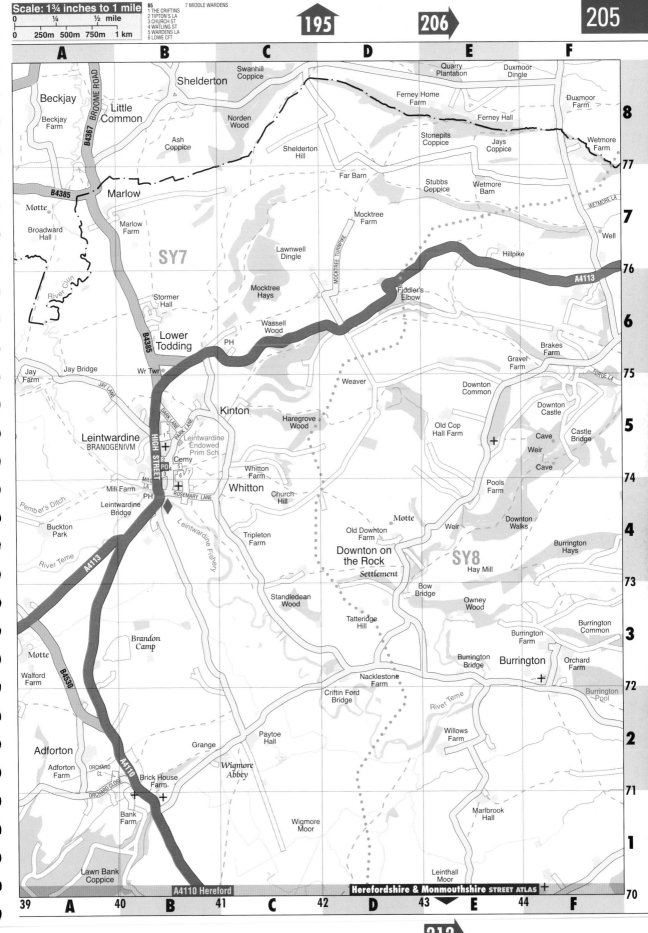

Scale: 1¾ inches to 1 mile
0   ¼   ½   mile
0   250m 500m 750m 1 km

B5
1 THE CRIFTINS
2 TIPTON'S LA
3 CHURCH ST
4 WATLING ST
5 WARDENS LA
6 LOWE CFT
7 MIDDLE WARDENS

A   B   C   D   E   F

Beckjay
Beckjay
Farm

Shelderton
Swanhill
Coppice

Little
Common

BROOME ROAD
B4367

Ash
Coppice

Norden
Wood

Shelderton
Hill

Quarry
Plantation

Duxmoor
Dingle

Ferney Home
Farm

Duxmoor
Farm

Ferney Hall

Stonepits
Coppice

Jays
Coppice

Wetmore
Farm

8

B4385

Marlow

Far Barn

Stubbs
Coppice

Wetmore
Barn

Wetmore
Barn

WETMORE LA

77

Motte

Marlow
Farm

SY7

Mocktree
Farm

Mocktree
Hays

Lawnwell
Dingle

MOCKTREE TURNPIKE

Hillpike

Well

A4113

7

Broadward
Hall

River Clun

Stormer
Hall

Lower
Todding

B4385

Wassell
Wood

PH

Fiddler's
Elbow

76

Jay
Farm

Jay Bridge

Wr Twr

Weaver

Brakes
Farm

Gravel
Farm

FORGE LA

6

JAY LANE

Kinton

Haregrove
Wood

Downton
Common

Downton
Castle

Cave

Castle
Bridge

75

Leintwardine
BRANOGENIVM

DARK LANE

PARK LANE

HIGH STREET

Leintwardine
Endowed
Prim Sch

Old Cop
Hall Farm

Cave

Weir

5

Mill Farm

Cemy
PO

Whitton
Farm

Pools
Farm

Downton
Walks

Leintwardine
Bridge

PH

MILL LA

ROSEMARY LANE

Whitton

Church
Hill

Motte

Weir

Hay Mill

SY8

Burrington
Hays

4

Pember's Ditch

Buckton
Park

Tripleton
Farm

Old Downton
Farm

Downton on
the Rock

Burrington
Common

73

River Teme

A4113

Leintwardine Fishery

Standledean
Wood

Settlement

Bow
Bridge

Owney
Wood

Burrington
Farm

Burrington
Bridge

Burrington

Orchard
Farm

72

Brandon
Camp

Tatteridge
Hill

Nacklestone
Farm

Burrington
Pool

3

Motte

Walford
Farm

B4530

Criftin Ford
Bridge

River Teme

2

Adforton

Grange

Paytoe
Hall

Willows
Farm

Adforton
Farm

ORCHARD
CL

Brick House
Farm

Wigmore
Abbey

Marlbrook
Hall

71

A4110

ORCHARD CLOSE

Bank
Farm

Wigmore
Moor

1

Lawn Bank
Coppice

Leinthall
Moor

70

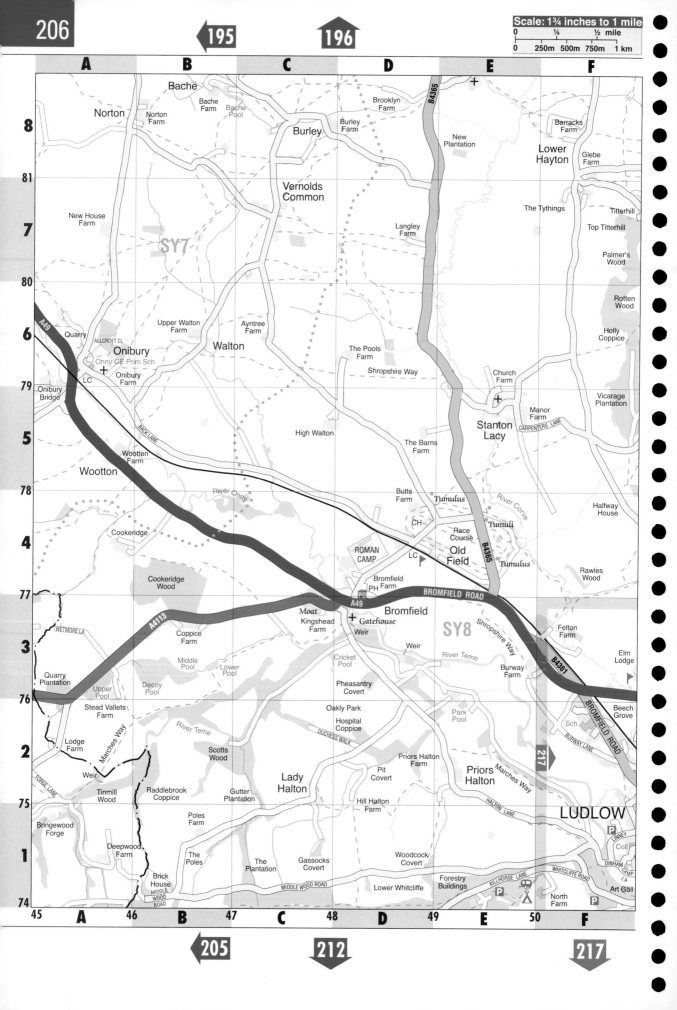

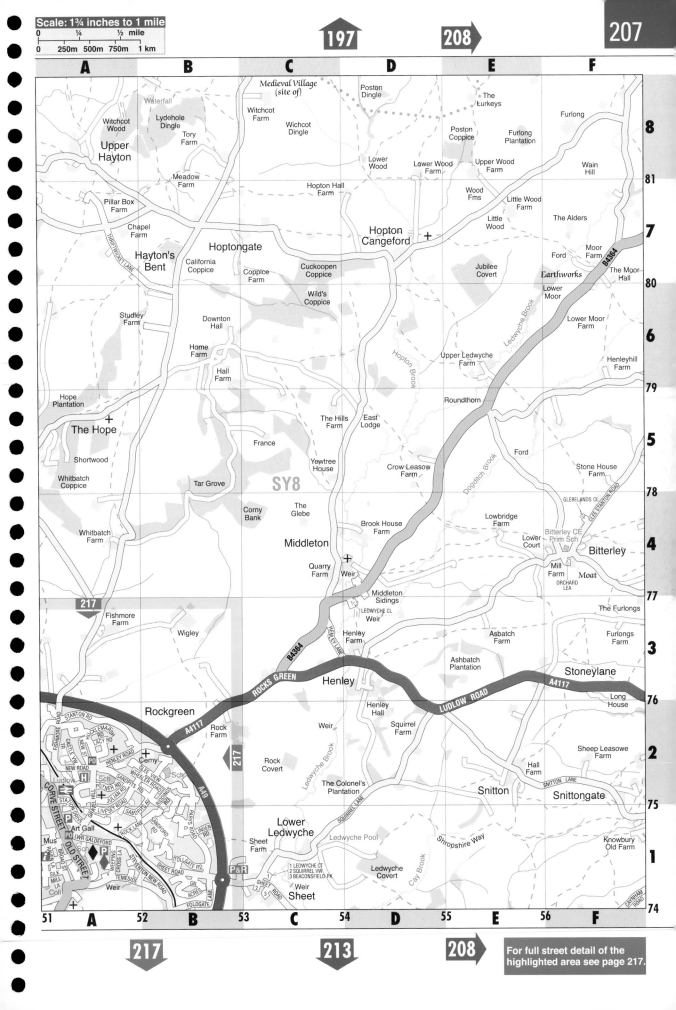

Scale: 1¾ inches to 1 mile

0   ¼   ½   mile
0   250m   500m   750m   1 km

197

208

207

A   B   C   D   E   F

Medieval Village (site of)

Poston Dingle

The Lurkeys

Furlong

Waterfall

Witchcot Farm

Witchcot Wood

Lydehole Dingle

Wichcot Dingle

Poston Coppice

Furlong Plantation

Upper Hayton

Tory Farm

Lower Wood

Lower Wood Farm

Upper Wood Farm

Wain Hill

8

81

Meadow Farm

Hopton Hall Farm

Wood Fms

Little Wood Farm

Pillar Box Farm

Chapel Farm

Hoptongate

Hopton Cangeford

Little Wood

The Alders

7

Hayton's Bent

California Coppice

Coppice Farm

Cuckoopen Coppice

Jubilee Covert

Ford

Moor Farm

The Moor Hall

B4364

Studley Farm

Wild's Coppice

Earthworks

Lower Moor

80

Downton Hall

Lower Moor Farm

6

Home Farm

Hope Plantation

Hall Farm

Upper Ledwyche Farm

Henleyhill Farm

79

The Hope

The Hills Farm

East Lodge

Roundthorn

Shortwood

France

Crow Leasow Farm

Ford

Stone House Farm

5

78

Whitbatch Coppice

Yewtree House

Tar Grove

SY8

Lowbridge Farm

GLEBELANDS CL

CLEE STANTON ROAD

Whitbatch Farm

Corny Bank

The Glebe

Brook House Farm

Lower Court

Bitterley CE Prim Sch

Bitterley

4

Middleton

Quarry Farm

Weir

Mill Farm

Moat

ORCHARD LEA

77

217

Fishmore Farm

Middleton Sidings

LEDWYCHE CL

Weir

Asbatch Farm

The Furlongs

Wigley

Henley Farm

B4364

Ashbatch Plantation

Furlongs Farm

3

ROCKS GREEN

HENLEY LANE

Henley

Stoneylane

A4117

Long House

Rockgreen

A4117

Rock Farm

217

Henley Hall

LUDLOW ROAD

76

FISHMORE ROAD

STANTON RD

HUCKLEMASH RD

LACY RD

CASTLE VIEW

NEW ST

HENLEY ROAD

Cemy

GLEE VIEW

WHEELER ROAD

Sch

Weir

Squirrel Farm

Sheep Leasowe Farm

2

NEW ROAD

PO

Ludlow

H

Sch

A49

SANDPITS

POYNER RD

JULIAN RD

SANDPITS LAY

RUDDINGS RD

Rock Covert

Hall Farm

STA.

CORVE STREET

LIVESEY ROAD

SANDPITS

Snitton

SNITTON LANE

Snittongate

75

P

Art Gall

GRAVEL HILL

ROCK LANE

SANDFORD

LINGEN RD

PARYS ROAD

The Colonel's Plantation

SQUIRREL LANE

PO

Mus

LWR GALDEFORD

Lower Ledwyche

Knowbury Old Farm

1

i

BROAD ST

KEEPING

CROSS LA

STRETTON NEW ROAD

TOLLGATE RD

Sheet Farm

Ledwyche Pool

Shropshire Way

SILK MILL LA

OLD STREET

TEMESIDE

GN

ACRES

SHEET ROAD

P&R

1 LEDWYCHE CT
2 SQUIRREL VW
3 BEACONSFIELD PK

Ledwyche Covert

Cay Brook

CAYNHAM ROAD

Coll

Weir

FOLDGATE LANE

Sheet

74

A   B   C   D   E   F

51   52   53   54   55   56

217

213

208

For full street detail of the highlighted area see page 217.

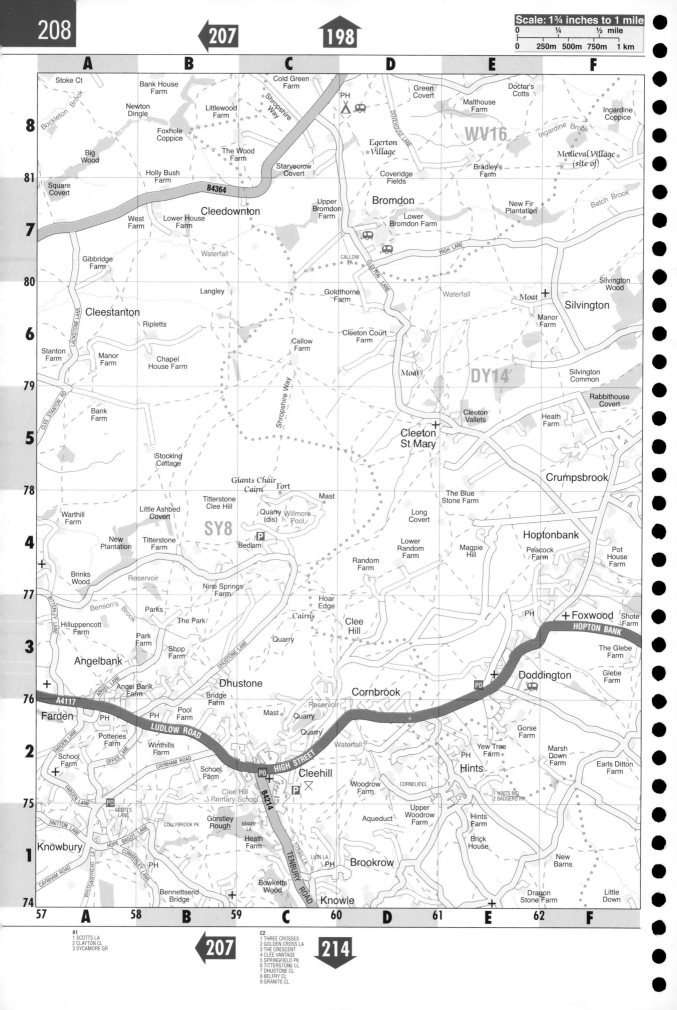

207
198

Scale: 1¾ inches to 1 mile

0   ¼   ½   mile
0   250m   500m   750m   1 km

A   B   C   D   E   F

Stoke Ct
Bockleton Brook
Bank House Farm
Cold Green Farm
Shropshire Way
PH
Green Covert
Malthouse Farm
Doctor's Cotts
Ingardine Coppice
Newton Dingle
Littlewood Farm
WV16
Ingardine Brook
8
Foxhole Coppice
The Wood Farm
Egerton Village
Bradley's Farm
Medieval Village (site of)
Big Wood
Starvecrow Covert
Coveridge Fields
New Fir Plantation
Batch Brook
81
Square Covert
B4364
Cleedownton
Upper Bromdon Farm
Bromdon
Lower Bromdon Farm
Silvington Wood
Silvington
7
West Farm
Lower House Farm
Waterfall
CALLOW
High Lane
Moat
Manor Farm
Gibbridge Farm
CLEETON LANE
Waterfall
80
Langley
Goldthorne Farm
Silvington Common
Cleestanton
Ripletts
Callow Farm
Cleeton Court Farm
DY14
Rabbithouse Covert
6
LACKSTONE LANE
Stanton Farm
Manor Farm
Chapel House Farm
Moat
Cleeton St Mary
Cleeton Vallets
Heath Farm
79
CLEE STANTON RD
Bank Farm
Cleeton St Mary
Crumpsbrook
5
Stocking Cottage
Shropshire Way
The Blue Stone Farm
Giants Chair Cairn
Fort
Mast
Hoptonbank
78
Little Ashbed Covert
Titterstone Clee Hill
Quarry (dis)
Willmore Pool
Long Covert
Peacock Farm
Pot House Farm
SY8
Lower Random Farm
Magpie Hill
4
Warthill Farm
New Plantation
Titterstone Farm
Bedlam
Random Farm
Brinks Wood
Reservoir
Nine Springs Farm
Hoar Edge
Clee Hill
PH
Foxwood
Shote Farm
77
Benson's Brook
Parks
Cairns
HOPTON BANK
The Glebe Farm
3
Hilluppencott Farm
The Park
Quarry
Doddington
Glebe Farm
Angelbank
Park Farm
Shop Farm
DHUSTONE LANE
Dhustone
Cornbrook
PO
BITTERLEY LANE
Angel Lane
Angel Bank Farm
Bridge Farm
Mast
Quarry
Reservoir
Gorse Farm
76
A4117
PH
Pool Farm
Quarry
Waterfall
Yew Tree Farm
Marsh Down Farm
Earls Ditton Farm
Farden
LUDLOW ROAD
Potteries Farm
Winthills Farm
HIGH STREET
Cleehill
PH
Hints
2
FARDEN LANE
School Farm
OFFICE LANE
CAYNHAM ROAD
School Farm
PO
CORNELIE CL
Woodrow Farm
Hints Farm
Brick House
1 HINTS RD
2 BADGERS RI
75
PO
SCOTTS LANE
Clee Hill Primary School
B4214
Aqueduct
Upper Woodrow Farm
SNITTON LANE
Collybrook Pk
Gorstley Rough
KNAPP LA
Heath Farm
Knowbury
HOPE BAGGOT LANE
CUMBERLEY LANE
PH
LION LA
PH
Brookrow
New Barns
1
CAYNHAM ROAD
WHITEWAYHEAD LA
Bennettsend Bridge
Bowketts Wood
TENBURY ROAD
TITTRILA
Knowle
Dragon Stone Farm
Little Down
74
57   A   58   B   59   C   60   D   61   E   62   F

207
214

A1
1 SCOTTS LA
2 CLAYTON CL
3 SYCAMORE GR

C2
1 THREE CROSSES
2 GOLDEN CROSS LA
3 THE CRESCENT
4 CLEE VANTAGE
5 SPRINGFIELD PK
6 TITTERSTONE CL
7 DHUSTONE CL
8 BELFRY CL
9 GRANITE CL

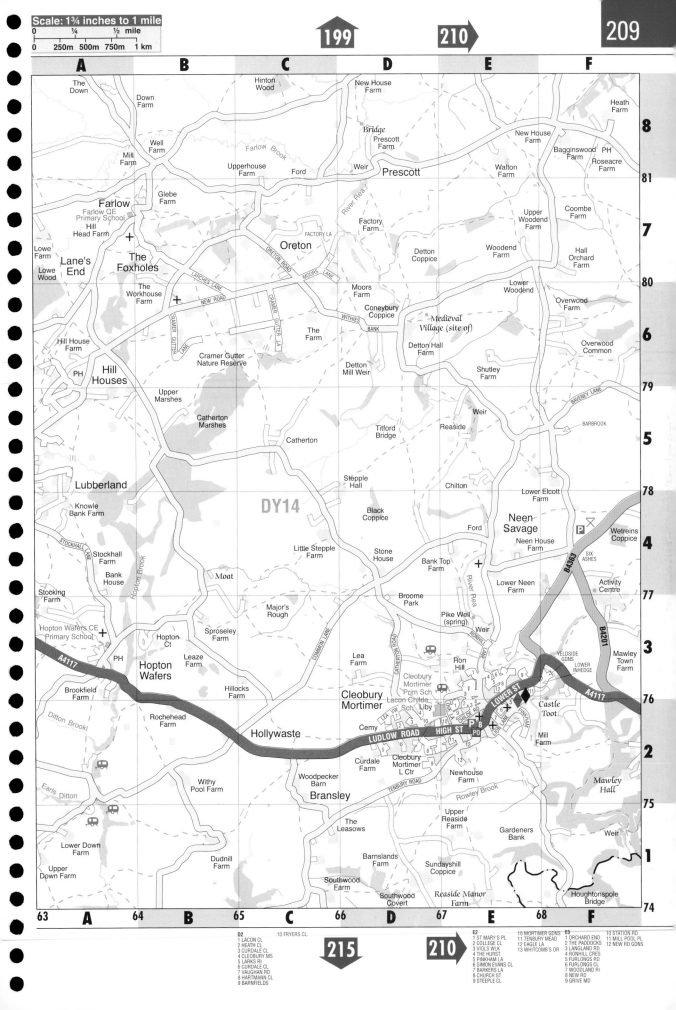

A   B   C   D   E   F

8
81
7
80
6
79
5
78
4
77
3
76
2
75
1
74

The Down
Down Farm
Mill Farm
Well Farm
Glebe Farm
Farlow
Farlow CE Primary School
Hill Head Farm
Lowe Farm
Lane's End
Lowe Wood
The Foxholes
The Workhouse Farm
Hill House Farm
PH
Hill Houses
Cramer Gutter Lane
Cramer Gutter Nature Reserve
Lubberland
Knowle Bank Farm
Stockhall Lane
Stockhall Farm
Bank House
Stocking Farm
Hopton Wafers CE Primary School
PH
Brookfield Farm
Ditton Brook
Hopton Wafers
Hopton Ct
Leaze Farm
Sproseley Farm
Rochehead Farm
Hollywaste
Earls Ditton
Withy Pool Farm
Lower Down Farm
Upper Down Farm
Dudnill Farm

Hinton Wood
Upperhouse Farm
Ford
Oreton Road
Larches Lane
New Road
Oreton
FACTORY LA
The Farm
Moors Lane
Upper Marshes
Catherton Marshes
Catherton
Little Stepple Farm
Moat
Major's Rough
Hillocks Farm
Woodpecker Barn
Bransley
The Leasows
Southwood Farm
Southwood Covert

New House Farm
Bridge
Prescott Farm
Weir
Prescott
River Rea
Factory Farm
Moors Farm
WITHIES
BANK
Coneybury Coppice
Detton Mill Weir
Titford Bridge
Stepple Hall
Black Coppice
Stone House
Little Stepple Farm
Broome Park
Pike Well (spring)
Common Lane
Catherton Road
Lea Farm
Cleobury Mortimer Prim Sch
Lacon Childe Sch
Cleobury Mortimer
Cemy
Cleobury Mortimer L Ctr
Curdale Farm
Ludlow Road
High St
Tenbury Road
Barnslands Farm
Sundayshill Coppice
Reaside Manor Farm

Detton Coppice
Medieval Village (site of)
Detton Hall Farm
Reaside
Weir
Chilton
Ford
Reaside
Shutley Farm
Woodend Farm
Upper Woodend Farm
Walton Farm
New House Farm
Lower Woodend
Overwood Farm
Overwood Common
Lower Elcott Farm
Neen Savage
Neen House Farm
Lower Neen Farm
Bank Top Farm
Ron Hill
Lacon Liby
Love La
High St
PO
Childe Rd
Lion Lane
Newhouse Farm
Rowley Brook
Upper Reaside Farm
Gardeners Bank

Heath Farm
Bagginswood Farm
PH
Roseacre Farm
Coombe Farm
Hall Orchard Farm
BAVENEY LANE
BARBROOK
Wetreins Coppice
P
SIX ASHES
B4363
Activity Centre
B4201
Mawley Town Farm
YELDSIDE GDNS
LOWER INHEDGE
Lower St
Castle Toot
A4117
Mill Farm
Mawley Hall
Weir
Houghtonspole Bridge

DY14

A4117

215   210

63   64   65   66   67   68

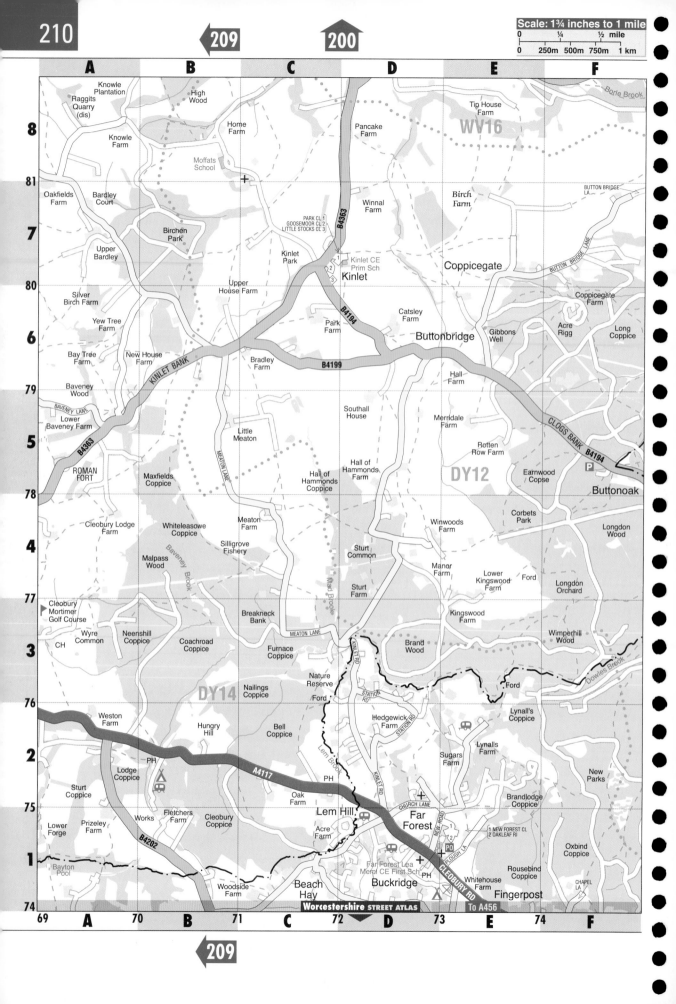

Borle Brook

Knowle Plantation

Raggits Quarry (dis)

High Wood

WV16

Tip House Farm

Knowle Farm

Home Farm

Moffats School

Pancake Farm

BUTTON BRIDGE LA

Oakfields Farm

Bardley Court

Winnal Farm

Birch Farm

PARK CL 1
GOOSEMOOR CL 2
LITTLE STOCKS CL 3

B4363

Birchen Park

Kinlet Park

Kinlet CE Prim Sch

Coppicegate

BUTTON BRIDGE LANE

Upper Bardley

Kinlet

Silver Birch Farm

Upper House Farm

Coppicegate Farm

Yew Tree Farm

Park Farm

Catsley Farm

B4194

Buttonbridge

Gibbons Well

Acre Rigg

Long Coppice

Bay Tree Farm

New House Farm

Bradley Farm

B4199

KINLET BANK

Hall Farm

Baveney Wood

BAVENEY LANE

Southall House

Merridale Farm

CLOGS BANK

B4194

Lower Baveney Farm

B4363

Little Meaton

MEATON LANE

Rotten Row Farm

DY12

Earnwood Copse

Buttonoak

ROMAN FORT

Maxfields Coppice

Hall of Hammonds Coppice

Hall of Hammonds Farm

P

Cleobury Lodge Farm

Whiteleasowe Coppice

Meaton Farm

Silligrove Fishery

Winwoods Farm

Corbets Park

Longdon Wood

BAVENEY BROOK

Malpass Wood

Sturt Common

Manor Farm

Lower Kingswood Farm

Ford

Longdon Orchard

Cleobury Mortimer Golf Course

Breakneck Bank

MAD BROOK

Sturt Farm

Kingswood Farm

Wimperhill Wood

CH

Wyre Common

Neenshill Coppice

Coachroad Coppice

Furnace Coppice

MEATON LANE

Brand Wood

DOWLES BROOK

Ford

Nature Reserve

KINLET RD

DY14

Nailings Coppice

Ford

STATION RD

Ford

Lynall's Coppice

Weston Farm

Hungry Hill

Bell Coppice

Hedgewick Farm

STATION RD

LEM BROOK

Lynalls Farm

Sugars Farm

PH

Lodge Coppice

A4117

KINLET RD

PH

New Parks

Sturt Coppice

Oak Farm

CHURCH LANE

Far Forest

Brandlodge Coppice

PO

Works

Fletchers Farm

Cleobury Coppice

Lem Hill

NEW ROAD

1

1 NEW FOREST CL
2 OAKLEAF RI

Lower Forge

Prizeley Farm

Acre Farm

Buckridge

PLOUGH LA

PO

Oxbind Coppice

B4202

Far Forest Lea
Meml CE First Sch

PH

CLEOBURY RD

Whitehouse Farm

Rousebind Coppice

CHAPEL LA

Bayton Pool

Woodside Farm

Beach Hay

Fingerpost

To A456

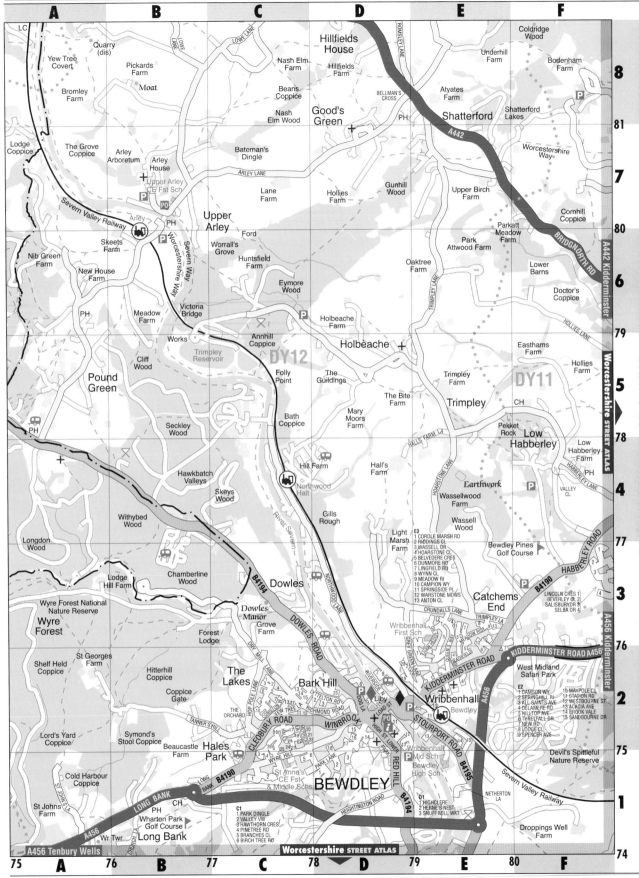

8
81
7
80
6
79
5
78
4
77
3
76
2
75
1
74

C2
1 RUSSETT WY
2 LAXTON DR
3 LAMBOURNE DR
4 NEWTON CL
5 DERWENT DR
6 MERTON CL
7 ELAN CL
8 LLESMERE DR
9 BRAMLEY WY
10 CONISTON WY
11 YEW TREE CL
12 MUSKOKA
13 THE LAKES RD
14 YORK RD
15 TUDOR RD
16 WATERLOO RD
17 ELTON RD
18 GROSVENOR WD
19 WHITE HEART CL
20 FORT-MAHON PL
21 OAKWOOD RD
22 FOREST CL
23 HALES PK
24 IRONSIDE CL
25 CHERRY CL
26 SEVERN WY
27 LAKES CT

C1
1 PARK DINGLE
2 VALLEY VW
3 HAWTHORN CRES
4 PINETREE RD
5 BRANCHES CL
6 BIRCH TREE CL

D2
1 WOODTHORPE DR
2 LANCASTER RD
3 COBHAM CRES
4 CHURCH VW
5 GREENACRES LA
6 SABRINA DR
7 NURSERY RD
8 RIVERWAY DR
9 DOG LA
10 SEVERN SIDE N
11 SEVERN SIDE S
12 PRITCHARD CT
13 GARDNERS MDW
14 PARK CL
15 ORCHARD RI
16 TELFORD DR
17 ROSENHURST DR
18 BARRATTS STILE CL
19 CLARENCE WY
20 GLOUCESTER WY
21 MARCH GR
22 MORTIMER GR
23 WOODTHORPE DR

E3
1 CORDLE MARSH RD
2 RIDDINGS CL
3 WASSELL DR
4 HOARSTONE CL
5 BELVEDERE CRES
6 DUNMORE RD
7 LINGFIELD RD
8 WYNN CL
9 MEADOW RI
10 CAMPION WY
11 SPRINGSIDE PL
12 WARSTONE MDWS
13 ANTON CL

E2
1 DAMSON WY
2 SPRINGHILL RI
3 ALL SAINTS AVE
4 DELAMERE RD
5 HILLTOP AVE
6 THREEFALL DR
7 NEW RD
8 LODGE CL
9 SPENCER AVE
10 MAYPOLE CL
11 STATION RD
12 WESTBOURNE ST
13 ACACIA AVE
14 BROOK VALE
15 SANDBOURNE DR

D1
1 HIGHCLERE
2 HERNE'S NEST
3 SNUFF MILL WKT

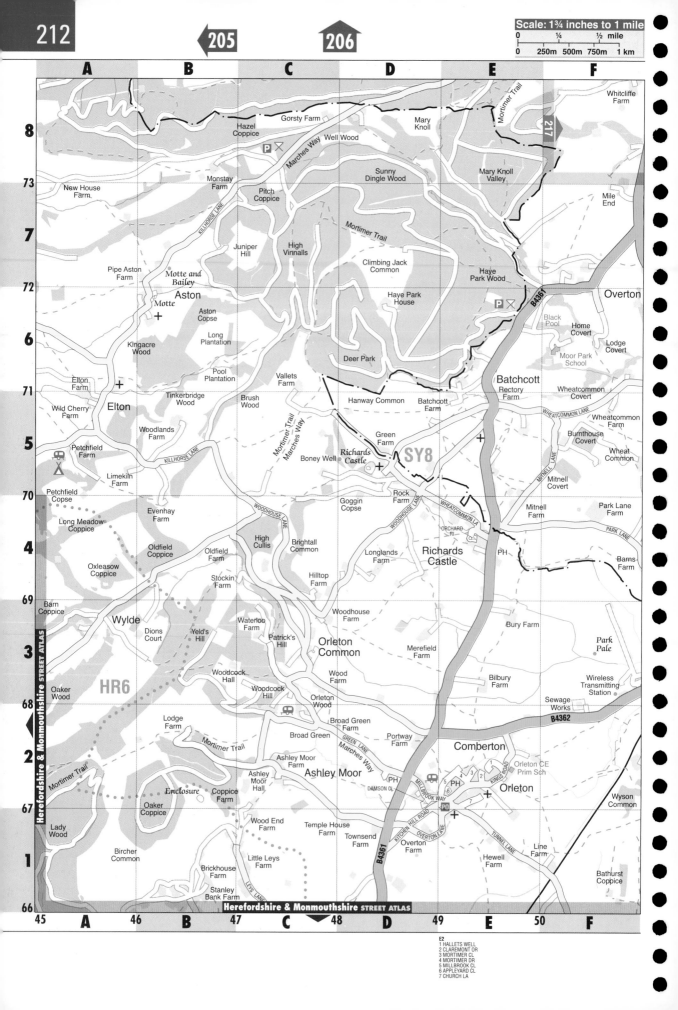

212

205

206

Scale: 1¾ inches to 1 mile

0 ¼ ½ mile
0 250m 500m 750m 1 km

A B C D E F

8

73

7

72

6

71

5

70

4

69

3

68

2

67

1

66

45 A 46 B 47 C 48 D 49 E 50 F

217

SY8

HR6

Herefordshire & Monmouthshire STREET ATLAS

Whitcliffe Farm
Mortimer Trail
Gorsty Farm
Hazel Coppice
Mary Knoll
Well Wood
Marches Way
Monstay Farm
Pitch Coppice
Sunny Dingle Wood
Mary Knoll Valley
Mile End
New House Farm
KILLHORSE LANE
Juniper Hill
High Vinnalls
Mortimer Trail
Climbing Jack Common
Haye Park Wood
Pipe Aston Farm
Motte and Bailey
Aston
Motte
Aston Copse
Haye Park House
Deer Park
B4361
Overton
Long Plantation
Black Pool
Home Covert
Moor Park School
Lodge Covert
Kingacre Wood
Pool Plantation
Vallets Farm
Batchcott
Elton Farm
Tinkerbridge Wood
Brush Wood
Hanway Common
Batchcott Farm
Rectory Farm
Wheatcommon Covert
Wheatcommon Farm
Wild Cherry Farm
Elton
Green Farm
WHEATCOMMON LANE
Wheatcommon Farm
Wheat Common
Woodlands Farm
Mortimer Trail Marches Way
Richards Castle
Burnthouse Covert
Petchfield Farm
KILLHORSE LANE
Boney Well
Mitnell Covert
Limekiln Farm
MITNELL LANE
Petchfield Copse
Evenhay Farm
WOODHOUSE LANE
Goggin Copse
Rock Farm
WOODHOUSE LANE
WHEATCOMMON LA
Mitnell Farm
Park Lane Farm
PARK LANE
Long Meadow Coppice
High Cullis
Brightall Common
ORCHARD RI
PH
Oldfield Coppice
Oldfield Farm
Longlands Farm
Richards Castle
Barns Farm
Oxleasow Coppice
Hilltop Farm
Stockin Farm
Barn Coppice
Woodhouse Farm
Bury Farm
Park Pale
Wylde
Dions Court
Yeld's Hill
Waterloo Farm
Orleton Common
Merefield Farm
Patrick's Hill
Wood Farm
Bilbury Farm
Wireless Transmitting Station
Oaker Wood
Woodcock Hall
Woodcock Hill
Orleton Wood
B4362
Sewage Works
Lodge Farm
Broad Green Farm
GREEN LANE
Portway Farm
Comberton
Orleton CE Prim Sch
Mortimer Trail
Broad Green
Marches Way
Ashley Moor Farm
PH
KINGS ROAD
Mortimer Trail
Enclosure
Coppice Farm
Ashley Moor Hall
Ashley Moor
DAMSON CL
MILLBROOK WAY
PH
Orleton
Wyson Common
Oaker Coppice
PO
Lady Wood
Wood End Farm
Temple House Farm
Townsend Farm
KITCHEN HILL ROAD
OVERTON LANE
Overton Farm
TUNNEL LANE
Line Farm
Bircher Common
LEYS LANE
Little Leys Farm
B4361
Hewell Farm
Bathurst Coppice
Brickhouse Farm
Stanley Bank Farm

E2
1 HALLETS WELL
2 CLAREMONT DR
3 MORTIMER CL
4 MORTIMER DR
5 MILLBROOK CL
6 APPLEYARD CL
7 CHURCH LA

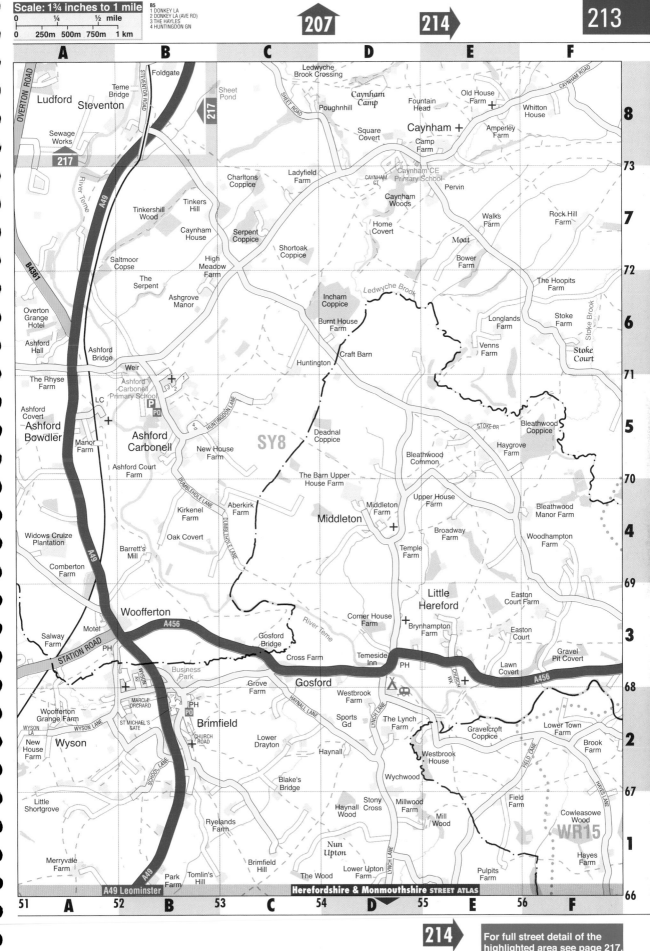

Scale: 1¾ inches to 1 mile

0   ¼   ½   mile
0   250m 500m 750m 1 km

B5
1 DONKEY LA
2 DONKEY LA (AVE RD)
3 THE HAYLES
4 HUNTINGDON GN

207
214

A **B** **C** **D** **E** **F**

Overton Road

Ludford
Steventon
Teme Bridge
Foldgate

Sheet Pond

217

Ledwyche Brook Crossing
Poughnhill
Caynham Camp
Square Covert
Fountain Head
Old House Farm
Whitton House

Caynham
Amperley Farm

Sewage Works

217

River Teme

Charltons Coppice
Ladyfield Farm

CAYNHAM CT

Caynham CE Primary School
Pervin

A49

Tinkershill Wood
Tinkers Hill
Caynham House

Serpent Coppice
Shortoak Coppice

Caynham Woods
Home Covert
Walks Farm
Moat
Rock Hill Farm

B4361

Saltmoor Copse
The Serpent
Ashgrove Manor
High Meadow Farm

Ledwyche Brook

Incham Coppice
Bower Farm
The Hoopits Farm

Stoke Brook

Overton Grange Hotel
Ashford Hall
Ashford Bridge
Weir

Burnt House Farm
Craft Barn
Huntington

Longlands Farm
Stoke Farm
Stoke Court

The Rhyse Farm

Ashford Carbonell Primary School
LC
PO

Venns Farm

STOKE DR
Bleathwood Coppice

Ashford Covert
Ashford Bowdler
Manor Farm

Ashford Carbonell
Huntingdon Lane

SY8

Deadnal Coppice

Bleathwood Common
Haygrove Farm

Ashford Court Farm
New House Farm
Aberkirk Farm

The Barn Upper House Farm

Upper House Farm
Bleathwood Manor Farm

Widows Cruize Plantation
Kirkenel Farm
Dumblehole Lane
Oak Covert

Middleton Farm
Middleton

Broadway Farm
Woodhampton Farm

Comberton Farm
Barrett's Mill

A49

Temple Farm

Little Hereford

Easton Court Farm

Woofferton
A456

Gosford Bridge
Cross Farm

Corner House Farm
Brynhampton Farm

Easton Court

Salway Farm
Motel
PH
Station Road

Temeside Inn
PH
CHURCH WK

Lawn Covert
Gravel Pit Covert
A456

Gosford

Business Park
Grove Farm
Haynall Lane
Westbrook Farm
Sports Gd
LYNCH LANE
The Lynch Farm

Gravelcroft Coppice
Lower Town Farm
Brook Farm

Woofferton Grange Farm
MARCLE ORCHARD
PH
PO
St Michael's Gate
Brimfield
CHURCH ROAD

Lower Drayton
Haynall

Westbrook House
Wychwood
FIELD LANE
HAYES LANE

New House Farm
Wyson
Little Shortgrove
Ryelands Farm
Blake's Bridge

Haynall Wood
Stony Cross
Millwood Farm
Mill Wood

Field Farm
Cowleasowe Wood
WR15

SCHOOL LANE

Brimfield Hill
Tomlin's Hill

Nun Upton
LYNCH LANE
The Wood
Lower Upton Farm

Pulpits Farm
Hayes Farm

Merryvale Farm
Park Farm
A49

A49 Leominster

Herefordshire & Monmouthshire STREET ATLAS

8
73
7
72
6
71
5
70
4
69
3
68
2
67
1
66

51 **A** 52 **B** 53 **C** 54 **D** 55 **E** 56 **F**

214

For full street detail of the highlighted area see page 217.

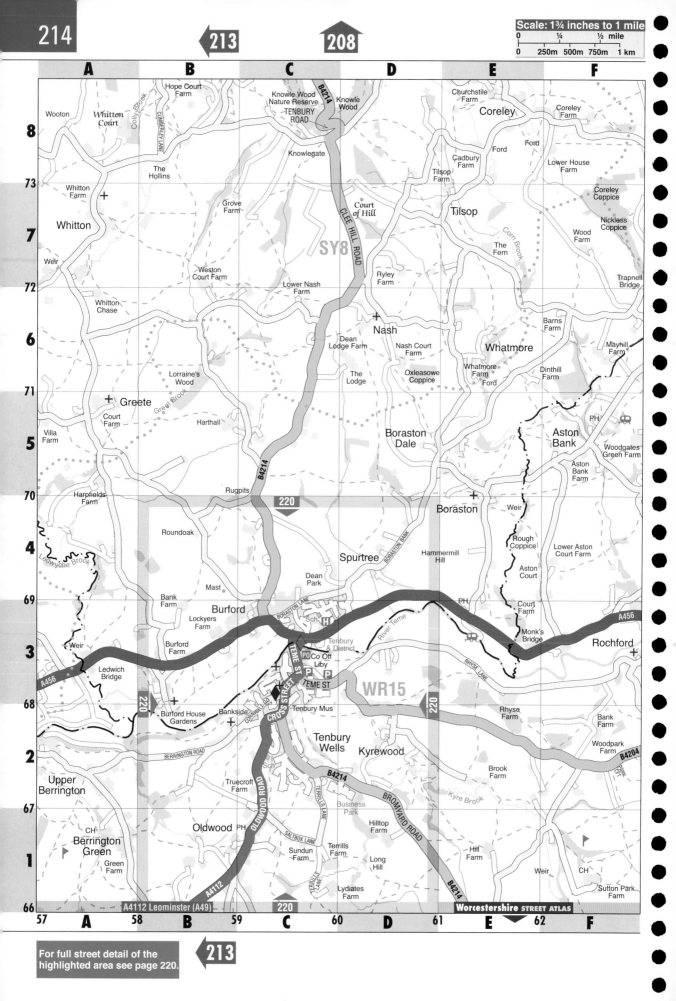

214

213

208

Scale: 1¾ inches to 1 mile

0   ¼   ½ mile
0 250m 500m 750m 1 km

A   B   C   D   E   F

8

Wooton

Whitton Court

Hope Court Farm

Knowle Wood Nature Reserve

TENBURY ROAD

Knowle Wood

B4214

Churchstile Farm

Coreley

Coreley Farm

The Hollins

Knowlegate

Cadbury Farm

Ford

Ford

Lower House Farm

73

Whitton Farm

Grove Farm

Tilsop Farm

Coreley Coppice

Nickless Coppice

7

Whitton

CLEE HILL ROAD

Court of Hill

Tilsop

Corn Brook

Wood Farm

Weir

SY8

The Fern

Trapnell Bridge

72

Weston Court Farm

Lower Nash Farm

Ryley Farm

Barns Farm

Whitton Chase

Dean Lodge Farm

Nash

Whatmore

Dinthill Farm

Mayhill Farm

6

Nash Court Farm

The Lodge

Oxleasowe Coppice

Whatmore Farm

Whatmore Ford

PH

Aston Bank

71

Lorraine's Wood

Great Brook

Harthall

Boraston Dale

Woodgates Green Farm

Greete

Court Farm

Aston Bank Farm

5

Villa Farm

Boraston

Weir

Rough Coppice

Lower Aston Court Farm

70

Harpfields Farm

Rugpits

B4214

220

Aston Court

Court Farm

4

Ledwyche Brook

Roundoak

Spurtree

BORASTON BANK

Hammermill Hill

Dean Park

River Teme

PH

Monk's Bridge

A456

Rochford

69

Bank Farm

Burford

BORASTON LANE

Sch

H

Mast

Lockyers Farm

RHYSE LANE

3

Weir

Ledwich Bridge

A456

Burford Farm

TEME ST

PO

Co Off Liby

P

P

Tenbury & District

Rhyse Farm

Bank Farm

68

220

Burford House Gardens

Bankside

CORNWALL RD

CROSS STREET

TEME ST

Tenbury Mus

WR15

220

Rhyse Farm

Woodpark Farm

B4204

2

BERRINGTON ROAD

Tenbury Wells

Kyrewood

Brook Farm

Upper Berrington

Truecroft Farm

OLDWOOD ROAD

Sch

B4214

TERRILLS LANE

Business Park

Kyre Brook

BROMYARD ROAD

67

Oldwood

PH

SALTBOX LANE

Hilltop Farm

Hill Farm

1

CH

Berrington Green

Green Farm

A4112

Sundun Farm

Terrills Farm

TERRILLS LANE

Long Hill

Weir

CH

Sutton Park Farm

B4214

Lydiates Farm

66

57   A   58   B   59   C   60   D   61   E   62   F

213

For full street detail of the highlighted area see page 220.

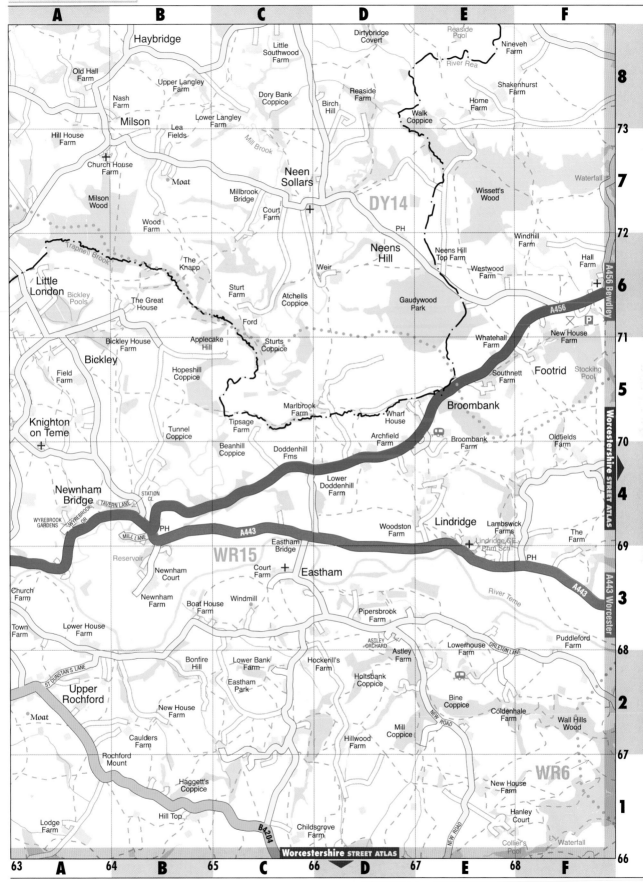

A   B   C   D   E   F

8
73
7
72
6
71
5
70
4
69
3
68
2
67
1
66

Haybridge

Old Hall Farm

Nash Farm

Milson

Hill House Farm

Milson Wood

Church House Farm

Moat

Upper Langley Farm

Lea Fields

Lower Langley Farm

Little Southwood Farm

Dory Bank Coppice

Dirtybridge Covert

Reaside Pool

Nineveh Farm

River Rea

Shakenhurst Farm

Home Farm

Walk Coppice

Reaside Farm

Birch Hill

Neen Sollars

Mill Brook

DY14

Wissett's Wood

Waterfall

Millbrook Bridge

Court Farm

PH

Neens Hill

Neens Hill Top Farm

Windhill Farm

Westwood Farm

Hall Farm

A456 Bewdley

Trapnell Brook

Wood Farm

The Knapp

Little London

Bickley Pools

The Great House

Sturt Farm

Weir

Atchells Coppice

Gaudywood Park

Whatehall Farm

New House Farm

Stocking Pool

A456

Bickley House Farm

Applecake Hill

Ford

Sturts Coppice

Southnett Farm

Footrid

Bickley

Field Farm

Hopeshill Coppice

Marlbrook Farm

Wharf House

Broombank

Oldfields Farm

Knighton on Teme

Tunnel Coppice

Tipsage Farm

Beanhill Coppice

Doddenhill Fms

Archfield Farm

Broombank Farm

Newnham Bridge

STATION CL

TAVERN LANE

WYREBROOK GARDENS

WYREBROOK DR

MILL LANE

PH

A443

Lower Doddenhill Farm

Woodston Farm

Lindridge

Lambswick Farms

Lindridge CE Prim Sch

The Farm

PH

Eastham Bridge

Reservoir

WR15

Court Farm

Eastham

River Teme

A443

A443 Worcester

Church Farm

Town Farm

Lower House Farm

Newnham Court

Newnham Farm

Boat House Farm

Windmill

Pipersbrook Farm

ASTLEY ORCHARD

Astley Farm

Lowerhouse Farm

ORLETON LANE

Puddleford Farm

ST DUNSTAN'S LANE

Bonfire Hill

Lower Bank Farm

Hockerill's Farm

Holtsbank Coppice

NEW ROAD

Bine Coppice

Coldenhale Farm

Wall Hills Wood

Upper Rochford

Moat

Caulders Farm

New House Farm

Eastham Park

Hillwood Farm

Mill Coppice

WR6

Rochford Mount

New House Farm

Hanley Court

Lodge Farm

Haggett's Coppice

Hill Top

B4204

Childsgrove Farm

Collier's Pool

Waterfall

63   64   65   66   67   68
A   B   C   D   E   F

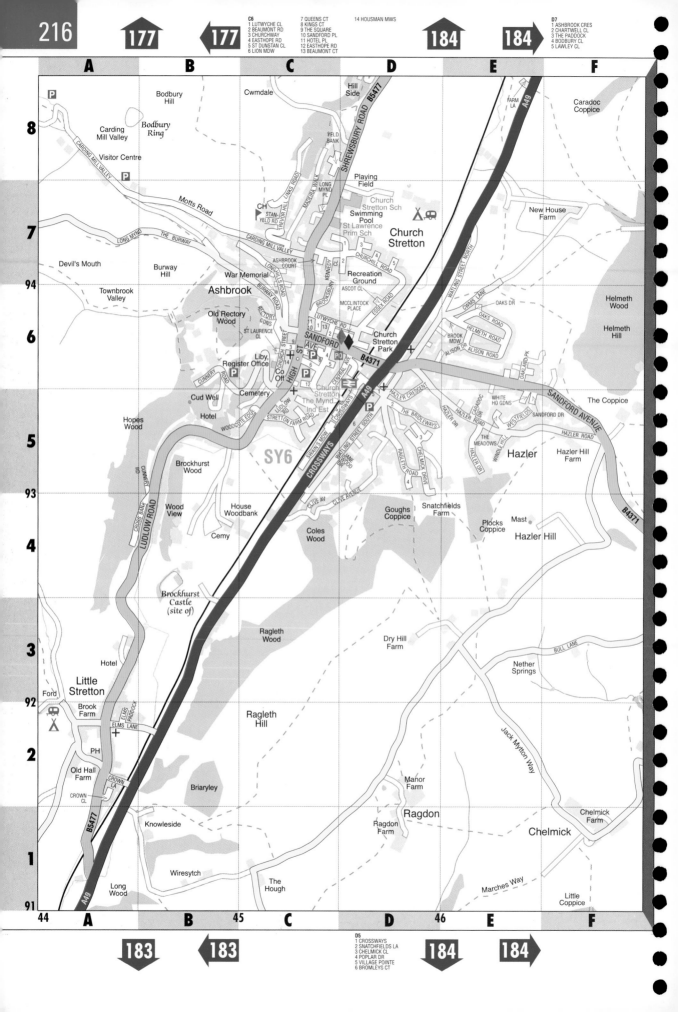

177 →

← 177

184 →

← 184

C6
1 LUTWYCHE CL
2 BEAUMONT RD
3 CHURCHWAY
4 EASTHOPE RD
5 ST DUNSTAN CL
6 LION MDW

7 QUEENS CT
8 KINGS CT
9 THE SQUARE
10 SANDFORD PL
11 HOTEL PL
12 EASTHOPE RD
13 BEAUMONT CT

14 HOUSMAN MWS

D7
1 ASHBROOK CRES
2 CHARTWELL CL
3 THE PADDOCK
4 BODBURY CL
5 LAWLEY CL

D5
1 CROSSWAYS
2 SNATCHFIELDS LA
3 CHELMICK CL
4 POPLAR DR
5 VILLAGE POINTE
6 BROMLEYS CT

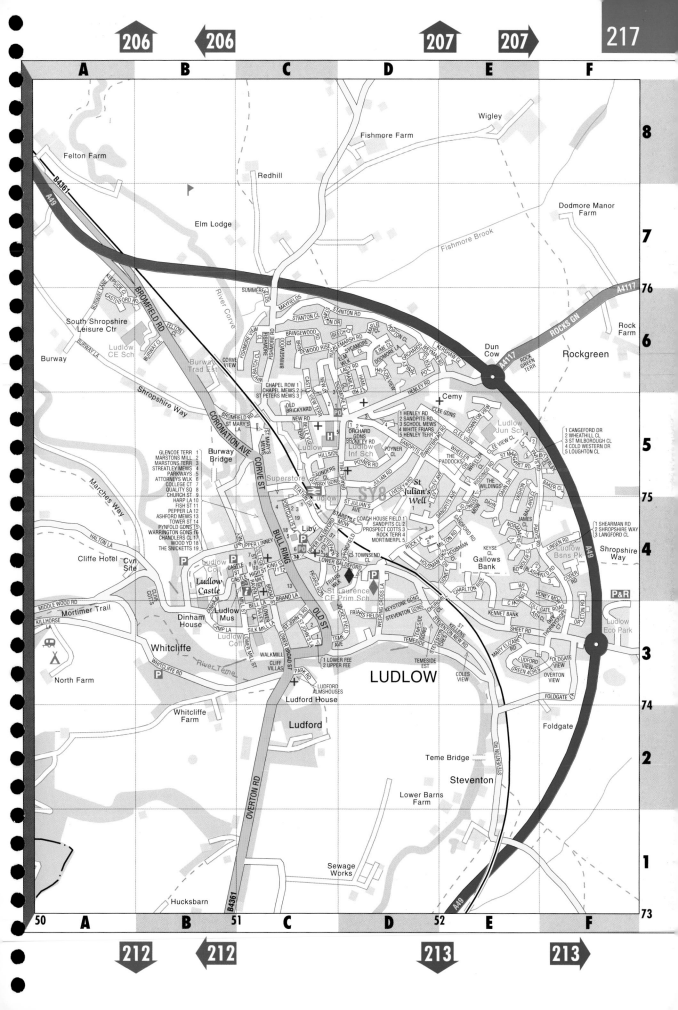

A B C D E F

8
7
76
6
5
75
4
74
2
1
73

LUDLOW

Felton Farm

South Shropshire Leisure Ctr
Burway
Ludlow CE Sch

Fishmore Farm
Wigley
Redhill
Elm Lodge

Dodmore Manor Farm
Fishmore Brook

Rock Farm
Rockgreen

Dun Cow

BROMFIELD RD
Shropshire Way
CORONATION AVE
CORVE ST

Burway Trad Est
Burway Bridge

Marches Way
Cliffe Hotel
Cvn Site
Mortimer Trail
KILLHORSE LA
North Farm
Whitcliffe
Whitcliffe Farm

MIDDLE WOOD RD
WHITCLIFFE RD

Ludlow Coll
Ludlow Castle
Ludlow Mus
Dinham House

Ludlow Jun Sch
St Julian's Well
Gallows Bank
Keyse Cl
The Wildings
The Paddocks

Ludlow Bsns Pk
Shropshire Way

P&R
Ludlow Eco Park

St Laurence CE Prim Sch

Ludford Almshouses
Ludford House
Ludford

Overton View
Foldgate View
Green Acres
Foldgate

Teme Bridge
Steventon
Lower Barns Farm

Sewage Works

Hucksbarn

1 GLENCOE TERR 1
MARSTONS MILL 2
MARSTONS TERR 3
STREATLEY MEWS 4
PARKWAYS 5
ATTORNEYS WLK 6
COLLEGE CT 7
QUALITY SQ 8
CHURCH ST 9
HARP LA 10
FISH ST 11
PEPPER LA 12
ASHFORD MEWS 13
TOWER ST 14
PYNFOLD GDNS 15
WARRINGTON GDNS 16
CHANDLERS CL 17
WOOD YD 18
THE SNICKETTS 19

CHAPEL ROW 1
CHAPEL MEWS 2
ST PETERS MEWS 3

1 HENLEY RD
2 SANDPITS RD
3 SCHOOL MEWS
4 WHITE FRIARS
5 HENLEY TERR

COACH HOUSE FIELD 1
SANDPITS CL 2
PROSPECT COTTS 3
ROCK TERR 4
MORTIMER PL 5

1 CANGEFORD DR
2 WHEATHILL CL
3 ST MILBOROUGH CL
4 COLD WESTERN DR
5 LOUGHTON CL

1 SHEARMAN RD
2 SHROPSHIRE WAY
3 LANGFORD CL

1 LOWER FEE
2 UPPER FEE

50 51 52

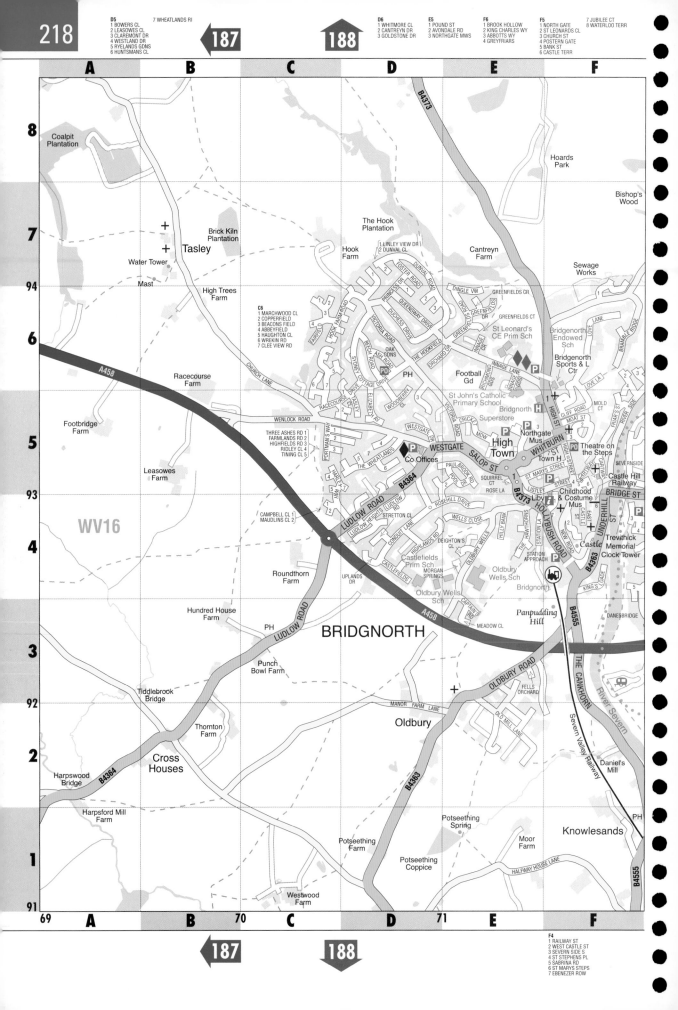

187

188

D5
1 BOWERS CL
2 LEASOWES CL
3 CLAREMONT DR
4 WESTLAND DR
5 RYELANDS GDNS
6 HUNTSMANS CL

7 WHEATLANDS RI

D6
1 WHITMORE CL
2 CANTREYN DR
3 GOLDSTONE DR

E5
1 POUND ST
2 AVONDALE RD
3 NORTHGATE MWS

F6
1 BROOK HOLLOW
2 KING CHARLES WY
3 ABBOTTS WY
4 GREYFRIARS

F5
1 NORTH GATE
2 ST LEONARDS CL
3 CHURCH ST
4 POSTERN GATE
5 BANK ST
6 CASTLE TERR

7 JUBILEE CT
8 WATERLOO TERR

C6
1 MARCHWOOD CL
2 COPPERFIELD
3 BEACONS FIELD
4 ABBEYFIELD
5 HAUGHTON CL
6 WREKIN RD
7 CLEE VIEW RD

THREE ASHES RD 1
FARMLANDS RD 2
HIGHFIELDS RD 3
RIDLEY CL 4
TINING CL 5

CAMPBELL CL 1
MAUDLINS CL 2

F4
1 RAILWAY ST
2 WEST CASTLE ST
3 SEVERN SIDE S
4 ST STEPHENS PL
5 SABRINA RD
6 ST MARYS STEPS
7 EBENEZER ROW

Coalpit Plantation

Hoards Park

Bishop's Wood

Brick Kiln Plantation

Tasley

Water Tower

Mast

High Trees Farm

The Hook Plantation

Hook Farm

1 LINLEY VIEW DR
2 DUNVAL CL

Cantreyn Farm

Sewage Works

Greenfields CR

Greenfields CT

St Leonard's CE Prim Sch

Bridgenorth Endowed Sch

Bridgenorth Sports & L Ctr

Racecourse Farm

Footbridge Farm

Church Lane

Racecourse Farm

Leasowes Farm

Wenlock Road

Football Gd

St John's Catholic Primary School

Bridgnorth Superstore

Northgate Mus

High Town

Town H

Theatre on the Steps

Castle Hill Railway

WESTGATE

SALOP ST

WHITBURN ST

Co Offices

WV16

Paul Brook Rd

Pool Rd

Squirrel CT

Rose LA

St Marys Street

Childhood & Costume Mus

Library

BRIDGE ST

Trevithick Memorial Clock Tower

Ludlow Heights

Stretton CL

Rosehill Drive

Wells Close

Castlefields Prim Sch

Morgan Springs

Oldbury Wells Sch

Oldbury Wells Sch

Roundthorn Farm

Uplands Dr

Station Approach

Bridgnorth

Panpudding Hill

Danesbridge

Hundred House Farm

PH

BRIDGNORTH

Oldbury

Fells Orchard

Punch Bowl Farm

Tiddlebrook Bridge

Thornton Farm

Cross Houses

Manor Farm Lane

Old Mill Lane

Harpswood Bridge

Harpsford Mill Farm

Potseething Spring

Moor Farm

Knowlesands

Potseething Farm

Daniel's Mill

Severn Valley Railway

River Severn

Potseething Coppice

Westwood Farm

Halfway House Lane

THE CANKHORN

187

188

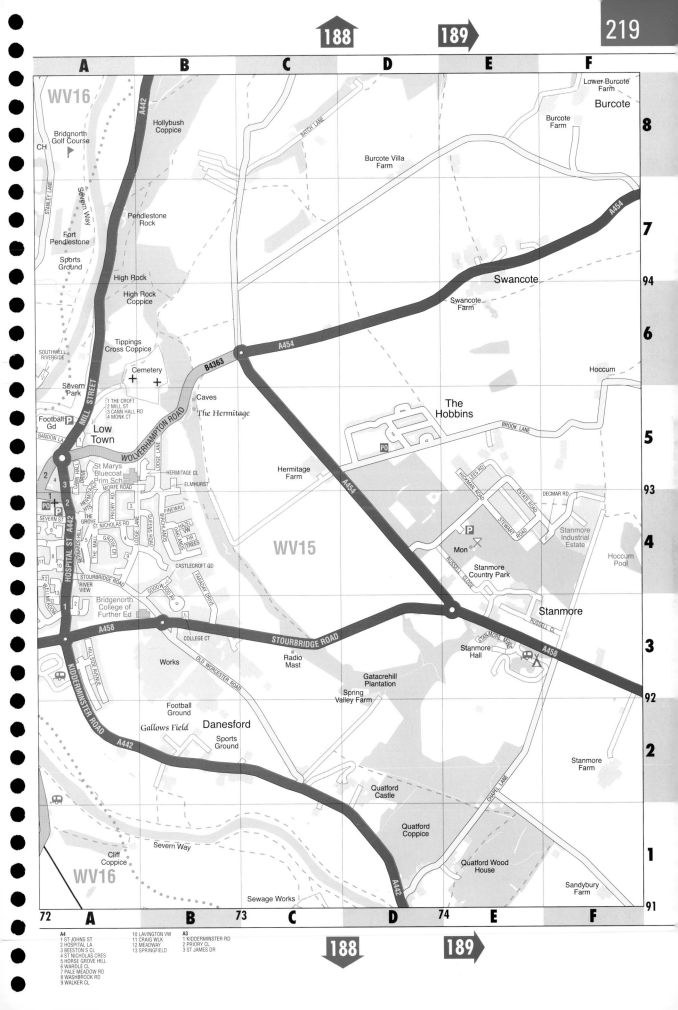

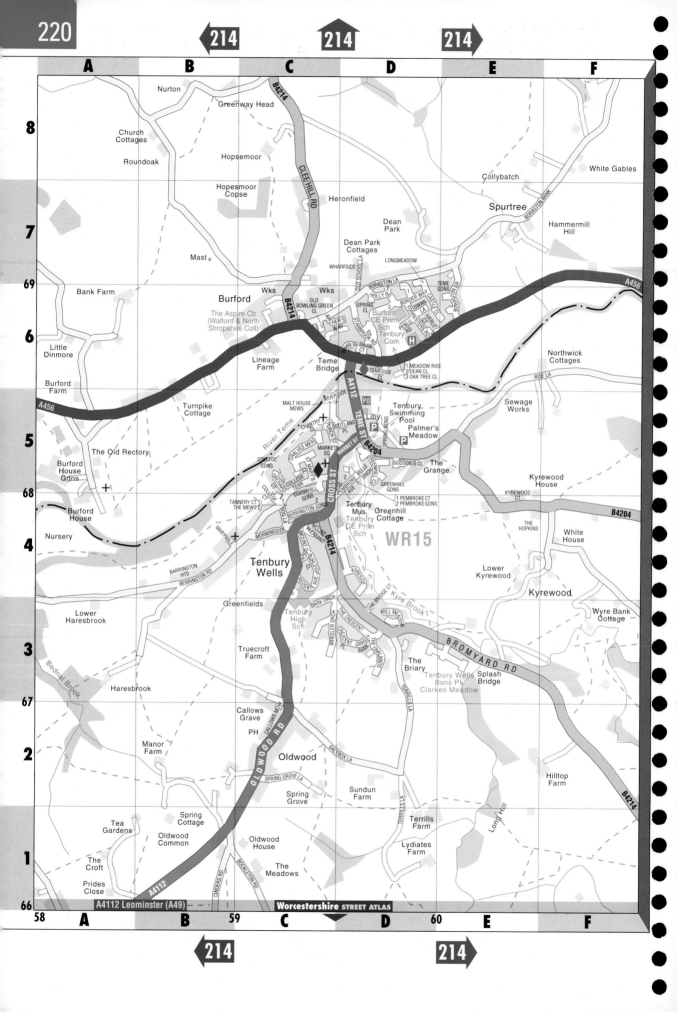

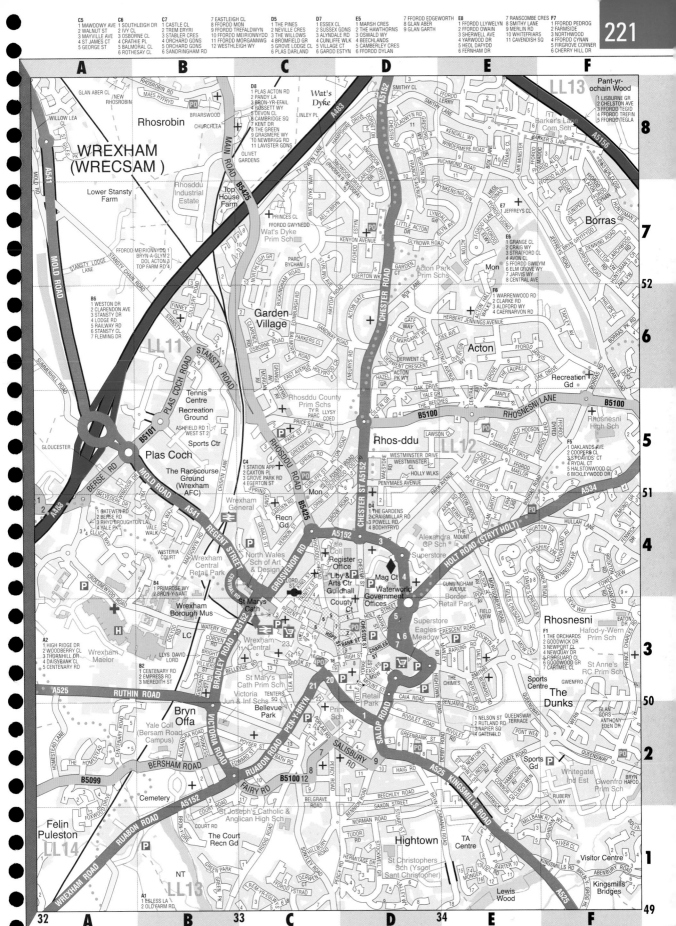

Index

Place name May be abbreviated on the map

Location number Present when a number indicates the place's position in a crowded area of mapping

Locality, town or village Shown when more than one place has the same name

Postcode district District for the indexed place

Page and grid square Page number and grid reference for the standard mapping

Church Rd 6 Beckenham BR2..........53 C6

Cities, towns and villages are listed in CAPITAL LETTERS

Public and commercial buildings are highlighted in magenta   **Places of interest** are highlighted in blue with a star*

Abbreviations used in the index

Acad	Academy	Comm	Common	Gd	Ground	L	Leisure	Prom	Promenade
App	Approach	Cott	Cottage	Gdn	Garden	La	Lane	Rd	Road
Arc	Arcade	Cres	Crescent	Gn	Green	Liby	Library	Recn	Recreation
Ave	Avenue	Cswy	Causeway	Gr	Grove	Mdw	Meadow	Ret	Retail
Bglw	Bungalow	Ct	Court	H	Hall	Meml	Memorial	Sh	Shopping
Bldg	Building	Ctr	Centre	Ho	House	Mkt	Market	Sq	Square
Bsns, Bus	Business	Ctry	Country	Hospl	Hospital	Mus	Museum	St	Street
Bvd	Boulevard	Cty	County	HQ	Headquarters	Orch	Orchard	Sta	Station
Cath	Cathedral	Dr	Drive	Hts	Heights	Pal	Palace	Terr	Terrace
Cir	Circus	Dro	Drove	Ind	Industrial	Par	Parade	TH	Town Hall
Cl	Close	Ed	Education	Inst	Institute	Pas	Passage	Univ	University
Cnr	Corner	Emb	Embankment	Int	International	Pk	Park	Wk, Wlk	Walk
Coll	College	Est	Estate	Intc	Interchange	Pl	Place	Wr	Water
Com	Community	Ex	Exhibition	Junc	Junction	Prec	Precinct	Yd	Yard

Index of towns, villages, streets, hospitals, industrial estates, railway stations, schools, shopping centres, universities and places of interest

Abb–Ard

A

Abbeyfield 4 WV16.....218 C6
Abbey Fields TF3 .....144 D3
Abbey Foregate 1 SY2..125 D5
Abbey La SY5...........168 D5
Abbey Lawn Bsns Pk
  SY2.................125 D6
Abbey Rd TF1...........131 A2
Abbey Walls 4 TF2 ....132 A4
Abbey Way TF9 ....36 D2
Abbots Cl TF2 ....132 A3
Abbotsfield Dr SY2....125 F3
Abbots Gn SY2.........126 A6
Abbots Pl 4 SY2.......125 F7
Abbots Rd SY2.........125 F7
Abbot St 17 LL11.......221 C3
Abbots Way
  Hodnet TF9...........69 C6
  Shrewsbury SY2.......126 A7
Abbotts Way 3 WV16..218 F6
ABCOTT..............194 F1
ABDON...............198 A5
Abdon Cl 9 WV16......200 E3
Abdon Ct 1 TF2........132 A3
Abelia Way TF2........132 F1
Abenbury Rd LL13......221 F1
Abingdon Rd
  3 Albrighton WV7....156 F8
  Shrewsbury SY2.......126 A7
Abney Ave WV7.........156 F5
Abraham Cl 6 TF1.....144 B1
Abraham Darby Sch TF7.152 E5
Acacia Ave 13 DY12...211 E2
Acacia Dr TF1.........131 A5
Access Sch SY4........83 C6
Acer Cl TF3...........143 E8
ACKLETON.............164 D2
Acorn Cl 4 SY11........41 F2
Acorn Mews 11 TF5....130 C7
Acorn Rise SY21.......170 B7
Acorn Way TF5.........130 C8
ACTON
  Lydbury North........193 A3
  Wrexham.............221 E6
ACTON BURNELL.......179 C5
Acton Burnell Castle*
  SY5.................179 C4

Acton Gate LL11 ....221 D6
Acton Gdns LL11.......221 E7
Acton Hall Walks LL12..221 E6
Acton Pk Prim Schools
  LL11................221 D7
Acton Pk Way LL12....221 D6
Acton Rd LL11.........221 C5
ACTON REYNALD........84 F3
ACTON ROUND.........187 A6
ACTON SCOTT.........196 A8
Acton Scott Historic Working
  Farm* SY6..........196 A8
Adams Cl TF10........109 E3
Adams Cres TF10......109 E3
Adams' Gram Sch TF10.109 E3
Adamson Dr TF4.......143 D3
Adams Ridge 1 SY3...125 E3
ADDERLEY.............19 A4
Adderley CE Prim Sch
  TF9.................18 F5
Adderley Rd TF9.......19 A2
Addison Rd TF1........130 C3
Addisons Way TF10....121 C4
Adelaide Dr SY21......170 B7
ADENEY..............108 C1
Adeney Rd TF10.......108 C1
ADFORTON............205 A2
ADMASTON............130 B6
Admaston Cl TF4......153 C7
Admaston Rd TF1......130 C5
Admaston Spa 8 TF5..130 B7
Admirals Cl TF1.......146 A6
Admirals Way TF11....146 A6
Adswood Gr SY3.......124 F1
Aelybryn LL11.........221 C7
Agden House La SY13...1 A5
Agnes Hunt Cl 2 SY4..81 A1
Agnes Hunt Meml Bglws
  SY11................41 B6
Ainsdale Dr
  Dawley TF2..........144 E8
  Shrewsbury SY1......113 E3
Aintree Cl TF1........131 A5
Alan Gutridge Dr SY13..124 E5
Albacore Rd TF1.......131 A7
ALBERBURY...........168 D5
Alberbury Dr SY1......114 B3
Alberbury Rd SY5......169 B4
Albert Dr 1 DY3.......190 F1
Albert Gdns 1 SY1.....113 F7
Albert Mews 7 SY11...40 E1

Albert Pl
  Donnington TF2.......132 C8
  24 Oswestry SY11....58 E8
Albert Rd
  Albrighton WV7......156 F4
  2 Oswestry SY11....58 E8
  Shrewsbury SY1......113 F2
  Wellington TF1.......130 E4
Albert Sq
  4 Shrewsbury SY1...113 F3
  Weston Rhyn SY10...23 C4
Albert St
  8 Oakengates/Donnington
    TF2...............132 C3
  6 Shrewsbury SY1...125 D7
  7 Wrexham LL13.....221 D2
Albert Terr 8 SY21....170 B6
Albion Hill 12 SY11....58 E8
Albion St TF1..........132 C3
Albridge La SY10.......76 E8
ALBRIGHTON
  Donington...........157 A6
  Pimhill..............101 D1
Albrighton By-pass WV7.157 B6
Albrighton Inf Sch WV7.157 A4
Albrighton Jun Sch WV7.157 A4
Albrighton Moat & Gdns*
  WV7................157 B7
Albrighton Sta WV7...157 B5
ALCASTON............196 A6
Alder Dr 1 SY5........172 E4
Alderley La SY4........66 E7
Aldermead Cl TF5.....130 A7
Alder Rd TF9...........53 A8
Alders La SY13.........30 D1
Alderslee Cl 5 TF2....132 E2
Aldersley Way 3 SY4..80 A1
ALDERTON.............83 C4
Aldford Way 3 LL12...221 F6
ALDON...............195 E2
Aldon View 19 SY7....195 E5
Aldridge Cl 16 TF2....132 F1
Aldwick Dr SY3........124 F2
ALE OAK..............192 B7
Alexander Fleming Prim Sch
  TF7.................153 C4
Alexandra Ave SY3....125 A2
Alexandra CP Sch LL12.221 D4
Alexandra Rd
  11 Market Drayton TF9..36 B1
  10 Oswestry SY11....40 D1
  4 Wellington TF1....130 D3
  Wrexham LL13........221 B2

Alfred St SY2..........125 E5
Algernon Ct TF2.......132 C8
Alison Dr SY6.........216 E6
Alison Rd SY6.........216 E6
ALKINGTON............14 E3
Alkington Gdns 1 SY13.15 A6
Alkington Rd SY13.....14 F6
Allcroft Cl SY7........206 A6
Allerton Rd 6 SY1.....114 B3
Allertons Mdw 6 TF5..130 B8
Allestree Cl 6 SY1....113 E5
Alley The TF6.........142 D2
Allgold Dr SY2........126 A5
Allmans La TF9.........72 A4
Alness Cl 1 SY2.......126 B7
Alloe Brook SY4.......169 E6
All Saints Ave 3 DY12..211 E3
All Saints CE (C) Prim Sch
  WV5.................190 D4
ALLSCOTT.............188 D2
ALLSCOTT.............129 C6
ALL STRETTON........184 B6
Alma Ave TF4.........143 F5
Alma Cl SY11...........78 D7
Alma Fields TF4.......143 F5
Alma Rd 2 LL20.........6 A7
Alma St SY3...........125 B6
ALMINGTON............37 C2
Almond Ave SY11......41 A7
Almond Cl 7 TF2......132 E8
Almond Dr 3 TF1......131 B6
Almond Dr 7 SY12....27 A2
Almond Gr LL13.......221 F4
Alms Ct 3 SY3........125 B2
ALPORT..............175 A1
Alport Rd SY13..........2 A1
Alton Gr TF10.........109 E1
Alton Terr 1 SY3......125 D4
Alvaston Way SY2.....126 A8
ALVELEY.............201 A3
Alveley Ind Est WV15..201 A3
Alveley Prim Sch WV15.201 B3
Alverley Cl
  4 Shrewsbury SY3...124 F6
  7 Wellington TF1....130 E4
Alvin Cl SY4...........65 F5
Alyndale Rd 3 LL12...221 D7
Amber Hill SY3........124 E4
Amblecote Dr 4 SY3..137 A5
Ambleside SY1........113 F4
Ambleside Rd 19 SY11..58 E8
Ambleside Way 3 TF2.132 E6
ANCHOR..............191 C7
Anchor Cl SY13........15 B7

Andreas Dr 14 TF2....132 F8
ANGELBANK...........208 A3
Angel La SY8.........208 A3
Annefield Cl 4 TF9....36 D2
ANNSCROFT..........136 A4
Anslem Ct 2 TF3......144 A1
Anson Dr 3 TF1.......131 B6
Anson Rd WV7........156 B7
Anstice Rd TF7.......153 A5
Anstice Sq 5 TF7.....153 B5
Anthony Eden Dr LL13..221 F2
Anton Cl 13 DY12.....211 E3
Anvil Cl TF10.........107 E5
Apley Ave TF1.........130 E5
Apley Castle TF1......130 E7
Apley Ct 4 TF1........130 D6
Apley Dr TF1..........130 E5
Apley Wood Prim Sch
  TF1.................131 A7
Apple Acre WV16......188 D1
Applebrook TF11......145 F3
Appledore 9 SY3......124 D7
Appledore Gdns TF1...130 D2
Apple Gr TF9...........36 A1
Applewood Cl
  6 Offa LL13.........221 D1
  West Felton SY11....78 D7
Applewood Hts SY11...78 D7
Appleyard Cl 6 SY8...212 E2
Apse Cl 9 WV5.......190 F4
Aqualate Cl 5 TF10...110 A4
AQUEDUCT............152 F8
Aqueduct La TF3......144 B1
Aqueduct Rd TF3......153 A8
Aragorn Way 5 TF4...153 A8
Aralia Cl 6 TF2.......132 F1
Aran Rd LL12.........221 E4
Arboretum The TF9....89 B7
Arbour La SY9.........182 B8
Arbourne Gdns 8 SY3.125 C4
Archers Way SY1......113 E6
Archer's Way
  Tenbury Wells WR15..220 C6
  5 Wrexham LL13.....221 E4
Arden Cl
  4 Shrewsbury SY2...125 C8
  Wem SY4............66 B8
Arden Way 11 WV15...201 B3
Ardern Ave TF4.......143 F4
Ardmillan Cl 5 SY11...58 F8
Ardmillan Ct SY11.....58 F8
Ardmillan La 4 SY11...58 F8

BETCHCOTT 177 E5
Betley La SY3 137 A5
Betnell Gr 2 TF7 153 A5
BETTISFIELD 29 C3
BETTON 37 A6
Betton Dingle Nature Reserve★ SY5 171 E1
Betton Rd TF9 36 E2
Betton St SY3 125 D4
BETTON STRANGE 137 F7
BETTWS-Y-CRWYN 191 F3
Betty's La CW3 5 A1
Beulah Dr 8 TF9 36 B1
Bevan Cl TF1 131 D4
Bevan Way TF9 36 B3
Beveley Rd TF2 131 E2
Beverley Cl DY11 211 F3
BEWDLEY 211 D1
Bewdley High Sch DY12 211 D1
Bewdley Sta DY12 211 E2
Bewdley Wribbenhall Mid Sch DY12 211 E2
Bickerstaff Ct TF1 130 D2
BICKLEY 215 A5
Bickleywood Dr 6 LL13 221 F5
BICTON 193 C5
Bicton CE Prim Sch SY3 169 F5
BICTON HEATH 124 A7
Bicton La SY3 169 F6
Bieston Cl LL12 221 F8
Big Walls 5 SY4 80 A1
Bilberry Cl TF3 143 F7
BILLINGSLEY 200 C3
Billingsley Cl 2 SY9 181 F3
BILMARSH 83 C7
BINGS HEATH 103 A1
Binweston La
Forden with Leighton & Trelystan SY21 170 F2
Worthen with Shelve SY5 171 C3
Birbeck Dr TF7 152 E4
Birch Cl
Llandysilio SY22 94 B1
7 Market Drayton TF9 52 F8
6 Ruyton-XI-Towns SY4 80 A1
Birch Coppice 17 WV5 190 F3
Birch Dale Ave 1 TF2 132 A4
Birch Dr
6 Hanwood SY5 173 F8
Shawbury SY4 103 F7
Birchfield Sch WV7 157 D5
Birch Gr
Alveley WV15 201 B3
Ruyton SY4 80 A1
Birch Hill Ave 30 WV5 190 F3
Birchill Pl 31 WV5 190 F3
Birch La LL13 10 D8
Birchlands WV15 219 B4
Birchlee Cl 2 TF2 132 E1
Birch Mdw TF12 152 D1
Birch Mdw Rd 4 TF12 152 C1
Birchmore 12 TF3 144 B1
Birch Rd SY12 27 C2
Birch Row TF12 161 C8
Birch St 5 LL13 221 D2
Birch Tree Rd 6 DY12 211 C2
Birchwood Cl 5 TF2 132 E8
Birchwood Dr
2 Shrewsbury SY1 113 D2
Whittington SY11 41 F2
Birchwood Gr SY13 32 E5
BIRDSGREEN 201 C4
BIRTLEY 184 C1
Bishopdale TF3 153 B8
BISHOP'S CASTLE 181 E3
Bishop's Castle Bsns Pk SY9 181 F3
Bishop's Castle Com Hospl SY9 181 F3
Bishop's Castle Prim Sch SY9 181 E3
Bishop's Castle Rly Mus★ SY9 181 F3
Bishops Castle St SY15 174 B3
Bishops Cl 3 SY11 78 D8
Bishops La 9 TF9 36 B1
Bishop St SY2 125 E6
Bishops Wlk TF2 132 D7
BISHOPS WOOD 148 F8
Bishton Rd WV7 156 F4
BITTERLEY 207 F4
Bitterley CE Prim Sch SY8 207 F4
Bitterley Cl SY8 217 F5
Bitterley La SY8 208 A3
Blackbird Cl TF3 131 D1
Blackbridge La SY10 76 A3
BLACKFORD 198 B1
Blackfriars SY11 59 A8
Black Gate St 17 SY11 58 E8
Blackmere Cl TF10 109 D2
BLACKMORE 171 E8
Blackmore Gr SY13 15 A8
BLACKOE 14 B3
BLACK PARK
Chirk 7 A5
Whitchurch Urban 2 E2
Blackpit La WV5 190 F5
Black Pk Rd
Whitchurch SY13 15 B8
Whitchurch Urban SY13 2 E2
Blacksmiths Dr 3 TF2 131 F1
Blacksmiths La SY4 85 F5
Blackstone Dr 3 TF2 132 D3
Blackthorn Gr 9 TF5 130 C8
Blaizefield Cl CW3 5 A2
Blakemere Cl 2 SY13 2 B1
Blakemore TF3 153 C8
Blakemore's Bank SY3 137 B6
Blakenham Ct 5 TF4 143 D2
Blakeway Cl TF12 161 E7
Blakeway Hollow TF13 159 C4
Blakeway Mews 5 SY3 124 A7
Blashfield Rd SY8 217 F4
Bleachfield 10 SY5 173 F8
Blenheim Cl SY11 41 A1
Blenheim Cres 1 WV7 156 F8
Blenheim Rd 11 TF1 131 A7
BLETCHLEY 51 E8
Bletchley Rd SY13 34 D3
Blews Hill 11 TF4 143 E4
Blews Hill Ct TF4 143 E4
BLISTS HILL 153 B3
Blists Hill Victorian Town★ TF7 153 A3
Blithe Cl TF12 152 D2
Blodwel Bank SY10 75 D5
Bloomfield Cl 3 WV5 190 E3
Bloomsbury Ct 1 TF2 120 D1
BLOREHEATH 37 E3
Blore Rd TF9 37 E1
BLUEBELL 128 F1
Bluebell Cl 10 SY21 170 B7
Bluebell Coppice 4 TF1 131 E1
Blue Bell Dr 9 SY21 170 B7
Bluebell Rd TF6 128 F2
Bluegate 2 TF11 146 A4
Blue House La WV7 157 B7
BLYMHILL 135 F5
Blythe Gdns TF2 132 D5
Blything Ct 10 WV16 200 E2
Boatwell Mdw
Dawley Hamlets TF4 152 D8
Dawley TF4 143 D1
BOBBINGTON 189 F1
Bockleton Rd WR15 220 C1
Bodbury Cl 4 SY6 216 D7
Boddington Cres 1 TF3 144 D4
Bodhyfryd 4 LL12 221 D4
Body Rd TF2 120 D3
Bogey La SY5 173 B4
Bog Hall La TF9 71 D4
Bog La WR15 220 C4
BOG THE 176 C4
BOLAS HEATH 107 B8
Bollingale Ave 5 TF2 132 A4
BOMERE HEATH 100 F4
Bomere Heath CE Prim Sch SY4 100 E3
BONINGALE 157 B2
Boningale Cl 13 TF3 144 C1
BOOLEYBANK 86 A8
Booley La SY4 85 F5
Booley Rd SY4 85 F5
Boot St
15 Welshpool SY21 170 B6
Whittington SY11 41 F3
BORASTON 214 E4
Boraston Bank WR15 220 E7
BORASTON DALE 214 D5
Boraston Dr WR15 220 E6
Boraston La WR15 220 D7
Border Cl 3 SY11 58 F7
Border Ret Pk LL13 221 E3
Border The TF3 144 B6
Borderway WR15 220 D6
Borfa Gn SY21 170 B7
Borle Brook Ct WV16 200 E2
BORRAS 221 F7
Borras Pk Rd LL12 221 F6
Borras Rd LL12 221 F5
Boscobel Cl 6 TF3 144 D1
Boscobel Dr 3 SY1 113 D2
Boscobel House★ ST19 148 F5
Boscobel Pl TF9 52 D4
Boscobel Rd TF9 52 D4
Bostock Cl 3 TF5 130 A7
Bostock Cres TF3 153 B8
Botany Bay Cl 3 TF4 144 A1
Botfield Cl
Albrighton WV7 157 B6
Telford Dawley TF3 144 C3
Botfield Rd TF11 146 A5
Botterham La DY3 190 F2
Boughey Rd TF10 109 E2
Bould La TF12 161 D2
BOULDON 197 D4
Boulmer Ave WV7 156 D8
Boulton Grange 5 TF3 144 D3
Bournbrook Gdns TF3 153 B8
Bournside Dr TF3 153 B8
BOURTON 186 C7
Bourton Cl 5 TF3 144 C1
Bourton Rd TF13 159 D4
BOWBROOK 124 B5
Bowbrook Grange SY5 124 B5
Bowdler Cl SY8 217 E4
Bowens Field SY4 66 A7
Bower End La CW3 5 F5
Bowers Cl 1 WV16 218 D5
Bower Yd TF8 152 C3
Bowkers La SY13 13 D5
Bowland Cl TF3 143 D8
Bowlers Alley WV7 156 C8
Bowling Gn Cl 14 SY9 181 F3
Bowling Gn La
Albrighton WV7 156 D5
20 Knighton LD7 203 B3
9 Welshpool SY21 170 B6
Bowling Gn Way 6 TF13 159 E4
BOWLING GREEN 87 F8
Bowring Gr TF1 130 D2
Bow Way SY4 100 F4
Box La LL12 221 E8
Boyd Cl TF3 144 C7
Bracewell Dr 8 SY3 124 E4
Brackenfield TF3 153 B8
Bracken Gr TF1 131 A3
Bracken Rise 3 SY12 27 A3
Bracken Way 3 TF10 109 F4
Brackley Dr SY3 124 D7
Bradbury La DY7 201 F6
Bradeley Gn La SY13 1 F6
Brades Rd SY13 49 B7
Bradford St
Shifnal TF11 145 F4
Shrewsbury SY2 125 E6
Bradley Ct 4 TF2 132 E6
Bradley Farm La SY14 1 C7
Bradley Fields
Donnington TF2 132 D6
Oswestry SY11 58 C8
BRADLEY GREEN 1 A8
Bradley Rd
Oakengates/Donnington TF2 132 D6
Wrexham LL13 221 B3
Bradleys The 1 SY1 114 B3
BRADNEY 189 B6
Braemar Rd 7 WV6 166 C2
Braggington La SY5 168 A5
Braithwaite Row TF1 130 D2
Bramble Ridge WV16 218 F6
Brambles The
Crewgreen SY5 167 F6
1 The Rock TF3 143 E7
Bramblewood TF12 152 D1
Bramblewood Cl LL14 23 E6
Bramley Cl 5 SY1 125 B8
Bramley Way 9 DY12 211 C2
BRAMPTON BRYAN 204 E3
Brampton Rd
Bishop's Castle SY9 181 F2
Lydbury North SY7 182 A1
Bramwell Cl 3 TF2 132 C3
Branches Cl 5 DY12 211 C1
BRANDHILL 195 D2
Brand La SY8 217 C4
Brandlee TF4 143 E4
Brandon Ave TF5 130 B7
Brandon Gr 4 TF1 131 A7
Brands Farm Way TF3 144 D4
Brands Mdw 16 TF2 132 F8
BRANDWOOD 64 E1
Brandywell Rd TF12 152 D1
BRANSLEY 209 C2
Brantley Cres 1 DY7 189 F1
Brantley La
Claverley WV5 189 F2
Trysull & Seisdon WV5 190 A6
Brassey Cl 2 SY3 125 D4
Bratch Comm Rd WV5 190 F4
Bratch La WV5 190 F4
Bratch Pk 1 WV5 190 F4
BRATCH THE 190 F4
BRATTON 130 A8
Bratton Rd TF5 130 A7
BREADEN HEATH 28 E6
Bream Cl 5 TF2 132 A6
Brecknock Ct 2 TF1 131 A4
Bredon Cl WV7 157 A5
Breidden Cl 5 SY10 58 C7
Breidden Mdw SY21 167 D3
Breidden Pl
Trewern SY21 167 B2
Wellington TF1 130 C6
Breidden View
Frankwell SY3 125 A6
Middletown SY21 167 D3
Breidden Way SY3 136 E6
Brereton TF3 153 C8
Brewery Pl 14 LL11 221 C3
Briar Cl 4 SY5 172 E4
Briars The SY12 63 D7
Briarswood LL11 221 B8
Briarwood 9 TF3 144 B1
Brickbridge La WV5 190 F3
Brickhill La TF2 131 E3
Brick Kiln Bank TF7 152 D7
Brickkiln La SY13 2 D2
Brick Kiln La TF7 153 E3
Brick Kiln Way 9 TF2 132 E7
Bricklin Mews TF1 131 E5
Bridge Bank TF12 152 C3
Bridge Cl 8 TF2 132 A6
Bridgeend La SY7 204 B5
Bridgeford Way 6 SY2 125 F8
Bridge La SY5 169 F1
Bridgeman Ct TF11 135 F2
Bridgeman Rd SY11 58 F8
BRIDGEMERE 4 D8
Bridgemere CE Prim Sch CW5 4 C8
Bridgemere Gdn World★ CW5 4 F4
Bridgemere Mews CW5 4 D8
Bridgenorth Rd WV5 190 C3
Bridgenorth Sports & Leisure Ctr WV16 218 F6
Bridge Rd
Alveley WV15 201 B3
Broseley TF12 152 B1
Dawley TF4 143 C3
2 Market Drayton TF9 36 A1
Much Wenlock TF13 159 D4
2 Wellington TF1 130 D3
BRIDGES 177 A3
Bridges Bsns Pk The TF4 143 C3
Bridge Sea Mdw SY7 204 B5
Bridge Sq TF2 132 A5
Bridge St
Bridgnorth WV16 218 F4
8 Clun SY7 193 D3
Knighton LD7 203 B3
1 Oakengates/Donnington TF2 132 A2
18 Shrewsbury SY1 125 B6
21 Wrexham LL13 221 C3
Bridgewater Cl SY4 83 B1
Bridgewater Dr 14 WV5 190 F4
Bridgewater St 7 SY13 15 A7
Bridge Way
Oakengates/Donnington TF2 120 E1
Shawbury SY4 103 D8
BRIDGNORTH 218 D3
Bridgnorth Ave 49 WV5 190 F3
Bridgnorth Castle★ WV16 218 F4
Bridgnorth Coll of Further Ed WV15 219 A3
Bridgnorth Endowed Sch Tech Coll WV16 218 F6
Bridgnorth Hospl WV16 218 E5
Bridgnorth Rd
Broseley TF12 161 D7
Dawley Hamlets TF3 153 B8
Highley WV16 200 E2
Madeley TF7 153 C7
Much Wenlock TF13 159 E4
Stockton TF11 163 B5
Sutton Maddock TF11 154 A1
Trysull & Seisdon WV6 190 C7
Wolverley & Cookley DY11 211 F7
Wombourne WV5 190 F3
Bridgnorth Sta WV16 218 F4
Bridgwater Cl 6 TF4 144 A2
Bridgwood 16 TF3 144 C1
Bridle Ct TF7 153 A6
Bridle Rd 4 TF7 152 F5
Bridle Terr TF7 153 A5
Bridleways The SY6 216 D5
Bridleway The 5 TF9 36 B1
Briery Bank TF7 152 D6
Briery La SY3 124 A6
Briggs La SY10 76 A1
Briggs Way TF2 132 C4
Bright St LL13 221 B3
Brightwell SY3 125 E2
BRIMFIELD 213 B2
Brimstree Dr TF11 145 F3
Brindley Cl
5 Albrighton WV7 157 A5
1 Wombourne WV5 190 E3
Brindleyford TF3 153 B8
BRINETON 135 F8
Bringewood Cl SY8 217 C6
Bringewood Rd SY8 217 C6
Bringewood Rise SY8 217 C6
Britannia Way TF1 131 C5
Britons La WV16 187 E8
Britten Ct 3 TF1 130 E3
Brixton Way SY1 113 F4
Brixton Way Ret Pk SY1 113 F4
BRJ Cath Coll The TF1 130 E6
Broadhaven Cl 1 SY1 113 C2
Broadhay Rd SY13 49 F4
Broadlands Way 6 SY11 59 B8
BROAD LANES 201 D7
Broad Mdw La TF7 152 D6
BROADOAK 113 D7
BROAD OAK 201 D7
Broad Oak Cres SY3 137 A6
Broad Oaks 7 TF3 144 D3
Broad St
Knighton LD7 203 B2
Ludlow SY8 217 C4
9 Montgomery SY15 174 B3
BROADSTONE 197 C8
Broadstone Mews 2 TF4 152 F8
Broadway
Hadley TF1 131 D3
Newport TF10 110 A3
Shifnal TF11 145 F5
Broadway Ave TF2 132 A6
Broadway Cl
10 Shifnal TF11 145 F5
Shrewsbury SY2 125 F1
Broadwell La WV6 166 B2
Broadwell The 13 SY3 124 F3
Brockford Glade TF5 130 B7
Brock Hollow 3 TF4 143 D3
BROCKTON
Church Aston 121 B6
Lydbury North 193 F8
Stanton Long 186 B4
Sutton Maddock 153 F4
Worthen with Shelve 171 E3
Brockton CE Prim Sch TF13 186 A5
Brockton Cl TF7 153 C7
Brockton Mdw SY5 171 E3
Brockton Way TF7 153 D6
Brockwood Copse 7 TF1 130 B7
Bro Gwilym LL14 6 B8
BROGYNTYN 40 A2
BROMDON 208 D7
BROMFIELD 206 D3
Bromfield Dr 2 SY3 125 E3
Bromfield Gr 4 LL12 221 D5
Bromfield Rd SY8 217 B6
BROMLEY
Hordley 62 C2
Worfield 188 E6
Bromley Rd
Ludlow SY8 217 D5
Bromley Rd *continued*
Shrewsbury SY3 124 A7
Bromleys Ct 6 SY6 216 D5
Bromley Way 5 TF2 132 C2
BROMLOW 175 F8
BROMPTON 139 B5
BROMSTEAD 123 E7
BROMSTEAD COMMON 111 E1
BROMSTEAD HEATH 123 E7
Bromyard Rd WR15 220 E3
BRONCROFT 197 D5
BRONINGTON 13 A3
Bronington Pk SY13 13 B3
Bronington VA Prim Sch SY13 13 B4
Bronwylfa SY22 93 F8
Bronwylfa Rd 12 SY21 170 B7
Bronydre LL13 221 B1
BRONYGARTH 22 E7
Bronygarth Rd SY10 23 C4
Bron-y-nant 2 LL13 221 B4
Bron-yr-efail 3 LL12 221 D8
Brook Cl SY5 137 B1
Brookdale
2 Hadley TF1 131 B4
3 Hadley TF1 131 C5
5 Shifnal TF11 145 F5
Brook Dr SY4 65 F5
Brookes Rd 6 TF12 161 E7
Brookfield
Bayston Hill SY3 136 E6
Stirchley TF3 144 C2
Whitchurch SY13 14 E8
Brookfield Cl SY10 23 D4
Brookfield Rd SY21 170 B7
Brookfields SY10 23 C4
BROOKHAMPTON 185 F1
Brook Hollow 1 WV16 218 F6
Brookhouse Rd SY11 58 E8
Brookhurst Way 2 TF2 132 F8
Brook La
Hanmer SY13 11 F5
Worfield WV15 219 E5
BROOKLANDS 1 E1
Brooklands Ave 3 TF11 145 F3
Brooklands Pk SY7 195 E6
Brooklands Rd WV7 157 B5
Brooklands The 10 DY3 190 F1
Brooklea Cl SY10 57 E2
Brooklyn Rd SY10 76 B1
Brook Mdw
Church Stretton SY6 216 E6
5 Wellington TF5 130 B8
Brook Rd
Bomere Heath SY4 100 F4
Craven Arms SY7 195 D6
Madeley TF7 153 C6
Pontesbury SY5 173 A4
Shrewsbury SY3 125 D5
Whitchurch SY13 15 B7
10 Wombourne WV5 190 F3
Brook Rise 6 SY5 173 A4
BROOKROW 208 D1
Brooksbury SY6 216 C6
BROOKSIDE 144 C1
Brookside
Bicton SY3 112 A2
2 Oakengates/Donnington TF2 120 E1
Pontesbury SY5 173 A5
6 Worthen with Shelve SY5 171 F3
Brookside Ave
Dawley TF3 153 B8
Newport TF10 109 E1
Stirchley & Brookside TF3 144 D1
Brookside Cl
Shifnal TF11 145 F6
15 Wombourne WV5 190 F3
Brookside Dr WV15 189 C6
Brookside Gdns
2 Brewood ST19 148 E8
1 Westbury SY5 169 B1
Brook St
Shrewsbury SY3 125 C3
6 Welshpool SY21 170 B6
Wrexham LL13 221 C3
Brook Vale 14 DY12 211 E2
Brookvale Rd 13 TF2 132 F1
Brook Vessons Nature Reserve★ SY5 176 F7
BROOMBANK 215 E5
Broom Dr
2 Minsterley SY5 172 E4
The Rock TF3 143 F7
BROOME
Cardington 179 B1
Hopesay 195 B4
Broome Cl SY7 195 B3
Broome Pl 2 SY1 125 C7
Broome Rd
Clungunford SY7 195 A1
Hopesay SY7 195 A4
Broome Sta SY7 195 A3
Broomfield Cl TF10 109 D3
Broomfield Pl TF10 109 D3
Broomfield Rd
Admaston TF5 130 A6
Newport TF10 109 D3
BROOMFIELDS 169 D8
Broom Gr 5 LL13 221 F4
Broomhall Cl SY11 58 C6
Broomhall La
Oswestry Rural SY10 58 B7
Pimhill SY4 101 B2
Broomhurst Way 7 TF2 120 F1
BROSELEY 152 D1

Longnor CE Prim Sch SY5 178 E3
Longnor Rd TF1 130 C6
LONG OAK 78 E3
Long Pack SY1 114 B4
Long Row 3 SY1 113 E1
LONGSLOW 35 F3
Longslow Cl 4 TF9 36 B1
Longslow Rd 10 TF9 36 B1
Longthorpe Dr TF1 131 C6
Longueville 1 LL13 221 C1
Longueville Dr SY11 59 B8
LONGVILLE IN THE DALE 185 C4
Longville Rd 6 SY1 113 D4
Longwithy La TF10 108 F4
Lonsdale Dr SY3 125 A1
LOPPINGTON 64 D7
Loppington Hse FE Unit & Adult Ctre SY4 46 E1
Lord Murray Dr TF7 152 E7
Lords Dr 1 TF2 132 E3
Lord Silkin Sch TF3 144 D2
Lord St
5 Oswestry SY11 58 D8
1 Wrexham LL11 221 C3
Lordstone La SY5 172 A1
Lorne St
8 Oswestry SY11 40 E1
Wrexham LL11 221 C4
LOSTFORD 51 E3
Lostford La TF9 51 E4
Loton Butts 9 SY2 125 F8
LOUGHTON 198 F2
Loughton Cl SY8 217 E5
Loughton La WV16 198 D1
Lovat Cl SY2 126 A7
Love La
Bishop's Castle SY9 181 F3
Bridgnorth WV16 218 F6
Cleobury Mortimer DY14 209 E2
Lydham SY9 182 A4
Wem SY4 66 B8
Lovell Cl TF11 146 A6
Loveridge Dr SY4 99 B7
LOWE 47 D2
Lowe Croft 6 SY7 205 B5
Lowe Hill Gdns SY4 65 F7
Lowe Hill Rd SY4 65 F6
Lowe La
Alveley WV15 201 B1
Upper Arley DY12 211 B8
LOWER ALLSCOT 188 E7
Lower Bar TF10 109 E3
LOWER BEOBRIDGE 189 D2
Lower Broad St SY8 217 C3
Lower Brook St SY11 58 D7
Lower Claremont Bank 10 SY1 125 B6
LOWER COMMON 178 A8
Lower Cross Lanes SY7 197 F4
LOWER DINCHOPE 196 A3
Lower Dingle 7 TF7 152 F4
LOWER DOWN 194 A7
LOWER FAINTREE 199 C7
Lower Fee SY8 217 C3
LOWER FORGE 200 E8
LOWER FRANKTON 43 B4
Lower Galdeford SY8 217 D4
Lower Hafod 1 SY11 58 C8
LOWER HAYTON 206 F8
Lower Heath CE Prim Sch SY13 50 A6
LOWER HENGOED 40 F6
LOWER HOPTON 97 D6
LOWER HORDLEY 62 A7
Lower Inhedge DY14 209 F3
Lower La SY7 183 E1
LOWER LEDWYCHE 207 C1
Lower Mill St SY8 217 C3
Lower Minst
Oswestry SY11 58 C8
Wrexham LL12 221 E8
LOWER NETCHWOOD 186 F2
LOWER PENN 190 F6
Lower Pk DY12 211 D2
Lower Pk Dr 5 TF1 130 C7
Lower Pulley La SY3 137 B7
Lower Raven La SY8 217 C3
Lower Rd
Myddle & Broughton SY4 82 E4
7 Pontesbury SY5 173 A4
LOWER RIDGE 42 D7
Lower St DY14 209 E2
LOWER TODDING 205 B6
Lower Wood TF3 143 E7
Loweswater Cl 1 TF2 144 E8
Lowfield 5 SY2 125 F8
LOW HABBERLEY 211 F5
Lowry Cl 10 TF5 130 B8
LOW TOWN 219 A5
Low Valley Cl TF1 131 D3
Loxdale 15 SY3 124 F3
LUBBERLAND 209 A5
Lucerne Cl 2 TF1 131 C5
Luciefelde Rd SY3 125 B4
Ludford Almshouses SY8 217 C3
Ludford Dr
15 Dawley TF3 144 C1
Shrewsbury SY1 113 D3
Ludford View SY8 217 E3
LUDLOW 217 D3
Ludlow Bsns Pk SY8 217 F4
Ludlow Castle* SY8 217 B4
Ludlow CE Sch SY8 217 A6
Ludlow Coll
Ludlow SY8 217 B4
Ludlow Coll *continued*
Ludlow SY8 217 C3
Ludlow Dr TF3 144 B2
Ludlow Eco Pk SY8 217 F3
Ludlow Hospl SY8 217 C5
Ludlow Hts WV16 218 D4
Ludlow Inf Sch SY8 217 D5
Ludlow Jun Sch SY8 217 E5
Ludlow Mus* SY8 217 C4
Ludlow Rd
Aston Eyre WV16 187 D5
Bitterley SY8 207 D2
Bridgnorth WV16 218 C3
Caynham SY8 208 B2
Church Stretton SY6 216 A3
Cleobury Mortimer DY14 209 D2
Craven Arms SY7 195 E5
Knighton LD7 203 C2
Ludlow Sta SY8 217 C5
LUDSTONE 189 F5
Ludstone Hall* WV5 189 E5
Lurkenhope Wood Nature Reserve* LD7 203 C4
LUSHCOTT 185 D6
Lutton Cl SY11 58 D7
Lutwyche Cl 1 SY6 216 C6
Lutwyche Rd SY6 216 C6
Lydbury Cl 8 TF3 144 C1
Lydbury N CE Prim Sch SY7 194 C8
LYDBURY NORTH 194 C8
LYDE 175 E8
LYDHAM 182 A6
Lydham Rd SY1 113 D4
Lyle Ct 17 TF1 130 E4
Lymehurst Ct 7 SY1 113 C1
Lymore View 5 SY15 174 B3
LYNCHGATE 194 E8
Lynch La SY8 213 D2
Lyncroft WV7 157 A5
Lyndale Gr LL12 221 D7
Lyndhurst Dr
1 Bayston Hill SY3 137 A5
6 Oakengates/Donnington TF2 132 A6
LYNEAL 45 E7
Lyneal La SY12 28 D2
LYNN 123 B4
Lyons La SY5 137 E1
Lysander Ave WV7 156 B7
Lytham Gn TF2 133 A8
LYTHBANK 136 C3
Lyth Hill Rd SY3 136 F4
Lythwood Rd SY3 136 E6
Lyttelton Rd DY12 211 C2

M

McClintock Pl SY6 216 D6
McCormick Dr TF1 130 C7
McGredy Dr 3 SY2 125 F5
McKinley Way SY4 85 D1
McLean Dr 3 TF2 132 F1
Maddocks TF7 153 A5
Maddocks Ct TF1 130 E3
Madebrook Cl TF7 153 D5
Madeira Hill 2 LL13 221 D2
Madeira Wlk SY6 216 C7
MADELEY 153 A5
Madeley Acad TF7 153 B6
Madeley Cl TF9 52 D4
Madeley Ct Sports Ctr TF7 153 B6
Madeley Inf Sch TF7 153 A4
Madeley Rd TF7 152 D4
MADELEYWOOD 152 E4
Madeley Wood View 10 TF7 152 F4
Madely Rd TF11 163 B8
Madog Pl 13 SY11 58 E8
Madras Sch LL13 10 E4
Maelor Sch LL13 10 F4
Maer La TF9 36 D3
Maes Alwyn SY10 23 D4
MAESBROOK 95 A7
Maesbrook Rd 4 SY3 125 B1
MAESBURY 77 B8
Maesbury Cty Prim Sch SY10 77 B8
MAESBURY MARSH 77 D6
Maesbury Rd
Oswestry Rural SY10 59 A2
Oswestry SY11 58 F6
Maes Celyn 5 LL13 221 C1
Maes Chwarae SY15 175 A1
Maes Glas 11 LL13 221 C2
Maesgwyn Rd LL13 221 B4
Maes Hafren 1 SY5 167 F6
Maes Hyfryd LL11 221 B8
Maesllwyn Cl SY13 13 A4
Maesllwyn La SY13 12 F4
Maes Neuadd SY15 175 A1
Maes Uchaf SY22 92 B6
Maes y Berwyn LL14 6 E3
Maes y Brllan 2 SY22 93 F6
Maes-y-clawdd SY10 59 A4
Maesydre Rd LL12 221 D5
Maes-y-felin SY21 174 A6
Maes y Foel SY22 92 B5
Maes-y-garreg SY22 92 B6
Maes-y-llan SY22 92 B6
Maes y Llan SY10 56 A4
Maes y Parc LL14 7 A5
Maes-yr-eglwys SY22 92 B6
Maesywaun LL14 6 E1
Mafeking Dr 9 TF2 132 C5
Mafeking Rd TF1 131 C4
Magister Rd WV7 156 B7
Magna Cl
Dawley TF4 143 F2
Whitchurch Rural SY13 16 A4
Magnolia Cl SY4 100 F3
Magnolia Dr
9 Ellesmere SY12 27 A2
5 The Rock TF3 143 E8
Magpie Way 4 TF3 153 A8
Main Rd
Condover SY5 178 C6
Maesbury Marsh SY10 77 C6
Norton in Hales TF9 20 C1
Oakengates/Donnington TF2 131 F1
Pontesbury SY5 173 B5
Wrexham LL11 221 B8
Main St 2 WV15 189 A6
MAINSTONE 181 A2
Maitlands The 6 SY5 178 C6
Majestic Way
Aqueduct TF4 153 D8
Dawley Hamlets TF4 152 F8
Dawley TF4 144 A1
Malcolm Davies Dr 2 TF2 132 B6
Maldwyn Way 12 SY15 174 B3
MALEHURST 172 F5
Malinsgate TF3 144 A6
MALINSLEE 144 A4
Malinslee Ctr TF3 144 A5
Mallard Cl
Dawley TF3 153 D8
7 Shrewsbury SY1 114 B4
Mallards Cl 9 WV15 201 B3
Mall The WV15 219 A4
Malory Dr TF3 144 A1
Malory Rd SY11 58 F8
Malthouse Bank TF6 142 D2
Malthouse Cl
3 Trefonen SY10 57 D2
7 Whittington SY11 41 E3
Malthouse La
Atcham SY5 139 A7
4 Trefonen SY10 57 D2
Maltings Cl WV6 164 D2
Maltings The
3 Bayston Hill SY3 137 A6
1 Wellington TF1 130 D3
West Felton SY11 78 D7
Maltkiln La
Whitchurch Rural SY13 31 E7
Whixall SY13 30 C2
Malt Rise 2 SY5 167 F6
Malvern Cl SY2 125 E2
Malvern Cres TF4 143 E1
Manchester Dr TF1 131 A7
Manley Rd LL13 221 D3
Mannerley La
5 Ketley TF3 131 E1
1 The Rock TF3 143 E8
Manor Cl
Hinstock TF9 72 A1
6 Market Drayton TF9 36 C1
Shifnal TF11 145 F3
Manor Crest 1 SY5 169 C4
Manor Dr
Oakengates/Donnington TF2 132 C1
3 Swindon DY3 190 F1
Manor Farm SY4 126 D8
Manor Farm Dr TF9 72 A1
Manor Farm La WV16 218 D2
Manor Gdns
9 Albrighton WV7 157 A5
Dawley TF4 143 F2
Market Drayton TF9 36 C1
1 Pontesbury SY5 173 B5
Manor House Cl 1 TF13 159 E5
Manor House La SY13 32 E3
Manor House National Nature Reserve Base* SY13 30 E6
Manor La
Bobbington DY7 190 B2
Prees SY13 32 F2
Manor Pk 6 SY5 173 A5
Manor Pl SY13 32 E3
Manor Rd
Dawley TF4 143 E2
Edgmond TF10 109 A3
6 Wellington TF1 131 A2
Manor Rise TF1 131 B2
Manor Way SY2 126 B6
Manse Cl TF1 131 C4
Mansell Rd TF1 130 D3
Manse Rd TF1 131 C4
Maple Ave
4 Ellesmere SY12 27 A3
Oswestry SY11 59 A7
Wrexham LL12 221 E5
Maple Cl
3 Craven Arms SY7 195 D6
Ludlow SY8 217 D6
Market Drayton TF9 52 F8
Oakengates/Donnington TF2 132 A5
Shifnal TF11 145 F5
Maple Cres 1 WV15 201 B3
Maple Dr 5 SY1 113 D3
Maplehurst Dr 2 SY11 41 A1
Maple Wood 11 TF3 144 D3
MARBURY 2 E8
MARCHAMLEY 68 F7
MARCHAMLEY WOOD 50 E3
Marche La SY5 168 A1
Marches Mdw SY4 80 C1
Marches Sch & Tech Coll The SY11 58 C6
March Gr 21 DY12 211 D2
March Way SY1 113 E5
Marchwood Cl 1 WV16 218 C6
Marcle Orch SY8 213 B2
Mardol 11 SY1 125 C6
Mardol Head 10 SY1 125 C6
Mardol Quay 14 SY1 125 B6
MARDU 192 F7
Mardu La SY7 193 A6
MARDY 23 C1
Margaret Ct 4 TF1 131 C3
Marigold Ct 2 TF1 131 E2
Marine Terr 8 SY1 125 D5
MARKET DRAYTON 36 B2
Market Drayton Cottage Hosp TF9 53 C8
Market Drayton Inf Sch TF9 36 C1
Market Drayton Jun Sch TF9 53 B8
Market Drayton Swimming Ctr TF9 53 D8
Market La WV4 190 F7
Market Mews 5 TF10 109 F3
Market Pl TF11 145 F4
Market Sq
3 Bishop's Castle SY9 181 F3
Tenbury Wells WR15 220 C5
8 Wellington TF1 130 D4
Market St
11 Craven Arms SY7 195 E5
4 Ellesmere SY12 27 B2
7 Knighton LD7 203 B3
Ludlow SY8 217 C4
2 Oakengates/Donnington TF2 132 B2
2 Shrewsbury SY1 125 C5
Tenbury Wells WR15 220 D5
11 Wellington TF1 130 E4
2 Wem SY4 66 A6
Wrexham LL12 221 D3
Marlborough Ct 7 SY1 114 A2
Marlborough Rd TF1 131 E5
Marlborough Way TF3 143 D8
Marlbrook La WV6 166 B2
Marlburn Way 11 WV5 190 F3
Marlcroft 1 SY4 66 A8
Marlebrook Way TF6 116 A6
MARLEY GREEN 3 B8
Marley Mount Cres 6 TF9 36 C2
MARLOW 205 B7
Marlow Dr TF2 132 B6
Marlpool Cl 4 SY3 124 F4
Marne Cl 1 SY4 66 B8
Marquis Terr TF2 132 B1
Marrion's Hill TF2 132 C2
Marshalls Ct 4 SY1 125 D8
MARSHBROOK 183 E4
Marshbrook Way TF2 132 E8
Marsh Cres 1 LL12 221 E5
Marshgate 3 SY3 124 D6
MARSH GREEN 117 B1
Marsh La
Cheswardine TF9 73 A8
Hinstock TF9 72 B1
Sheriffhales TF11 134 D3
Marsh Mdw Cl 4 TF1 130 C7
Marsh Rd
Edgmond TF10 108 F6
Sheriffhales TF11 134 D4
MARSH THE
Chirbury with Brompton 175 E5
Hinstock 90 B8
Marsland Cl SY11 25 A6
Marstons Mill SY8 217 C4
Marstons Terr SY8 217 C4
Mart Ave 4 TF2 132 D1
Martingale Way TF4 143 D6
Martin Rd TF1 130 C4
Martins Cl SY10 57 E2
Martins Fields SY10 57 E2
Martin Wilson Prim Sch The SY1 125 E8
MARTON
Chirbury and Broughton 171 B1
Myddle and Broughton 81 D4
Marton Dr
Shrewsbury SY1 113 D2
Wellington TF1 130 C6
Mary Elizabeth Rd SY8 217 E3
Maryvale WR15 220 B4
Mary Webb Cl 2 SY5 173 A5
Mary Webb Rd SY3 125 B1
Mary Webb Sch SY5 173 B4
Mary Webb Sports Ctr SY5 173 B4
Masefield Cl 4 TF9 53 A7
Maserfield SY11 58 C7
Maserfield Cl 4 SY11 58 C7
Maslan Cres TF10 107 D5
Mason Ave 12 LL13 221 D2
Mason Dr 3 TF7 152 F5
Mason's Pl TF10 109 E5
Massey Cres SY1 113 E5
Matlock Ave 6 TF4 144 A4
Maudlins Cl WV16 218 C4
Maurice Chandler Sports Ctr TF9 70 C8
Maurice Lee Ave 4 TF2 132 A3
Mawddwy Ave 1 LL11 221 C5
Mawley Ct 7 SY2 125 F2
Maws Craft Ctr* TF8 153 A2
Mayfair Cl 4 WV7 157 A5
Mayfair Gr 3 TF2 132 F2
Mayfield TF7 153 A5
Mayfield Ave 6 SY7 195 E5
Mayfield Dr 5 SY2 125 F4
Mayfield Gdns SY2 126 A4
Mayfield Gr SY3 136 E6
Mayfield Pk SY2 126 A4
Mayfield Rd 3 WV7 156 F5
Mayfields SY8 217 C6
Maynards Croft 4 TF10 109 F4
Maypole Cl 10 DY12 211 E2
Maypole Rd TF12 152 C2
Maythorne Cl TF7 153 C4
Mayville Ave 3 LL11 221 C5
Meadcroft 1 TF7 153 A5
Meadlands The 3 WV5 190 F3
Meadow Bank TF9 19 A4
Meadow Brook SY3 136 F6
Meadowbrook Cl 12 WV15 201 B3
Meadow Brook Cl TF7 153 B5
Meadow Cl
Aston Eyre WV16 187 D4
Bridgnorth WV16 218 E3
Cressage SY5 149 E4
7 Madeley TF7 153 C5
Market Drayton TF9 36 A1
Morville WV16 187 D5
Oakengates/Donnington TF2 131 F6
8 Oswestry SY11 41 A1
4 Shrewsbury SY1 114 A2
Wem SY4 66 A8
Meadowcroft 3 SY13 14 E8
Meadow Dale Dr 1 TF5 130 A6
Meadow Dr
5 Gobowen SY11 41 A7
Shifnal TF11 146 A6
Meadow Farm Dr SY1 114 A3
Meadowlea 6 TF7 153 A5
Meadow Lea
7 Oswestry SY11 41 A1
Wrexham LL13 221 E3
MEADOWLEY 187 E3
Meadow Pl 1 SY1 125 C6
Meadow Rd
Albrighton WV7 157 B5
Clive SY4 84 A5
1 Craven Arms SY7 195 E5
8 Dawley TF4 143 E4
Gnosall TF10 111 A2
8 Newport TF10 109 F3
6 Oakengates/Donnington TF2 132 E8
3 Wellington TF1 130 C2
Meadow Rise
9 Bewdley DY12 211 E3
Oswestry SY11 41 A1
Tenbury Wells WR15 220 D6
Meadows Prim Sch TF1 131 D1
Meadows Prim Sch The SY11 41 A1
Meadows The
Church Stretton SY6 216 E5
6 Gobowen SY11 41 A7
Lawley TF4 143 B6
2 Oakengates/Donnington TF2 132 A1
2 Pant SY10 76 A1
Meadowsweet Dr 4 TF2 132 E1
Meadow Terr SY1 125 C6
Meadow The TF9 69 D5
MEADOWTOWN 175 E8
Meadow View
Llandrinio SY22 167 B8
Prees SY13 49 D8
2 Westbury SY5 169 B1
Meadow View Cl TF10 110 A3
Meadow View Rd
Newport TF10 110 A3
Whitchurch SY13 14 F7
Meadow Way 7 SY11 41 A7
Meadway 12 WV15 219 A4
Mead Way TF11 146 A4
Meaton La DY14 210 B5
Medlar Cl 1 TF3 143 F8
MEDLICOTT 177 B1
Meese Cl TF1 130 D6
MEESON 106 E5
Meeson Cl WV7 157 B5
MEESON HEATH 106 F4
Meifod Pl 13 LL13 221 C2
Melbourne Cl 7 TF4 144 A4
Melbourne Rise 7 SY3 124 A7
Mellor Cl 4 TF7 152 F4
Melrose Cres 3 TF9 53 B8
Melrose Dr SY2 125 E1
Melrose Gdns TF1 130 C3
Melton Way 17 SY3 124 F3
MELVERLEY 168 A7
Melverley Craft Ctr* SY22 168 A7
MELVERLEY GREEN 167 F8
Melverley View SY5 168 A6
Mendip Cl TF4 143 E1
Mentone Cres TF10 109 B4
MEOLE BRACE 125 B2
Meole Brace Infants Sch SY3 125 A1
Meole Brace Jun Sch SY3 125 A1
Meole Brace Ret Pk SY2 125 C1
Meole Brace Sch SY3 125 A2
Meole Cres SY3 125 B2
Meole Rise 6 SY3 125 C3
Meole Wlk SY3 125 A2
Merchant Cl 2 WV6 166 C3

Mercia Dr 5 TF1 . . . 131 A5
Mercian Cl SY3 . . . 124 F1
Mercian Ct 4 TF9 . . . 36 C1
Mere Cl
2 Newport TF10 . . . 109 F4
Shifnal TF11 . . . 146 A3
Shrewsbury SY2 . . . 125 F2
Mere Gn Ct SY3 . . . 124 F3
Mere Gr 4 TF5 . . . 130 C8
Mere La DY7 . . . 201 F6
Mereside SY2 . . . 125 F2
Meres Visitor Ctr* SY12 . . 27 D2
MERETOWN . . . 110 B5
Merevale Way TF2 . . . 120 E1
Merganser Cl 1 TF1 . . . 131 A6
Merlin Coppice 8 TF1 . . 131 A7
Merlin Rd
Shrewsbury SY3 . . . 124 D7
9 Wrexham LL12 . . . 221 E8
Merricks La DY12 . . . 211 C2
Merridale Cres TF1 . . . 130 E5
MERRINGTON . . . 100 E6
Merrington Rd
3 Oakengates/Donnington TF2 . . . 120 F1
Pimhill SY4 . . . 100 E5
Merry La
Grinshill SY4 . . . 84 A1
Hadnall SY4 . . . 83 F1
Merton Cl 6 DY12 . . . 211 C2
Methodist Hill 4 LL20 . . . 6 A7
Mews The WR15 . . . 220 C4
Meyrick Rd 4 TF1 . . . 130 D5
MICKLEY . . . 51 C6
Mickley La TF9 . . . 51 C5
Middle Croft Rd TF10 . . . 107 D5
Middlegate SY1 . . . 113 D5
MIDDLEHOPE . . . 196 E7
Middle La TF6 . . . 105 F7
Middle Rd 3 TF2 . . . 132 B4
Middle St 4 LL14 . . . 6 D8
MIDDLETON
Bitterley . . . 207 C4
Little Hereford . . . 213 D4
Oswestry Rural . . . 59 C7
MIDDLETON BAGGOT . . . 186 F1
Middleton Cl 10 SY11 . . . 59 A8
MIDDLETON PRIORS . . . 186 E1
Middleton Rd
Oswestry Rural SY11 . . . 59 C7
Oswestry SY11 . . . 58 E7
MIDDLETON SCRIVEN . . . 199 F6
MIDDLETOWN . . . 167 C3
Middletown Residential Pk SY21 . . . 167 D3
Middletown Sq 3 SY2 . . 126 A8
Middle Wardens 7 SY7 . 205 B5
Middle Wood Rd
Bromfield SY8 . . . 206 E1
Ludlow SY8 . . . 217 A3
Midgley Ct TF10 . . . 109 E3
Mid Wales Airport SY21 . 170 B3
Mile Bank Rd SY13 . . . 2 B2
MILEBROOK . . . 203 E3
MILE OAK . . . 59 A4
Mile Oak Ind Est SY10 . . . 58 F5
Milfields Way WV16 . . . 199 F8
MILFORD . . . 98 F6
Milford Rd SY4 . . . 99 A7
Milk St 7 SY1 . . . 125 C5
Mill Bank TF1 . . . 130 F3
Millbank Rise LL13 . . . 221 E1
Millbrook Cl 5 SY8 . . . 212 E2
Millbrook Dr SY4 . . . 103 D8
Millbrook Prim Sch TF1 . 131 A5
Millbrook Way SY8 . . . 212 D2
Mill Cl 3 WV15 . . . 189 A6
Mill Ct 7 LL13 . . . 9 C8
Miller Pl 7 TF2 . . . 132 B6
Millers Gn SY1 . . . 113 E1
Millers Vale 12 WV5 . . . 190 E3
Millers Way 4 TF2 . . . 132 F8
Mill Farm Dr TF3 . . . 144 D4
Mill Field Cl 23 LD7 . . . 203 B3
Millfield Dr TF9 . . . 36 F2
Millfield Grange TF9 . . . 36 F2
Millfields Rd 3 TF1 . . . 130 F3
Millfields Way 9 WV5 . . 190 E3
Mill Gn 2 LD7 . . . 203 B3
MILL GREEN . . . 71 E5
Millichope Pk* SY7 . . . 197 B7
Millington Cl 1 SY4 . . . 81 A1
Mill La
Blymhill & Weston-under-Lizard TF11 . . . 135 C2
Bronington SY13 . . . 13 A4
Broseley TF12 . . . 161 C8
Diddlebury SY7 . . . 196 F4
Donington WV7 . . . 147 F1
Hadnall SY4 . . . 102 C6
Hanwood SY5 . . . 169 F1
Kemberton TF11 . . . 154 C6
Knighton on Teme WR15 . . 215 B4
Kynnersley TF6 . . . 119 C6
Leintwardine SY7 . . . 205 B4
Madeley TF7 . . . 153 B5
Prees Higher Heath SY13 . . 32 F3
Smestow DY3 . . . 190 E2
Stoke upon Tern TF9 . . . 88 E3
Tibberton TF10 . . . 107 E5
Tong TF11 . . . 147 D7
Uffington SY4 . . . 126 D8
Wellington TF1 . . . 130 F3
Welshpool SY21 . . . 170 B6
Millman Gr TF4 . . . 143 C6
Mill Mdw
3 Shrewsbury SY2 . . . 125 E3
Tenbury Wells WR15 . . . 220 D3
Millmead Dr 4 SY2 . . . 125 F3
Mill Pk SY13 . . . 15 C7
Mill Pool Cl 11 WV5 . . . 190 E3
Mill Pool Pl 11 DY14 . . . 209 E3
Millpool The WV5 . . . 190 C5
Mill Rd
Bronington SY13 . . . 13 A5
Hodnet TF9 . . . 51 E1
Knighton LD7 . . . 203 B2
Newcastle on Clun SY7 . . 192 D5
Shrewsbury SY3 . . . 125 B2
Millside 20 WV5 . . . 190 F3
Mill St
Bridgnorth WV15 . . . 219 A5
Hopesay SY7 . . . 195 A4
Ludlow SY8 . . . 217 C3
Prees SY13 . . . 49 C8
Wem SY4 . . . 66 A5
Whitchurch SY13 . . . 15 A7
Millstream 5 SY5 . . . 171 F3
Millstream Way 5 TF1 . . 131 B6
Millward Cl TF2 . . . 132 B8
Mill Way 4 TF2 . . . 132 A6
Millwood Rise 9 LL13 . . . 9 C8
Milners Ct 7 TF4 . . . 143 E6
Milners La TF4 . . . 143 E5
Milnthorpe Cl 5 SY3 . . . 125 A1
MILSON . . . 215 B8
Milton Cl 6 SY1 . . . 125 E8
Milton Dr
1 Madeley TF7 . . . 152 F5
1 Market Drayton TF9 . . . 36 C2
Milton Rd SY8 . . . 217 E4
Mimosa Cl TF7 . . . 153 B3
Minchers Rise TF3 . . . 143 E8
Miners Mdw TF12 . . . 161 D8
Mines The TF12 . . . 152 B2
Minshall Pl SY11 . . . 59 B7
MINSTERLEY . . . 172 D4
Minsterley Prim Sch SY5 . . . 172 E3
Minsterley Rd SY5 . . . 173 A5
MINTON . . . 183 D5
Minton Cl TF7 . . . 152 F7
Mitcham Ct 7 SY3 . . . 124 D7
Mitchel Way 2 TF7 . . . 152 F5
Mitnell La SY8 . . . 212 E5
Moat Cl 8 TF1 . . . 130 C7
Moat Croft 1 TF11 . . . 145 F3
Moat Hill SY9 . . . 181 C4
Moat House The WV16 . . 188 D1
Moat St WV16 . . . 218 F5
Mocktree Turnpike SY7 . 205 D6
Modra Pk SY10 . . . 58 D5
Moffats Sch DY12 . . . 210 B8
Mold Ct WV16 . . . 218 F5
Mold Rd LL11 . . . 221 A7
Mole Way TF5 . . . 130 C7
MONDAYTOWN . . . 172 B6
Monet Cl 6 TF5 . . . 130 B7
Moneybrook Way SY3 . . . 125 B1
Monger Rd LL13 . . . 221 E1
MONKHOPTON . . . 186 F4
MONKMOOR . . . 126 B7
Monkmoor Ave
3 Oswestry SY11 . . . 58 F8
Shrewsbury SY2 . . . 125 E7
Monkmoor Cl 1 SY11 . . . 58 F8
Monkmoor Cres 3 SY2 . . 125 E7
Monkmoor Ct SY11 . . . 40 F1
Monkmoor Ind Est SY2 . . 126 A8
Monkmoor Pool Nature Reserve* SY2 . . . 126 C8
Monkmoor Rd
Oswestry SY11 . . . 58 F8
7 Shrewsbury SY2 . . . 126 A8
Monkmoor Recn Ctr SY2 125 F7
Monks Cl 13 WV5 . . . 190 F3
Monks Ct WV15 . . . 219 A5
Monksfield 5 TF9 . . . 36 A1
Montague Pl SY3 . . . 125 D3
MONTFORD . . . 169 D5
MONTFORD BRIDGE . . . 169 E6
MONTGOMERY . . . 174 A3
Montgomery Castle* SY15 . . . 174 B3
Montgomery Mews 2 TF1 . . . 131 A7
Montgomery Rd
3 Wellington TF1 . . . 130 C4
Wrexham LL13 . . . 221 E4
Montgomery Way 5 SY1 . . . 114 A2
Montrose Pl SY3 . . . 124 A6
Moorfield Ct TF10 . . . 109 E2
Moorfield Foundation Sch TF10 . . . 109 E1
Moorfield La TF10 . . . 109 D1
Moorhead Cl 2 LL13 . . . 221 F4
Moorhouse Cl TF1 . . . 130 C3
Moor La WV6 . . . 166 D2
Moorland Ave LL13 . . . 221 F4
Moorland Dr 14 TF2 . . . 132 F1
Moorland Rd 3 TF10 . . . 109 E2
Moor Pk Sch SY8 . . . 212 F6
Moor Rd TF4 . . . 143 F4
Moors La
Farlow DY14 . . . 209 C7
St Martin's SY11 . . . 24 D4
Moors The
Cressage SY5 . . . 149 E5
1 Diddlebury SY7 . . . 196 F4
Moors View The 2 SY7 . 196 F4
MORDA . . . 58 D4
Morda Bank SY10 . . . 58 D4
Morda CE Prim Sch SY10 . 58 D4
Morda Cl SY11 . . . 58 D6
Morda Rd SY11 . . . 58 D6
Morden Cl 6 TF2 . . . 132 C2
MORE . . . 182 B6
MORETON . . . 123 D7
Moreton Bsns Pk SY10 . . . 23 E5
MORETON CORBET . . . 85 E3
Moreton Corbet Castle* SY4 . . . 85 E3
Moreton Cres SY3 . . . 125 D4
Moreton Hall Sch SY10 . . . 23 F4
MORETON SAY . . . 35 A1
Moreton Say CE Prim Sch TF9 . . . 34 A2
Moreton St SY13 . . . 32 D1
MORETONWOOD . . . 34 E3
Morfe La DY7 . . . 201 F5
Morfe Rd WV15 . . . 219 A5
Morgan Ave LL11 . . . 221 C6
Morgans Cotts 9 SY1 . . . 113 E1
Morgansfield SY6 . . . 185 A3
Morgan Springs WV16 . . 218 E4
Morgan Way 2 TF1 . . . 131 D2
Morningside WR15 . . . 220 C4
Mornington Cl 4 SY3 . . . 124 D6
Morrellswood La
Leighton & Eaton Constantine SY5 . . . 141 E1
Little Wenlock SY5 . . . 142 A1
Morris Cl SY1 . . . 113 D5
Morris Dr TF2 . . . 132 C8
Mortimar SY1 . . . 113 E4
Mortimer Cl 3 SY8 . . . 212 E2
Mortimer Dr 4 SY8 . . . 212 E2
Mortimer Gdns 10 DY14 . 209 E2
Mortimer Gr 22 DY12 . . . 211 D2
Mortimer Pl SY8 . . . 217 D4
Mortimer Rd TF9 . . . 52 E5
MORTON . . . 76 E5
MORTON COMMON . . . 76 E6
Morton Ct 7 TF4 . . . 143 E4
Morton La SY10 . . . 77 B8
MORTON MILL . . . 86 B2
MORVILLE . . . 187 E5
Morville CE Sch WV16 . . 187 E5
Morville Dr TF1 . . . 130 C6
Morville Hall & Gdns* WV16 . . . 187 D4
MORVILLE HEATH . . . 187 F4
Morville Rd SY1 . . . 113 D3
Mosclay Rd 6 TF2 . . . 132 D2
MOSE . . . 189 A1
Mossbank Way SY3 . . . 124 D7
Mossey Gn 2 TF1 . . . 131 F1
Mossey Gn Way TF2 . . . 131 F1
Mossfield TF9 . . . 73 A6
Moss La
Bronington SY13 . . . 13 B3
Cheswardine TF9 . . . 55 C3
Ellesmere Rural SY12 . . . 26 C6
Hanmer SY13 . . . 12 C2
Norton in Hales TF9 . . . 36 F6
Moss Rd TF2 . . . 132 C4
MOSTON . . . 67 E2
Moston Gn 6 SY1 . . . 114 A3
Moston Rd SY1 . . . 114 B3
Mottershead 3 SY1 . . . 113 D4
Mound Way TF2 . . . 152 F6
Mountbatten Cl 1 TF11 . 146 A6
Mount Bradford La SY11 . 25 A7
Mount Cl
5 Pontesbury SY5 . . . 173 A4
22 Welshpool SY21 . . . 170 B6
Mount Cres
Oswestry SY11 . . . 40 C1
Whitchurch SY13 . . . 14 F8
Mount Dr 1 SY11 . . . 58 D8
Mount Gilbert TF1 . . . 130 F2
Mount Gilbert Sch
Dawley TF4 . . . 144 A3
Wellington TF1 . . . 130 D5
Mount La
Market Drayton TF9 . . . 53 C8
Stoke upon Tern TF9 . . . 70 F6
Mount Orch WR15 . . . 220 C4
MOUNT PLEASANT . . . 113 D2
Mount Pleasant
3 Clun SY7 . . . 193 C3
3 Oakengates/Donnington TF2 . . . 132 B1
Tenbury Wells WR15 . . . 220 C4
2 Trewern SY21 . . . 167 D3
Mount Pleasant Ave 10 WV5 . . . 190 F4
Mount Pleasant Dr TF3 . . 153 B8
Mount Pleasant Inf Sch SY1 . . . 113 D1
Mount Pleasant Jun Sch SY1 . . . 113 D1
Mount Pleasant Rd
2 Madeley TF7 . . . 153 C5
Shrewsbury SY1 . . . 113 D2
Mount Rd
1 Dawley TF4 . . . 143 F4
2 Oswestry SY11 . . . 58 D8
Mount Rise SY11 . . . 40 C1
Mounts Cl TF7 . . . 153 C5
Mount Side TF1 . . . 131 D2
Mount St
Shrewsbury SY3 . . . 125 B7
Welshpool SY21 . . . 170 B6
Wrexham LL11 . . . 221 D3
Mount The
Rhosnesni LL12 . . . 221 E4
Shrewsbury SY3 . . . 124 F7
Whitchurch SY13 . . . 14 F8
Mount View SY6 . . . 184 C3
Mount View Rd 2 TF2 . . 132 B1
Mount Way 4 SY5 . . . 173 A4
Mountwood Pk SY3 . . . 124 E7
Mousecroft La SY3 . . . 124 F2
Moveage The 11 SY1 . . . 113 C2
MUCH WENLOCK . . . 159 D4
Much Wenlock Leisure Ctr TF13 . . . 159 F6
Much Wenlock Mus* 7 TF13 . . . 159 E4
Much Wenlock Prim Sch TF13 . . . 159 F3
Much Wenlock Rd TF8 . . 151 B4
MUCKLETON . . . 104 E7
Muckleton La TF6 . . . 104 F4
Muckleton Rd SY4 . . . 104 B8
MUCKLEY . . . 187 B6
MUCKLEY CROSS . . . 187 C6
Mulberry Ave 5 SY12 . . . 27 A2
Mulberry Cl TF10 . . . 109 F1
Mulberry Ct
Hadley TF1 . . . 131 C5
6 Oswestry SY11 . . . 58 D7
Mullinder Dr TF2 . . . 144 A8
MUNSLOW . . . 197 A6
Murivance 5 SY1 . . . 125 B5
Museum of the Gorge* TF8 . . . 152 B4
Muskoka 12 DY12 . . . 211 C2
Musk Rose Cl 12 TF2 . . . 132 E8
Musley La LL13 . . . 9 D6
MUXTON . . . 120 E1
Muxton Cty Prim Sch TF2 . . . 132 F8
Muxton La
Lilleshall & Donnington TF2 . . . 133 A8
Oakengates/Donnington TF2 . . . 120 F1
MYDDLE . . . 82 D4
Myddle CE Prim Sch SY4 . 82 D4
MYDDLEWOOD . . . 82 A4
Myford TF4 . . . 143 B2
MYND . . . 204 C6
Mynd Cl SY2 . . . 126 A6
Mynd Ind Est The SY6 . . . 216 C5
MYNDTOWN . . . 182 F4
Mynd View 5 SY7 . . . 195 E5
Myrtle Dr 2 SY21 . . . 170 B6
Mythstories Mus* SY4 . . . 66 B6
MYTTON . . . 169 F8
Mytton Cl 3 SY11 . . . 41 E3
Mytton Gr 7 SY3 . . . 124 E6
Mytton Oak Rd SY3 . . . 124 C5
Mytton Pk 6 SY3 . . . 124 E6
Mytton Rd SY4 . . . 103 F7

N

Nabb Cl 5 TF2 . . . 132 C3
Nabb The 3 TF2 . . . 132 B3
Naird La
Hollinswood & Randlay TF11 . . . 145 A5
Stirchley & Brookside TF11 144 F2
Nairn Rdbt TF11 . . . 145 A5
Nanny Murphy's La TF11 134 B1
NANT . . . 22 F1
Nant La SY10 . . . 58 C3
NANTMAWR . . . 75 B5
Nantmawr Bank SY10 . . . 75 C6
Nantmawr Quarry (Outdoor Activity Centre)* SY10 . . 75 C6
Nantwich Rd
Whitchurch Urban SY13 . . . 15 E7
Woore CW3 . . . 4 F2
NANT Y CAWS . . . 58 D2
NANT-Y-GOLLEN . . . 57 B7
Napier Sq LL13 . . . 221 E2
NAPLEY . . . 37 F8
Napley Dr TF9 . . . 20 D2
NAPLEY HEATH . . . 21 A1
Napley Rd TF9 . . . 20 D1
Napoleon Dr SY3 . . . 124 C6
Narrow La TF9 . . . 71 D2
NASH . . . 214 D6
Neachley La TF11 . . . 147 A3
Near Vallens TF1 . . . 131 D4
NEDGE HILL . . . 144 F3
NEEN SAVAGE . . . 209 E4
NEEN SOLLARS . . . 215 C7
NEENTON . . . 199 B6
NEFOD . . . 24 B5
Nefod La SY11 . . . 24 B6
Nelson Ct 2 TF11 . . . 146 A6
Nelson St LL13 . . . 221 E2
Nelson Way 2 TF2 . . . 120 F1
NESSCLIFFE . . . 97 E3
Nesscliffe Hill Ctry Pk* SY4 . . . 97 F4
Netherfield 8 WV16 . . . 200 E3
NETHER SKYBORRY . . . 203 A4
NETHERTON . . . 200 E1
Netherton La
Bewdley DY12 . . . 211 E1
Highley WV16 . . . 200 E2
Nether Way 5 SY3 . . . 124 F4
Netley Rd SY3 . . . 125 B1
Nettles La 4 SY3 . . . 125 B6
Neufchatel Cl SY13 . . . 15 B7
Neville Cres 2 LL12 . . . 221 D5
Nevil Rd 2 TF1 . . . 130 C4
NEWBRIDGE
Cefn . . . 6 D8
Oswestry Rural . . . 77 A8
Newbridge Rd LL14 . . . 6 C8
New Bridge Rd TF8 . . . 152 D4
Newbrigg Rd 10 LL12 . . . 221 D8
New Brookdale TF1 . . . 131 B4
Newbrook Dr 2 SY3 . . . 137 A5
NEWCASTLE . . . 192 E5
Newcastle CE Prim Sch SY7 . . . 192 D5
Newcastle Rd
Market Drayton TF9 . . . 36 F2
Woore CW3 . . . 5 D2
New Church Rd TF1 . . . 130 E3
New Coll TF11 . . . 130 F3
Newcomen Way TF7 . . . 152 D5
NEWDALE . . . 143 C7
Newdale Prim Sch TF3 . 143 D8
Newent Cl 2 SY1 . . . 125 E8
Newfield Cl 2 TF11 . . . 145 F5
Newfield Ct TF2 . . . 132 A5
Newfield Dr
Oakengates/Donnington TF2 . . . 132 A5
Shrewsbury SY1 . . . 125 D7
New Forest Cl DY14 . . . 210 E1
Newgate WV6 . . . 166 C3
Newgate Ct 7 SY11 . . . 58 D7
Newhall Gdns SY2 . . . 125 E5
New Hall La SY13 . . . 13 B4
New Hall Rd TF1 . . . 130 E3
Newham Way SY3 . . . 124 E3
Newhouse La
Albrighton WV7 . . . 157 A4
Church Pulverbatch SY5 . . 173 F2
Condover SY5 . . . 178 A6
New Houses SY4 . . . 169 D6
Newill Gr 1 TF5 . . . 130 B7
NEWINGTON . . . 195 D6
Newington Way SY7 . . . 195 E6
NEW INVENTION . . . 203 C7
Newlands Rd
12 Oakengates/Donnington TF2 . . . 132 B2
1 Oakengates TF2 . . . 132 B1
NEW MARTON . . . 25 C2
New Mills La SY5 . . . 173 B6
NEWNES . . . 26 E1
NEWNHAM BRIDGE . . . 215 A4
New Options Coll TF11 . 164 A6
Newpark St SY1 . . . 125 D7
New Pk Cl SY1 . . . 125 D8
New Pk Rd SY1 . . . 125 D7
New Pk St SY1 . . . 125 D7
NEWPORT . . . 109 D3
Newport Bsns Pk TF10 . . 109 F2
Newport CE Jun Sch TF10 . . . 109 F2
Newport Cl 3 LL13 . . . 221 F1
Newport Cres TF11 . . . 145 F5
Newport Dr SY2 . . . 125 F1
Newport High Sch TF10 . 109 E2
Newport Inf Sch TF10 . . . 109 F2
Newport Pl 13 SY1 . . . 125 C6
Newport Rd
Albrighton WV7 . . . 156 E8
Donington TF11 . . . 147 D1
Edgmond TF10 . . . 109 C4
Gnosall ST20 . . . 111 E5
Hinstock TF9 . . . 71 F3
1 Oswestry SY11 . . . 41 A1
Perton WV7 . . . 157 F2
Shifnal TF11 . . . 145 F5
Sutton upon Tern TF9 . . . 53 E7
Tong TF11 . . . 147 D3
Whitchurch SY13 . . . 15 A7
Newport St SY7 . . . 193 D4
Newport Swimming Pool TF10 . . . 109 F3
Newquay Dr 4 LL13 . . . 221 F1
New Rd
7 Bewdley DY12 . . . 211 E3
Bridgnorth WV16 . . . 218 F4
8 Cleobury Mortimer DY14 . . . 209 E3
Dawley TF4 . . . 143 F2
Farlow DY14 . . . 209 B6
7 Gobowen SY11 . . . 41 A8
Hanley WR6 . . . 215 E1
Hanmer SY13 . . . 12 B2
Ironbridge TF8 . . . 152 C4
Loggerheads TF9 . . . 54 F8
Ludlow SY8 . . . 217 C5
Madeley TF7 . . . 153 A5
Montgomery SY15 . . . 174 B4
Much Wenlock TF13 . . . 159 E5
6 Oakengates/Donnington TF2 . . . 132 C5
Rock DY14 . . . 210 D1
Swindon DY3 . . . 190 D2
New Rd Gdns 12 DY14 . . . 209 E3
New Rhosrobin LL11 . . . 221 A8
New River Cl 7 TF1 . . . 130 C7
New Row
4 Hollinswood TF3 . . . 144 B6
Horsehay TF4 . . . 143 C3
New St
6 Bishop's Castle SY9 . . . 181 F3
Clive SY4 . . . 84 A5
1 Dawley TF4 . . . 143 E3
Ford SY5 . . . 169 C4
Ludlow SY8 . . . 217 C6
Newport TF10 . . . 109 E3
Oakengates/Donnington TF2 . . . 132 A3
15 Oswestry SY11 . . . 58 E8
Shrewsbury SY1 . . . 125 A6
Welshpool SY21 . . . 170 B6
Wem SY4 . . . 66 A7
NEWSTREET LANE . . . 34 F7
Newton 14 SY7 . . . 195 E5

NEWTON
Welshampton and Lyneal 28 A1
Worfield 188 D8
Newton Cl
1 Albrighton WV7 156 E7
4 Bewdley DY12 211 C2
Newtonmere Dr
8 Shrewsbury SY1 113 D2
6 Wellington TF1 130 C5
NEWTON ON THE HILL 83 B3
Newton St
12 Craven Arms SY7 195 E5
Wrexham LL13 221 E2
NEWTOWN 81 B1
Newtown TF9 53 D8
NEWTOWN 159 D5
Newtown TF10 109 E1
NEWTOWN 47 A4
Newtown 8 SY13 15 A8
New Town TF4 143 F4
Newtown CE Prim Sch SY4 46 F4
Newtown Gdns SY4 99 A8
New Trench Rd
Lilleshall & Donnington TF2 120 E2
Oakengates/Donnington TF2 132 C8
NEW WOODHOUSES 16 E8
NEW WORKS 143 A6
New Works La TF6 143 A6
NIB HEATH 98 F2
Nickless Way 4 TF4 143 E5
Nightingale Way 2 TF1 130 F6
Nightingale Wlk SY1 113 D5
Noble St SY4 66 A6
NOBOLD 124 E1
Nobold SY4 99 A8
Nobold Cl SY4 99 A8
Nobold La SY5 124 E1
Noel Hill Rd SY5 138 F4
No Man's Gn La DY7 201 F3
NONELEY 64 F4
Noneley Rd SY4 64 E7
Nook La
Bronington SY13 12 F1
Cuckoo's Corner SY13 29 F8
Prees SY4 49 F3
Norbroom Ct 10 TF10 110 A4
Norbroom Dr TF10 110 A4
NORBURY 182 D8
Norbury Prim Sch SY9 182 D7
Norbury Rd ST20 111 E8
NORDLEY 188 A8
Norfield View 4 TF3 144 D4
Norfolk Rd LL12 221 F7
Normandie Cl SY8 217 E4
Norman Rd LL13 221 D1
North Cl 9 SY3 125 C4
North Dr SY10 41 B5
North Gate 1 WV16 218 F5
Northgate Mews 3 WV16 218 E5
Northgate Mus★ WV16 218 E5
North Hermitage 6 SY3 125 C4
Northlands CW3 5 A1
Northleigh Gr LL11 221 C7
North Rd
Pant SY22 93 F7
Wellington TF1 130 D5
Northside Cl 8 SY1 114 C3
North St
2 Oakengates/Donnington TF2 132 C2
Shrewsbury SY1 125 D7
Northumberland Pl 3 SY1 125 D8
North Wales Sch of Art & Design LL11 221 B4
NORTHWOOD 46 C7
Northwood 3 LL12 221 F7
Northwood Halt Sta DY12 211 C4
Northwood La
Kidderminster Foreign DY12 211 D3
Stottesdon WV16 199 F3
Northwood Rd SY2 126 B6
Northwood Terr TF3 144 B3
NORTON
Culmington 206 A8
Stockton 163 B5
Wroxeter and Uppington 139 F8
Norton Cl TF7 153 C7
Norton Dr
1 Dawley TF3 144 B1
Wroxeter & Uppington SY4 127 E1
NORTON IN HALES 20 D2
Norton in Hales CE Prim Sch TF9 20 C1
Norton St 4 LD7 203 B3
Norwich Dr TF3 144 D3
Novers The 5 SY9 181 E3
NOX 169 C1
Nuffield Hospl SY3 124 F2
Nurseries The SY10 76 B2
Nursery Cl 2 SY11 78 D8
Nursery Dr 2 WV5 190 F2
Nursery Mdws SY1 125 C8
Nursery Rd 7 DY12 211 D2
NURTON 166 F4
NURTON HILL 166 D4
Nurton Hill Rd WV6 166 E5

O

Oadby Way 1 SY3 124 C6
Oakapple Cl 3 ST19 148 E8
Oak Ave
Newport TF10 109 F1
Penley LL13 10 F3
Oak Bridge Ct WR15 220 D3
Oak Cl
Llandysilio SY22 94 A1
Madeley TF7 153 C6
Weston Rhyn SY10 23 D4
Oakcroft LL14 23 D8
Oak Dr
10 Ellesmere SY12 27 A2
2 Minsterley SY5 172 E3
Oswestry SY11 58 F6
Shawbury SY4 103 D7
Trysull & Seisdon WV5 190 C5
Whitchurch SY13 14 F6
Wrexham LL12 221 E6
Oak Edge View SY5 176 A8
OAKENGATES 132 A2
Oakengates Leisure Ctr TF2 132 B5
Oakengates Rd TF2 132 C6
Oakengates Sta TF2 132 B2
Oakengates Theatre★ TF2 132 B3
Oak Farm La SY11 78 E8
Oakfield 3 LL13 221 E1
Oakfield Cl
Bronington LL13 13 B3
3 Shrewsbury SY3 124 F5
St Martin's SY11 25 A6
Worthen with Shelve SY5 171 E3
Oakfield Dr SY3 124 E5
Oakfield Pk TF13 159 E3
Oakfield Rd
14 Market Drayton TF9 36 B1
Shifnal TF11 145 F5
Shrewsbury SY3 124 E5
Wellington TF5 130 C8
Oakfields SY22 92 D6
Oak Gdns WV16 218 D6
Oakhurst Ave SY11 40 D1
Oakhurst Rd SY11 40 D1
Oak La
Oswestry Rural SY10 75 D8
8 Shrewsbury SY3 124 B6
Oakland Cty Prim Sch SY3 137 A6
Oakland Pk SY6 216 E6
Oaklands
Bicton Heath SY3 124 B7
Bridgnorth WV15 219 B4
Oaklands Ave 1 LL12 221 F5
Oaklands Dr
Oakengates/Donnington TF2 132 A7
Whittington SY11 41 E2
Oaklands Rd LL14 23 E6
Oaklands The WR15 220 D3
Oakleaf Rise DY14 210 E1
OAKLEY 37 C6
Oakley Ave SY3 125 C3
Oakley Cl SY4 63 B1
Oakley La TF9 37 A6
Oakley Manor Gdns 7 SY3 125 C3
Oakley St SY3 125 C4
Oak Mdw 4 SY9 181 F4
Oak Rd
2 Hanwood SY5 173 F8
The Rock TF3 143 E8
Oak Ridge 6 SY21 170 B7
OAKS 173 D3
Oak St Head 2 SY3 125 C3
Oaks Cres TF1 130 B2
Oaks Dr SY6 216 E6
Oaks Rd
Church Stretton SY6 216 E6
1 Craven Arms SY7 195 D5
Oak St
Highley WV16 200 E3
Oswestry SY11 58 D8
Shrewsbury SY3 125 C3
Oak Tree Cl WR15 220 D6
Oak Tree Cres SY7 194 B8
Oak Tree Dr SY3 136 E7
Oaktree La WV16 198 F4
Oakvale Ct 2 SY5 178 C6
Oakwood Cl 5 SY11 41 F2
Oakwood Dr
2 Oakengates/Donnington TF2 132 A6
Shrewsbury SY1 113 D3
Oakwood Pk LL13 10 F4
Oakwood Rd
21 Bewdley DY12 211 C2
Cleobury North WV16 198 E6
Oatfield Cl 3 SY13 15 A6
OBLEY 203 F8
Occupation La WV16 200 D6
Oerley Cl 4 SY10 58 C8
Oerley Way SY10 58 C8
Offa LL14 6 E3
Offa Dr SY11 40 F1
Offas Cl SY10 75 D7
Offas Dyke Rd SY22 94 A1
Office La SY8 208 A2
Offoxey Rd TF11 147 E5
Okehampton Rd TF1 131 B7
Old Armoury The 5 TF9 53 C8
Old Bedstone Rd 3 SY7 204 C5
Old Bell Mus The★ SY15 174 B3
Old Bowling Gn Cl WR15 220 C6
Old Brickyard SY8 217 C5
OLDBURY 218 D2
Oldbury Rd WV16 218 E3
Oldbury Wells WV16 218 E4
Oldbury Wells Sch WV16 218 E4
Old Chads La SY13 1 C8
Old Chapel Ct 26 SY11 58 E8
Old Chirk Rd SY11 23 F1
OLD CHURCH STOKE 175 B1
Old Coach Rd ST19 148 F7
Old Coleham 3 SY3 125 D5
OLD COPPICE 136 D3
Old Coppice Grange 7 TF3 143 F8
Oldcroft TF2 132 A3
Old Dalelands 5 TF9 53 B8
Olden La
Ruyton SY4 80 A1
Ruyton-XI-Towns SY4 79 E1
Old Farm La TF10 121 C3
Old Farm Rd
2 Esclusham LL14 221 A1
Hadnall SY4 102 C4
OLDFIELD 199 E7
OLD FIELD 206 E4
Oldfield Rd 3 TF4 144 A2
Oldford Cl 27 SY21 170 B6
Oldford Inf Sch SY21 170 B6
Oldford La 26 SY21 170 B6
Oldford Rise SY21 170 B5
Oldford View 28 SY21 170 B6
Old Fort Rd SY11 40 E1
Old Hall Cl
Albrighton WV7 156 F5
1 Wellington TF1 130 F2
Old Hall Sch The TF1 130 F4
OLD HARDWICK 26 B1
Old Heath SY1 113 E2
OLDINGTON 188 D8
Old Mapsis Way SY10 58 D4
OLD MARTON 25 E1
Old Mill Cl 4 SY5 171 F3
Old Mill La WV16 218 E2
Old Nursery Cl TF7 153 B6
Old Office Cl TF4 143 E5
Old Office Rd TF4 143 E5
Old Oswestry (Hillfort)★ SY10 40 F3
OLD PARK 144 A7
Old Pk Prim Sch TF4 144 A5
Old Pk Rd 5 TF2 132 B1
Old Pk Way TF3 143 F7
OLDPOOL 86 D1
Old Post Office La SY10 57 D2
Old Potts Way SY3 125 D5
Old Rectory Gdns SY11 78 C7
Old Roman Rd SY3 125 A3
Old Sch Cl 6 WV16 200 F2
Old Sch La
Tenbury Wells WR15 220 D7
Westbury SY5 168 C2
Old Sch Mews 1 LL13 9 C8
Old Shackerley La WV7 148 A1
Old Smithy Cl 3 WV6 166 C3
Old Smithy Rd TF10 107 E5
Old St SY8 217 C3
Old Toll Gate TF2 132 C3
Old Top House Cotts SY4 126 D8
Old Vicarage Rd TF4 143 F1
Old Weston Rd ST19 148 E8
Old Wharf TF3 144 A5
Old Willow Rd TF2 120 E1
OLDWOOD 220 C2
OLD WOODHOUSES 3 D2
Oldwood Rd WR15 220 C2
OLD WOODS 100 B5
Old Worcester Rd
Albrighton WV7 156 D6
Bridgnorth WV15 219 B3
Oleander Cl 6 TF3 131 E1
Oliver Ct 1 TF1 130 E4
Olivet Gdns LL11 221 C8
OLLERTON 88 E7
Ollerton La
Childs Ercall TF9 70 F1
Stoke upon Tern TF9 88 E8
OLLERTON LANE 88 E8
ONIBURY 206 A6
ONNELEY 5 E3
Onnybrook Dr SY7 195 E6
Onny CE Prim Sch SY7 206 A6
Onny Gr TF2 132 D4
Onslow Dr
Shrewsbury SY1 113 D2
4 Wellington TF1 130 C5
Orchard Cl
Adforton SY7 205 A1
Church Aston TF10 121 E8
5 Claverley WV5 189 E4
Cressage SY5 149 E5
4 Eardington WV16 188 C1
Hadley TF1 131 D2
Little Wenlock TF6 142 D2
Pattingham WV6 166 C3
Waters Upton TF6 106 B4
Orchard Croft SY22 167 B8
Orchard Ct WR15 220 C5
Orchard Dr
Bridgnorth WV16 218 D6
1 Minsterley SY5 172 E3
1 West Felton SY11 78 D8
Orchard End 1 DY14 209 E3
Orchard Fields SY4 84 B5
Orchard Gdns
Ludlow SY8 217 D5
4 Wrexham LL11 221 C7
Orchard Gn SY22 93 E6
Orchard La
Great Hanwood SY5 173 E8
The Gorge TF8 152 D4
Orchard Lea SY8 207 F4
Orchard Pk SY10 94 F7
Orchard Rd
3 Eardington WV16 188 C1
3 Shifnal TF11 145 F5
Orchard Rise
15 Bewdley DY12 211 D2
2 Market Drayton TF9 53 A8
Richards Castle (Hereford) SY8 212 E4
Orchard Sch The SY21 167 E3
Orchard St
4 Highley WV16 200 F2
7 Oswestry SY11 58 E8
Orchards The 1 LL13 221 F1
Orchard The
Albrighton WV7 157 A5
Bewdley DY12 211 C2
17 Bicton Heath SY3 124 A7
Orchard Way
Wellington TF1 130 F3
Wem Urban SY4 66 B6
Orchid Cl 5 TF2 132 E7
ORETON 209 C7
Oreton Rd DY14 209 C7
Oriel Way 8 SY3 124 E3
ORLETON 212 E2
Orleton CE Prim Sch SY8 212 E2
ORLETON COMMON 212 C3
Orleton La
Eastham WR15 215 E3
Wellington TF1 130 C4
Orleton La Inf Sch TF1 130 B4
Orleton Rd SY8 217 F3
Orleton Terr TF1 130 C3
Ormsdale Cl 8 TF2 132 F8
ORSLOW 123 E3
Orsons Mdw 15 SY3 124 A7
Orton La WV4 190 F6
OSBASTON
Ercall Magna 104 F2
Kinnerley 77 E2
Osborne Cl
5 Oswestry SY11 59 B8
3 Wrexham LL11 221 C6
Osborne Rd LL11 221 C6
Osmere Cl 1 SY13 2 B1
Osprey Gr 5 TF1 131 A7
Osterley Gr 3 TF2 132 F8
Oswald Pl 3 SY11 58 D7
Oswald Rd SY11 58 E8
Oswald Row 25 SY11 58 E8
Oswalds Cl SY11 58 D7
Oswald's Well La SY11 58 C7
Oswald Way 3 LL12 221 E5
Oswell Rd SY2 125 F8
OSWESTRY (CROESWALLT) 58 B8
Oswestry Inf Sch SY11 58 F8
Oswestry Leisure Ctr SY11 59 A7
Oswestry Rd
12 Ellesmere SY12 27 A2
Oswestry Rural SY10 57 E2
Whittington SY11 41 E3
Oswestry Sch SY11 58 C7
Oswestry Transport Mus★ SY11 58 F8
Oswestry Visitor & Ex Ctr★ SY11 58 D7
OTELEY 27 E2
Oteley Rd
Atcham SY2 126 A1
Shrewsbury SY2 125 C2
Ottley Way TF9 52 E5
Oulton La TF10 111 A8
OUNSDALE 190 E4
Ounsdale Rd WV5 190 F4
Our Lady & St Oswald's Rcp Sch SY11 58 D7
Outwood 1 SY1 113 D5
OUTWOODS 111 B1
Oval Cl 2 TF2 132 E3
Oval The
Albrighton WV7 156 E8
Bicton SY3 112 A2
Market Drayton TF9 53 C8
Newport TF10 110 A3
Overcross SY3 125 E3
OVERDALE 143 D8
Overdale
8 The Rock TF3 131 E1
The Rock TF3 143 E8
Overdale Rd SY3 136 E6
Overley Hall Sch TF6 129 C2
OVERS 177 A2
Overstone 2 SY1 113 D5
OVERTON 212 F6
Overton Cl SY1 114 C2
Overton La SY8 212 D1
OVERTON/OWRTYN 9 D8
Overton Rd
Ludlow SY8 217 C2
St Martin's SY11 24 E6
Overton View SY8 217 E3
Overton Way LL12 221 E6
Owen Cl TF3 144 E2
Owl's La SY15 181 F6
Oxford Rd
5 Dawley TF4 144 A4
Great Dawley TF4 143 F3
Oxford St
4 Oakengates/Donnington TF2 132 B2
Oxford St *continued*
3 Wrexham LL13 221 E3
Oxlip Cl 16 TF2 132 E8
Oxon Bsns Pk SY3 124 C7
Oxon CE Prim Sch SY3 124 B6

P

Packwood Haugh Sch SY4 80 A3
Paddock Cl TF1 130 C5
Paddock Ct TF4 143 F3
Paddock La TF11 154 A6
Paddocks The
Baschurch SY4 81 A6
2 Cleobury Mortimer DY14 209 E3
16 Knighton LD7 203 B3
Ludlow SY8 217 E5
Market Drayton TF9 36 B1
4 Shawbury SY4 103 D6
3 Shrewsbury SY3 124 B6
Paddock The
3 Church Stretton SY6 216 D7
7 Claverley WV5 189 E4
Much Wenlock TF13 159 E4
10 Oakengates/Donnington TF2 120 F1
1 Shifnal TF11 145 F4
2 Wem SY4 66 B8
22 Wombourne WV5 190 F3
PADDOLGREEN 47 E5
Padmans Alley 1 TF12 152 C1
Pageant Dr
Dawley Hamlets TF4 143 F1
Dawley TF4 144 A1
Painsbrook La SY4 102 E6
Painswick Cl 6 SY3 124 B7
PAINTERS GREEN 13 E7
Painters La SY13 50 D6
Painters Pl 10 SY3 124 C7
Pale Mdw Rd 7 WV15 219 A4
Palmer St 4 LL13 221 E3
Pandy La 2 LL12 221 D8
Panorama 2 TF2 132 B3
PANPUNTON 203 B4
PANT 76 B1
PANT-GLAS 40 A5
Pant La SY12 8 E4
Pantulf Rd SY4 66 B8
PAPERMILL BANK 85 D8
Parade The
Donnington TF2 132 C7
Wellington TF1 130 E4
Paradise TF8 152 B4
Parc Bychan LL11 221 C7
Parc Caradog SY21 167 A1
Parc Hafod SY22 94 A2
Parc Offa SY22 94 A2
Pargeter Cl 1 TF3 144 A1
Parish Cl TF4 143 E2
Parish Dr TF1 131 D5
Park Ave
Madeley TF7 153 B5
Oswestry SY11 58 D8
Shawbury SY4 103 D7
Shrewsbury SY3 125 A6
Wem SY4 66 A5
Whitchurch SY13 15 A7
Wrexham LL12 221 D4
Park Bank SY4 80 A2
Park Cl
14 Bewdley DY12 211 D2
Kinlet DY12 210 C7
3 Oakengates/Donnington TF2 132 E2
Park Cres SY11 41 B4
Park Croft WR15 214 F2
Park Ct TF7 152 E6
Parkdale TF1 131 C5
Park Dingle 1 DY12 211 C1
Park Dr SY11 40 D1
Park End TF10 109 F5
Parker Bowles Dr 1 TF9 52 F8
Parker Leighton Way SY10 58 E4
Parkers Cl LL11 221 C6
Parker's Pl 10 SY21 170 B6
Park Fechan Gdns 6 SY11 41 E3
PARK HALL 41 A4
Park Hall Countryside Experience★ SY11 41 B4
Park Hall Stadium (The New Saints FC) SY11 41 C3
PARK HEATH 73 C3
Parkhill La SY7 193 A1
Park Issa Gdns 2 SY11 41 E3
Park La
Bewdley DY12 211 D1
Craven Arms SY7 195 C4
Ercall Magna TF6 116 D7
Leintwardine SY7 205 B5
Loggerheads TF9 55 D8
Madeley TF7 152 E6
Munslow SY7 197 B6
Richard's Castle (Shropshire) SY8 212 F4
Shifnal TF11 145 F2
The Rock TF3 143 F8
24 Welshpool SY21 170 B6
Whittington SY11 41 B3
Park La Ave TF7 152 F5
Parklands TF1 130 D5

Queensway Dr WV16 .... 218 D6
Queensway Terr LL13 ... 221 E2
Queenswood Cl 2 TF2 .. 144 B8
Queenswood Prim Sch TF2 .... 144 B8
Quendale WV5 .... 190 F3
Quillets The SY4 .... 80 C1
QUINA BROOK 48 C7
Quines Cl 9 TF2 .... 132 E8
Quinta Fields SY10 .... 23 C4
Quinta Terr LL14 .... 23 D5
Quinton Cl 11 SY3 .... 124 C7
Quorn Gr 2 TF9 .... 52 F8

R

Raby Cres SY3 .... 125 C4
Racecourse Ave SY2 .... 125 E6
Racecourse Cres SY2 ... 125 F6
Racecourse Dr WV16 .... 218 C5
Racecourse Gn 1 SY2 .. 125 F6
Racecourse La SY3 ...... 124 B6
Racecourse Rd TF13 .... 159 E4
Rack La SY13 .... 30 F1
Radbrook Cty Prim Sch SY3 .... 124 F3
Radbrook Rd SY3 .... 124 E4
Radford La WV4 .... 190 F7
Radfords Field SY11 ...... 58 F6
RADLITH 173 C4
RADMOOR 87 F6
Radmore La ST20 .... 111 C7
Radnor Ct 3 TF1 .... 131 A4
Radnor Dr 5 LD7 .... 203 B3
Rad Valley Gdns SY3 .... 124 E5
Rad Valley Rd SY3 ..... 124 E5
RAF Tern Hill TF9 .... 52 C2
RAGDON 216 D1
Ragged Robins Cl 2 TF2 .... 132 D3
Ragleth Gdns SY2 .... 126 A6
Ragleth Rd SY6 .... 216 D5
Railway La 2 SY2 .... 125 D6
Railway St 1 WV16 ..... 218 F4
Rampart Ct Ret Pk TF3 .. 144 C7
Rampart Way TF3 .... 144 B7
Ramsey Mdws 6 SY1 ... 114 B4
Ramshurst Ct TF2 ...... 132 A3
RANDLAY 144 E3
Randlay Ave TF3 .... 144 C3
Randlay Ctr TF3 .... 144 C4
Randlay Fields TF3 ..... 144 D3
Randlay Intc TF3 .... 144 E4
Randlay Prim Sch TF3 ... 144 C3
Ranford Way SY4 .... 66 B7
Range Rd 18 LL13 ...... 221 E1
Ranscombe Cres 7 LL12 .... 221 E8
RATLINGHOPE 177 B4
Ravenhill Dr 5 TF2 ..... 131 F1
Raven La SY8 .... 217 C4
Raven Mdws SY1 .... 125 C6
Ravenscourt Wlk SY3 ... 124 D5
Ravenscroft Gdns 9 SY2 .... 125 F3
Ravensdale Dr 15 TF2 ... 132 F8
Raven Sq 2 SY21 ...... 170 A6
Raven St SY21 .... 170 A6
Rays Farm* WV16 .... 200 C2
REABROOK 172 D3
Reabrook Ave SY3 ...... 125 E4
Rea Dr TF1 .... 130 D6
Rea St SY3 .... 125 E4
Rectory Cl SY10 .... 57 E2
Rectory Dr TF11 .... 135 F2
Rectory Gdns
Church Stretton SY6 ..... 216 C6
Hanwood SY5 .... 173 F8
3 Worthen with Shelve SY5 .... 171 F3
Rectory La
Adderley TF9 .... 19 B4
Pant SY22 .... 93 F6
Rectory Rd WV7 .... 156 F6
Red Bank
Market Drayton TF9 ...... 53 B8
Welshpool SY21 .... 170 B7
Red Bank La 7 TF9 ...... 53 B8
Red Bank Rd 6 TF9 ...... 53 B8
Red Barn La SY3 .... 125 B4
REDBROOK 13 F7
RED BULL 37 C3
Redburn Cl 7 TF2 ...... 132 A1
Redchurch Cl TF12 ..... 152 D2
Redfern Cl 7 SY3 ...... 125 D3
Redfield 1 SY1 .... 113 C1
Redfield Cl TF12 .... 152 D1
Redford Dr 7 WV7 ..... 157 A5
Redgate Ave WR15 ..... 220 C4
Red Hall La LL13 .... 9 F3
REDHILL
Bayston Hill 136 D7
Lilleshall and Donnington . 132 E3
Red Hill DY12 .... 211 D2
Redhill Dr SY5 .... 136 D7
Redhill Prim Sch TF2 .... 132 F2
Redhill Way TF2 .... 132 E4
Red Kite Cl TF1 .... 131 B6
Red La
Broseley TF12 .... 162 A7
Hopesay SY7 .... 195 A6
Llanfair Waterdine LD7 .... 192 A2
Welshpool SY21 .... 170 A5
RED LAKE 131 F2
Redlake Mdw 5 SY7 .... 204 C5
Redlands Rd TF1 .... 131 E5
Red Lees TF1 .... 131 D2
REDNAL 61 A4
Rednal Fields TF4 .... 143 F1
Rednal Ind Est (Site A) SY11 .... 61 B4
Rednal Ind Est (Site B) SY11 .... 61 C6
Redstone Dr 8 WV16 ... 200 E2
Redwing Cl 3 TF1 ...... 130 F5
REDWITH 77 A5
Redwood Cl 3 TF5 ...... 130 A8
Redwood Dr SY7 .... 195 A4
Redwood La SY7 .... 194 D1
Reed Cl 1 TF2 .... 132 C3
Reedham Rd SY1 .... 113 C2
Reet 3 LL13 .... 221 B2
Reeves La LD7 .... 203 F1
Regent Dr 9 TF2 .... 132 C2
Regents Dr SY1 .... 125 E8
Regent St
Wellington TF1 .... 130 F3
8 Wrexham LL11 .... 221 C3
Rembrandt Dr 4 TF5 ... 130 B7
Renshaw Wood La WV8 . 148 F2
Rest The 3 LL14 .... 6 C8
Retreat Gdns The 4 WV6 .... 166 C3
Revells Cl SY12 .... 26 C6
Reynards Coppice TF7 .. 153 B3
Reynards Mdw TF7 ...... 153 B4
Reynaulds Cl 4 SY2 .... 126 A5
Reynolds Cl
2 Ditton Priors WV16 ... 198 D8
8 Swindon DY3 .... 190 F1
Reynolds Dr 9 TF2 ..... 132 B2
Reynolds Wharf TF8 .... 153 B1
Rhallt La SY21 .... 170 C8
RHEWL
Overton 9 B4
Selattyn and Gabowen 24 B1
Rhew Level La SY10 ...... 94 A8
Rhewl La SY10 .... 24 B1
Rhewl The SY10 .... 24 B1
RHIEWS 35 B7
Rhiw Refail 3 SY10 ...... 94 A8
Rhodes Ave 3 TF4 ...... 143 F5
RHOS
Llandrinio 167 A8
Weston Rhyn 23 A4
RHOS COMMON 94 C1
RHOS-DDU 221 D5
Rhosddu Cty Prim Schools LL11 .... 221 C5
Rhosddu Ind Est LL11 .... 221 B7
Rhosddu Rd LL11 .... 221 C4
Rhos Ddu Rd 5 LL11 .... 221 C3
RHOSNESNI 221 F3
Rhosnesni High Sch LL13 .... 221 F5
Rhosnesni La LL12 ...... 221 E5
RHOSROBIN 221 B8
Rhosrobin Rd LL11 ...... 221 B8
RHOSWIEL 23 E5
RHOSYGADFA 24 E1
Rhyd Broughton La LL11 . 221 A4
Rhyd-esgyn La SY21 .... 167 A5
Rhyd Galeo SY10 .... 24 A1
RHYDYCROESAU 39 A2
RHYD-Y-CWM 191 C3
RHYN 24 B7
Rhyn La SY11 .... 7 C1
Rhyn Pk Sch SY11 .... 24 C5
RICHARDS CASTLE 212 E4
Richards Rd TF2 .... 120 C2
Richmond Ave TF2 ...... 132 A6
Richmond Cl 9 TF10 .... 109 F1
Richmond Ct 3 TF1 ..... 130 D5
Richmond Dr SY3 .... 124 F6
Richmond Gdns
Bridgnorth WV16 .... 218 E6
3 Chirk LL14 .... 6 E3
Richmond Rd
Bewdley DY12 .... 211 C2
Wrexham LL12 .... 221 D8
Richmond Terr 2 SY13 .. 15 B7
Riddings Cl
2 Bewdley DY12 .... 211 E3
3 Broseley TF12 .... 161 E7
Hadley TF1 .... 131 D1
Riddings La WV16 .... 199 E3
Riddings Mdw SY8 ...... 217 E4
Riddings Rd SY8 .... 217 E5
Riders Lea 16 SY3 ...... 124 F3
Ridgebourne Rd SY3 .... 124 F4
Ridge The
4 Bishop's Castle SY9 ... 181 E3
1 Pant SY10 .... 94 A8
RIDGWARDINE 19 E1
Ridgway TF6 .... 116 E8
Ridings Cl 1 TF9 .... 36 B1
Ridings The 2 SY3 ..... 124 B6
Ridley Cl WV16 .... 218 C5
RINDLEFORD 188 F6
Ringers Way 4 TF5 ..... 130 A6
Ripley Cl 1 TF1 .... 131 C5
Ripple Cl 3 SY2 .... 125 F2
Rise La
Rochford WR15 .... 214 E3
Tenbury Wells WR15 ..... 220 F6
Riven Rd TF1 .... 131 E5
River Cl LL13 .... 221 F1
River Gdns SY4 .... 103 E7
River La TF6 .... 106 A3
Riverside WR15 .... 220 C5
River Side WV16 .... 218 F5
Riverside Ave TF8 .... 153 B1
Riverside Dr
7 Clun SY7 .... 193 D3
Ternhill TF9 .... 52 C4
Riverside N DY12 .... 211 D2
River View
Bridgnorth WV15 .... 219 A4
Pen-y-bont Llan Emrys SY10 74 A4
Riverway Dr 8 DY12 .... 211 D2
Rivington Ave 2 SY3 .... 125 A1
Rivulet Rd LL13 .... 221 E2
Robert Jones & Agnes Hunt Orthopaedic Hospl SY10 41 B5
Robert Jones Cl 3 SY4 .. 99 B8
Robert Jones Way SY4 .. 114 B6
Roberts Dr TF4 .... 143 D5
Robertson Way SY2 ..... 125 F6
Roberts Rd TF7 .... 152 D5
Robin Cl
Ellesmere Urban SY12 ..... 27 B3
Shrewsbury SY1 .... 114 C4
Robin La TF10 .... 109 A3
Robins Dr TF7 .... 152 D6
Robinsford Cl 6 SY3 .... 124 B6
Rocfield Terr TF2 .... 132 B4
Rochester Cl 10 TF3 .... 144 D3
ROCHFORD 214 F3
Rock Acres TF10 .... 121 B3
Rockall Way TF3 .... 143 F7
Rock Cl SY9 .... 182 F8
Rocke's Mdw LD7 .... 203 C2
Rocke St SY3 .... 125 E4
Rock Gn Terr SY8 .... 217 E6
ROCKHILL 193 B2
Rock La
Edgmond TF10 .... 108 F3
Hanmer LL13 .... 11 B8
Ludlow SY8 .... 217 D4
Rock Rd TF3 .... 143 E7
Rocks Gn
Ludford SY8 .... 207 C3
Ludlow SY8 .... 217 F6
Rocks The 4 SY3 .... 125 C3
Rock Terr
Ludlow SY8 .... 217 D4
St Georges TF2 .... 132 D2
ROCK THE 143 E7
Rock The
Sheriffhales TF11 .... 134 B4
The Rock TF3 .... 143 E8
Rockwell La SY10 .... 76 A1
Roddam Ct 2 TF10 ...... 109 E2
RODEN 116 A6
Roden Cl TF1 .... 130 D5
Roden Gr SY4 .... 65 F5
Rodenhurst La SY4 ...... 116 D2
Roden La TF6 .... 115 D5
RODINGTON 116 E2
RODINGTON HEATH 116 C2
Rodney Cl 6 TF11 .... 146 A6
Rodney's View 1 SY22 ... 94 A1
Rodney View SY10 .... 76 D5
RODWAY 107 A1
Roe Deer Gn TF10 .... 109 E5
Roft St SY11 .... 58 E7
Roman Fold SY7 .... 195 E8
Roman Gr 3 TF2 .... 132 C2
Roman Rd SY3 .... 125 A3
Roman Rd Sports Ctr SY3 .... 125 A2
Roman Way
Hinstock TF9 .... 72 A2
Whitchurch SY13 .... 14 F8
ROMSLEY 201 D1
Romsley Dr SY2 .... 125 E3
Romsley La DY12 .... 201 D1
Romsley View 6 WV15 .. 201 B3
Ronhill Cres 4 DY14 .... 209 E3
Ronhill La DY14 .... 209 E3
Rookery La SY4 .... 50 F2
Rookery Rd TF2 .... 132 D4
Rookery The 2 TF7 ..... 153 B5
Rope Wlk Ct 17 SY3 ..... 125 B6
RORRINGTON 175 D7
Rosebury Gr 9 WV5 .... 190 F3
Rose Cres TF1 .... 130 E3
Rosedale 7 SY1 .... 114 A3
Rose Gr TF1 .... 130 E3
ROSEHILL 53 A1
Rosehill Ave SY11 .... 41 D2
Rosehill Cl SY11 .... 41 E2
Rosehill Dr
Bridgnorth WV16 .... 218 D4
Whittington SY11 .... 41 D2
Rose Hill Rd TF9 .... 70 F6
Rose La WV16 .... 218 E5
Roselyn SY1 .... 113 F3
Rosemary La
Leintwardine SY7 .... 205 B4
Whitchurch SY13 .... 15 A7
Rosemary Way 5 SY5 ... 173 B4
Rosemede 3 SY1 .... 113 F3
Rose Mount Dr 1 SY10 ... 76 A1
Rosemount Gdns WV6 ... 164 D2
Rosenhurst Dr 17 DY12 . 211 D2
Rose Tree Cl 4 TF3 ..... 143 F8
Roseway
Shrewsbury SY1 .... 113 F3
Wellington TF1 .... 130 E3
Rose Way 2 SY5 .... 171 F3
Rosewood Ave 9 LL13 ... 221 F4
Roslyn Rd TF1 .... 130 E4
Rossett Way 4 LL12 .... 221 D8
Rosthwaite TF1 .... 130 E3
Rotherfield SY1 .... 113 F1
Rothesay Cl 6 LL11 ..... 221 C6
Rothesay Gr 9 TF2 ..... 132 A1
Rothley Cl SY3 .... 124 F4
Rothley Dr 3 SY3 .... 124 A6
Rough La TF12 .... 161 E7
ROUGHTON 189 A5
Round Hill Cl SY1 .... 125 B8
Round Hill Gn SY1 .... 125 B8
Round Hill La SY1 .... 125 B8
Round House Pk TF4 .... 143 B1
ROUND OAK 195 A7
Round Oak Dr 4 TF1 .... 130 D7
Roundway SY3 .... 125 E2
Roundwood Cl 9 SY11 ... 59 A8
Roushill SY1 .... 125 C6
Rowallan Way 4 TF2 ... 132 F1
Rowan Ave
5 Dawley TF4 .... 144 A2
Great Dawley TF4 .... 143 F2
Rowan Cl
4 Ellesmere SY12 .... 27 A2
3 Gobowen SY11 .... 41 A7
2 Llandysilio SY22 .... 94 A1
Rowan Dr 7 TF10 .... 109 F1
Rowan Rd TF9 .... 36 D2
Rowe La
Maelor South SY12 .... 29 A4
Munslow TF13 .... 185 E1
Welshampton & Lyneal SY12 .... 28 F4
Rowland Gate 6 TF1 .... 130 D4
ROWLEY 171 D5
Rowley Cl 5 TF7 .... 152 F4
Rowley Ct 2 SY2 .... 125 F2
Row The SY6 .... 184 A6
ROWTON
Alderbury with Cardeston 168 D3
Ercall Magna 105 C4
Rowton Ave SY5 .... 168 E3
Rowton Cl 5 TF1 .... 130 F5
Rowton Rd SY2 .... 125 F1
Royal Air Force Mus* WV7 .... 156 C7
Royal Oak Dr
4 Brewood ST19 .... 148 E8
5 Hadley TF1 .... 131 A6
Royal Shrewsbury Hospl SY3 .... 124 D6
Royal Way
Dawley TF3 .... 144 A6
1 Great Dawley TF4 ..... 143 F6
Ruabon Rd LL13 .... 221 A1
Rubery Way LL13 .... 221 F2
Rubicon SY13 .... 14 E7
RUCKLEY 179 C3
RUDGE 190 A8
RUDGE HEATH 189 E6
Rudge Heath Rd WV15 .. 189 E6
Rudge Rd
Pattingham & Patshull WV6 .... 166 B1
Rudge WV6 .... 190 A8
Rudge The SY5 .... 141 B1
Ruewood Mdw Nature Reserve* SY4 .... 65 D4
Ruith Field TF5 .... 130 B8
Rural Cotts SY5 .... 141 A2
Rushbrooke Way 1 SY2 . 126 A8
RUSHBURY 185 A2
Rushbury CE Prim Sch SY6 .... 185 A2
Rushbury Rd
Rushbury SY6 .... 185 A3
1 Wellington TF1 .... 130 C5
Rushey La WV7 .... 165 D8
Rush La TF9 .... 36 A2
Rushmoor La TF5 .... 117 E1
RUSHTON 141 B5
Rushton Rd 7 SY2 ...... 125 F8
Rushwater Cl 21 WV5 ... 190 F3
Ruskin Way 7 TF3 ...... 144 A1
Russell Cl WV15 .... 219 E4
Russell Field 2 SY3 ..... 124 F5
Russell Gr LL12 .... 221 E5
Russell Rd TF7 .... 153 B5
Russell Ridge 1 SY3 .... 124 F4
Russell Sq 4 TF7 .... 153 B5
Russell St 8 LD7 .... 203 B3
Russett Way 1 DY12 .... 211 C2
RUTHALL 198 C8
Ruthall Cl 1 WV16 ...... 198 D8
Ruthin Rd LL13 .... 221 A3
Rutland SY1 .... 113 E5
Rutland Gn 1 TF1 .... 131 A4
Rutland Rd LL13 .... 221 E2
Ruyton Castle (remains of)* SY4 .... 80 A1
RUYTON-XI-TOWNS 80 B1
Rydal Ave
Shrewsbury SY1 .... 113 F3
Whitchurch SY13 .... 15 B7
Rydal Ct 4 LL13 .... 221 F5
Ryder Dr TF2 .... 133 A7
RYEBANK 48 A3
Ryebank Rd TF2 .... 131 F1
Ryefield Way 2 SY13 .... 15 A6
Ryelands SY3 .... 124 E4
Ryelands Gdns 5 WV16 . 218 D5
RYTON 155 C2
Ryton Cl
5 Shrewsbury SY3 ...... 125 B1
Tweedale TF7 .... 153 D6
Ryton Hall TF11 .... 155 C2
Ryton Rd
Beckbury TF11 .... 164 C8
Ryton TF11 .... 155 C1
Ryton Way TF3 .... 144 B1

S

Sabrina Dr 6 DY12 ..... 211 D2
Sabrina Rd 5 WV15 ..... 218 F4
Saddlers SY5 .... 172 E4
Sadlers Fold 11 TF2 .... 132 A1
Saggars Cl TF7 .... 152 E4
St Agathas Cl TF1 .... 130 C7
St Alkmond Mdw 3 SY13 . 14 F8
St Alkmond's Pl 5 SY1 .. 125 C5
St Andrews CE Prim Sch
Great Ness SY4 .... 97 E4
Shifnal TF11 .... 145 F2
St Andrews Cl
Hope Bowdler SY6 .... 184 C3
9 Shifnal TF11 .... 145 F5
St Andrews Rd 3 SY3 ... 124 E3
St Andrews Way 4 TF10 121 E8
St Anne's CE Fst & Mid Schools DY12 .... 211 C1
St Annes Dr SY10 .... 58 D4
St Anne's RC Prim Sch LL13 .... 221 F3
St Anne's Rd 7 SY3 ..... 124 E3
St Antony's Rd 10 SY3 .. 124 E3
St Aubin Dr 2 TF4 ...... 143 E6
St Austin's Friars 9 SY1 125 B6
St Austin's St 12 SY1 .... 125 B6
St Barbaras Pl SY11 ...... 41 C4
St Brelade Cl 3 TF4 .... 143 E6
St Bride's Way SY22 ...... 92 C5
St Catherines Cl TF1 .... 130 E6
St Catherine's Dr 1 SY3 124 E3
St Chads CE Prim Sch WV6 .... 166 C3
St Chads Cl 8 WV6 ..... 166 C2
St Chad's Cl 6 TF1 ..... 130 D5
St Chad's Terr 2 SY1 .... 125 B5
St Chads Way TF9 .... 20 C2
St Christophers Sch / Ysgol Sant Christopher LL13 . 221 D1
St Christophers Way 3 TF4 .... 143 F6
St Cuthberth's Cres WV7 156 E5
St Davids Cl
5 Dawley TF4 .... 143 F6
4 Gobowen SY11 .... 41 A7
St David's Cres LL13 .... 221 E4
St Davids' Ct 3 LL13 .... 221 F5
St Dunstan Cl 5 SY6 .... 216 C6
St Dunstan's La WR15 ... 215 A2
St Eatas La SY5 .... 139 A7
ST GEORGE'S 132 C2
St Georges CE Prim Sch
Clun SY7 .... 193 C3
Oakengates/Donnington TF2 .... 132 D2
St George's Cres 5 LL12 .... 221 D3
St Georges Ct SY3 ...... 125 B6
St George's Ct SY13 ...... 15 B8
St Georges Gdns 3 SY5 . 173 B4
St Georges Jun Sch SY3 . 124 F6
St George's Pl SY7 ...... 193 C3
St Georges Rd TF2 ...... 132 D5
St George's St SY3 ...... 125 B7
St Giles CE Prim Sch SY2 .... 126 A5
St Giles Cl 2 TF1 .... 131 A2
St Giles Cres LL13 ...... 221 E4
St Giles Prim Sch LL13 .. 221 D2
St Giles' Rd 2 SY2 ..... 125 F4
St Giles Way 1 LL13 .... 221 D2
St Giles Way / Ffordd San Silyn 20 LL13 .... 221 C3
St Gregorys Cl WV16 .... 187 E5
St Helens Cl TF1 .... 130 E6
St Helier Dr TF4 .... 143 E6
St James Cl 3 SY11 ...... 59 A8
St James Cres 3 TF3 ... 144 B1
St James Ct
6 Wellington TF1 .... 130 D3
4 Wrexham LL11 .... 221 C5
St James Dr 3 WV15 .... 219 A3
St James Rd SY2 .... 126 B6
St John's Cath Prim Sch WV16 .... 218 E5
St Johns CE Fst Sch ST19 .... 148 E7
St John's CE Prim Sch DY3 .... 190 F2
St John's Cl
4 Ellesmere SY12 .... 27 C2
Swindon DY3 .... 190 E1
St John's Cres 4 SY7 ... 195 D5
St John's Ct 4 WV16 .... 198 D8
St John's Dr TF2 .... 132 A6
St John's Hill
Ellesmere SY12 .... 27 C2
3 Shrewsbury SY1 ...... 125 B5
St John's La
Bewdley DY12 .... 211 A1
Ludlow SY8 .... 217 C3
St John's Pk 5 SY13 ..... 15 A8
St John's Rd SY8 .... 217 C3
St Johns St 1 WV15 ..... 219 A4
St John's St
4 Whitchurch SY13 .... 15 A8
Wrexham LL13 .... 221 E2
St John St TF1 .... 130 E3
St John the Baptist CE Prim Sch SY4 .... 80 A1

Addresses

Name and Address	Telephone	Page	Grid reference

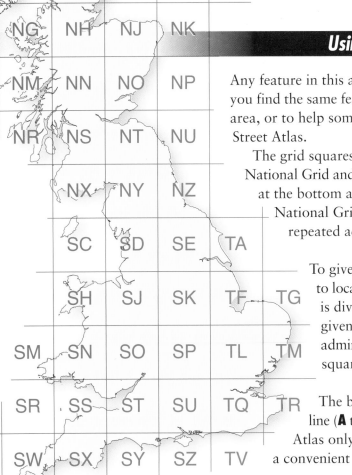

Any feature in this atlas can be given a unique reference to help you find the same feature on other Ordnance Survey maps of the area, or to help someone else locate you if they do not have a Street Atlas.

The grid squares in this atlas match the Ordnance Survey National Grid and are at 500 metre intervals. The small figures at the bottom and sides of every other grid line are the National Grid kilometre values (**00** to **99** km) and are repeated across the country every 100 km (see left).

To give a unique National Grid reference you need to locate where in the country you are. The country is divided into 100 km squares with each square given a unique two-letter reference. Use the administrative map to determine in which 100 km square a particular page of this atlas falls.

The bold letters and numbers between each grid line (**A** to **F**, **1** to **8**) are for use within a specific Street Atlas only, and when used with the page number, are a convenient way of referencing these grid squares.

Example *The railway bridge over DARLEY GREEN RD in grid square B1*

Step 1: Identify the two-letter reference, in this example the page is in **SP**

Step 2: Identify the 1 km square in which the railway bridge falls. Use the figures in the southwest corner of this square: Eastings **17**, Northings **74**. This gives a unique reference: **SP 17 74**, accurate to 1 km.

Step 3: To give a more precise reference accurate to 100 m you need to estimate how many tenths along and how many tenths up this 1 km square the feature is (to help with this the 1 km square is divided into four 500 m squares). This makes the bridge about **8** tenths along and about **1** tenth up from the southwest corner.

This gives a unique reference: **SP 178 741**, accurate to 100 m.

Eastings (read from left to right along the bottom) come before Northings (read from bottom to top). If you have trouble remembering say to yourself "Along the hall, THEN up the stairs"!

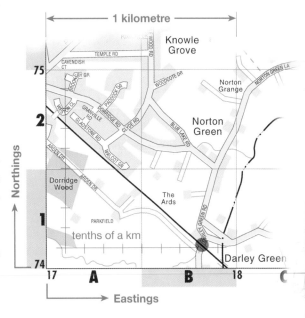

PHILIP'S MAPS

the Gold Standard for drivers

◆ **Philip's street atlases cover every county in England, Wales, Northern Ireland and much of Scotland**

- ◆ Every named street is shown, including alleys, lanes and walkways
- ◆ Thousands of additional features marked: stations, public buildings, car parks, places of interest
- ◆ Route-planning maps to get you close to your destination
- ◆ Postcodes on the maps and in the index
- ◆ Widely used by the emergency services, transport companies and local authorities

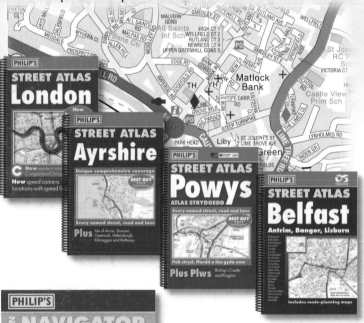

For national mapping, choose
Philip's Navigator Britain
the most detailed road atlas available of England, Wales and Scotland. Hailed by Auto Express as 'the ultimate road atlas', the atlas shows every road and lane in Britain.

Street atlases currently available

England

Bedfordshire and Luton	Surrey
Berkshire	East Sussex
Birmingham and West Midlands	West Sussex
Bristol and Bath	Tyne and Wear
Buckinghamshire and Milton Keynes	Warwickshire and Coventry
Cambridgeshire and Peterborough	Wiltshire and Swindon
Cheshire	Worcestershire
Cornwall	East Yorkshire Northern Lincolnshire
Cumbria	North Yorkshire
Derbyshire	South Yorkshire
Devon	West Yorkshire
Dorset	
County Durham and Teesside	**Wales**
Essex	Anglesey, Conwy and Gwynedd
North Essex	Cardiff, Swansea and The Valleys
South Essex	Carmarthenshire, Pembrokeshire and Swansea
Gloucestershire and Bristol	Ceredigion and South Gwynedd
Hampshire	
North Hampshire	Denbighshire, Flintshire, Wrexham
South Hampshire	Herefordshire Monmouthshire
Herefordshire Monmouthshire	Powys
Hertfordshire	
Isle of Wight	**Scotland**
Kent	Aberdeenshire
East Kent	Ayrshire
West Kent	Dumfries and Galloway
Lancashire	Edinburgh and East Central Scotland
Leicestershire and Rutland	Fife and Tayside
Lincolnshire	Glasgow and West Central Scotland
Liverpool and Merseyside	Inverness and Moray
London	Lanarkshire
Greater Manchester	Scottish Borders
Norfolk	
Northamptonshire	**Northern Ireland**
Northumberland	County Antrim and County Londonderry
Nottinghamshire	County Armagh and County Down
Oxfordshire	Belfast
Shropshire	County Tyrone and County Fermanagh
Somerset	
Staffordshire	
Suffolk	

How to order

Philip's maps and atlases are available from bookshops, motorway services and petrol stations. You can order direct from the publisher by phoning **0207 531 8473** or online at **www.philips-maps.co.uk**
For bulk orders only, e-mail philips@philips-maps.co.uk